State-Initiated Restraints of Competition

State-Initiated Restraints of Competition

Edited by

Josef Drexl

Director, Max Planck Institute for Innovation and Competition, Munich, Germany

Vicente Bagnoli

Professor of Law, Mackenzie Presbyterian University – Law School, São Paulo, Brazil

ASCOLA COMPETITION LAW

Edward Elgar PUBLISHING

Cheltenham, UK • Northampton, MA, USA

Published by
Edward Elgar Publishing Limited
The Lypiatts
15 Lansdown Road
Cheltenham
Glos GL50 2JA
UK

Edward Elgar Publishing, Inc.
William Pratt House
9 Dewey Court
Northampton
Massachusetts 01060
USA

A catalogue record for this book
is available from the British Library

Library of Congress Control Number: 2014952144

This book is available electronically in the **Elgar**online
Law Subject Collection
DOI 10.4337/9781784714987

FSC www.fsc.org MIX Paper from responsible sources FSC® C013056

ISBN 978 1 78471 497 0 (cased)
ISBN 978 1 78471 498 7 (eBook)

Typeset by Columns Design XML Ltd, Reading
Printed and bound in Great Britain by T.J. International Ltd, Padstow

Contents

Figures

Tables

Contributors

Arthur Barrionuevo, Professor at Fundação Getúlio Vargas (FGV)/São Paulo Business Administration School; specialist in competition and regulation; former Commissioner of CADE (the Brazilian competition authority).

Gilberto Bercovici, Full Professor of Economic Law and Political Economy at the Faculty of Law of the University of São Paulo (Brazil); Professor at the Faculty of Law of Mackenzie Presbyterian University (Brazil).

Leonor Bettencourt Nunes, LL.M. in European Law, King's College, London.

S. Chakravarthy, competition policy and law consultant, India.

Thomas K. Cheng, B.A. (Yale), J.D. (Harvard); Associate Professor at the Faculty of Law of the University of Hong Kong.

Claudia Curiel Leidenz, Economist; Professor at the Universidad Católica Andrés Bello, Caracas, Venezuela.

Josef Drexl, Dr. iur. (Munich), LL.M. (UC Berkeley); Director of the Max Planck Institute for Innovation and Competition, Munich; Honorary Professor at the University of Munich.

Pedro Dutra, Lawyer specialized in competition law and regulatory law; Pedro Dutra Advogados, São Paulo.

Deborah Healey, LL.M. (Hons.) (Syd.), Senior Lecturer, Faculty of Law, University of New South Wales, Sydney.

Thomas Jaeger, Dr. iur. (Salzburg), LL.M. (Leuven), Senior Researcher at the Max Planck Institute for Innovation and Competition (Munich); Substitute Professor at the University of Hanover; Lecturer at the Law Faculty of the University of Munich.

Maria Manuel Leitão Marques, Lawyer, PhD in economics (Coimbra); Professor at the Faculty of Economics of the Universidade de Coimbra; Professor at the Law Faculty of the Universidade Nova de Lisboa, Portugal.

Gesner Oliveira, PhD in economics (UC Berkeley); GO Associados, São Paulo, Brazil; former president of CADE (the Brazilian competition authority).

Rudolph J.R. Peritz, Professor of Law; Director, IProgress Project, New York Law School.

Simonetta Vezzoso, Lawyer, PhD in Economics (Witten/Herdecke); Senior Researcher and Adjunct (Aggregato) Professor at the Department of Economics and Management at the Università degli Studi di Trento, Italy.

Tania Zúñiga-Fernández, LL.M. (ESAN University, Lima, Peru); Professor of Competition Law; Associated member of CEPIC-ESAN, Institute for Intellectual Property, Competition, Consumer and Trade.

Preface

This book assembles various contributions that are based on talks given to the Seventh Conference of the Academic Society of Competition Law (ASCOLA), which was held at the Mackenzie Presbyterian University of São Paulo (Brazil) on 12–14 April 2012. Some other contributions are made by ASCOLA members who were not able to attend the conference.

In recent years the market economy has gained ground all around the world. Privatization and trade liberalization have not only characterized the economic policy of the more advanced economies, these policies also characterize economic reform in the many emerging and developing economies. In short, the state seems to get out of the economy almost everywhere and, thereby, seems to leave more room for private economic actors. Therefore, there is a temptation to assume that the state as the source of the restraints of competition is fading away, while competition law enforcers will have to concentrate on controlling restraints of competition by private parties.

Yet this book shows a much more complex picture. Of course the topic of the book – which was also the topic of the conference – was chosen with a purpose. Especially as countries in Latin America have a legacy of state-run economies. State-owned enterprises still exist in many of these countries, and regulators may have a hard time to switch from interventionism to pro-competitive regulation. Yet the kind of state interventions that take place in the market economy may be very multifaceted. In more advanced jurisdictions, competition law has been complemented by pro-competitive public procurement regimes and subsidy (state aid) control. Also, privatization and trade liberalization have not reduced the need for state intervention. Quite on the contrary, such policies have increased the need for a different kind of regulation. Historically, there were often good reasons, such as the public service argument, why certain sectors of the economy were exempted from competition in favour of state-owned monopolists. Such reasons have not disappeared with liberalization. Rather, diverse policy goals and public interest grounds also need to be taken account of today in the framework of sector-specific regulation. At the same time, this raises the question as to how such regulation interfaces with general competition law and policy.

In sum, the book was conceived on the assumption that 'state-related restraints' can take very diverse forms and that it is very timely to discuss those restraints and how they are handled in different jurisdictions.

The book addresses the topic in four parts. Part 1 deals with state-owned enterprises, as the classical form of state-initiated restraints. Part 2 presents examples of 'pro-competitive regulation' in a broader sense, that is, beyond the topic of state-owned enterprises, namely, in the context of sector-specific regulation or where specific forms of regulation and even competition law are used as a means to enhance competition with the state as an addressee. Part 3 assembles contributions on 'anti-competitive' state intervention and regulation where the authors criticize the state or the regulator for distorting competition and failing to achieve the goals of competitive markets. Part 4 finally contains two contributions that provide snapshots of the law on public procurement and subsidy control from the perspective of two individual jurisdictions.

Part 1 opens with a contribution on the Australian 'competitive neutrality' policy by Deborah Healey. This policy is designed to combat distortions of competition arising from privileges granted to state-owned enterprises. Many other jurisdictions could learn from such a more principled approach to controlling state-owned enterprises. In the next contribution, Gilberto Bercovici analyses the role Petrobrás, as the state monopolist in the oil sector, still today plays in Brazil's economic energy and innovation policy and how competition issues, including pricing and purchaser power exercised by Petrobrás are handled. In another contribution Tania Zúñiga-Fernández illustrates that Latin American jurisdictions can also adopt more principled approaches – namely, based on the constitutional principle of subsidiarity in Peru – to deciding whether the state must or must not entertain state-owned enterprises. In the last contribution of Part 1, Josef Drexl addresses the regulation of so-called public sector information (PSI) in the European Union at the interface with competition law. The contribution highlights how difficult, but important, it is to distinguish between economic activity by a state – in the sense of a 'public undertaking' – and original state function. By evaluating this form of regulation through the lenses of competition policy, Josef Drexl simultaneously introduces Part 2 of the book.

Part 2 starts with two contributions that analyse broader policy instruments by which jurisdictions address state administrative actions that distort competition. In the first one, Maria Manuel Leitão Marques and Leonor Bettencourt Nunes demonstrate how the European legislature enhanced cross-border competition among EU Member States in the framework of the Services Directive. Similarly, Thomas Cheng analyses the rules of the Chinese Anti-Monopoly Law on 'administrative monopolies' after some years of experience. These competition rules are designed to prevent Chinese provinces and lower territorial entities from restricting imports from other parts of China through regional trade regulation. The question of this analysis is above all how effective these rules can be. The remaining two contributions of Part 2 deal with more sector-specific issues. Gesner Oliveira looks at the regulation of the water and sanitation services market in Brazil in order to find out which pro-competitive policy measures can deliver the fastest universal coverage of these services in the country. In the last contribution of Part 2, Simonetta Vezzoso addresses a more recent and very important challenge of competition law, namely the interface of competition policy and data protection regulation. The latter has quite some tradition in the European Union in particular. It was initially inspired by concerns about data collection and processing activities of state entities. More recently, however, the focus moved to large private entities, such as Google, that build their business model and even market power on the control of personal data of individuals.

In the first contribution to Part 3, Claudia Curiel Leidenz shows through a thorough analysis of the economic policy development in Venezuela that countries can also completely turn around market liberalization by increasing state intervention in the economy, thereby also destroying the first impressive steps in the direction of building up a workable competition system. Then, Arthur Barrionuevo and Pedro Dutra criticize how the Brazilian sector-regulator went beyond its statutory powers by aiming to impose investment targets on providers of pay-TV. In contrast, the authors sketch an alternative model of regulation that not only respects the limitation of the regulatory powers but, more importantly, also achieves the goals of innovation and broader coverage of the country by relying on competitive pressure. In the last contribution to Part 3, Rudolph Peritz strikes an almost provocative tone by describing intellectual property law as anti-competitive regulation and by claiming that the far-reaching rejection of a duty to license under US antitrust law should be reconsidered in the light of the recent *eBay* case-law of US courts according to which public interest reasons can justify a denial of injunctive relief in intellectual property infringement cases.

Public procurement decisions and subsidies are other forms by which states can distort competition among firms. In Part 4, S. Chakravarthy recommends that India seriously consider joining the WTO Agreement on Government Procurement. He thereby argues that this Agreement would not prevent India from taking into account development needs, including privileged treatment of micro and smaller enterprises from

India. In the second contribution, Thomas Jaeger turns to state aid control in the European Union. In comparison with the anti-subsidies regime of the WTO, he also criticizes the European approach. Due to an inappropriate delineation between public and private subsidies many state-initiated restraints escape control despite their nevertheless equally distortive effect on competition.

Neither the conference nor the book was meant to present a full analysis of the very diverse forms of 'state-initiated restraints of competition'. The contributions of the book present analyses of various sub-topics and examples from several jurisdictions, offering numerous insights that will hopefully attract the interest of the reader. Yet, also across the various contributions, there are a number of common threads of learning.

First of all, the variety of different forms of state-initiated restraints is quite astonishing. They cannot be captured by the three areas of the control of state-owned enterprises, public procurement and state subsidies. Most importantly, trade liberalization requires policymakers and regulators to use competition policy analysis as a means to enhance pro-competitive regulation and avoid the fallacy of anti-competitive regulation.

Secondly, the international perspective shows that the topic cannot be dealt with uniformly across different jurisdictions. By definition, state-initiated restraints of competition can only be understood and appropriately addressed in the historical and socio-political context of an individual country. Yet this does not mean that countries cannot learn from the experience of other countries. Quite the contrary, countries typically share the same policy goals and the same economic features of markets that are in need of regulation.

Thirdly, some of the contributions (Drexl, Jaeger) show how important it is to identify the scope of legal instruments correctly to achieve maximum positive effects in terms of competition, whether this concerns if certain state activity fulfills the requirements for an 'economic activity' of an undertaking and, consequently, makes the state an addressee of competition law, or whether it is about certain forms of regulation that can be considered a subsidy.

Fourthly, some authors (Oliveira, Chakravarthy) also contribute to the growing research on competition law in developing countries. In emerging and developing countries, public services are still in need of extending distribution networks in order to attain a degree of universal provision of all consumers, while developed countries liberalized public service markets after having attained universal coverage often through a state monopolist. Oliveira's contribution demonstrates that competition policy is also the right approach in the field for developing countries. Chakravarthy explains how important government procurement rules are for developing countries despite justified development concerns against fully opening up national procurement markets to international competition.

Moreover, many contributions highlight the relevance of state-initiated restraints in multi-level (federal) jurisdictions, whether this is about China or the European Union. The upper level cannot accept that lower level state entities distort competition in the larger market. Of course, in a globalized world such concerns have long attained the level of international law with the WTO law and many bilateral agreements that nowadays address public procurement and state subsidies.

And finally, several of the contributions explore the interface of competition law and sector-specific regulation. None of them favoured exclusive competence of the sector regulators. They all supported pro-competitive regulation as well as parallel application of the sector-specific rules and general competition law. This makes state-initiated restraints of competition and anti-competitive regulation also an issue for competition agencies and courts.

This book would not have been possible without the conference held at Mackenzie Presbyterian University in São Paulo. Therefore, the editors would like to thank Mackenzie Presbyterian University, Mackenzie Presbyterian Institute and Mackenzie Law School, which recognized the potential of the Conference and provided a unique opportunity to bring together academics from different nations and universities. As regards the burden of organizing the conference, the editors would also like to thank, from the Mackenzie Competition Law Studying Group, Tatiana Coutinho, Amanda Navas, Patrícia Calderon, Mariana Cavichioli Almeida, Ana Cláudia Stein, Maria Fernanda Madi, Paulo André Nogueira Lima, Murilo Sampaio Ferraz and Israel Sayão.

Some other people were involved in the preparation of this book to whom the editors are greatly indebted. The editing of the book took place at the Max Planck Institute in Munich, where Delia Zirilli collected the contributions and brought them into a uniform style. Most important and time consuming was the work done by Allison Felmy. She reviewed all the contributions by the non-native speakers from a linguistic point of view. Last but not least, the editors are very grateful to the staff of Edward Elgar, especially to John Paul McDonald, who strongly supported the book throughout the time of its coming into existence.

June 2014
Vicente Bagnoli
Josef Drexl

Abbreviations

ABA	American Bar Association
ABC	Australian Broadcasting Corporation
ACCC	Australian Competition and Consumer Commission
ACTA	Anti-Counterfeiting Trade Agreement
AGCNCO	Australian Government Competitive Neutrality Complaints Office
AIC	Administration for Industry and Commerce (China)
AIS	Australian Institute of Sport
Am. Econ. Rev.	American Economics Review
Am. J. Sociology	American Journal of Sociology
ANATEL	Agência Nacional de Telecomunicações (National Telecommunication Agency of Brazil)
ANP	Agência Nacional de Petróleo (National Oil Agency of Brazil)
Antitrust Bull.	Antitrust Bulletin
Antitrust L.J.	Antitrust Law Journal
AQSIQ	Administration of Quality Supervision, Inspection and Quarantine (China)
ASC	Australian Sports Commission
ASEAN	Association of South-East Asian Nations
BEUC	Bureau Européen des Unions de Consommateurs (The European Consumer Organisation)
CAC Act	Commonwealth Authorities and Companies Act (Australia)
CAPEX	capital expenditure
CCNCO	Commonwealth Competitive Neutrality Complaints Office (Australia)
CCTV	China Central Television
CHP	combined heat and power

Cir.	U.S. Circuit Court of Appeals
CJEU	Court of Justice of the European Union
C.M.L. Rev.	Common Market Law Review
CNP	Conselho Nacional do Petróleo (National Oil Council of Brazil)
CNU	Competitive Neutrality Unit (Victoria)
COAG	Council of Australian Governments
Colum. L. Rev.	Columbia Law Review
Comp. Eur. Pol.	Comparative European Politics
CSO	community service obligation
DBCDE	Department of Broadband, Communications and the Digital Economy (Australia)
DTH	direct-to-home
EC	(former) European Community; European Community Treaty
ECJ	(former) European Court of Justice (now CJEU)
ECLR	European Competition Law Review
ECR	European Court Reports
EDIPE	Escritório de Distribuição de Produtos de Petróleo (Office of Distribution of Oil By-Products of Brazil)
E. L. Rev.	European Law Review
EStAL	European State Aid Law Quarterly
Eur. Const. L. Rev.	European Constitutional Law Review
Fed. Cir.	US Court of Appeals for the Federal Circuit
FRAND	fair, reasonable and non-discriminatory
FTC	Federal Trade Commission (United States)
F.3rd	Federal Reporter, Third Series
GBE	Government Business Enterprise (Australia)
GDP	gross domestic product
Geo. Mason L. Rev.	George Mason Law Review
GFR	general financial rules (India)
GPA	Agreement on Government Procurement
GPS	Global Positioning System
HCA	High Court of Australia
Harv. Int'l Rev.	Harvard International Review

IIC	International Review of Intellectual Property and Competition Law
INDECOPI	Instituto Nacional de Defensa de la Competencia y de la Protección de la Propiedad Intelectual (National Institute for the Protection of Competition and Intellectual Property of Peru)
Int'l Data Priv. L.	International Data Privacy Law
IPART	Independent Pricing and Review Tribunal (Australia)
IPRs	intellectual property rights
IRA	internal rate of return
IWA	International Water Association
J. Am. Stat. Ass.	Journal of the American Statistical Association
J. Comp. L. & Econ.	Journal of Competition Law and Economics
J. Development Stud.	Journal of Development Studies
J. Pol. Econ.	Journal of Political Economy
LAPSI	Legal Aspects of Public Sector Information
LGT	Lei Geral de Telecomunicações (General Telecommunication Law of Brazil)
lit.	littera (letter)
Md. L. Rev.	Maryland Law Review
MEQR	measure of equivalent effect as quantitative restrictions
Mich. L. Rev.	Michigan Law Review
MINCI	Ministero para la Comunicación y la Información de la República Bolivariana de Venezuela (Ministry for Communication and Information of the Bolivarian Republic of Venezuela)
MMDS	Multichannel Multipoint Distribution Service
NAFTA	North American Free Trade Agreement
NBN	national broadband network
NCC	National Competition Council (Australia)
N.C. L. Rev.	North Carolina Law Review
NCP	National Competition Policy (Australia)
NDRC	National Development and Reform Commission (China)

NPV	net present value
NSW	New South Wales
Nw. J. Tech. & Intell. Prop.	Northwestern Journal of Technology and Intellectual Property
Nw. U. L. Rev.	Northwestern University Law Review
OECD	Organisation for Economic Cooperation and Development
OJ C	Official Journal Part C (European Union)
OJ L	Official Journal Part L (European Union)
PNAD	Pesquisa Nacional por Amostra de Comincílios (National Housing Sample Survey of Brazil)
PNSB	Pesquisa Nacional de Saneamento Básico (National Basic Sanitation Survey of Brazil)
POSC	point of single contact
PPP	public-private partnership
PSI	public sector information
PSU	public sector undertaking
Pub. Contr. L.J.	Public Contract Law Journal
QCA	Queensland Competition Authority
RAND J. Econ.	RAND Journal of Economics
Rev. Eur. Adm. L.	Review of European Administrative Law
SAIC	State Administration for Industry and Commerce (China)
SCM Agreement	Agreement on Subsidies and Countervailing Measures
S. Ct.	US Supreme Court Reporter
SeAC	serviço de acesso condicionado (conditional access service)
SEP	standard-essential patent
SNIS	Sistema Nacional de Informações sobre Saneamento (National Information System on Sanitation of Brazil)
Stan. L. Rev.	Stanford Law Review
SVO	State Valuation Office (Australia)
TEC	(former) Treaty on the European Community
TEU	Treaty on the European Union
TFEU	Treaty on the Functioning of the European Union

Trade Practices L.J.	Trade Practices Law Journal
TRIPS	Agreement on Trade-Related Aspects of Intellectual Property Rights
TVC	cable television
UNCITRAL	United Nations Commission on International Trade Law
USC	United States Code
Utilities Pol'y	Utilities Policy
WACC	weighted average cost of capital
West Eur. Pol.	West European Politics
WTO	World Trade Organization

PART 1

State-owned enterprises

1. Competitive neutrality: addressing government advantage in Australian markets

Deborah Healey

1. INTRODUCTION

The activities of government in the market have significant capacity to impede effective competition.[1] Government impacts the level playing field of competition by making laws and regulations that restrict competition, by the less than comprehensive application of competition law to the entities which it owns and controls, including state-owned enterprises, and by the exemptions or exceptions it grants to itself or other favoured groups. Even where competition law expressly applies to government entities there are advantages that accrue to government-owned or controlled bodies merely because of government ownership or control. Policy designed to address this latter issue is termed competitive neutrality policy.

The foundation of competitive neutrality policy is the principle that government business activities conducted in competition with the private sector should not have competitive advantage simply by virtue of their government ownership and control. Competitive neutrality policy implements mechanisms to ensure that advantages of this kind do not occur. This is a recognized problem worldwide and various jurisdictions have taken steps to redress the competitive balance.[2] This chapter outlines the

[1] See D.D. Sokol 'Anticompetitive Government Regulation', in I. Lianos and D. Sokol (eds) *The Global Limits of Competition Law* (Stanford University Press 2012) 83–88.

[2] OECD, 'Competitive Neutrality: Maintaining a Level Playing Field between Public and Private Business: Report on OECD and National Best Practices on Competitive Neutrality' DAF/COMP (2012)7/FINAL. See also A. Capobianco and H. Christiansen, 'Competitive Neutrality and State-Owned Enterprises: Challenges and Policy Options', OECD Corporate Governance

substantial steps taken under Australian competition law and policy to deal with the impact of government on the market and particularly with the issue of competitive neutrality. A detailed structured policy was implemented in 1995 to address competitive neutrality issues and substantial progress has been made to level the playing field for the private sector where government participates in the market. Along with corporatization and privatization of government businesses, competitive neutrality has become an accepted feature of the Australian business landscape. Complaints in this area continue to be processed and the chapter examines a representative selection of complaints and their outcomes, and looks in particular at two recent examples of the examination of complaints about competitive neutrality. This chapter also raises several outstanding issues that continue to exist despite the comprehensive nature of Australian reforms in the area.

2. COMPETITION LAW AND POLICY REFORM IN AUSTRALIA

Australia implemented broad-ranging reforms to its long-standing competition law and policy in 1995 following a comprehensive 1993 review that was undertaken with the agreement of the Commonwealth and the states and territories.[3] The review was undertaken in response to the economic position of Australia at that time and was directed at creating a true national market in Australia within a broader competition-policy framework.

At the time of the review, competition law had developed greatly since its initial enactment in 1906 but a number of important areas of business were not subject to the existing competition law, the Trade Practices Act 1974, mainly for constitutional reasons. Australia is a federation of states and territories and the Australian Parliament's specific powers to legislate under the Constitution at that time did not allow the enactment of a truly

---

Working Papers No. 1, May 2011, available at http://www.oecd-ilibrary.org/governance/competitive-neutrality-and-state-owned-enterprises_5kg9xfgjdhg6-en (accessed 31 December 2013).

[3] Report by the Independent Committee of Inquiry into National Competition Policy (Canberra: AGPS 1993) (the Hilmer Report).

comprehensive competition law.[4] It was difficult, for example, for the Australian Parliament to enact a law to catch bodies such as partnerships and co-operatives, which were not deemed to be constitutional 'corporations', or to catch individuals not engaged in constitutional 'trade and commerce'. It was also difficult for a Commonwealth competition law to catch bodies owned and controlled by the states, although the 1974 Act expressly caught bodies owned and controlled by the Commonwealth. Nor was it possible for the Commonwealth to unilaterally stop states enacting laws in their own jurisdictions that overrode the competition law or exempted particular specified conduct or persons from its application, which was often done for anti-competitive or protectionist purposes.[5]

The outcome of the review, the Hilmer Report, emphasized that competition policy encompasses far more than just the competition law alone, and determined that Australian competition policy needed to address not only the anti-competitive conduct of firms but also areas such as unjustified regulatory restrictions on competition; the inappropriate structure of public monopolies; the denial of access to essential facilities; monopoly pricing; and competitive neutrality.[6] The Hilmer Report recommended significant reforms to the law[7] and the implementation of significant policy mechanisms, which were ultimately agreed to and adopted by the Australian government and the governments of each of the states.[8] The reforms expressly sought to maximize community

---

[4] Commonwealth of Australia Constitution Act, s. 51(xx); s. 51(i). Subsequent judicial interpretation of the constitutional power with respect to corporations suggests a broader view may now be taken: *New South Wales v Commonwealth* [2006] HCA 52.

[5] For a detailed explanation of these issues see generally D. Healey, 'Australia' in M. Williams (ed.) *The Political Economy of Competition Law in Asia* (Edward Elgar Publishing 2013) 344.

[6] See Hilmer Report (n. 3 above) 7.

[7] The amendments were made in 1995 to the Trade Practices Act 1974. That Act was amended most recently in 2010 and its name was changed to the Competition and Consumer Act 2010. The most recent amendments dealt mainly with consumer law, which has also traditionally been contained in the Australian competition law.

[8] See Competition Principles Agreement; Conduct Code Agreement; Agreement to Implement National Competition Policy and Related Reforms. A National Competition Council was established as part of these reforms to provide advice about competition policy matters and make various recommendations in relation to the statutory access regime contained in Part IIIA of the Trade Practices Act 1974.

resources to improve efficiency, increase productivity and encourage innovation, to the benefit of the whole community.

The reforms that were ultimately made became known as National Competition Policy (NCP) reforms, and these included amendments to the competition law itself and the formal agreement by the states to enact and keep in place identical state laws to cover the gaps in application (that is, those areas that could not be the subject of Commonwealth law under the Constitution). They also included review by governments at Commonwealth and state level of all laws restricting competition; structural reform of public monopolies to facilitate competition; introduction of third-party access regimes to cover significant 'essential' infrastructure facilities at Commonwealth and state levels;[9] some limited price oversight; and the introduction of competitive neutrality policy in all jurisdictions.[10] A body called the National Competition Council (NCC) was established to support the implementation of the NCP reforms.[11] Financial incentives to complete the reform process were agreed between the Commonwealth and the states based on estimated efficiency savings. Between 1998 and 2003 a total of AU$834 million was paid by the Commonwealth to the states when they reached various milestones. These reforms fuelled substantial productivity growth.[12]

3. AUSTRALIAN MARKETS AND THE ROLE OF GOVERNMENT

The background to many of the NCP reforms, and particularly the competitive neutrality policy, was the substantial representation of government in the market and high levels of market regulation at both Commonwealth and state levels. The government in Australia has traditionally been responsible for the delivery of a wide range of services to

---

[9] Part IIIA was introduced into the Trade Practices Act 1974.

[10] The commitments to introduce competitive neutrality by each of the jurisdictions were included in the Competition Principles Agreement at clause 3, which is set out in Appendix A.

[11] Following completion of the NCP agenda, some functions relating to competitive neutrality policy were referred to the Productivity Commission, where an autonomous office called the Australian Government Competitive Neutrality Complaints Office was established. See http://www.pc.gov.au/agcnco (accessed 31 December 2013).

[12] Productivity Commission, Review of National Competition Policy (2005) xvii, available at: http://www.pc.gov.au/projects/inquiry/ncp/docs/finalreport (accessed 31 December 2013).

its citizens in areas such as utilities, transport and telecommunications. It has been suggested that this dependence on government originated from the original isolation of Australian colonists from Europe and even the other Australian colonies due to the fragmented nature of the population centres almost from the outset of colonization. This situation continues today, with population still mainly centred on widely dispersed large cities in coastal areas due to the inhospitable nature of much of the landscape. This is said to have fostered and supported an attitude whereby the citizens expected central governments to provide for them.[13] This feature meant, however, that reform of government businesses was particularly important to the continued productivity of the Australian economy.

When Australian economic progress faltered in the 1980s a more robust approach to the market was taken and the domestic economy was opened up to international trade. Reforms aimed at improving government efficiency were undertaken at that time.[14] However, the significant impact of government businesses on the Australian economy continued, and studies emphasized the significant shortcomings of their operations, particularly their pricing practices and productivity.[15] Realization of the impact of these factors led to governments pursuing a variety of reforms such as corporatization,[16] commercialization, privatization and competitive tendering and contracting, even prior to NCP.

4. COMPETITIVE NEUTRALITY POLICY AS A RESPONSE TO MARKET DISTORTION

4.1 Specific Factors in Distortion

It was also well recognized that the differential treatment of government businesses may lead to serious distortions in resource allocation in the community as well as being inequitable when, for example, consumers

---

[13] See P.D. Finn, *Law and Government in Colonial Australia* (OUP 1987) 2.

[14] See generally D. Healey (n. 5 above) 4.

[15] National Competition Council, Competitive Neutrality Reform: Issues in Implementing Clause 3 of the Competition Principles Agreement (2007) 2.

[16] The Hilmer Report (n. 3 above) 300 recognized that corporatization alone would not fulfil the requirements of an appropriate model. The model required embodies five basic principles: clarity and consistency of objectives; management authority and accountability; performance monitoring; effective rewards and sanctions; and competitive neutrality.

chose to purchase from a lower-priced government provider. In such cases 'the production and investment decisions of that business and actual and potential competitors will be influenced. If the government-owned business is not the least-cost producer when costs are measured on an equivalent basis, the allocation of resources towards production by this business would be inefficient'.[17]

Distortions identified in the Hilmer Report arose from market features such as there being no requirement for government businesses to recover costs or to price efficiently; the non-accountability of managers for their business performance; the conferral of monopoly rights on businesses, sheltering them from competitive pressures and disciplines; exemptions from paying various taxes; immunity from regulatory requirements; explicit or implicit government guarantees on debts; concessional rates of interest on loans; not being required to account for depreciation expenses; and effective immunity from bankruptcy.[18] Distortions arising from this type of government conduct were said to be 'less deliberate and transparent, and typically flow from a failure to reform laws, policies and practices to keep abreast of developments as bureaucratic and monopolistic enterprises move to more commercial and competitive operating environments'.[19]

The Hilmer Report also noted that there may be competitive disadvantages arising from government ownership, such as greater accountability obligations, community-service obligations, reduced managerial autonomy, requirements to comply with various government policies on wages, employment and industrial relations. Administrative review and onerous reporting requirements that do not apply to private businesses competing in the same market are examples of competitive disadvantage regularly experienced by government-owned or controlled entities.

4.2 Competitive Neutrality Recommendations of the Hilmer Report

Some initiatives such as some privatization and corporatization had already commenced, but the Hilmer Report for the first time recommended a comprehensive programme of reforms to address issues arising from government ownership. While it acknowledged that competition policy does not require all firms to compete on an equal footing, and that differences of size, assets, experience and culture are 'a hallmark of a

---

[17] See Australian Government, National Competition Policy Report 2005–2007 (2008) 46.

[18] See Hilmer Report (n. 3 above) 295–297.

[19] Ibid., 295.

competitive market economy', it did recognize that in terms of market distortions: 'by far the most systematic distortions appear to arise when government businesses participate in competitive markets. In particular, government businesses were often seen as enjoying a unique set of competitive advantages by virtue of their ownership, including exemption from tax'.[20]

The Hilmer Report recommended issues of competitive neutrality being dealt with in a 'systematic, nationally consistent manner' as part of NCP, recognizing that differences in approach could lead to further distortion.[21] Where privatization or corporatization were not practical, competitive neutrality policy should ensure that the full economic costs of resources deployed were reflected in pricing. 'Under this approach, government businesses would be required to account for costs incurred by the business itself (such as wages), other associated costs (such as accommodation) and implicit costs (such as commercial rate of return and income tax equivalents)'.[22]

However, accounting measures of this kind were acknowledged to be less effective than privatization or corporatization.

4.3 Adoption of Competitive Neutrality Policy in Australia

As a result of the Hilmer Report, the Australian state and territory governments agreed to a set of principles supported by institutional arrangements aimed at addressing these problems in the framework of a competitive neutrality policy. A co-operative model was adopted under which all governments agreed to the principles but were individually responsible for their implementation. There was a significant degree of autonomy for individual governments in implementing the principles. The competitive neutrality principles adopted were, in summary:

- Government businesses should not enjoy any net competitive advantage by virtue of their ownership when competing with other businesses …
- Government businesses competing against other firms within their traditional markets should be subject to measures that effectively neutralise any net competitive advantage flowing from their ownership. Unless exceptional circumstances exist, those advantages should be neutralised within one year of the introduction of competition:

---

20 Ibid., 293.
21 Ibid., 293.
22 Ibid., 302.

(a) where the government business has traditionally provided services directly to the public, there should be a presumption that this be achieved through corporatisation; and
(b) where the government business has traditionally provided services only to other government entities, this may be achieved through corporatisation or the application of effective pricing directions …

- Government businesses should not compete against other businesses outside their traditional markets without being subject to measures that effectively neutralise any net competitive advantage flowing from their ownership. No transition period should be permitted in this setting:
  (a) where the government business has traditionally provided services directly to the public, there should be a presumption that this be achieved through corporatisation; and
  (b) where the government business has traditionally provided services only to other government agencies, this may be achieved through corporatisation or the application of effective pricing directions.[23]

Competitive neutrality policy was formally implemented under the Intergovernmental Competition Principles Agreement, signed by each of the Commonwealth, states and territories as part of the NCP.[24] Under the competitive neutrality policy, significant Government Business Enterprises (GBEs),[25] classified by the Australian Bureau of Statistics as Public Trading Enterprises and Public Financial Enterprises, were subject to full Commonwealth, state and territory taxes or tax-equivalent systems, debt-guarantee fees directed towards offsetting the competitive advantages of these, and the regulations to which private-sector businesses were normally subject, such as those relating to protection of the environment, planning and approval processes, as though they were

[23] Ibid., 306 et seq.

[24] The Intergovernmental Competition Principles Agreement was signed on 25 February 1994. The Agreement implemented the arrangements for reform of NCP between the Commonwealth, the states and territories, and thus also provided for independent price oversight of government business enterprises which are monopoly or near monopoly suppliers of goods, structural reform of public monopolies, legislative review and the establishment of access regimes for natural monopolies; it also set up the National Competition Council. A summary of the obligations under clause 3 of the Competition Principles Agreement is set out in Appendix A.

[25] A Government Business Enterprise (GBE) is a Commonwealth authority or Commonwealth company as defined by the Commonwealth Authorities and Companies Act 1997 (CAC Act) and prescribed as a GBE under the Commonwealth Authorities and Companies Regulations 1997 (CAC Act Regulations).

private businesses.[26] Other agencies undertaking significant business activities as part of a broader range of functions were to implement these processes if appropriate, or at least ensure prices charged for goods or services take those issues into account and reflect full cost attribution for the activities.[27] Importantly, the competitive neutrality policy was implemented 'only to the extent that the benefits to be realized from implementation outweigh the costs'.[28]

As noted, governments had considerable flexibility in implementing competitive neutrality policy in their individual states and territories, but needed to document their responses and progress.[29] The implementation of competitive neutrality policy was timetabled, and governments agreed to adopt individual policy statements on competitive neutrality, to set up fair and transparent individual complaints mechanisms and to report annually on progress in implementing the competitive neutrality reforms.[30]

4.4 Measuring Competitive Advantage

The Hilmer Report recognized that in some situations it would be difficult to determine the net competitive advantage or disadvantage with any precision. Where there are net competitive advantages, however,

---

26 Intergovernmental Competition Principles Agreement clause 3(4). Various terms have been used over time in laws and policies to describe government entities and businesses. In this chapter the use of a capitalised description for government entities describes a defined type of government entity with specific characteristics. Some of these are no longer used. The Public Performance and Accountability Act 2013 (fully operative 1 July 2014), for example, refers to 'government business enterprise' which is not capitalised, and refers to 'a Commonwealth entity of Commonwealth company that is prescribed by the rules'.

27 Ibid., clause 3(5).

28 Ibid., clause 3(6).

29 For information about the various states see e.g., New South Wales, available at: http://www.ipart.nsw.gov.au/Home/About_Us/What_We_Do/Competitive_Neutrality; Victoria, available at: http://www.vcec.vic.gov.au/Competitive-Neutrality; Queensland, available at: http:www.treasury.qld.gov.au/office/knowledge/docs/ncp/ncp-competitive-neutrality.pdf; Tasmania, available at: http://www.economicregulator.tas.gov.au/domino/otter.nsf/price-v/002 (all accessed 31 December 2013).

30 Payments made to state and territory governments for compliance with their obligations under the NCP included assessment of competitive neutrality obligations: Intergovernmental National Competition Policy and Related Reforms Agreement.

government businesses may be able to price below more efficient or equally efficient commercial rivals. It found that competitive neutrality concerns had greater impact in markets where a GBE had not traditionally operated. Different concerns arose in traditional monopoly markets. In markets opened up to competition it was not appropriate for government businesses to enjoy continuing advantages against newer and possibly more efficient competitors. In newer markets new entry by government businesses had the capacity to take away business from more efficient competitors if issues of competitive neutrality were not addressed. Competitive neutrality policy recognized that the adoption of its principles could encourage greater efficiency in resource allocation even where there is no actual or potential competition because governments are better informed about the actual cost of providing goods or services.[31] Competitive neutrality policy also assists public-sector managers to more accurately assess whether the government should retain responsibility for some business activities or whether alternative means of service provision should be considered.[32]

5. IDENTIFIED PUBLIC BENEFITS OF COMPETITIVE NEUTRALITY POLICY

Identified benefits of competitive neutrality policy include:

- more efficient pricing, with resources allocated to their best uses;
- longer-term performance efficiency gains as a result of Government Business Enterprises (GBE) operating in a more competitive environment;
- savings to government from better utilization of infrastructure;
- transparency and greater efficiency in the provision of community-service obligations; and
- increased service quality as a result of better performance monitoring.[33]

---

[31] See National Competition Council, Competitive Neutrality Reform: Issues in Implementing Clause 3 of the Competition Principles Agreement (Canberra) (2007) 7.

[32] See Commonwealth Competitive Neutrality Guidelines for Managers (1998) 1.

[33] National Competition Council, Competitive Neutrality Reform: Issues in Implementing Clause 3 of the Competition Principles Agreement (1997) 2. See

In November 2000, the Council of Australian Governments (COAG) clarified some implementation issues, agreeing that:

- Where a government business such as a university is not subject to the executive control of government it may adopt a 'best endeavours approach' to implementing competitive neutrality policy.[34]
- The term 'full cost attribution' in clause 3 of the Agreement would be satisfied by a range of costing methods, including fully distributed cost, marginal cost and avoidable cost.
- Governments are not required to undertake a competitive process for the delivery of community service obligations (CSOs).[35]

Subsequent to the completion of the NCP reforms, a new National Reform Agenda, also agreed to and implemented by the all governments through the Council of Australian Governments (COAG), continued the competitive neutrality reforms.[36] The provisions of the Competition and Infrastructure Reform Agreement 2006, which implemented this continuation, are set out in Appendix B.

The preceding material discussed the principles behind the adoption of a competitive neutrality policy in Australia. The remainder of the chapter addresses more practical issues.

6. WHAT BUSINESSES AND ACTIVITIES ARE COVERED?

Government needs to be clear on what activities are subject to competitive neutrality policy. Bodies classified as public trading enterprises and public financial enterprises include major commodity marketing authorities, electricity authorities, railway authorities, port authorities and, at

---

also National Competition Council, Assessment of Government Progress in Implementing the National Competition Policy and Related Reforms (2003) para. 2.2.

[34] For an example of a university policy on competitive neutrality see the University of New South Wales Policy available at http://www.gs.unsw.edu.au/policy/documents/commercialactivitiesguide.pdf (accessed 31 December 2013).

[35] A. Trembath, 'Competitive Neutrality: Scope for Enhancement. National Competition Council Staff Discussion Paper' (2002) 8.

[36] As to the National Reform Agenda generally see D. Healey (n. 5 above).

local government level, water and sewerage businesses, government-owned banks and government-owned insurance companies.[37] As noted, clause 3(5) of the Competition Principles Agreement extends to other significant businesses that are not public trading enterprises or public financial enterprises but that undertake activities substantially funded by revenue and earn profits, or potentially earn profits. The classification of businesses as 'significant' varies from jurisdiction to jurisdiction,[38] as a business activity may be operated on a commercial basis in one jurisdiction but be part of government in another jurisdiction. 'Significant' in this context is not just a measure of the size of a business but also its influence on the relevant market, and its contribution to the economy at its own level.[39]

The Commonwealth Competitive Neutrality Policy Statement, for example, deems all GBEs and their subsidiaries 'significant business enterprises'. A 'business' for these purposes involves the following features:

- It charges for goods and services;
- It is an actual or potential competitor either in the private or public sector – users must not be prohibited by law or policy from choosing alternative sources of supply;
- Its managers must have a degree of independence in relation to production and pricing.[40]

In addition, other commercial activities of non-GBE SOE agencies prescribed by regulation under the Financial Management and

---

[37] For further comment, see Commonwealth Competitive Neutrality Policy Statement (1996), available at: http://archive.treasury.gov.au/documents/275/PDF/cnps.pdf (accessed 31 December 2013).

[38] A number of sources have compared the differences in approach between various jurisdictions. See, e.g., I. Hanrahan, 'Becoming Competitively Neutral – Removing the Gilded Edge of Government Business' (2004) 12 *Trade Practices L.J.* 19 (Queensland and Victoria); Trembath (n. 35 above) (Commonwealth and all states and territories); and most recently, Victorian Competition and Efficiency Commission, Competitive Neutrality Interjurisdictional Comparison Paper (2013), available at: http://www.vcec.vic.gov.au/Competitive-Neutrality/Policy-documentation, under heading 'Competitive neutrality inter-jurisdictional comparison paper February 2013.pdf' (accessed 31 December 2013).

[39] A full and detailed list of the types of business activities NCC thought 'should be considered for competition reform' in this context appears in National Competition Council (n. 33 above) 11.

[40] National Competition Policy Report 2005–2007 (n. 17 above) 48.

Accountability Act 1997, Commonwealth authorities or departments with a commercial turnover of at least AU$10 million per annum, baseline costing activities for market-testing purposes and public-sector bids are considered 'significant' for the purposes of the policy.

While competitive tendering and contracting out were not mandated by the NCP, they complement competitive neutrality outcomes and, where government bids against the private sector, are subject to competitive neutrality principles. In these circumstances private bidders are more likely to consider that government does not have an unfair advantage.[41]

Other business activities may choose to apply a competitive neutrality policy, and may be the subject of complaint. Non-profit entities that are legally required or directed by the government to operate on a 'non-profit' basis are exempt from the requirements of competitive neutrality.[42]

The competitive neutrality policy also applies to local governments, with states applying policies similar to those regarding state businesses.[43]

7. RELATIONSHIP WITH OTHER POLICY OBJECTIVES

Importantly, competitive neutrality policy is not intended to override the policy obligations of government agencies or the range of social, environmental, economic and regional responsibilities of government agencies, which are all relevant to determining whether the application of competitive neutrality is in the public interest.[44]

Where public-interest issues are raised to justify the non-application of competitive neutrality policy, however, the government body concerned must conduct a transparent public-interest analysis to justify any decision not to apply full cost adjustments. Factors relevant to the public interest in this context have been identified as including:

- laws and policies relating to the environment;
- social welfare and equity;

---

41 See Trembath (n. 35 above) 39; see also Commonwealth Government Competitive Neutrality Policy Statement 1996.

42 Australian Government, Australian Government Competitive Neutrality Guidelines for Managers (2004) 2.

43 See Trembath (n. 35 above) 41 ff.

44 See, for example, Competitive Neutrality Guide to Implementation Victoria 2000, 'Foreword' (copy with author).

- laws and policies relating to matters such as occupational health and safety, industrial relations, access and equity;
- economic and regional development, including employment and investment growth;
- the interests of consumers generally or of a class of consumers;
- the competitiveness of Australian businesses; and
- the efficient allocation of resources.[45]

In respect of the Commonwealth, responsibility for compliance rests with the responsible minister and in addition the GBEs and Commonwealth Companies must have their arrangements approved by the Minister for Finance.

8. IMPLEMENTATION OF THE COMPETITIVE NEUTRALITY POLICY AT A PRACTICAL LEVEL

8.1 Business Pricing Decisions

The application of the competitive neutrality policy at its most basic level requires the making of government business pricing decisions comparable with private-sector organizations by identifying all direct costs and adding competitive neutrality components where necessary.[46] The first step is identifying the direct costs of a function. The second step is adjusting for relevant costs or margins that apply in the private sector and may not be fully accounted for in the direct costs to government, including things like commercial rate of return, payment of all relevant Commonwealth and state taxes, regulatory neutrality and debt neutrality. Factoring in of community-service obligations is an important consideration; however, under the competitive neutrality policy, community-service obligations are only able to be implemented on a non-commercial basis at the explicit direction of legislation, cabinet decision or public directions from shareholder ministers.[47] This process allows for consideration of the true cost to the community of these community-service

[45] See Hanrahan (n. 38 above) 25, citing National Competition Council, 'Local Government and National Competition Policy' (2000) 2, available at: www.ncc.gov.au/pdf/CICOmLg-001.pdf viewed 9 February 2004 (accessed 31 December 2013).

[46] See Commonwealth Competitive Neutrality Guidelines (1998) 7. See also Competition Policy Report 2005–2007 (n. 17 above) 49.

[47] See Commonwealth Competitive Neutrality Guidelines (1998) 19.

obligations. A change in November 2000 means that governments are free to determine how community-service obligations should be implemented, subject to them being 'transparent, appropriately costed and funded directly by government'.[48]

8.2 Determining 'Net Competitive Advantage'

Whether particular competitive neutrality reforms are appropriate in a particular case depends on whether the benefits of a particular reform outweigh the costs, in accordance with the Competition Principles Agreement.[49] The concept of 'net competitive advantage' is thus central to competitive neutrality. Factors that are relevant to the consideration of the benefits and detriments to an individual organization include matters relating to the interests of consumers, the competitiveness of the business generally, ecologically sustainable development, social welfare and equity, industrial relations, occupational health and safety, access and equity, economic growth and regional development, and the efficient allocation of resources.[50] Areas of potential net advantage identified in the NCP are: exemption from taxation liability, access to capital at concessional rates, exemption from aspects of business regulation, and pricing policies that do not take account of full production costs.[51] The NCC has stated: 'every factor which contributes to an ownership-related advantage or disadvantage should be identified and, to the extent practicable, the advantage or disadvantage eliminated'.[52]

The NCC has emphasized that the term 'net competitive advantage' does not mean that 'advantages' in one area compensate for 'disadvantages' in another, as clearly the weighing up involved in these circumstances is unlikely to lead to efficient resource-allocation outcomes and makes little sense. Rather, in each case an individual consideration of the actual facts and circumstances must occur.

---

[48] See Trembath (n. 35 above), 50, also as to market testing.

[49] Clause 1(3).

[50] See National Competition Council (n. 33 above) 12.

[51] Competition Principles Agreement clauses 3(4), 3(5).

[52] See National Competition Council (n. 33 above) 8. The NCC also recommended using 'proxies' such as tax-equivalent regimes where advantages or disadvantages cannot be removed or transaction costs of the removal are too high.

9. COMPETITIVE NEUTRALITY COMPLAINTS

9.1 Complaints Procedures

Complaints mechanisms set up under the competitive neutrality policy are the way in which interested parties pursue their concerns about government policy, conferring competitive advantages on government-owned businesses. Complaints may allege, for example, that a business has not been exposed to competitive neutrality arrangements or is not complying with the relevant arrangements, or that the arrangements are not effective. A complaints process requires an independent arbitrator of genuine complaints, with formal advice on outcomes and reasons being given to the parties, and prompt rectification of any legitimate issues. The Commonwealth and each of the states and territories have mechanisms for the investigation of complaints through independent bodies, which report and make recommendations based on the investigations.

9.2 Consideration of Case Examples

Concerted implementation of structural and other mechanisms at Commonwealth, state and territory levels have led to a relatively small number of complaints about breach of competitive neutrality principles. Analysis of some of these illustrates the way in which the complaints process works and how competitive neutrality principles are viewed in various jurisdictions. The numbers of complaints investigated in the Commonwealth, the states and the territories vary widely, from one complaint in New South Wales, the most populous state with the largest economy, to 63 complaints in Victoria, the state that has the second-largest population and the second-largest economy.[53] Whether the disparities reflect more effective corporatization and implementation of the competitive neutrality policy in New South Wales, some other feature of the individual economies, different business behaviour, or some factor such as the ease of making a complaint is difficult to discern. Victoria is, however, the only jurisdiction to have more than 20 complaints.

---

[53] Victorian Competition and Efficiency Commission, Competitive Neutrality Inter-jurisdictional Comparison Paper (2013) 9, available at http://www.vcec.vic.gov.au/Competitive-Neutrality/Policy-documentation, under heading 'Competitive neutrality inter-jurisdictional comparison paper February 2013.pdf' (accessed 31 December 2013).

The examples below are a random selection of complaints from a number of jurisdictions.[54]

9.3 Commonwealth Government Businesses

There have been a total of 15 complaints involving the Commonwealth government. A selection of these is set out below.

9.3.1 NBN Co

This recent consideration of competitive neutrality policy implementation in a complex regulatory environment warrants detailed consideration, particularly because of the phase of the business at the time of the complaints. Three competitors made various complaints about the conduct of NBN Co, which was established in 2009 as a GBE wholly owned by the Commonwealth to design, build and operate a wholesale-only national broadband network (NBN) across Australia.[55] The NBN was intended to connect around 93 per cent of Australian homes, schools and workplaces via fibre-to-the-premises, and to deliver broadband speeds of up to 100 megabits per second.[56] Its broad purposes were to address perceived failures in the telecommunications market such as the failure of business to invest in high-speed broadband, a lack of competition in regional broadband services and a lack of uniform national wholesale pricing in the supply of broadband. Rollout of the fibre network for the NBN was expected to continue until 2020.

NBN Co had a corporate plan and an independent board and management team. The intention was that it would be funded with government equity until NBN Co had sufficient cash flows to support private-sector debt without explicit government support.[57] In the longer term the government expected NBN Co to be self-funding and intended to sell down its interest within five years after the NBN was fully operational.

The government expected NBN Co to operate in a commercial manner and in accordance with a written statement of expectations, and that its approach to pricing would recognize the importance of maintaining

---

[54] For instance, from other jurisdictions; see Victoria, available at: http://www.vcec.vic.gov.au//Competitive-Neutrality/Invetigation-reports (accessed 31 December 2013).

[55] National Broadband Companies Act 2011.

[56] Australian Government Competitive Neutrality Complaints Office (2011) *NBN Co*, Investigation No. 14, at 3, available at: http://www.pc.gov.au/agcnco/publications/investigation/nbnco (accessed 31 December 2013).

[57] Ibid., 7.

affordability to drive take-up rates.[58] It was intended that NBN Co would provide and charge for one of the two cost components faced by retail service providers in supplying services to customers over the NBN. NBN Co would charge for access to the network (fibre, wireless or satellite) to the point of interconnection. Retail service providers would then need to transport their data from the point of interconnection to the point of presence (the backhaul). End-user prices were expected to vary because of different costs of providing the backhaul link, and where this would have the greatest impact on retail prices NBN Co was required to provide a 'transit backhaul service', such as a link to connect rural and remote areas of the network to the main competitive backhaul network. NBN Co was preparing a special-access undertaking to be approved by the Australian Competition and Consumer Commission (ACCC) under the Competition and Consumer Act 2010 to finalize pricing for its part of the NBN.

9.3.1.1 The complaints Three competitors alleged that NBN Co was not complying with the competitive neutrality policy in a number of respects, and that policy development had granted NBN Co commercial advantages. OPENetworks submitted that, while NBN Co had been announced as a provider of last resort to greenfield developments, it had actively sought business in commercially viable developments. Its pricing in those developments was allegedly contrary to competitive neutrality principles, because infrastructure and connections were being provided at no cost, an option that was unavailable to private providers. In addition, and in these circumstances, the projected rate of return of 7 per cent was impossible. The complainant also alleged that there were possible competitive neutrality breaches arising from ministerial determinations of technical specifications. Comverge Networks raised similar issues in relation to greenfield developments. It also alleged that NBN Co did not follow a fair and transparent tender process when seeking to build networks in new developments, resulting in a 'capture of intellectual property from … competitors'.[59] NBN Co's negotiations with Telstra for transfer of existing and new networks were alleged to put smaller players at a significant disadvantage. In addition, it was alleged that NBN Co's operational standards were presented as new industry standards to which all operators must adhere. The third complainant, Service Elements, characterized the greenfield development as a position in which 'NBN is

---

[58] Ibid., 3.

[59] Ibid., 2.

able to act as a provider of "first resort" rather than a provider of "last resort"' due to financial backing by the government. Its pricing of infrastructure was said to be contrary to current industry practice of charging capital costs to developers rather than to retail service providers. The complainant also alleged that its 7 per cent target rate of return did not represent a commercial rate of return as required by the competitive neutrality policy, and that NBN Co was afforded regulatory advantages as a consequence of ministerial determinations and its role in defining the footprint for the national broadband network. It made claims similar to those of the other complainants about the tender process.

9.3.1.2 The process The Australian Government Competitive Neutrality Complaints Office (AGCNCO) considered whether NBN Co was being conducted or was likely to be conducted in accordance with competitive neutrality arrangements. This involved assessing NBN Co's actual or intended compliance with the policy's requirements on taxation, debt, regulatory neutrality and commercial rate of return.[60] The fact that the business activity of NBN Co was in its infancy meant that the business model had not been sufficiently implemented to yield data on what would be viewed as normal costs and revenues and in some respects required examination of whether NBN Co was in *ex ante* breach of the competitive neutrality policy, rather than looking at commercial results achieved up to that point. New developments across the country had access to fibre technology as it was built, and this installation was done by the private sector. The government had announced that the NBN Co would be the infrastructure provider of last resort in new developments. Developers were obliged to prepare and fund certain installations to NBN Co specifications.

9.3.1.3 Assessment of complaints AGCNCO determined that issues relating to the status of NBN Co as a provider of last resort, its long-term contracts with Telstra and the tender process to establish a panel of infrastructure providers fell outside the competitive neutrality policy. The determination on 'provider of last resort' turned on the government's own view of what those words meant. In addition, AGCNCO emphasized that the competitive neutrality policy does not mean that government businesses cannot compete with private businesses.[61] Competitive advantages conferred by market position were not part of the competitive neutrality

---

[60] Ibid., 4.
[61] Ibid., 19.

policy, as 'matters of business type, size, location and market position can be exploited by all businesses'.[62] NBN Co's use of profile to promote itself to the development industry was an operational decision and not a breach of the competitive neutrality policy. The NBN's long-term contracts with Telstra were characterized as 'a deliberate decision by the Government to establish a company of sufficient size and balance sheet strength to achieve the scale of reform required to create a structurally separated telecommunications industry in Australia'.[63] The AGCNCO characterized this advantage as one of size, not one of government ownership.

Complaints about the tender process really related to NBN Co securing sensitive information submitted by tenderers. This complaint was characterized as one outside the competitive neutrality policy and in that respect NBN Co advised that tenders were conducted in accordance with government tender requirements.

9.3.1.4 Pricing of infrastructure in greenfield developments The competitive neutrality policy requires government businesses to set prices to earn a commercial rate of return overall. In this regard, the outcome of overall activities of a business, not the price of particular products or services, is relevant. AGCNCO noted that this approach gives the same flexibility to government businesses in setting prices as applies in the private sector, and means that a pricing model with adverse impact on competition in a particular market sector would not breach the competitive neutrality policy (although it would be subject to general competition law). In the greenfield developments example, NBN Co supplied fibre and active equipment at no cost with developer obligations being limited to meeting the cost of 'pit and pipe' construction. The cost of fibre and active equipment was recovered from retail service providers, meaning that pricing between brownfield and greenfield markets was consistent. This was a different model from that used by private providers, and would have an effect on competition in that market segment because developers would have a clear incentive to use NBN Co to reduce costs. The Department of Broadband Broadcasting and the Digital Economy (DBCDE) advised AGCNCO that the pricing model reflected the government's objective of achieving a common entry-level broadband price structure for all Australian premises across all technologies used in the rollout. AGCNCO concluded that NBN Co's pricing model for individual

62 Ibid., 20.
63 Ibid., 21.

goods or services in particular market segments was not in itself a breach of the competitive neutrality policy.

9.3.1.5 Expected rate of return on assets and related issues The complainants alleged that the NBN Co's estimated rate of return of 7 per cent and the timeframe over which it was expected to be achieved represented a breach of the competitive neutrality policy. They claimed that: it was not achievable under the planned pricing structure; it was not a true commercial rate of return; it was not achievable within a reasonable timeframe; and it was not representative of the cost of meeting NBN Co's shareholder loans.

In response, DBCDE argued that the published 7 per cent internal rate of return was net of the estimated tax payments made after 2028, and on a pre-tax basis could be closer to 8 per cent. AGCNCO stated that the issue was whether the return from the project would deliver a commercial return commensurate with its weighted average cost of capital (WACC). At the time the complaints were considered there was no data yet available on NBN Co's financial performance to verify the achievement or otherwise of a commercial rate of return. Given the 'infancy' of NBN Co, AGCNCO approached the issue by examining the processes used by NBN Co to determine its forecast revenue and costs, stating:

> In this *ex ante* context, important considerations in relation to the pricing model are:
>
> - the presence of sound processes for setting cost estimates and pricing
> - the presence of appropriate sensitivity testing around the assumptions that underpin the business case
> - recognition that NBN Co has adopted a 'cross-subsidy' pricing model in order to achieve the government's stated objective of offering a common entry level broadband price structure.[64]

NBN Co had undertaken to update its corporate plan annually and an independent report considered the plan to 'be in line with a range of available domestic and international benchmarks and consistent with the stated policy objectives of government with respect to the NBN'.[65] NBN Co's pricing model was also subjected to sensitivity testing and would be under ACCC scrutiny to gain approval for the proposed special-access undertaking.

---

64 Ibid., 27.
65 Ibid., 28.

AGCNCO cited the Competitive Neutrality Guidelines for Managers, which provide guidance on how to determine a commercial rate of return when, as in this case, a benchmark has not been set by the government. Relying on the Guidelines, AGCNCO looked at risk broadbanding rather than the WACC because a comparable WACC was not easily determined and managers were only able to approximate the market risk of the business. Using risk broadbanding, analysis showed that the expected after-tax internal rate of return of 7 per cent would not deliver a commercial rate of return.[66] DBCDE and NBN Co argued that NBN Co's commercial rate of return should be viewed in the context that NBN Co had been established to deliver both commercial and social benefits. NBN Co was not, however, transparently funded for delivery of non-commercial benefits that the government required and AGCNCO had not been provided with quantification of the non-commercial benefits expected. In these circumstances AGCNCO was unable to determine whether the difference between a commercial rate of return and the 7 per cent projected was adequately explained by the non-funded community service obligations. AGCNCO concluded that there was a potential *ex ante* breach of the competitive neutrality policy. It recommended that the government arrange for an analysis of the non-commercial benefits required and put in place accountable and transparent community service obligations funding. It also recommended that NBN Co adjust its pricing model by taking into account funding by the government for its community service obligations, and show how the adjusted pricing model would achieve a commercial rate of return that reflected its risk profile.

The complainants also argued that the 30-year model with positive cash flows from 2022 was unreasonable from a commercial perspective and represented a breach of the competitive neutrality policy. AGCNCO noted that the competitive neutrality policy and guidelines provided limited guidance on what was a reasonable timeframe to earn a commercial rate of return. The reasonableness of the length of the start-up phase was the real issue here. AGCNCO concluded that in the absence of a quantification of NBN Co's CSOs the expected timeframe for achieving a commercial rate of return (12 years) represented a potential *ex ante* breach of the competitive neutrality policy.

Another argument of the complainants was that the government's commitment of funds to NBN Co represented a shareholder loan and should be viewed as a debt when looking at competitive neutrality compliance. The competitive neutrality policy, however, only requires

66 Ibid., 32.

debt neutrality provisions to be applied when monies are borrowed from the government or raised in the market. AGCNCO concluded that the equity funding of NBN Co was not subject to the debt-neutrality provisions of the competitive neutrality policy.

As to the complaint about ministerial determinations, AGCNCO found that as no ministerial determinations had been made, there had been no breach of the competitive neutrality policy in that respect. In any event, if determinations did not exempt NBN Co from regulations that applied to other competitors, there would not be a breach of the regulatory neutrality requirements of the competitive neutrality policy.[67]

9.3.2 Complaint re AIS Swim School

The AIS Swim School was a commercial activity of the Australian Sports Commission (ASC), the body responsible for sports development at elite and grass-roots levels. The ASC conducted learn-to-swim classes, recreational swimming, aqua-aerobics and other aquatic activities at the Australian Institute of Sport (AIS) facilities. A competitor swim school lodged a complaint with the Minister for Sport and Tourism and the AIS. The complaint alleged that the AIS Swim School was subsidized by the ASC, its government owner, and that its costing and pricing policy did not comply with the competitive neutrality policy. The complaint also stated that it was inappropriate for the AIS Swim School to replicate services already available in the area in the private sector, and that if it was to continue in this way it should adopt a corporatized model.

Legislation setting up the AIS required it to allow individuals and community groups to have access to AIS facilities, and expressly provided for provision of commercial services at AIS facilities.

The CCNCO (Commonwealth Competitive Neutrality Complaints Office, predecessor of AGCNCO) agreed that AIS Swim School was a business activity under the Commonwealth Competitive Neutrality Policy Statement. It found, however, that it was inappropriate for AIS Swim School to be subject to competitive neutrality arrangements because it had no significant net competitive advantage resulting from government ownership. For the purposes of this consideration, the costs of providing AIS Swim School services were the avoidable costs of providing the services, given that the pool facilities were constructed and operated primarily to meet the core purpose of the Australian Sports Commission – the servicing of the development of elite athletes. The same principle would be applied to other swim schools using facilities predominantly

67 Ibid., 37.

associated with other users such as schools or health clubs. The incremental costs associated were embodied in a facilities rent charge to the AIS Swim School, so that in effect the AIS Swim School's costs were not being subsidized by the AIS.

In any event, CCNCO found that the AIS Swim School was not advantaged by not applying competitive neutrality principles. There was no significant competitive advantage from its tax-exempt status because of its size and the nature of its operations. It had no significant advantage as a result of government ownership. It costed and priced its activities consistently with normal commercial behaviour. CCNCO did recommend, however, that the AISSS be subject to appropriate competitive neutrality arrangements, as this would involve negligible cost.[68]

9.3.3 ABC production facilities

The Australian Broadcasting Corporation (ABC), the national Australian broadcaster, owned production facilities and equipment and employed staff to produce television programmes for broadcast on its network. The ABC Production Portfolio (ABC Productions) also tendered on a commercial basis to provide production facilities and labour to other film and television producers. A competitor complained that ABC and ABC Productions were not complying with competitive neutrality principles, on the basis that ABC Productions had access to resources purchased for non-commercial production that enabled it to provide services at a lower cost than its competitors. The Commonwealth Competitive Neutrality Statement identified the sale of consumer goods and studio rentals as business activities subject to competitive neutrality despite the fact that the turnover for the studio-rentals business fell below the threshold for automatic application. CCNCO emphasized that it was not usually necessary to examine the internal costing or pricing policies of a stand-alone GBE to determine whether it was complying with the competitive neutrality principles because the assessment could be based on its aggregate performance. However, where a business unit draws heavily on assets and resources of a non-commercial parent agency the level of costs allocated to the unit could determine its profitability. In this situation both the level of profits and the construction of the cost base were examinable, but investigation of individual transactions was not required. Here the key question was whether the prices set generated

---

[68] Commonwealth Competitive Neutrality Complaints Office (1999) *Australian Institute of Sport Swim School*, Investigation No. 2, available at: http://www.pc.gov.au/__data/assets/pdf_file/0010/5401/report2.pdf (accessed 31 December 2013).

sufficient revenue to cover all relevant costs. This required assessment of whether there was an appropriate methodology for allocating costs to the commercial activity; whether there were appropriate accounting and internal control systems to demonstrate that the costing methodology was followed in practice; and whether the revenue was sufficient to cover all relevant costs, including taxes, that a private business would pay. CCNCO found that the method of costing labour and facilities used by ABC Productions exceeded the minimum cost benchmark consistent with competitive neutrality principles. The accounting and control system provided a basis for ensuring that all relevant costs were identified and its costing and pricing approach was followed in practice. Even allowing for the impact of taxation, ABC Productions generated a commercial level of profits in 1998–1999. The allocation of costs to ABC Productions was found to be consistent with competitive neutrality principles and no action was required.[69]

9.3.4 Meteorological services to aviation

A subsidiary of a New Zealand government meteorological body (Metra) lodged a complaint alleging that the Civil Aviation Safety Authority's administration of aviation regulations conferred a regulatory advantage on the Bureau of Meteorology (Bureau) by preventing Metra from competing in the market for the supply of meteorological services to the aviation industry. The Bureau was a statutory authority funded by the Commonwealth budget to provide weather forecasting and other meteorological services within Australia, and it also provided services to the aviation industry on a cost-recovery basis. The aviation services were regulated by the Civil Aviation Safety Authority (CASA). The Bureau resisted the introduction of full competition arguing that a fully competitive commercially viable aviation weather service does not exist anywhere in the world. Submissions indicated that the Airports Association of Australia was happy with the current arrangement, although other interested parties favoured a more competitive model.

CCNCO found that a component of the Bureau's services constituted a business activity for the purposes of the competitive neutrality policy. Various interested parties had different views on whether the market was contestable or not contestable. CCNCO looked at whether there could be competition for the market or in the market and concluded that some of

---

[69] Commonwealth Competitive Neutrality Complaints Office (2000) *ABC Production Facilities, Investigation* No. 4, available at: http://www.pc.gov.au/__data/assets/pdf_file/0012/5403/report4.pdf (accessed 31 December 2013).

the suggestions lay outside competition policy. The complainant thought that three models of competition could exist:

- a basic value-adding service which could entail Metra adding further detail and precision to the existing service for specific critical destinations and route-forecast elements;
- an expanded value-added service whereby Metra would become the sole supplier for its own customers. Data collection and basic collation would continue to be undertaken by the Bureau, funded under cost-recovery arrangements;
- a competitive tendering model whereby the government would make particular products contestable.

CCNCO noted that the Bureau and the Minister for Environment and Heritage had cited several reasons why the market should be reserved for the Bureau, including the nature of the good supplied, safety considerations and Australia's international aviation obligations. The CCNCO determined that there was not a case for preventing competition for value-added services on safety grounds. Australia's obligations under the Chicago Convention did not act to limit competition in the provision of meteorological services that were beyond the requirements of international conventions.

Ultimately the CCNCO did not consider that there was a case for restricting competition in the provision of value-added meteorological services to the aviation industry. The costs would be low and the overall impact on efficiency was likely to be positive. The Parliamentary Secretary to the Minister for the Environment and Heritage indicated to the CCNCO that other models of competition were under active investigation. The CCNCO recommended that the government should complete its consideration of the options for introducing competition in the provision of these services as soon as possible, and if no other model was likely to deliver greater net benefits to the community than competitive provision of value-added services, that approach should be implemented forthwith.[70]

9.3.5 Defence Housing Australia

AGCNCO received a complaint from the Real Estate Institute of Australia (REIA) regarding Defence Housing Australia (DHA)'s exemptions

---

[70] Commonwealth Competitive Neutrality Complaints Office (2001) *Meteorological Services to Aviation*, Investigation No. 7, AusInfo, Canberra.

from licensing requirements for the provision of property sales and management services. REIA alleged that DHA, a statutory body with responsibility for providing housing for members of the defence forces and other government agencies, acted as an estate agent and that its exemptions were anti-competitive because they provided a more favourable business environment for DHA than for private-sector real-estate agents. DHA did not need to comply with requirements such as those on continuing professional development for agents, maintaining a registered office and complying with prudential requirements such as trust accounts for bonds paid by tenants and insurances.

DHA was identified in the government's Competitive Neutrality Policy Statement as a government business activity subject to the competitive neutrality policy. AGCNCO considered whether DHA could be viewed as operating a real-estate business and should be subject to the same regulatory requirements applying to real-estate agents. Legislation regulating real-estate agents was introduced to safeguard individuals in their dealings with agents, to establish a process whereby only 'suitable' persons with appropriate qualifications could act as agents and to protect consumer transactions. AGCNCO noted that agents act on behalf of others for reward in transactions. The key issue was whether DHA operated as a real-estate agent in its transactions, and to determine this issue AGCNCO considered whether DHA would be required to comply with the relevant laws if it was trading as a private business in each state or territory. It concluded that while its activities were of a similar nature they were performed on its own behalf and not on behalf of a third party. DHA itself characterized its activities as similar to a private-sector property developer rather than an agent. In the circumstances DHA did not gain a regulatory advantage as a result of being government owned and had not breached the regulatory neutrality provisions.[71]

9.4 New South Wales

9.4.1 State Valuation Office

In *State Valuation Office*, the only case from New South Wales, three private valuation firms complained that the State Valuation Office (SVO) had failed to comply with the competitive neutrality policy in tendering for specific contracts to provide land-valuation services for the NSW

---

71 Australian Government Competitive Neutrality Complaints Office (2008) *Defence Housing Australia*, Investigation No. 13, available at: http://www.pc.gov.au/__data/assets/pdf_file/0004/79330/report13-defencehousing.pdf (accessed 31 December 2013).

Valuer General and a Victorian Council. At the time of the complaints the SVO operated as a commercial business unit in the NSW Department of Commerce and it competed with private-sector firms to provide land-valuation services to the NSW Valuer General and private clients. The work was awarded each year following tenders for NSW Local Government areas and the contracts were generally for three or four years.[72]

In a detailed consideration the Independent Pricing and Review Tribunal (IPART) found that the pricing methodology employed by SVO was consistent with the NSW competitive neutrality policy. In applying the methodology, however, SVO in two cases underestimated the resources it would require to fulfil the contracts. IPART made no finding on whether this was done in breach of competitive neutrality principles or was done in error. Some adjustments were required to the costing of insurance premiums, which appears to be lower than that of private-sector valuers. SVO's profit calculations were distorted by the exclusion of some corporate overheads. For the future, IPART recommended that SVO should improve its documentation to assist with further compliance reviews.[73]

9.5 Queensland

9.5.1 Cattletrain

In the *Cattletrain* complaint against Queensland Rail's livestock transport service, Cattletrain alleged that Queensland Rail breached competitive neutrality principles in Central Queensland because it priced its services lower than a private operator could by offering more favourable prices to selected customers to attract business, discounting livestock freight rates to particular businesses and employing procedures and operational advantages relating to animal-welfare transport standards. It was alleged that Queensland Rail influenced the development of these standards in a way that gave Queensland Rail an advantage over private-sector competitors.

The Queensland Competition Authority (QCA) found that Queensland Rail did enjoy a competitive advantage and priced these services below a

---

[72] In investigating these complaints, IPART referred to the NSW Treasury documents Policy Statement on the Application of Competitive Neutrality, January 2002, and Guidelines for Pricing of User Charges, June 2001.

[73] Independent Pricing and Review Tribunal (2004) *Investigation of Competitive Neutrality Complaints against State Valuation Office*, available at: http://www.ipart.nsw.gov.au/files/637ea1f8-f819-42a5-b485-9f670093fae2/Investigation_of_Competitive_Neutrality_Complaints_against_the_State_Valuation_Office_-_8_October_2004.pdf (accessed 31 December 2013).

level that a private organization could attain. Slightly more favourable prices were provided to certain clients in the form of volume discounting without supporting financial information, and this could only have been done by an entity that did not cover its costs, that is, that was government-owned or controlled. Other discounts to customers in exchange for operational efficiencies did not result from government ownership or control, and were in fact also applied by some commercial operators. The substitution of larger wagons for smaller wagons at the same price was due to operational requirements rather than as a result of government ownership. The complaint in relation to animal-welfare issues was not substantiated, as no advantage arose from government ownership.

Open-ended financial arrangements between Queensland Rail and the Queensland government that had applied at the time of the complaints had ceased so no further action was necessary.[74]

9.6 Victoria

9.6.1 City of Ballarat childcare centres

In a case from Victoria, the City of Ballarat ran two childcare centres. A competitor complained to the Victorian Competitive Neutrality Unit (CNU) that the Council childcare centres operated at a considerable loss and were subsidized by the City Council. A further complaint was made that the Council was paying their childcare workers wages above the level prescribed by the Federal Award which applied to all childcare centres.

The childcare services were found to be business activities, as they were provided for a fee. They were 'significant' because of their size relative to the size of businesses in the relevant market, comprising approximately 13 per cent of the market, in which there were a reasonable number of competitors of a moderate size. Under the Victorian competitive neutrality policy[75] government agencies falling within this definition were required to determine costing and pricing for their business activities. Where competitive neutrality measures were at risk of jeopardizing other public policy objectives, options for achieving all policy objectives, including competitive neutrality pricing, were explored

---

[74] Queensland Competition Authority (2001) Complaint by a Road Transport Operator against Queensland Rail, Final Report; available at: http://ncp.ncc.gov.au/docs/Queensland's%20sixth%20annual%20report%20on%20implementing%20the%20NCP,%20March%202002.pdf (accessed 31 December 2013).

[75] Victoria, Competitive Neutrality Policy 2000 (copy with author).

through a documented public-interest process.[76] The Council undertook a public-interest test process looking at the issue of community need and weighing it against competitive neutrality obligations against the background of an identified shortfall of childcare services in the relevant area. The Council had determined that the imposition of full-cost pricing of services would affect the ability of the community to access the services. As a result, the Council was required to subsidize services to meet community needs. No commercial rate of return could thus be achieved. CNU found that the Council had undertaken a thorough review of its public-policy objectives and had justified its childcare programme subsidy. CNU determined that the Council had not breached Victoria's competitive neutrality policy. The CNU noted that the Council had not become involved in developing new childcare centres to cater for identified need but had commenced an assessment of needs that it intended to provide to commercial stakeholders in the area.[77] This example is useful because the competitive neutrality policy breach was justified in all of the circumstances by a detailed consideration of the public-interest test.

10. MEASUREMENT OF PROGRESS IN COMPETITIVE NEUTRALITY REFORM

An early analysis of competitive neutrality implementation indicated concern because some governments identified significant business enterprises by size alone, which would have exempted many government business activities having a significant market influence arbitrarily from reform.[78] The NCC indicated that specific business activities should be identified that would be subject to competitive neutrality principles. The NCC was also concerned because the mechanisms for complaints handling established by some governments lacked transparency. Adoption of a competitive neutrality framework was particularly important in relation

76 Competitive Neutrality Unit, Department of Treasury and Finance (2003) Competitive Neutrality Complaint Investigation *Re City of Ballarat* 1 (copy with author).

77 Ibid.

78 National Competition Council, Annual Report 1995–1996, 14, available at: http://ncc.gov.au/publications/C41 (accessed 31 December 2013).

to competitive tenders where an in-house provider participated in the tender process.[79]

An assessment of the progress of governments by the NCC in 2003 indicated that most jurisdictions had committed to full-cost attribution for their significant business activities but that they had struggled to deal with some issues, including the application of marginal pricing or competitive pricing strategies in the short term. Coverage of the governments' competitive neutrality policies was generally satisfactory, although it could be improved.[80] Slow policy implementation allowed in some industries detracted from the results. Complaints handling could be improved in some respects.[81]

In its 2005–2006 Annual Report, the last before the formal finalization of National Competition Policy, the NCC stated that progress in relation to competitive neutrality had been mixed. All states and territories had corporatized major government businesses, and other significant businesses had been exposed to competitive neutrality principles. Competitive neutrality complaints units had been established. There was, however, scope for improving coverage of competitive neutrality principles and the operation of complaints mechanisms.[82] Both the NCC and the Productivity Commission[83] stated that commitment to better governance was required to ensure NCP reform objectives. The Productivity Commission stated: 'failure to meet this objective has potentially serious consequences given that government-owned enterprises have combined assets of more than A$174 billion and generate A$55 billion in revenue annually'.[84]

The Productivity Commission noted in particular that the majority of government-owned enterprises monitored failed to obtain commercial

---

[79] The NCC noted that it would place particular weight, in assessing the compliance of a jurisdiction with implementing the competitive neutrality policy, on allegations of non-compliance and how they were dealt with. Ibid., 15.

[80] National Competition Council (n. 33 above) 28. New South Wales' coverage was potentially broadest as it had assumed that competitive neutrality principles would apply unless an individual government business presented a case that costs exceeded benefits. West Australia had not required businesses operated by public hospitals to apply competitive neutrality principles.

[81] Ibid., at 2.13.

[82] National Competition Council, Annual Report 2005–2006, 59, available at: http://ncc.gov.au/publications/C41 (accessed 31 December 2013).

[83] Productivity Commission (2005) (n. 12 above).

[84] Ibid.

rates of return.[85] In 2004–2005, aggregate profitability increased in areas such as electricity, water and urban transport, but declined in railways, forestry and ports.[86]

The numbers of actual complaints about competitive neutrality policy issues are small when compared to the substantial areas of business conducted by government bodies. This may be because there are necessarily many variants in the implementation of individual competitive neutrality policies. Alternatively, it may be that not many businesses consider themselves to be disadvantaged when competing with government businesses or recognize that they are so disadvantaged.

Significant steps have been taken in implementing a competitive neutrality policy in Australia by the Australian government and the states and territories. This chapter has attempted to provide a snapshot of the reasons for implementation of the Australian competitive neutrality policy, how it was implemented and some of the issues arising. Continued diligence should provide additional economic rewards in the more efficient delivery of competitive government services to the benefit of the community as a whole.

11. REMAINING QUESTIONS

The success of the NCP reforms in Australia was underpinned by recognition by all governments of the urgency of comprehensive reform, broad agreement on priority areas, a solid conceptual framework, and highly effective procedural and institutional mechanisms.[87] The conclusions of the Productivity Commission on the issue of profitability indicate that despite elaborate systems for addressing the issue of competitive neutrality, levelling the playing field by insisting on a commercial rate of return for all government businesses is still a long way off. This suggests that even with the advantages provided by government ownership or control, these bodies struggle to achieve profitability. Of course on that score they are not alone: many private businesses are not profitable. The *ex ante* nature of the consideration in the *NBN Co* case cast no light on that issue. The general failure to

---

[85] As to the measurement of rates of return in a competitive neutrality context, see generally Commonwealth Competitive Neutrality Complaints Office Research Paper 'Rate of Return Issues' (1998), available at: http://www.pc.gov.au/agcnco/publications/research/cnror (accessed 31 December 2013).

[86] Productivity Commission (n. 12 above).

[87] Ibid., xxiii.

achieve profitability raises the issue of whether the profitability of government businesses should be considered and measured in identical fashion to private businesses. This issue may need to be addressed in the context of the on-going policy development in the area.

Issues of competition law and policy are a complex mix. Circumstances are never precisely the same in individual examples, for reasons that include the political economy of particular jurisdictions and the aims and coverage of particular competition laws in a jurisdiction. Australian competition law, for example, takes a substantial economic approach but allows for public-benefit consideration in a number of respects, particularly in areas of market failure. The Australian methodology for tackling the role of the government in the market is comprehensive and is considered to be a successful approach to dealing with the issue of competitive neutrality.

The Australian approach will not be appropriate for all jurisdictions. Just as competition laws vary between jurisdictions, so will approaches to achieving competitive neutrality. In many developing jurisdictions the realization that competitive neutrality is an issue and that implementation of some form of competitive neutrality policy should be considered is a truly significant step towards levelling the playing field between private and government businesses. Australia does, however, provide one example of a country that has adopted a competitive neutrality policy with considerable success.[88]

Despite the comprehensive competition policy initiatives of the last 20 years, further change is foreshadowed. A new Australian government elected in September 2013 has instituted an 'independent "root and branch" review' of Australia's competition law and policy 'in recognition of the fact that the Australian economy has changed markedly since …

---

[88] At the time of publication Australia had embarked on a further comprehensive review of competition law and policy: http://www.competitionpolicyreview.gov.au/terms-of-reference, March 2014. A key area of consideration is government involvement in markets. The draft report of September 2014, available at http://www.competitionpolicyreview.gov.au/draft-report, contains overwhelming support for the concept of competitive neutrality. It calls for governments to re-commit to competitive neutrality; review and updating of policies; and greater transparency of compliance and the findings of investigations by further public reporting – see Recommendations p. 36, and full details in Ch. 11. The final report is expected in March 2015.

1993'.[89] The review is the most comprehensive since the Hilmer Review.[90] It is very wide ranging, and is based on the following policy objectives:

1.1. no participant in the market should be able to engage in anti-competitive conduct against the public interest within that market and its broader value chain;
1.2. productivity boosting microeconomic reform should be identified, centred on the realisation of fair, transparent and open competition that drives productivity, stronger real wage growth and higher standards of living;
1.3. government should not be a substitute for the private sector where markets are, or can, function effectively or where contestability can be realised; and
1.4. the need to be mindful of removing wherever possible, the regulatory burden on business when assessing the costs and benefits of competition regulation.[91]

Among its 'key areas of focus', the review will look at 'government involvement in markets through GBEs, direct ownership of assets and competitive neutrality policy, with a view to reducing government involvement where there is no longer a clear public interest need'.

This suggests that there is an appetite for further privatisation of government businesses which would once again reduce the impact of government on competition in the market, reducing the need for competitive neutrality policy initiatives.

Despite its comprehensive nature the review is to report within 12 months. The approach to issues of competitive neutrality and, hence, the outcome of this review are still unknown. It may recommend a lesser involvement by Government in contestable markets; however, while there is any government involvement at all in contestable markets, competitive neutrality policy, in one form or another, will continue to be an important tool for ensuring a level playing field between government business and private market participants.

---

[89] See Competition Policy Review Terms of Reference: available at: http://competitionpolicyreview.gov.au/terms-of-reference/ (accessed 31 March 2014). These Terms of Reference were released in March 2014.

[90] The Dawson Review, which reported in 2003, was more concerned with amendment of the competition law itself, rather than competition policy. See http://tpareview.treasury.gov.au/content/termsofref.asp for the Dawson Terms of Reference and http://tpareview.treasury.gov.au/content/report.asp for the Report (accessed 31 March 2014).

[91] See Competition Policy Review Terms of Reference (n. 89 above).

APPENDIX A: CLAUSE 3 OF THE COMPETITION PRINCIPLES AGREEMENT[92]

(1) The objective of competitive neutrality policy is the elimination of resource allocation distortions arising out of the public ownership of entities engaged in significant business activities: Government businesses should not enjoy any net competitive advantage simply as a result of their public sector ownership. These principles only apply to the business activities of publicly owned entities, not to the non-business, non-profit activities of these entities.

(2) Each Party is free to determine its own agenda for the implementation of competitive neutrality principles.

(3) A Party may seek assistance with the implementation of competitive neutrality principles from the Council. The Council may provide such assistance in accordance with the Council's work program.

(4) Subject to subclause (6), for significant Government business enterprises which are classified as 'Public Trading Enterprises' and 'Public Financial Enterprises' under the Government Financial Statistics Classification:

(a) the Parties will, where appropriate, adopt a corporatisation model for these Government business enterprises (noting that a possible approach to corporatisation is the model developed by the intergovernmental committee responsible for GTE National Performance Monitoring); and

(b) the Parties will impose on the Government business enterprise:

(i) full Commonwealth, State and Territory taxes or tax equivalent systems;

---

[92] These principles were refined by further agreement of the Council of Australian Governments (COAG), which agreed at its November 2000 meeting that:

- the NCC's assessment of governments' application of the competitive neutrality policy to government businesses over which they had no executive control (such as universities) should be based on a 'best endeavours' approach;
- the term 'full cost attribution' could cover a range of methods, including fully distributed cost, marginal cost and avoidable cost;
- governments were not required to establish a competitive process for their delivery of CSOs; and
- governments are free to determine who should receive a CSO payment or subsidy, but such payments should be transparent, appropriately costed and budget funded.

As noted in National Competition Council, Assessment of Governments Progress in Implementing the National Competition Policy and Related Reforms (2003) Volume 1, at 2.1.

(ii) debt guarantee fees directed towards offsetting the competitive advantages provided by government guarantees; and
(iii) those regulations to which private sector businesses are normally subject, such as those relating to the protection of the environment, and planning and approval processes, on an equivalent basis to private sector competitors.

(5) Subject to subclause (6), where an agency (other than an agency covered by subclause (4)) undertakes significant business activities as part of a broader range of functions, the Parties will, in respect of the business activities:
(a) where appropriate, implement the principles outlined in subclause (4); or
(b) ensure that the prices charged for the goods and services will take into account, where appropriate, of the items listed in paragraph 4(b) and reflect full cost attribution for these activities.

(6) Subclauses (4) and (5) only require the Parties to implement the principles specified in those subclauses to the extent that the benefits to be realised from implementation outweigh the costs.

(7) Subparagraph (4)(b)(iii) shall not be interpreted to require the removal of regulation which applies to a Government business enterprise or agency (but which does not apply to the private sector) where the Party responsible for the regulation considers the regulation to be appropriate.

(8) Each party will publish a policy statement on competitive neutrality by June 1996. The policy statement will include an implementation timetable and a complaints mechanism.

(9) Where a State or Territory becomes a Party at a date later than December 1995, the Party will publish its policy statement within six months of becoming a Party.

(10) Each Party will publish an annual report on the implementation of the principles set out in subclauses (1), (4) and (5), including allegations of non-compliance.

APPENDIX B: COMPETITION AND INFRASTRUCTURE REFORM AGREEMENT OF 10 FEBRUARY 2006 – CHAPTER ON COMPETITIVE NEUTRALITY OF GOVERNMENT BUSINESS ENTERPRISES

6.1 The Parties agree to enhance the application of competitive neutrality principles to government business enterprises engaged in significant business activities in competition with the private sector:

Objectives

a. That the enterprise has clear commercial objectives.

b. That any non commercial objectives or obligations established for the enterprise are clearly specified and publicly reported.
c. That enterprises do not exercise regulatory or planning approval functions in circumstances in which they compete with private sector enterprises.

Governance

d. That the responsibilities of the governing board of the enterprise and the performance measures against which the board will be held accountable are published.
e. That the governing board is appointed on the basis of particular skills needed by the board.
f. That having received strategic guidance from the government about the achievement of its objectives, the enterprise has operational autonomy in the day to day management of its affairs.
g. That the dividend policy applicable to the enterprise should be clearly and publicly specified.
h. That any payments to the government as shareholder or for the purposes of competitive neutrality, such as taxes, tax equivalent payments, special dividends, capital repayments, are identified in a transparent manner.

Reporting

i. That at least annually the enterprise will report publicly on its commercial performance and on its performance of any non commercial activities.
j. That any directions given to the enterprise by the government are published.
k. That where the legislation establishing an enterprise derogates from competitive neutrality the derogation has been published.

2. Petrobrás: state monopoly and competition policy

Gilberto Bercovici

1. THE FORMATION OF THE FUEL MARKET IN BRAZIL

In Brazil, the oil sector is a monopoly of the state, but the state-owned enterprise responsible for the Brazilian oil policy, Petrobrás, needs to act following the principles of Brazilian competition policy, in at least two sectors: first, the fuel distribution market, the only branch of the oil sector not monopolized by the state; and, second, when Petrobrás uses its purchasing power.

Historically, we first notice a relevant interest in the market for oil and gas resources in Brazil by the time of the First World War. On the one hand, other countries experienced supply difficulties and a price increase as a result, especially in relation to coal, steel and fuel. On the other hand, in Brazil, there was a fear that foreign nations or economic groups would try to take control of such resources.

Indeed, the fuel supply market in Brazil was controlled by five subsidiaries of large foreign companies, namely Standard Oil of New Jersey, Anglo-American (affiliated with Royal Dutch Shell), Atlantic Refining Company, Texas Company and Caloric Company.[1] The fuel was imported from American and English refineries located at the Gulf of

---

[1] Internationally, the famous 'Seven Sisters' of the oil industry were Standard Oil of New Jersey (later Exxon), Royal Dutch Shell, Anglo-Iranian Oil Company (later British Petroleum), Texaco, Socony Mobil Oil, Gulf Oil and SOCAL (Standard Oil of California). Later, the companies Gulf, SOCAL and Texaco merged into Chevron. Sometimes, an eighth sister is included: Compagnie Française des Pétroles (CFP). On the origins of the 'Seven Sisters', three of which derive from the early Standard Oil founded in 1870 by J.D. Rockefeller, see A. Sampson, *The Seven Sisters: The Great Oil Companies and the World They Shaped* (Bantam Books 1976) 21–69.

Mexico and Aruba, in the Dutch Caribbean. Elevated prices, as well as tax advantages and foreign exchange rates, which highly benefited the foreign distributing companies, gave rise to many conflicts throughout the 1930s.[2]

On the eve of World War II, the share of oil products in the imports composition was extremely elevated in Brazil. Fuel imports were not just a serious problem to the balance of trade, but led to national dependency on foreign sources for the raw materials essential to the industrialization process, the transport and communication infrastructure as well as to the country's defense. In this context, the military authorities concentrated on the oil issue, emphasizing the strategic importance of controlling this resource, therefore drawing attention to the vulnerable position of Brazil resulting from its complete dependence on foreign fuel supply.[3]

Decree-Law No. 395 of 29 April 1938 declared of public interest the national oil supply market, including activities such as production, import, export, transport (including the construction of pipelines), distribution, trading and refining, regardless of the oil's origin (Article 1). The federal government retained the exclusive entitlement to act in this sector (Article 2), through the National Oil Council (Conselho Nacional do Petróleo – CNP) that was directly controlled by the President of the Republic (Article 4). The organization and assignment of the legal competence of the National Oil Council were established by Decree-Law No. 538 of 7 July 1938.

The Executive Power furthermore issued Decree-Law No. 3.236 of 7 May 1941, which withdrew the legal regime of oil and gas fields (including bituminous and pyrobituminous shale and rocks) from the Mining Code. Besides providing a better systematization for the subject, Decree-Law No. 3.236/1941 determines that oil and gas fields located in the national territory belong, not subject to prescription, exclusively to the domain of the federal government (Article 1, *caput*), reasserting as null and invalid any private registry (Article 1, sole paragraph). The research and exploitation of oil and gas should be authorized and supervised by the National Oil Council, and performed by national

---

2 J.D. Wirth, *A Política do Desenvolvimento na Era de Vargas* (Fundação Getúlio Vargas 1973) 116–118; L. Martins, *Pouvoir et Développement Économique: Formation et Évolution des Structures Politiques au Brésil* (Éditions Anthropos 1976) 284 et seq.

3 G. Cohn, *Petróleo e Nacionalismo* (Difel 1968) 41–44 and 46–48; Wirth (n. 2 above) 115 et seq. and 123–125; J.D. Wirth, 'Setting the Brazilian Agenda, 1936–1953' in J.D. Wirth (ed.) *Latin American Oil Companies and the Politics of Energy* (University of Nebraska Press 1985) 110–113.

companies or companies held by Brazilian shareholders or partners, with the participation of the federal government. Article 28, *caput*, of Decree-Law No. 3.236/1941 maintained the authorization by the federal government, acting through the National Oil Council, to research and exploit oil and gas fields and to process, trade and transport their products. The relevance of this Decree-Law is considerable; the legal regime governing oil was based on it and remained in force until the formal institution of the legal state oil monopoly and the constitution of Petrobrás in 1953, with the approval of Law No. 2.004 on 3 October of the same year by President Getúlio Vargas.

2. STATE MONOPOLY AND FUEL SUPPLY

After the creation of Petrobrás in the second Vargas presidency and its institutionalization during the Juscelino Kubitschek presidency,[4] the role of Petrobrás in the state monopoly system was expanded as a measure to enforce the monopoly itself. President João Goulart issued Decree No. 53.337 of 3 December 1963, by which Petrobrás was accorded the monopoly in imports of oil and oil by-products. This was intended, at first, as a way of controlling the balance of trade. More importantly, in the long term, it should bring a larger diversification of fuel supply sources, as well as providing better negotiation conditions regarding prices and freights, increasing national exports to those countries which supplied Brazil with oil and oil by-products.[5]

Law No. 2.004/1953 did not provide for the supply of oil by-products as a state monopoly. However, in 1962, when Francisco Mangabeira was head of Petrobrás, the company started its own supply business, with the creation of the Office of Distribution of Oil By-Products (Escritório de Distribuição de Produtos de Petróleo – EDIPE), which was planned to later be part of the state monopoly activities. The National Oil Council approved two resolutions: one assigned Petrobrás the role of distributor of by-products to government bodies and state-owned companies; the

---

[4] See G. Bercovici, *Direito Econômico do Petróleo e dos Recursos Minerais* (Quartier Latin 2011) 163–171.

[5] G. Carvalho, *Petrobrás: Do Monopólio aos Contratos de Risco* (Forense Universitária 1977) 174 et seq.; C. da Rocha Viana, *Reformas de Base e a Política Nacionalista de Desenvolvimento – De Getúlio a Jango* (Civilização Brasileira 1980) 143 et seq. and 152 et seq.; E. del Carmen Alveal Contreras, *Os Desbravadores: A Petrobrás e a Construção do Brasil Industrial* (Relume-Dumará/ANPOCS 1994) 88.

other authorized Petrobrás to act as distributor of oil by-products in the whole national territory. Resolution No. 8 of the National Oil Council of December 1963 provided for a forthcoming monopoly controlling the whole oil chain, a project which was unfortunately abandoned after the military coup of 1964.[6] In lieu thereof, the Petrobrás Fuel Distributor, established in January 1972,[7] became the indisputable market leader in the supply of oil by-products in Brazil, very much as a result of the creation of subsidiaries of several state-owned companies which aimed at the expansion of the role of Petrobrás.

In conformity with the Constitution of 1988, Fábio Konder Comparato asserts that state activity can no longer be taken as an intervention, but as the ordinary performance of a constitutional duty, as explicit in the principles and guidelines of the text of the Constitution. The state, thus, is constitutionally legitimated to conduct and condition the process of capital reproduction. Francesco Galgano affirms that state intervention in the economy means that the state decides, on the one hand, the amount of resources destined for capital reproduction, and, on the other hand, the amount which is designated for the social objectives contained in the emancipatory clauses of the Constitution. The state may, as well, withdraw one activity from the market if it acts as an obstacle to the achievement of the constitutional goals, establishing either a state monopoly or a public service regime, which, in Brazil, is inspired by the French tradition of 'service public'.[8]

In relation to its origin, the monopoly can be either natural or legal. From an economic point of view, monopoly studies define the concept as a deviation from the neoclassical model of perfect competition. The natural monopoly increases economic concentration, and the law acts to reduce the risk of abuse of market power, according to Article 173(4) of

---

[6] F. Mangabeira, *Imperialismo, Petróleo, Petrobrás* (Zahar 1964) 10 et seq. and 92–117; Carvalho (n. 5 above) 177 et seq.; J.L. de Mattos Dias and M.A. Quaglino, *A Questão do Petróleo no Brasil: Uma História da Petrobrás* (Ed. FGV/Petrobrás 1993) 153–155.

[7] Carvalho (n. 5 above) 178–180; de Mattos Dias and Quaglino (n. 6 above) 155 et seq. and 179–181; del Carmen Alveal Contreras (n. 5 above) 99. On oil distribution in Brazil, see also L. Randall, *The Political Economy of Brazilian Oil* (Praeger 1993) 157–162.

[8] F. Galgano, 'Pubblico e Privato nella Regolazione dei Rapporti Economici' in F. Galgano (ed.) *Trattato di Diritto Commerciale e di Diritto Pubblico dell'Economia* (CEDAM 1977) vol. 1, 123–125; E.R. Grau, *A Ordem Econômica na Constituição de 1988 (Interpretação e Crítica)* (12th edn, Malheiros 2007) 148–151; and F. Konder Comparato, 'Regime Constitucional do Controle de Preços no Mercado' (1991) *Revista de Direito Público* No. 97, 18.

the Brazilian Constitution.[9] The legal monopoly, however, is created to defend the public interest, setting apart a certain activity exclusively for the state. The constitutional concept of monopoly is always a public one, never that of a private monopoly. The difference between a public and a private monopoly is, as a matter of fact, attached to the economic goals of the exclusiveness itself, not to the legal regime. It is clear, then, that the state monopoly, in contrast to a private one, is not – and cannot be – controlled by competition law. Besides, the constitutional concept of monopoly always refers to a legal monopoly, and not a natural one.[10]

Eros Grau understands the state monopoly as a form of state action in the economic domain by absorption. In other words, the state monopoly can be defined as the complete control, by the state, of the means of production and/or change of a particular economic activity *stricto sensu*.[11] The state monopoly is a relevant tool of the collectivity in the modern interventionist state. It is, in fact, a technique, a procedure of state action, employed to accomplish a certain task in view of promoting the public interest.

German authors prefer, in this case, to employ the term 'administrative monopoly' (*Verwaltungsmonopol*), which perfectly emphasizes the relation between the monopoly and a public goal in favor of an entity of the public administration, or a private entity legally invested to act on its behalf. The rules that establish a state monopoly are of public character, originating from the externalization of public power, which does not prevent it from being managed by a private legal entity. The basis for the implementation and accomplishment of the monopoly lies in the necessary conducting of economic policies by the state. The state monopoly is a special form of public economic activity, justified in the light of economic policy and set up in conformity with the principles of the

---

[9] Article 173(4) of the Constitution of 1988 reads as follows: 'The law shall repress the abuse of economic power that aims at the domination of markets, the elimination of competition and the arbitrary increase of profits.'

[10] See F. Machlup, *The Political Economy of Monopoly: Business, Labor and Government Policies* (4th edn, The John Hopkins Press 1967) 37–39 and 48–50; P. Badura, *Das Verwaltungsmonopol* (Duncker & Humblot 1963) 3–5, 7–8, 10–22 and 24–30; H. Mayer, *Staatsmonopole* (Springer-Verlag 1976) 2–10; C. Tácito, 'Ordem Econômica. Concorrência e Monopólio. Gás Natural' in *Temas de Direito Público (Estudos e Pareceres 1997)* vol. 2, 1136 et seq. This does not mean that the abuse of economic power may not occur in respect of a state monopoly, a phenomenon called 'monopoly abuse', the control of which does not belong to the field of competition law. See Badura, op. cit., 260–280.

[11] Grau (n. 8 above), 127 et seq. and 148. On the concept of state monopoly, see also Mayer (n. 10 above) 1–32.

economic constitution and the rules of the Constitution which institute the goals of the state.[12]

The state monopoly implies that the legitimacy to exercise a certain activity in the public interest is withdrawn from the domain of free enterprise. A monopoly is related to the exclusiveness to perform an economic or entrepreneurial activity, not to the exclusive property of the means of production or to the state ownership. The essential feature of the monopoly is the exclusion of all other competitors from performing a particular activity, which leads to a broad control over it. The state is entitled to transfer the execution of such activities to third parties, as provided for by law. Usually, this performance is undertaken by legal entities, either public or private, attached to the public administration (government bodies or public companies). This was the case of the original text of the Constitution of 1988. Article 177(1) did not allow the federal government to grant any concession whatsoever involving the exploitation of oil and gas fields, except the participation of states and municipalities pursuant to Article 20(1) of the Constitution. There may be, however, in some circumstances, a state monopoly with a 'reservation to breach' (*Verwaltungsmonopol mit Durchbrechungsvorbehalt*), that is, with the power to grant a concession to private entities.[13]

The Ninth Amendment to the Constitution, approved on 9 November 1995, allowed the federal government to choose the system of direct public activity or to contract such activities out to public or private companies. The federal government, then, may still act directly in the oil sector, by means of a public company under its controlling interest (Article 62 of Law No. 9.478 of 6 August 1997 determines the controlling interest of the federal government over Petrobrás). It is important to emphasize that the Ninth Amendment abolished the state monopoly over the direct public activities in the oil industry, but the state monopoly in such activities continues to exist, as provided for in Article 177 of the Constitution. Until the Ninth Amendment of 1995, oil-related activities could only be performed by the state itself or by an entity directly controlled by the state (namely, Petrobrás). From that moment on, the federal government was given the possibility to exploit these very same activities – which still are a state monopoly – by itself, or by contracting them out to other public or private companies (current text of Article 177(1) of the Constitution).

---

12 Badura (n. 10 above) 1, 86–95 and 281 et seq.

13 Badura (n. 10 above) 1 et seq., 244–251 and 258 et seq.; M.B. Coma, *Constitución y Sistema Económico* (2nd edn, Tecnos 1988) 173–179 and 190–193; Konder Comparato (n. 8 above), 148 and 150–153.

The present state monopoly regime for the oil industry is a typical case of a state monopoly with a 'reservation to breach' (*Verwaltungsmonopol mit Durchbrechungsvorbehalt*) that entitles the federal government to contract with private entities, as well as to decide who may perform economic activities in this sector; in other words, there is a 'monopoly of choice by the public power'.[14] In short, the federal government has not changed its position as the legal monopolist in oil exploitation and refining, but now it may choose either to perform these activities by itself or by public companies, or to contract with private entities.

The effects of the state monopoly of oil exploitation and refining are extended to the oil by-products. The terms of authorization, regulation and control of the sale and distribution of oil fuels – including but not limited to gas, ethanol and renewable energy resources – are determined by federal law, according to Article 238 of the Constitution.

3. THE NATIONAL FUEL SUPPLY SYSTEM AS A PUBLIC UTILITY

As we have seen, the oil supply system was declared a public utility as early as 1938 (Decree-Law No. 395/1938), which included the production, import, export, transport, distribution and trade of oil and its by-products, as well as oil refining, whatever the origin of the oil is (Article 1).

In relation to the North American debate, the notion of 'public utility' refers to a private activity which is the object of particular attention from the state authorities, which create rules in order to assure that such activity will be performed in the interest of the collectivity.[15]

---

14 Badura (n. 10 above) 258 et seq.; A. de Moraes, 'Regime Jurídico da Concessão para Exploração de Petróleo e Gás Natural' (2001) *Revista de Direito Constitucional e Internacional* No. 36, 163 et seq. and 166 et seq.; A. Walmott Borges, *A Ordem Econômica e Financeira da Constituição e os Monopólios: Análise das Alterações com as Reformas de 1995 a 1999* (reprint, Juruá 2008) 138–141; A. Ruy Barbosa, 'A Natureza Jurídica da Concessão para Exploração de Petróleo e Gás Natural' in P. Valois Pires (ed.) *Temas de Direito do Petróleo e do Gás Natural II* (Lumen Juris 2005) 22–27; J.A. Bucheb, *Direito do Petróleo: A Regulação das Atividades de Exploração e Produção de Petróleo e Gás Natural no Brasil* (Lumen Juris 2007) 123 et seq.

15 L. de Anhaia Mello, *O Problema Económico dos Serviços de Utilidade Pública* (2nd edn, Prefeitura do Município de São Paulo 1940) 25 et seq. and 32–35; F. Bilac Pinto, *Regulamentação Efetiva dos Serviços de Utilidade Pública* (Forense 1941) 75et seq. and 182 et seq.; O. Braga, 'Serviços Públicos

The leading US case is the well-known: *Munn v. Illinois* of 1876. The syllabus includes part of the majority opinion drafted by Chief Justice Waite, which reads:

> When, therefore, one devotes his property to a use in which the public has an interest, he, in effect, grants to the public an interest in that use, and must submit to be controlled by the public for the common good, to the extent of the interest he has thus created. He may withdraw his grant by discontinuing the use, so long he maintains the use, he must submit to the control.[16]

The private activities of special relevance and usefulness for the collectivity must be regulated by the state, although they do not, as a result, become public services. Such activities are profoundly regulated by the state, which, in the case of absence of a private agent – by lack of interest or condition to render the services – must provide the service itself.[17]

The national fuel supply, which in 1938 was already considered a public utility, retained the same nature after the enactment of Law No. 9.847 of 26 October 1999. Due to its importance to the collectivity, all activities listed in Article 1(1) of this law are subject to prior authorization by the National Oil Agency. The following activities, but not limited to them, are included under the concept 'national fuel supply': 'production, import, export, refining, processing, treatment, transport, transfer, storage, distribution, sale, trading, evaluation and certification of oil, gas and its by-products'.[18]

As an indication of how closely the fuel supply is regulated by the state, for instance, the National Oil Agency defines to which retailers the distributor may sell its products, limited to monthly rates previously determined. The distributor is also required to inform and procure the previous approval of the agency of most of its operations (Articles 8(XV), (XVI), (XVII) and (XXI) of Law No. 9.478/1997 and Articles 16,

---

Concedidos', *Revista de Direito Administrativo – Seleção Histórica* (Renovar 1995) 111 and 125; L.G. Kaercher Loureiro, *A Indústria Elétrica e o Código de Águas: O Regime Jurídico das Empresas de Energia entre a Concession de Service Public e a Regulation of Public Utilities* (Sergio Antonio Fabris Editor 2007) 118–124.

16 *Munn v. Illinois*, 94 U.S., 113, 125 et seq. (1876).

17 C.A. Bandeira De Mello, 'Serviços Públicos e Serviços de Utilidade Pública – Caracterização dos Serviços de Táxi – Ausência de Precariedade na Titulação para prestá-los – Desvio de Poder Legislativo' in *Pareceres de Direito Administrativo* (Malheiros 2011) 216–218. See also C.A. Bandeira De Mello, *Curso de Direito Administrativo* (28th edn, Malheiros 2011) 693 et seq.

18 Bucheb (n. 14 above) 21–23; M. D'Assunção Costa Menezello, *Comentários à Lei do Petróleo: Lei Federal no. 9.478 de 6-8-1997* (Atlas 2000) 54.

16-A, 16-B and 20 of Order No. 29/1999 of the National Oil Agency).[19] The distributor is not allowed to act as a retailer, and the retailers are allowed to contract with only one distributor (Article 12 of Order No. 116 of 5 July 2000 of the National Oil Agency).

4. THE FUEL SUPPLY MARKET AND ADMINISTERED PRICES

In Brazil, fuel prices are, ultimately, determined by the public administration, and not by the market itself. The market for oil and by-products, as well as other fuels, is an example of a market with 'administered prices'.[20]

In the 1930s, Gardiner Means offered a classic and yet simple definition of administered price, setting it in opposition to market-built prices: 'By an administrated price I mean one which is set by administrated action and held constant for a period of time'.[21]

Since then, economists and their readers contrast two price concepts: on the one hand, 'administered prices', and, on the other hand, 'private prices'. Private prices are the result of the free market system and of the individual action of economic agents who act in this market.[22]

According to the law, the price of oil and its by-products, as well as of fuels in general, had to be fixed by the state with regard to other elements than just regular market fluctuations. The authority of the former National Oil Council to fix fuel prices and provide for their uniform application all over the country was mandatory, pursuant to Decree-Law No. 538/1938, Article 10(c). Also, Law No. 4.458 of 5 November 1954

---

[19] Oil and gas are rather destined for the domestic market and, taking into account national parameters, not subject to volatile international prices. The control of the balance of payments and external accounts demands a higher control of export and import of oil, gas and by-products. This is, as a matter of fact, the mission of the National System of Fuel Stocks, established by Law No. 8.176 of 8 February 1991.

[20] The price of kerosene is determined by different parameters, under great influence of applicable international prices. The price of ethanol, besides international prices and other parameters, is also influenced by the gasoline price.

[21] G.C. Means, 'Price Inflexibility and the Requirements of a Stabilizing Monetary Policy' (1935) 30 *J. Am. Stat. Ass.* 401.

[22] See B. Hauptkorn, *Preisrecht: Ökonomische Rationalität und praktische Vernunft des allgemeinen und besonderen Rechts der Bildung und Verlautbarung von Preisen* (Duncker & Humblot 2000) 32 et seq.

assigned to the National Oil Council the authority to fix consumer prices of oil by-products not submitted to any other governmental body with power to control supplies, stocks and prices (Articles 13 to 15). This very same authority was secured by Article 2 of Decree-Law No. 61 of 21 November 1966 and Decree-Law No. 1.599 of 30 December 1977. The equalization costs to match the prices of oil by-products all over the territory were covered by the state, which would, on the one hand, compensate the distributors for the transport costs and, on the other hand, subsidize the ethanol. As a source of the necessary funds, the Freight for Uniform Costs levy was established in 1984, pursuant to National Oil Council's Resolution No. 16 of 27 November 1984. Moreover, there were several cross-subsidies through gasoline, diesel oil, ethanol, LPG (liquefied petroleum gas) and naphtha. Petrobrás would report on a monthly basis to the National Oil Council the difference between costs and refundable expenditures, such as foreign exchange variation between oil import prices and domestic fixed prices, through the Oil Account, By-Products Account and Ethanol Account.[23]

From the 1990s on, the fuel supply policy changed in order to liberalize fuel prices; and the former Decree No. 4.071 of 12 May 1939 underwent important changes. The import of oil by-products was allowed by Article 60 of Law No. 9.478/1997. The equalization of consumer prices was abolished and the new regulation granted free access to pipelines, tanks and terminals (Article 58).

A first result of such policy was the entry of many new distributors into the fuel supply market. As an inconvenient outcome, fuel adulteration and tax evasion escalated. The National Oil Agency was not sufficiently structured to monitor and sanction these unlawful practices. It is important to notice that many large foreign distributors eventually left the market, since they could not compete against a monopolist supplier (Petrobrás) and a predatory mass of regional distributors. With the development of the National Oil Agency and the stabilization of the economy, the fuel supply market is expected to overcome this phase and consolidate itself.

Oil and oil by-products are still considered as a group of products with administered prices by the Central Bank of Brazil, and are included in the list of administered prices which compose the National Extended Consumer Price Index. Despite the rhetoric of price liberalization, the state

---

[23] For an analysis of the policy of fuel administered prices in Brazil, see, among others, Randall (n. 7 above) 165–184; and M.W. Lima Sathler and M. Tiomno Tolmasquim, 'A Formação de Preços Derivados de Petróleo no Brasil' (2001) 8(1) *Revista Brasileira de Energia* 1–5.

still preserves the tools capable of controlling the oil industry. For example, in cases of abusive practices, the government may temporarily establish maximum prices, as stated by Resolution of the Agência Nacional de Petróleo (ANP) No. 4 of 6 August 2002 (Article 1(1)).

The Brazilian state still controls the price formation of oil products through public companies, such as Petrobrás. As a legal monopolist of most oil industry-related activities (Article 177 of the Constitution of 1988), as well as the leader of the national oil market, it is not difficult for Petrobrás to control prices, though indirectly. The following figures confirm this conclusion: according to the National Oil Agency, in 2010, Petrobrás alone was responsible for more than 98 per cent of the oil refining in Brazil.[24] Due to the market share of the omnipresent Petrobrás, and its institutional and economic position, the state, which retains the controlling interest of the company, is able to determine price levels which influence the prices of the other competitors.

Administered prices are an exception to competitive price formation. In the case of prices completely determined by the state, factors such as economic scarcity or private choices do not play any role. Instead, political decisions are determinants, of course based on the law and focusing on the fulfillment of the public interest. Administered prices show, additionally, that some economic sectors are prone to less competition, or no competition at all, which demands a more active role of the state as a regulator, or, in some cases, as a substitute to competition.[25]

5. PURCHASING POWER OF PETROBRÁS, INDUSTRIAL POLICY AND COMPETITION POLICY

The Constitution of 1988 expressly states 'free competition' as a principle of the constitutional economic order (Article 170 (IV)). This principle is to be understood as a 'means', a 'tool' of the economic policies, and not an end in itself. Competition policy as a public policy itself, or as a means to a broader economic policy, can vary across different periods and legal systems.[26]

---

[24] Anuário Estatístico Brasileiro do Petróleo, Gás Natural e Biocombustíveis (2011) 97, available at: http://www.anp.gov.br (accessed 31 December 2013).

[25] Hauptkorn (n. 22 above) 41 et seq., 172 et seq. and 189 et seq. See also the seminal work of J.K. Galbraith, *A Theory of Price Control: The Classic Account* (3rd edn, Harvard University Press 1980) 70–75.

[26] J.A. Tavares Guerreiro, 'Formas de Abuso de Poder Econômico' (1987) *Revista de Direito Mercantil* No 66 49; Grau (n. 8 above) 208–214; P.A Forgioni,

Massimo Motta lists a roll of objectives of antitrust. For instance, competition policy may focus on: general economic welfare (the most elevated objective, in his opinion), consumer welfare, protection to small companies, economic integration (as in Europe), economic freedom, macroeconomic stability, and the guarantee of a fair and equal treatment of consumers and competitors. Motta assumes the influence of other factors over the competition policy, such as fighting inflation and unemployment (social reasons), reducing the market power of certain groups or agents (political reasons), and the enforcement of environmental, industrial and foreign trade policies (strategic reasons).[27] He states:

> To define competition policy (or antitrust policy as it is more often called in the US) is not an easy task. A possible definition might be as follows: the set of policies and laws, which ensure that competition in the marketplace is not restricted in a way that is detrimental to society, which is, not restricted in a way as to reduce economic welfare.[28]

In the context of the debate about competition policy as a public policy, it is relevant to notice, as Norbert Reich does, that the problem of competition policy may be reduced to a conflict among objectives of a different order, that is, social-political functions versus economic functions *stricto sensu*. By including free competition as a principle of the constitutional economic order in Brazil, the constitutional legislator assigned to competition an instrumental feature, by articulating the competition law to fulfill certain objectives of the general economic policy.[29]

Another aspect which must be considered, as we discuss competition policy as a means to implement a certain economic policy, is the relation

---

Os Fundamentos do Antitruste (2nd edn, RT 2005) 24–26, 87–93 and 190–199. See also N. Reich, *Markt und Recht: Theorie und Praxis des Wirtschaftsrechts in der Bundesrepublik Deutschland* (Luchterhand 1977) 243–245. A different understanding of the antitrust policy as both a means and an objective is professed by W. Fikentscher, *Wirtschaftsrecht* (C.H. Beck 1983) Vol. 2, 143–151. For an interpretation of the antitrust policy as an end in itself see E. Hoppmann, *Wirtschaftsordnung und Wettbewerb* (Nomos 1988) 185–188, 238–253 and 276–295.

27 M. Motta, *Competition Policy: Theory and Practice* (12th edn, Cambridge University Press 2009) 17–30.

28 Ibid., 30.

29 On this general debate see N. Reich (n. 26 above) 245 et seq. For a critique of the so-called 'instrumentalization of competition policy' (*Instrumentalisierung der Wettbewerbspolitik*), see Hoppmann (n. 26 above) 48–54.

between innovation and competition. The main agent of the innovation process is the enterprise, usually a large company, which owns the necessary financial, technical and human resources. By introducing innovations, the company modifies the relative power of the other economic agents in the market, changing, in its turn, its own competition conditions.[30] Innovation is a theme extensively studied by Joseph Schumpeter. According to Schumpeter, the main trigger of the capitalist development is innovation. Innovation is a form of competition which differs from price formation, namely, a form of 'non-price competition'. Simultaneously, innovations differentiate products tending to develop potential market power. Of course, such market power can only be assessed *ex post*, in case the innovation efforts succeed. The main characteristic of innovation is the uncertainty *ex ante* whether the investments will be profitable or not. Schumpeter rejects the 'static analysis' of competition, focused on the price level, as insufficient to grasp the relevance of innovations in the dynamics and transformation processes of the economic system.[31] Schumpeter asserts that monopolistic power encourages investments in research and development,[32] since the recovery of such investments has a high level of certainty. In case of a market with several competitors, it is uncertain that the innovation investments will ever be recovered. So, monopolies or markets with only a few competitors offer better conditions for innovation investments, whose results can only be verified *ex post*, and not *ex ante*.

An antitrust policy, according to Hovenkamp, contrasts the innovation resulting from collaboration among competitors, which may be harmful to competition, with the innovation internal to the company. Exclusive endogenous innovations seldom come into conflict with competition law. Economists emphasize that product differentiation through innovation brings larger profits to companies, and this is exactly what we see in

---

30 S. Possas, 'Concorrência e Inovação' in V. Pelaez and T. Szmrecsányi (eds), *Economia da Inovação Tecnológica* (Hucitec 2006) 32 and G. Arbix, *Inovar ou Inovar: A Indústria Brasileira entre o Passado e o Futuro* (Papagaio 2007) 38 et seq. and 49.

31 J.A. Schumpeter, *Business Cycles: A Theoretical, Historical, and Statistical Analysis of the Capitalist Process* (reprint, 1st edn, Bartleby's Books/Martino Publishing 2005) Vol. I, 91 et seq.; and M. Moura e Silva, *Inovação, Transferência de Tecnologia e Concorrência: Estudo Comparado do Direito da Concorrência dos Estados Unidos e da União Europeia* (Almedina 2003) 27–29 and 32–34.

32 Schumpeter (n. 31 above) Vol. I, 96 et seq. and 108 et seq.; J.A. Schumpeter, *Capitalism, Socialism and Democracy* (reprint, Harper Perennial 2001) 87–106.

developed countries. Again, a static analysis of antitrust policies is not enough to verify how innovation distinguishes competitors among them and affects competition in a target market, since the various economic agents may create, eliminate, increase or diminish their differences, therefore modifying the configuration of their products.[33]

It is no wonder that investment in innovation as well as research and development is a core goal of contemporary industrial policy, which does not clash with antitrust policy at all, since the goals which both pursue are part of the constitutional economic order.[34]

In 2010, a new law concerning the 'national purchasing power' was enacted (Law No. 12.349 of 15 December 2010 amending Law No. 8.666 of 21 June 1993), which determines that the state will use its best endeavors to implement preferential processes of purchasing national goods (up to 25 percent) and local services, thus contributing to the development of the national economy by means of supporting the industrial policy, consolidating protection of national businesses and increasing innovation in the private sector. Through this new legislation, the Brazilian state plays a substantial role as a main supporter of innovation ventures, focusing on the domestic market as the dynamic center of the development process.[35]

In the oil industry, Petrobrás plays a key role as a developer of industrial and innovation policies determined by the federal government.[36] The common competition law standards cannot be successfully

---

[33] Schumpeter, *Capitalism, Socialism and Democracy* (n. 32 above) 81 et seq., 84–86 and 100–106; Arbix (n. 30 above) 115 et seq.; Possas (n. 30 above) 15.

[34] C. Salomão Filho, *Direito Concorrencial: As Estruturas* (Malheiros 1998) 176–199 and 220–222; H. Hovenkamp, *The Antitrust Enterprise: Principle and Execution* (reprint, Harvard University Press 2008), 15; Arbix (n. 30 above) 28–33. See also M. Eifert, 'Innovationsfördernde Regulierung' in M. Eifert and W. Hoffmann-Riem (eds), *Innovationsfördernde Regulierung: Innovation und Recht II* (Duncker & Humblot 2009) 17.

[35] See also D. Borges Barbosa (ed.) *Direito da Inovação: Comentários à Lei Federal de Inovação, Incentivos Fiscais à Inovação, Legislação Estadual e Local, Poder de Compra do Estado (Modificações à Lei de Licitações)* (2nd edn, Lumen Juris 2011) 197–236 and 250–267.

[36] G. Philip, *Oil and Politics in Latin America: Nationalist Movements and State Companies* (reprint, Cambridge University Press 2006) 390–392; de Mattos Dias and Quaglino (n. 6 above) 128–131; J.B. Ortiz Neto and A.J. Dalla Costa, 'A Petrobrás e a Exploração de Petróleo Offshore no Brasil: Um Approach Evolucionário' (2007) 61(1) *Revista Brasileira de Economia* 100–102. A program devoted to the development of technology employed in deepwater oil

applied to examine the singularity of a giant company, which is protected by the legal state oil monopoly and is the recipient of, and likewise responsible for, the largest innovation efforts in the late history of Brazil.

production (PROCAP – *Programa de Capacitação Tecnológica em Águas Profundas*) received investments of up to 1 percent of the annual billings of Petrobrás, something unheard of in the history of technology development in Brazil. For further information about the projects financed by PROCAP, the innovations achieved and the trends of research and development investments by Petrobrás, see Ortiz Neto and Dalla Costa, op. cit., 102–106. On research and technology investments, see also Randall (n. 7 above) 241–251. Besides the PROCAP program, it is worth mentioning the CTPETRO, a sectorial fund established in 1988 with the purpose of financing developments in science and technology. The resources derive from oil royalties, and are jointly administered by the Ministry of Science and Technology and the National Oil Agency.

3. The principle of subsidiarity as the essential restriction on Peruvian state business activity under pro-competitive conditions

Tania Zúñiga-Fernández

1. INTRODUCTION

This chapter highlights the importance of the Peruvian experience in the area of the restriction of state business activity under the principle of subsidiarity explicitly recognized by the Constitution. In its main part it describes the requirements and the authorization for the state to engage in business activities. As a result of these requirements, under the principle of fair competition and economic pluralism, the state plays a facilitating, enabling and promoting role in the social market economy, which is the economic model of the country as established in the Peruvian Constitution.

The role of the government in the economy has considerably evolved over the constitutional history of Peru, which is reflected in 13 constitutions since the first Constitution of 1823 to the current 1993 Constitution.[1]

Until the entry into force of the 1993 Constitution, the Peruvian state had gone through a history of military dictatorships, *de facto* governments and inefficient management of state resources. The state had developed a clear business function; it often showed a predominantly interventionist attitude, with utter disdain for the respect of the principle of fair competition, and promoted state monopolies and price fixing.

[1] These 13 constitutions date from the following years: 1823, 1826, 1828, 1834, 1837, 1839, 1856, 1860, 1867, 1920, 1933, 1979 and 1993. See T. Zúñiga-Fernández, *Fusionskontrolle in einer 'small market economy' in Lateinamerika: Wettbewerbspolitische Untersuchung am Beispiel Peru* (Nomos 2009) 55.

Peru, like most Latin American countries, introduced economic neoliberal structural reforms in the 1990s after going through a severe economic and fiscal crisis accompanied by discredit in the international financial world. These reforms were motivated by the so-called Washington Consensus.[2] The main components of economic reforms in Peru were: (1) fiscal discipline; (2) trade and market liberalization; (3) deregulation and privatization; (4) the promotion and protection of free competition; and (5) liberalization of foreign investment and investment guarantees.

The current Peruvian legal system promotes an 'enabling' role of the state as a facilitator and guarantor of the private economic sector, thus consolidating legal security in business operations and fostering greater confidence of investors in Peru.

Indeed, the principle of subsidiarity is central to this new image of the state as guarantor, with an essential content which drastically restricts the power of the state to engage in business operations.

2. THE FREE COMPETITION PRINCIPLE OF THE SOCIAL MARKET ECONOMY IN THE CONSTITUTIONAL FRAMEWORK

The oldest legal record of competition law in Peru dates back to some criminal rules, but also to the constitutional provisions of 1920 and 1933, which for the first time stated an express prohibition of private monopoly, while also admitting state monopolies. The principle of free competition in the Constitution was only introduced in the 1990s and with it begins the development of competition law in Peru. At the same time, the national competition authority, INDECOPI, was created.

In the Constitutions of 1979 and 1993, to varying degrees, the foundation of the economic system was characterized as a social market economy.

The economic model of the social market economy introduced by the 1979 Constitution was related to the concept of the welfare state through

---

[2] See B. Kresalja and C. Ochoa, *Derecho Constitucional Económico* (Fondo Editorial PUCP 2009), 362; J. Williamson, *The Washington Consensus Revisited* (Institute for International Economics 1996) 39. J. Williamson, *Latin America Adjustment: How Much Has Happened?* (Institute for International Economics 1990) 1–3.

the following features: central planning, social collectivism, interventionism in economic activity with extraordinary transitional measures, economic activities exclusively reserved for the state and price control. This is stated in Article 115: 'Private sector business initiative is free. It is exercised in a social market economy. The State stimulates and regulates its exercise to comply with the public interest'.[3] Under this provision, the state adopted its business role with express powers to legally intervene in the economy in order to harmonize free business initiative and the public interest.

Moreover, the 1993 Constitution explains the concept of the social market economy as a goal to be reached through the promotion of free enterprise and free competition. Consequently, if free enterprise is the rule, intervention by the state in business activity must then be the exception, so that if public companies are set up, they must compete on equal terms with the private companies, without privileges.[4]

Thus, with the new constitutional framework, the state becomes an enabling state and guarantor. Article 58 of the Constitution states the following: 'Private sector business initiative is free. It is developed in a social market economy. The State leads the country's development under this system and mainly acts in the areas of employment promotion, health, education, security, public services and infrastructure'.

On this point, the Peruvian Constitutional Court has stated:

> [W]hen certain rights or individual freedoms enter into conflict with the prerogatives of the State, it is crucial to establish the legal and policy framework that safeguards these rights. Neither the guarantee of private property nor private autonomy are unrestricted *per se* in contemporary constitutionalism. What is important is that these rights are interpreted in light of the terms of the *social welfare state and the democratic rule of law*, otherwise, other equally valuable constitutional principles would be at risk of being deferred. Only in this way can the old and misleading postulate of a virtuous market *per se* and a minimum State *per se* be truly overcome, to be replaced by a new paradigm whose wording is: '*as much market as possible and as much State as necessary*'.[5]

---

[3] It has been stated that the drafting of this article was inspired by the Constitutions of Italy (1947) and Spain (1978), as well as by ordoliberal thought.

[4] Kresalja and Ochoa (n. 2 above) 360.

[5] Constitutional Court (Tribunal Constitucional), Resolution No. 0048-2004-PI/TC of 1 April 2005, para. 16, available at: http://www.tc.gob.pe/jurisprudencia/2005/00048-2004-AI.html (accessed 31 December 2013). (translation by the author; emphasis added).

The state assumes the role of promoter and vigilant protector of free competition,[6] combating all practices that limit it. The state is obliged to stimulate wealth creation, and does not assume the role of a promoter of the development nor is it directly involved in the economy. The private sector business initiative is called upon to be primarily responsible for the economic activity.[7] So states Article 61 of the Peruvian Constitution: 'The State facilitates and supervises free competition. It fights against any practices restricting free competition and abuse of dominant or monopolistic positions. No laws or arrangements can authorize or establish monopolies.' Furthermore, the Constitutional Court has stated the following:

> The *regulatory function of the State* is provided in Article 58 of the Constitution. … Article 61 assigns the duty to the State to prohibit and combat all practices that restrict free competition, as well as the abuse of dominant or monopolistic positions. … Consistent with such interpretation, *the existence of antitrust legislation* and development of regulatory frameworks that enable greater levels of competition *is justified*. In this way and with respect to the free private business initiative, the *guiding role of the State* aims at the development of the country, trying to *materialize the social component of the economic model under the Constitution*. … The State is not just an organization that acts as the guarantor of the legal system, but because it determines or participates in setting the 'rules of the game', thus defining the ultimate objective of promoting the common good. Thus, the State acts as regulator and catalyst of economic processes.[8]

With these statements, the unrestricted permissive approach to the state's business activity[9] is left behind. Today, according to liberal thought, the

---

[6] A. Céspedes Zavaleta, *El Estado Empresario: Verdades, Conjeturas y Mitos Jurídicos* (Ediciones Caballero Bustamante 2010) 88 et seq.

[7] B. Kresalja, *El principio de subsidiariedad en materia económica. Analisis de las constituciones peruanas de 1979 y 1993* (Palestra 2010) 97–100.

[8] Constitutional Court (Tribunal Constitucional), Resolution No. 0008-2003-AI/TC of 11 November 2003, paras 36–38 and 40, available at: http://www.tc.gob.pe/jurisprudencia/2003/00008-2003-AI.html (accessed 31 December 2013) (translation by the author; emphasis added).

[9] The sixth paragraph of the preamble of the 1979 Constitution states as follows: 'Determined to promote the creation of a just, free and educated society, without exploited or exploiters, free from any discrimination based on sex, race, creed or social status, where the economy is at the service of men and not men to serve the economy, an open society to higher forms of coexistence and suitable to receive and use the influence of the scientific, technological, economic and social revolution that changes the world.'

state is conceived as a regulator and facilitator in respect of the development of the economy.[10]

3. THE RESTRICTIVE ROLE OF THE PRINCIPLE OF SUBSIDIARITY FOR STATE BUSINESS ACTIVITY IN PERU

The principle of subsidiarity is also mentioned by different rules on the financing of state-owned enterprises[11] as well as rules of competition law,[12] such as Article 14.3 of Legislative Decree No. 1044 approving the Law on the Repression of Unfair Competition, which establishes that state business activity exercised contrary to the provisions stated in Article 60 of the 1993 Constitution is illicit.

3.1 The Constitutional Formula Restricting State Business Activity

Article 60 of the 1993 Constitution is the legal foundation for the restriction of state business activity anchored in the subsidiarity principle.[13] Thus Article 60 states:

> The State recognizes economic pluralism. The national economy is based on the coexistence of several forms of property and enterprise.
>
> Only as authorized by specific law can the State subsidiarily perform direct or indirect business activities where this is mandated by a high level of public interest or evident national interest.
>
> Corporative activity, public or not public, enjoys the same legal treatment.

The Peruvian Constitutional Court has recognized that free private initiative and free enterprise are the foundation of the principle of subsidiarity, and these are set out in Article 2(16) and Article 59 of the Constitution. Article 2(16) guarantees the right to property and inheritance. Article 59 states:

---

10 Kresalja and Ochoa (n. 2 above) 363.

11 Legislative Decree 1031 (June 2008), National Fund for Financing the State Business Activity (FONAFE).

12 Kresalja and Ochoa (n. 2 above) 362–366.

13 Zúñiga-Fernández 2009 (n. 1 above) 65. See also Kresalja (n. 7 above) 97 and 132–138.

> The State promotes wealth creation and ensures labor freedom, as well as free enterprise, free trade, and free industry. Exercising this freedom must not harm good morals, health or public security. The State provides overcoming opportunities to sectors suffering any kind of inequality; to this end, it promotes small enterprises in all their modalities.

It is important to note that the inefficiency of state-owned enterprises could be considered exceptionally justified when the benefits generated cannot be achieved otherwise. At the same time, the state is allowed to develop business activities in the field of production and distribution of products or services provided that this does not constitute the exercise of any power of *ius imperium* or ensues welfare benefits aimed at providing assistance to the lower-income population. The provision of such welfare benefits by virtue of specific laws does not qualify as business activity but constitutes an expression of central state functions, which inspired Peruvian constitutional thought and are linked to health, education and social security. In other words, when the state is obliged to provide such services, the state is not prevented from doing this by virtue of the principle of subsidiarity set out in the aforementioned Article 60.

3.2 Competition Rules Related to Restrictions on State Business Activity

The restriction of the state for doing business is also recognized in the Law on the Repression of Unfair Competition regulated by Legislative Decree No. 1044. Thus Article 14.3 of this law establishes:

> The business activity developed by a public entity or a State-owned enterprise not complying with Article 60 of the Peruvian Constitution represents a violation of the rules to be determined by the authorities under this law. Thereby, it is not required to demonstrate a significant advantage by the performer of such business activity.

The principle of subsidiarity was interpreted by the Board of Defense of Competition of the National Institute for the Protection of Competition and Intellectual Property (INDECOPI) in the following way:

> [T]he subsidiarity concept must be understood as the circumstance in which a State enterprise intervention is exceptionally tolerated due to the fact that there is no private offer or it is insufficient to meet the needs of consumers in a certain sector. Therefore, there will be no subsidiary role if it is found that

there is a real or potential offer provided by the private sector, as long as it is able to meet the demand of a particular relevant market.[14]

3.3 The Essential Content of the Principle of Subsidiarity

That the state is able to do business is a possible scenario, but only under certain conditions. First, the legal authorization by Parliament for engaging in business activity is mandatory. Parliament can only give this authorization in view of promoting the public or national interest. For that purpose, identifying the relevant market is the first step to determining whether the state-owned enterprise or the state entity does play a subsidiary role in contrast to the private sector. After that it will be important to determine the private offering available and whether it can meet the demand that the state-owned enterprise aims to respond to.[15]

3.3.1 Parliamentary authorization of the exercise of state business activity

The first prerequisite for carrying out business activity is the authorization of the national Parliament.[16] The reason for this is related to the principle of 'balance of powers': in order to exclude arbitrary decisions and margins of political discretion in the hands of government officials.[17]

3.3.2 Justified public interest or national interest

The above requirement is consistent with the second of the conditions, which requires that the authorization granted to the state to develop an economic activity must respond to the need of promoting a high-level public interest or evident national interest. Both the high-level public interest and the national interest are issues that require evaluation that should not be taken by any public authority, but by the Congress, a procedural requirement that corresponds to those applicable to the passing of laws.[18]

---

[14] INDECOPI, Resolution No. 2550-2010/SCGI-INDECOPI of 14 September 2010.

[15] INDECOPI, Resolution No. 3134-2010/SC1-INDECOPI, Fundament No. 82-83. Sie also Kresalja (n. 7 above) 144–147.

[16] This also finds support in Article 3 of Legislative Decree 1031, which states that the subsidiary performance of economic units in the state business activity (FONAFE) must be 'authorized by an Act of Congress'.

[17] INDECOPI, Resolution No. 3134-2010/SC1-INDECOPI, Fundament No. 68. See also Kresalja and Ochoa (n. 2 above) 361.

[18] INDECOPI, Resolution No. 3134-2010/SC1-INDECOPI of File No. 201-2008/CCD, Fundament No. 70.

Concepts such as public interest or national interest are indeterminate legal concepts that should be discussed and defined by Parliament. This also applies to business activities undertaken by any state agency, regional governments and local governments and the institutions under them.[19] The competition authority, for example, could not have the authority to evaluate or argue if the business activity serves a purpose of this nature.[20]

3.3.3 Non-existence or insufficiency of real or potential private offer

According to what has been stated above, once the relevant market has been determined, it is necessary to evaluate the relationship of supply and demand. There are three possible scenarios for this analysis.

First, two or more unrelated private companies compete with the government agency or state-controlled company in the relevant market. This scenario assumes that the competitive conditions are suitable and the private offer is sufficient. Therefore, the reported government agency or company has to prove, on the one hand, that the established private companies cannot satisfy the demand that would be released should it be withdrawn and, on the other, that there are high barriers to entry preventing the market entrance of new suppliers that would otherwise be capable of meeting the demand that would be released.

Second, a private company and a state-owned enterprise participate in the relevant market. In this scenario, the presumption that the private offer is sufficient does not apply; therefore, in order to conclude that the state intervention is not subsidiary, the authority must prove – from its investigation and the evidence provided by the complainant – that the private company has the capacity to meet the demand that will eventually be released, or that there are no barriers limiting the entry of potential competitors in case the established offer is not sufficient.

Third, only the state-owned enterprise or entity participates in the relevant market: There is no private offer; therefore, the presence of barriers to market entry will be assessed. Should there be no barriers – unlike the two first scenarios – then the state company plays a subsidiary role. If it is determined that there are significant entry barriers, the participation will also be subsidiary, unless it is determined that the presence of the state company or entity must cease, as this is itself the barrier discouraging the entry of private competitors.

---

19 INDECOPI, Resolution No. 3134-2010/SC1-INDECOPI of File N° 201-2008/CCD, Fundament No. 71.

20 INDECOPI, Resolution No. 3134-2010/SC1-INDECOPI of File No. 201-2008/CCD, Fundament No. 126 et seq.

4. CONCLUSION

According to the constitutional framework, state's business activity in Peru is restricted by the principle of subsidiarity. The state can only perform business activities under specific conditions: legal authorization by Parliament, the explicit justification by high-level public interest or evident national interest and the absence or insufficiency of real or potential private offers. On the other hand, the exercise of *ius imperium* or the mandatory provision of social security or pension benefits are issues set outside the scope of the concept of business activities. Free enterprise, economic pluralism and the principle of free competition represent the pillars of the subsidiarity principle which determines the level of state business activity and the conceptual dimension of the social market economy in the Peruvian legal system.

4. The competition dimension of the European regulation of public sector information and the concept of an undertaking

Josef Drexl*

1. INTRODUCTION

Many state bodies produce and hold a large stock of data that can be exploited commercially. These bodies, such as courts or land and company registries, often fulfil essential state functions. With regard to such data, every modern state today has to decide on the principles on whether and how to make that data available to the public for commercial re-use. In the European Union, already in 2003, the legislature decided to adopt a directive in this regard, the so-called Public Sector Information (PSI) Directive,[1] which was most recently revised in June 2013.[2] The

* The author was a member of the Legal Aspects of Public Sector Information (LAPSI) European Thematic Network of scholars, funded by the European Commission and coordinated by the NEXA Center for Internet and Society at the Polytechnic University of Turin, from 2010 through 2012. LAPSI assisted the Commission in preparing the 2013 revision of the PSI Directive. Several of the LAPSI recommendations influenced the 2013 Directive and will be referred to in the following. The author is also a member of the follow-on LAPSI 2.0 network coordinated by the University of Leuven in Belgium. Information on LAPSI is available at: http://www.lapsi-project.eu/ (accessed 30 December 2013). This chapter only reflects the opinion of its author and neither the opinion of any of the other LAPSI members or the LAPSI networks as such, nor of the European Commission.

[1] Directive 2003/98/EC of the European Parliament and of the Council of 17 November 2003 on the re-use of public sector information, [2003] OJ L 345, p. 90.

[2] Directive 2013/37/EU of the European Parliament and of the Council of 26 June 2013 amending Directive 2003/98/EC on the re-use of public sector

objectives of this legislation are twofold: as its primary object, the Directive seeks to promote access of private businesses to PSI, based on the assumption that better commercial use of such information may help to develop new information markets and, finally, enhance economic growth.[3] Secondly, by the time of its revision in 2013, the Directive had also become an important element of the EU's open-data policies that are designed to make publicly-held data widely available to the public.[4]

The European PSI regime draws our attention to a new kind of economic activity or, at least, economically relevant activity of state bodies that comes along with the emergence of the information society. In order to provide further guidance for the EU PSI policy, this chapter aims at clarifying the role of state bodies holding PSI both as providers of information for downstream added-value information services and as competitors in the relevant markets at the interface of sector-specific regulation and competition law.

From a methodological point of view, this chapter applies a competition-policy-oriented approach. The PSI Directive's goal of promoting the emergence of new information markets and of enhancing economic growth is complementary to the objectives of competition law and seems to react to the fact that public bodies hold a large stock of data, access to which is indispensable for private businesses to enter new markets for information services.[5] In this regard, PSI appears as a particular form of essential facility that is held by state bodies.

---

information, [2013] L 175, p. 1. In the following, unless otherwise indicated, references to the Directive relate to the consolidated version available at: http://eur-lex.europa.eu/LexUriServ/LexUriServ.do?uri=CELEX:02003L0098-20130717:EN:NOT (accessed 30 December 2013).

[3] On the economics of PSI see R. Pollock, 'The Economics of Public Sector Information', Cambridge Working Papers in Economics 0920, Faculty of Economics, University of Cambridge (2009), available at: http://ideas.repec.org/p/cam/camdae/0920.html (accessed 31 December 2013); P.N. Weiss, 'Borders in Cyberspace: Conflicting Public Sector Information Policies and their Economic Impacts' in G. Aichholzer and H. Burkert (eds), *Public Sector Information in the Digital Age* (Edward Elgar 2004) 137. From a more public-policy-oriented perspective see M. Blakemore and M. Caglia, 'Access to Public-Sector Information in Europe: Policy, Rights, and Obligations' (2006) 22 *The Information Society* 13.

[4] See Recitals 3 and 6 of Directive 2013/37/EU (n. 2 above).

[5] According to B. Lundqvist, '"Turning Government Data into Gold": The Interface Between EU Competition Law and the Public Sector Information Directive – With Some Comments on the Compass Case' (2013) 44 *IIC* 79, 80 et seq., the case-law on refusal to deal and refusal to license in EU competition law influenced the drafting of the PSI Directive as the main source of inspiration.

Yet there is also tension between the EU PSI regime and EU competition law. With the goal of promoting the emergence of new markets, the PSI Directive adopts an approach of industrial policy. It thereby goes beyond competition law, which is only designed to protect competition law in existing markets. In contrast to competition law, which is uniformly applicable to all different kinds of undertakings and economic sectors, the PSI Directive establishes a sector-specific regime for so-called 'public sector bodies' that are competitors or potential competitors of private businesses on the different levels of the generation of information, its processing and refinement and, finally, the provision of such information to the public. To the extent that the PSI Directive imposes obligations on public sector bodies that go beyond the rules of competition law, there is therefore the concern that the regime of the PSI Directive could distort competition. In this regard, a competition-policy-oriented analysis can be used as a yardstick to assess the pros and cons of the European PSI policy.

In practical terms, the PSI Directive and EU competition law overlap with regard to their respective scope of application. Parallel application of the two fields may produce particular benefits with a view to creating a more effective system of regulation. Yet the two regimes define the addressees of the obligations they contain in different ways. The PSI Directive applies to 'public sector bodies', EU competition law to 'undertakings'. Both of these concepts create legal uncertainties when state bodies act at the interface of the fulfilment of their public tasks and economic activity. Therefore, for fully assessing the complementarity of the two regimes, this chapter will also analyse to what extent the two regimes apply to the same kind of bodies and the same kind of activity. In this context, this chapter will also discuss the recent *Compass* judgment of the Court of Justice of the European Union (CJEU) and its rather cautious approach to applying competition law to public sector bodies that restrict access to PSI for commercial re-use.[6]

Finally, this chapter will also consider whether and to what extent the most recent evolution of the PSI regime into an instrument of open-data policy is compatible with the previous industrial-policy orientation of the Directive.

The analysis will be structured as follows: section 2 will explain the competition dimension of the re-use of PSI in general. Section 3 will present the EU sector-specific regulation under the PSI Directive. Section

---

[6] Case C-138/11 *Compass-Datenbank GmbH* [2012] ECR I-449. On this judgment see also Lundqvist (n. 5 above) 88–94.

4 will turn to a competition-policy evaluation of the Directive. Section 5 will focus on the classification of holders of PSI as undertakings in the sense of competition law and as public sector bodies in the sense of the PSI Directive. Finally, section 6 will assess the most recent trend, expressed by the 2013 revision of the PSI Directive, of integrating the PSI Directive in the context of a larger open-data policy.

2. THE COMPETITION DIMENSION OF PUBLIC SECTOR INFORMATION

Although the competition dimension of PSI was never particularly taken account of in European competition policy prior to the adoption of the PSI Directive in 2003, EU competition law has nevertheless produced cases in which PSI was an issue.

The most prominent judgment of the European courts in this regard is the one in *Magill* of 1995.[7] In the underlying case, the two public TV stations from the Republic of Ireland (RTE) and the United Kingdom (BBC), as well as one private TV station (ITV), refused to grant copyright licences for their programme listings to a private publisher (Magill) and thereby prevented comprehensive TV guides from entering the market. In this case, the European Court of Justice (ECJ, now CJEU) for the first time confirmed that a refusal to license an intellectual property right constituted an abuse of market dominance in the sense of former Article 86 EC Treaty (now Article 102 TFEU).[8] Thereby, the ECJ did not give any particular weight to the fact that two of the three TV stations belonged to the public sector. The fact that RTE and BBC were to be considered 'undertakings' for the purpose of applying competition law was not even mentioned by the ECJ. But the Court stressed the particular role of the information held by the TV stations. The TV stations were considered as market dominant in the upstream information market, since they were the only source from which another undertaking, like Magill, could receive the programme information for entering the downstream market for printed TV guides.[9] With the refusal to license, the TV stations managed to be the sole providers of printed TV guides,

---

[7] Joined Cases C-241/91 P and C-242/91 P *RTE and ITP v Commission* ('*Magill*') [1995] ECR I-743.

[8] This case-law was further developed by the ECJ and the Court of First Instance (now General Court) in Case C-418/01 *IMS Health* [2004] ECR I-5039; T-201/04 *Microsoft v Commission* [2007] ECR II-3601.

[9] *Magill* (n. 7 above) para. 47.

which, however, only included the programmes of the individual TV stations. Accordingly, the ECJ confirmed the previous Commission decision, where, following a leveraging theory, it was held that the TV station had excluded competition in the downstream publishing market by refusing to grant access to essential information produced in an upstream information market.

Beyond this competition law analysis, the facts of *Magill* mirror the characteristics of a PSI case in which a public sector body holds essential information that is needed for providing added-value information services in a downstream market.[10] In this regard, the *Magill* case can illustrate the advantages of sector-specific PSI regulation. The case took nine years from the complaint lodged to the Commission by Magill in 1986 to the ECJ's final judgment in 1995. Although the ECJ made a courageous step by applying European competition law to refusals to license intellectual property rights, competition law did not at all turn out to be an efficient means to provide quick and effective relief to the victims of such a competition law violation. Sector-specific regulation of PSI markets can improve the situation quite considerably by imposing an obligation on public sector bodies to provide access to PSI without the need to argue a complex competition case and without the need to rely on intervention by competition agencies.[11]

Yet, as far as the specific facts of *Magill* are concerned, even after its revision of 2013, the PSI Directive does not offer any relief. According to its Article 1(2)(d), the PSI Directive does not apply to public service broadcasters and their subsidiaries.

---

[10] The specific PSI features of Magill are also recognised by Lundqvist (n. 5 above) 86.

[11] Of course, also PSI cases can lead to disputes in the legal framework established by the Directive. According to Article 7(4) of the Directive, public sector bodies have to inform applicants for re-use of the means of redress relating to the decisions of public sector bodies on re-use. According to Recital 28 of Directive 2013/37/EU, these means of redress should include the possibility of review by an 'impartial review body'. The Recital further points out that this body could be the national competition authority.

3. SECTOR-SPECIFIC PSI REGULATION IN THE EUROPEAN UNION

3.1 Recognition of an Obligation to Allow Re-use of PSI

In 2003, the European legislature made a first move to address refusals to grant access to publicly-held data to private businesses that wanted to re-use that data for added-value information services. However, the 2003 Directive largely remained without teeth, since it left it to the Member States to decide on which data should be available for commercial re-use.[12] Accordingly, the Member States were even authorised to attribute the decision as to whether individual data should be available for commercial re-use to the individual public sector bodies holding that data. The role of the 2003 Directive was largely limited to establishing general and harmonised principles on *how* such re-use would be granted, while it was for the Member States to decide *whether and in which cases* private businesses have a right to re-use.[13]

This obvious lack of effectiveness was finally addressed by the 2013 Directive. Article 3(1) of the revised PSI Directive now formulates an obligation to allow commercial re-use, providing that 'Member States shall ensure that documents to which this Directive applies … *shall be re-usable* for commercial and non-commercial purposes'.[14]

3.2 Scope of Application of the Directive

Yet, also under the revised Directive, a decision is required with regard to the conditions under which particular data has to be made available for commercial re-use in the framework of defining the scope of application of the Directive. Here, the revised Directive takes an approach that has already previously been followed by some Member States. Today, whenever a Member State decides that certain data are generally accessible to the public, the PSI Directive makes it mandatory to also allow commercial re-use of such data. The Directive thereby combines the general access regimes under the domestic laws of the Member States with the EU re-use obligation. This system is legally implemented by a very broad definition of 'public sector information' and an exception

---

[12] See also Recital 7 of Directive 2013/37/EU.

[13] Cf. also Lundqvist (n. 5 above) 82 (referring to the law prior to the 2013 revision).

[14] Emphasis added.

from the scope of application of the Directive for all documents to which access is restricted by virtue of the access regimes in the Member States.[15] Hence, the scope of the obligation to allow commercial re-use still depends on national law and, therefore, may considerably differ between the Member States. Yet the revised Directive has now made commercial re-use automatic with the national decision to make data generally accessible to the public.

Article 1(1) of the Directive describes 'public sector information' as all 'documents held by public sector bodies of the Member States'. While the term 'document' seems to indicate a tangible manifestation, this is not confirmed by Article 2(3) of the PSI Directive, which defines a document as 'any content whatever its medium (written on paper or stored in electronic form or as a sound, visual or audiovisual recording)' and 'any part of such content'.

With the term 'public sector body' the Directive refers to the addressees of the obligations contained in the Directive. According to its Article 2(1), public sector bodies are to be understood as all 'State, regional or local authorities, bodies governed by public law and associations formed by one or several such authorities or one or several such bodies governed by public law'. As part of this definition, the use of the term 'public law' has the potential of creating legal uncertainties, since Member States may have very different concepts of public law. Therefore, Article 3(2) introduces a general European notion of a 'body governed by public law' requiring the fulfilment of three cumulative conditions: (i) the body needs to be 'established for the specific purpose of meeting needs in the general interest, not having an industrial or commercial character'; (ii) the body needs to have legal personality; and (iii) the body needs to be 'financed, for the most part by the State, or regional or local authorities, or other bodies governed by public law; or subject to management supervision by those bodies; or having an administrative, managerial or supervisory board, more than half of whose members are appointed by the State, regional or local authorities or by other bodies governed by public law'.

The concept of public sector information brings many different kinds of information within the scope of the PSI Directive, including judicial decisions, geographical or commercial data held by public registers,

---

[15] Article 1(2)(ca) of the revised PSI Directive. According to this provision, the exception also applies to rules whereby citizens or companies have to prove a particular interest to obtain access. Hence, if a Member State makes access to information contained in a land registry dependent on the showing of a particular interest, the PSI Directive will not give rise to a re-use obligation.

meteorological data, but also the contents of archives and public libraries as well as objects of art in public museums.[16]

Yet the Directive also has to acknowledge that there are prevailing legal reasons that limit access to and commercial re-use of such data. Accordingly, Article 1(2)(cc) of the revised PSI Directive excludes documents from its scope of application, access to which is restricted by virtue of the access regimes in the Member States, which, in particular, are designed to protect personal data. Article 1(4) of the PSI Directive safeguards the application of the EU and national law on data protection law in particular with regard to Directive 95/46/EC.[17]

In a similar vein, Article 1(2)(b) of the PSI Directive excludes re-use of PSI for 'documents for which third parties hold intellectual property rights'.[18] The wording of this provision, however, gives rise to some uncertainties. In a literal understanding, the exception would also apply to situations in which public sector bodies as licensees are able to grant sub-licences for the use of such documents. This reading seems to be confirmed by Recital 9 of Directive 2013/37/EU, which states that documents held by libraries, museums and archives should be considered documents for which third parties hold intellectual property rights as long as the term of protection of those rights has not expired. Yet such a reading goes beyond what is actually needed for the protection of intellectual property. If, pursuant to their contractual relationship with the initial right-holders, public sector bodies are authorised to sub-license the

---

[16] This is confirmed by Recital 4 of the PSI Directive, which mentions information arising from a wide range of activity, such as 'social, economic, geographical, weather, tourist, business, patent and educational information'.

[17] Directive 95/46/EC of the European Parliament and of the Council of 24 October 1995 on the protection of individuals with regard to the processing of personal data and on the free movement of such data, [1995] OJ L 281, p. 31. In general on the interface with data protection see E. Bassi, 'PSI, protezione dei dati personali, anonimizzazione' in D. Tiscornia (ed.), *Open Data and Re-use of Public Sector Information* (2011) XX/1-2 *Informatica e diritto* 65; B. van der Sloot, 'Public Sector Information & Data Protection: A Plea for Personal Privacy Settings for the Re-use of PSI' in D. Tiscornia (ed.), *Open Data and Re-use of Public Sector Information* (Edizioni Scientifiche Italiane 2011) XX/1-2 *Informatica e diritto* 219.

[18] Article 1(5) of the Directive also stresses that the Directive only applies in so far as its obligations are compatible with the provisions of international agreements on the protection of intellectual property rights. On the treatment of intellectual property rights by the PSI Directive see also A.M. Rovati, 'Prime note su proprietà intellettuale e riutilizzo dei dati pubblici' in D. Tiscornia (ed.), *Open Data and Re-use of Public Sector Information* (Edizioni Scientifiche Italiane 2011) XX/1-2 *Informatica e diritto* 153.

use of PSI, there is indeed no need to exclude the application of the Directive. Yet the Directive refrains from making a clear statement as to a general obligation of public sector bodies from granting re-use where this can be implemented by sub-licensing intellectual property rights. In Recital 22, the Directive only states that public sector bodies 'should ... exercise their copyright in a way that facilitates re-use'.

Sub-licensing is especially possible with regard to the media archives of public broadcasters. In Germany, the two major public TV stations, ARD and ZDF, recently tried to establish a joint online platform for the marketing of their digital media content, but finally gave up this project due to the intervention of the German competition agency, the *Bundeskartellamt*, which, based on merger control law, only wanted to allow the joint venture under certain conditions.[19] This case demonstrates that public TV stations try to commercially exploit their archives whether third-party intellectual property rights are involved or not. Since, however, the PSI Directive grants a sector-specific exemption to public broadcasters pursuant to its Article 1(2)(d), the Directive does not provide any remedy to private operators to gain access to such archives.

Under the 2003 Directive, a similarly broad exemption was provided for educational and research establishments as well as cultural establishments. Yet the revision of 2013 has now made the Directive applicable to libraries, including university libraries, museums and archives.[20] This extension of the scope of application is a reaction to the many digitisation projects that have created a significant amount of digital public domain content which can be exploited by commercial added-value services.[21] Yet, as Article 3(2) of the PSI Directive clarifies, the general obligation to allow commercial re-use does not apply to documents held by such

---

19 See '"Germany's Gold": ARD und ZDF stoppen geplante Online-Videothek' (16 September 2013), available at: http://www.spiegel.de/netzwelt/web/ard-und-zdf-beerdigen-onlinevideothek-germany-s-gold-a-922475.html (accessed 31 December 2013). The prohibition of a similar joint online platform of the two major private TV stations by the *Bundeskartellamt* was finally confirmed by the Düsseldorf Court of Appeals (*Oberlandesgericht*) on 8 August 2012 (Case VI-Kart 4/11). On this latter case see also P. Klocker, 'Aktuelle Entscheidungspraxis des Bundeskartellamtes 2012/2013' in Forschungsinstitut für Wirtschaft und Wettbewerb (FIW) (ed.), *Schwerpunkte des Kartellrechts 2013* (Carl Heymanns Verlag, 2013) 1, 11 et seq.

20 Article 1(2)(e) and (f) of the revised PSI Directive. See also Recital 14 of Directive 2013/37/EU.

21 See Recital 15 of Directive 2013/37/EU. Digitisation projects exist not only on a national, but also on an EU level. The most important European initiative is the Europeana platform. See http://www.europeana.eu.

libraries, museums and archives. Rather, as regards these institutions, the previous approach under the 2003 Directive applies, according to which it is for the Member States to decide 'where the re-use of such documents is allowed'.

3.3 Exceptions for Documents that Fall outside the Public Task

In Article 1(2)(a), the PSI Directive contains another rather peculiar exception for 'documents the supply of which is an activity falling outside the scope of the public task of the public sector bodies concerned'.

Since it is for the Member States to define what falls or does not fall within the 'public task' as part of their national law, binding rules or common administrative practice, 'provided that the scope of the public tasks is transparent and subject to review', Member States dispose of very broad discretion to further limit the scope of application of the Directive.

However, this exception is needed for establishing a level playing field between the public sector bodies and the commercial re-users as commercial suppliers of added-value information services in downstream markets.[22] For this purpose, Article 1(2)(a) of the PSI Directive draws a line between the production of documents that falls within the public task and the use of such documents by the public sector bodies that falls outside of that public task and that constitutes re-use by the public sector body itself.[23] Only with regard to the former documents are the public sector bodies under an obligation to make them available for re-use to private competitors. Hence, the exception contained in Article 1(2)(a) of the PSI Directive protects public sector bodies from an obligation to share the documents that they have produced for the purpose of providing added-value information services outside the scope of the fulfilment of their public tasks.

3.4 Who Decides on the Available Format?

Article 1(2)(a) of the Directive, which exempts documents the supply of which falls outside the scope of the public task, touches upon another

---

[22] See Recital 13 of Directive 2013/37/EU, according to which the public sector body retains the right to exploit any document that is made available for re-use.

[23] Recital 8 explicitly clarifies that use of PSI outside of the scope of the public tasks constitutes re-use.

aspect of the PSI Directive that deserves particular attention from both an economic and competition-oriented perspective. This aspect relates to the format in which public sector bodies are required to make their PSI available for re-use.

Indeed, PSI may be available in very different formats, in particular, in only analogue or digital format. Digitised data may be available in more or less refined versions. Electronic databases and digital platforms established by public sector bodies may be equipped with more or less refined utilities for users. Therefore, the question arises whether a public sector body should be under an obligation to digitise its PSI to facilitate commercial re-use of such information. In this regard, Article 5 of the Directive adopts a cautious approach. Article 5(1) only obliges public sector bodies to make their documents available in the pre-existing format. Beyond this, the same provision obliges public sector bodies to transfer their data in an open and machine-readable format where this is 'possible and appropriate'. According to Article 5(2), this does not imply an obligation to create or adapt documents if this 'involve[s] disproportionate effort, going beyond a simple operation'. And Article 5(3) clarifies that there is no requirement to 'continue the production and storage of a certain type of documents with a view to the re-use of such documents'.

Hence, Article 5 of the Directive needs to be read in the light of the concept of public tasks laid out in Article 1(2)(a) of the Directive. In principle, the public sector body is only under an obligation to make documents available that it has produced within the scope of the fulfilment of its public tasks. Since any further digital purification and refinement falls outside the scope of application of the Directive, the public sector body is neither under an obligation to make such documents available to private competitors nor, if such documents are made available, to respect the other principles of the Directive, such as in particular the limitations on the charging policy contained in Article 6 of the Directive.

3.5 Principles and Procedures Applicable to Re-use

Beyond the general obligation to allow re-use of PSI in Article 3(1), the Directive stipulates four major principles that govern the re-use of PSI that are designed to create an EU-wide level playing field for added-value information services.

First, Article 10(1) of the Directive stipulates a non-discrimination principle according to which the conditions for the re-use of documents need to be non-discriminatory for comparable categories of re-use.

Second, the principle of non-discrimination also applies where a public sector body acts as a competitor of private re-users in a downstream market for added-value services. In this regard, under Article 10(2) of the Directive, a public sector body that re-uses its PSI as input for its own commercial activities outside of the scope of its public tasks is obliged to apply the same charges and conditions to both its own commercial activity and to other re-users. The fulfilment of this obligation obviously requires the public sector body to clearly distinguish, at least as far as its financial constitution is concerned, between the production of the PSI within the scope of its public tasks and its commercial re-use of its own PSI outside of its public tasks.

Third, Article 6 of the Directive limits the discretion of the public sector body regarding its charging policy for re-use of its PSI.[24] The 2013 revision of the PSI Directive has strengthened the limitation on the charging regime as compared to the 2003 Directive. While former Article 6 allowed for a 'reasonable return on investment',[25] the new version of Article 6(1) only allows public sector bodies to charge a price that corresponds to the 'marginal costs' for the 'reproduction, provision and dissemination' of the documents. In this context, use of the term 'marginal costs' is misleading. While usually the term relates to the incremental costs incurred by the production of another unit as distinguished from the fixed costs that are incurred by production independent of the volume of production, the provision is sufficiently clear to relate to the specific costs of making available the documents for re-use as distinguished from the costs of producing the documents within the scope of the public sector body's public tasks.

However, Article 6(2) provides for a few exceptions from the marginal-cost standard. Most important is Article 6(2)(a), which enables public sector bodies to charge higher prices if they are required – obviously as a matter of the domestic legal regime in the Member States – to generate

---

[24] See also the LAPSI recommendations on charging: M. Ricolfi et al., 'The "Principles Governing Charging" for Re-use of Public Sector Information' in D. Tiscornia (ed.), *Open Data and Re-use of Public Sector Information* (Edizioni Scientifiche Italiane 2011) XX/1-2 *Informatica e diritto* 105, also available at: http://papers.ssrn.com/sol3/papers.cfm?abstract_id=2217405 (accessed 30 December 2013).

[25] On the interpretation of this standard see the recent EFTA Court judgment of 16 December 2013, Case E-7/13 *Creditinfo Lánstraust v Registers Iceland and the Icelandic State*, available at: http://www.eftacourt.int/cases/ (accessed 30 December 2013). This has so far remained the only judgment in which a European Court had to interpret the provisions of the PSI Directive.

revenue to cover a substantial part of their costs relating to the performances of their public tasks. Indeed, many public sector bodies, such as registers, fulfil a public task and nevertheless impose fees on the citizens and companies concerned. Article 6(2)(a) protects these citizens and companies from cross-subsidising the production of data for private businesses that want to exploit that data commercially. In a similar vein, Article 6(2)(b) exempts documents for which the public sector body is 'required to generate sufficient revenue to cover a substantial part of the costs relating to their collection, production, reproduction and dissemination'. Finally, Article 6(2)(c) exempts libraries, museums and archives. These institutions would be seriously limited in their possibilities to acquire new content if they were prevented from charging beyond marginal costs by Article 6(1) of the Directive.[26] With regard to all of these exceptions, Article 6(3) of the Directive maintains the 2003 regime by authorising public sector bodies to charge a price that also guarantees a 'reasonable return on investment'.

Fourth, Article 11 of the Directive considerably restricts the possibility of public sector bodies to grant exclusive rights for the re-use of PSI and, thereby, provides all potential market actors with non-discriminatory access to PSI. However, Article 11(2) allows for the grant of exclusive rights where this 'is necessary for the provision of a service in the public interest'. And, even more importantly, the 2013 revision has provided new rules on the grant of exclusive rights for the digitisation of cultural resources. These rules are most important for the large digitisation projects of public libraries and archives with regard to works in the public domain. These projects require major financial resources and are often implemented in the form of public-private partnerships (PPPs) with private actors, such as Google.[27] For these cases, the 2013 revision introduced a new Article 11(2a), which provides that exclusive rights for digitisation of cultural resources must in principle not exceed 10 years.[28] In addition, Article 11(2a)(3) makes it mandatory that the public sector

---

26 See also the LAPSI Recommendations in this regard: Ricolfi et al. (n. 24 above) 119 et seq.

27 Such a PPP with Google was entered into by the Bayerische Staatsbibliothek in 2007. See Bayerische Staatsbibliothek, 'Mass Digitisation within the Framework of a Public-Private Partnership between the Bayerische Staatsbibliothek and Google', available at: http://www.bsb-muenchen.de/Mass-Digitisation-within-the-F.1842+M57d0acf4f16.0.html (accessed 30 December 2013). As part of this PPP, Google has taken over the whole costs of digitisation.

28 An extension beyond ten years is allowed if the duration of the exclusive right is reviewed during the 11th year and every seven years thereafter.

body be provided free of charge with a copy of the digitised cultural resources and that the copy be available for re-use at the end of the exclusivity period.

4. COMPETITION POLICY EVALUATION OF THE PSI DIRECTIVE

The PSI Directive is based on the assumption that the public sector body is typically the only source for the specific information. Accordingly, the general principles of non-discrimination on the charging policy and the limitation on the grant of exclusive rights are very much inspired by the competition law prohibition of abuse of market dominance contained in Article 102 TFEU. Accordingly, the Directive confirms the competition law dimension of the PSI regime and even the applicability of competition law. Right in the very first recital, the Directive points out its objective to ensure that competition in the internal market is not distorted. Another recital points out that 'competition rules should be respected when establishing the principles for re-use of documents avoiding as far as possible exclusive agreements between public sector bodies and private partners'.[29]

Yet there are also aspects of the PSI Directive and its working that can create competition concerns: first, the question of whether public sector bodies are the only source of information may be less realistic today than in 2003. In particular, the Directive may generate a negative impact on the emergence of private competitors in the upstream market where information is produced (at 4.1 below). Second, the marginal-cost standard governing the charging policy might be questionable from an economic and competition-oriented perspective (at 4.2 below). Third, the grant of exclusive rights should not always be considered anti-competitive (at 4.3 below). Fourth, sector-specific exemptions from the PSI Directive could be as problematic as sector-specific exemptions from competition law (at 4.4 below). Finally, imposing a duty on public sector bodies to allow re-use without requiring an abuse of market dominance could be considered as an illegitimate intervention in the competitive market process (at 4.5 below).

---

[29] Recital 29 of Directive 2013/37/EU.

4.1 On the Prevention of Competition in the Upstream Market where Information is Produced

In 2003, when the PSI Directive was adopted, the European legislature wanted to react to a double problem. On the one hand, private market actors largely depended on access to publicly-held information for entering the market for added-value information services. On the other hand, many public sector bodies did not regard it as part of their public role to provide information in the pure commercial interest of private businesses. In the latter regard, the European legislature indeed sought to trigger a change of mentality among Member States and the officials of their public sector bodies.

Yet, especially with the introduction of an obligation to grant re-use, the revised Directive may now even risk producing anti-competitive results. Today, many commercial re-users have also extended their activities from the level of the re-use of PSI to the upstream level of producing information that from a competition perspective could be regarded as substitutable for information held by public sector bodies. A good example of this is Google, which is no longer only a customer of public sector bodies regarding PSI, but has become a major producer of large amounts of data that may well exceed what can be offered by public sector bodies.

This development calls into question the approach of the PSI Directive in two regards. On the one hand, in many instances, the assumption that public sector bodies are the only source of information may no longer hold true. Hence, the analogy to Article 102 TFEU as a justification for an obligation to grant re-use of PSI has become questionable. Therefore, in certain instances, public sector bodies can no longer be viewed as market dominant. On the other hand, the limitation of the charging policy of public sector bodies to the marginal-cost standard in 2013, which does not allow for charging for the full costs of the production and provision of the data, has the same potential of affecting competition in the upstream market for the generation of data similar to the practice of predatory pricing that produces an exclusionary effect on private actors in the upstream information market. Hence, the PSI Directive may excessively restrict the freedom of public sector bodies to act and, at the same time, prevent the emergence of more competition in the upstream market, where information is produced, by decreasing the incentives of private actors to invest in the generation of information.

These concerns should convince the Commission and the EU legislature to critically observe the development of the markets concerned. But there are also various factors that still argue for the maintenance of the current system.

First, due to the large variety of information, it is very difficult to define information markets based on the substitutability of individual information and, therefore, to distinguish the cases in which a public sector body is the only source of information from those in which competition is already taking place in the upstream market or in which such competition could develop. To define a new legal regime which takes care of all these eventualities of very diverse information markets, especially without giving up the obligation to grant re-use where this is needed, therefore appears practically impossible.

Second, although more and more private actors nowadays enter the market in which information is generated, such actors may still rely on the PSI regime for re-use of data that is already available. Access to PSI at prices under the marginal-cost standard will prevent firms from wasting economic resources by investing in unnecessary duplication of already available information. This can also be illustrated by the business strategy of Google. With regard to geographical data, for instance, Google would act completely rationally if it relied both on access to PSI and on information that it is constantly generating itself in offering its added-value Google Maps service. Based on access to PSI for re-use, Google can combine both ways of acquiring information in a most flexible and economically efficient way.

Thirdly, low prices charged by public sector bodies based on the marginal-cost standard will not prevent private businesses from generating their own data where such data generation is only the by-product of other commercial activity. This is again best illustrated by Google, which generates its data not through targeted investment in knowledge generation but by the use of its search engine by private users. With regard to business information, the data that Google produces through its search engine may well nowadays be superior in many regards to what company registers can offer to private market actors for their added-value information services. The PSI Directive has no negative impact on this kind of knowledge generation by private businesses.

Yet the emergence of new, especially digital information markets may, and should, convince Member States constantly to review their decisions on what should belong to the public tasks. Many forms of the production of information, such as of meteorological data, are traditionally considered to fall within the scope of public tasks since, at the time these were defined, it was hard to imagine that private businesses would have sufficient incentives to invest in such knowledge generation. The emergence of digital information markets, however, makes private investment in such activities more profitable and, therefore, may argue for a gradual withdrawal of the state from such activities.

4.2 On the Anti-competitive Effect of the Marginal-cost Standard

The pricing mechanism is key to the working of the market economy and competition. This includes, and requires, the freedom of market actors to take into account the full costs of producing and providing goods and services when they negotiate prices. By imposing the marginal-cost standard, the revised Directive might risk undermining this pricing mechanism although the requirements for a prohibition of excessive pricing pursuant to Article 102 lit. a) TFEU are not fulfilled.

From a competition perspective this can produce two negative effects. On the one hand, limiting the freedom to charge prices may reduce incentives of public sector bodies to engage in the production of information. This effect argues for an exception in cases in which a reduction of income from re-use has a negative impact on the volume of production of information through the public sector body. In many instances, such a causal link between income and the production of PSI will not exist. For instance, the number of judicial decisions rendered by courts does not depend on whether and how much courts can charge private businesses for publishing these decisions in the form of printed court reports or digital databases. The same holds true for many other public sector bodies such as land and company registers for which private parties using the registers have to pay fees. Yet, in the framework of Article 6(2)(b) of the PSI Directive, the revision of 2013 took account of the particular risk that the marginal-cost standard can reduce the production of PSI, by exempting those public sector bodies from the marginal-cost standard that have to rely on their own revenue to finance the collection, production, reproduction and dissemination of PSI. By providing for this exception, the Directive also safeguards the freedom of especially poorer Member States to co-finance public tasks through private re-users of PSI.[30]

Second, as already explained above (see 4.1), the marginal-cost standard might lead to exclusionary effects, similar to predatory pricing practices, and thereby reduce the investment of private businesses in the

[30] See also the arguments made in the LAPSI Recommendations regarding the principle of subsidiarity: Ricolfi et al. (n. 24 above) 121 et seq.

production of comparable data.[31] As has already been explained, there are, however serious doubts as to whether such an effect actually exists. Hence, at least for the time being, one should not rely on such a potential effect as an argument against applying the marginal-cost standard.

Yet another problem relating to the marginal-cost standard deserves to be mentioned. The marginal-cost standard is based on the idea that, within the scope of the fulfilment of public tasks, the state anyhow finances the generation of PSI. Hence, the potential of economic commercialisation of PSI constitutes nothing more than a by-product of the fulfilment of these public tasks and, therefore, should not justify prices beyond the marginal-cost standard. In this reasoning, however, it is overlooked that, under the marginal-cost standard, prices do not reflect the full costs of the production and provision of the information, and that, accordingly, private commercial re-use is at least cross-subsidised by tax payers' money.[32] In many instances, as has already been pointed out, individual citizens and companies are charged fees although the specific activity falls within the scope of the performance of public tasks. For instance, if the marginal-cost standard were to be applied to the publication of court decisions, the parties to the underlying proceedings, who finance these proceedings through their fees, would cross-subsidise the businesses of private publishers. The same can be argued for the large varieties of registers that act both in the public interest and on behalf of private parties. Hence, in this regard, it is welcomed that Article 6(2)(a) of the revised Directive provides for an exception of the marginal-cost standard for public sector bodies that are required to generate revenue to cover a substantial part of their costs relating to the performance of their public tasks beyond the cases in which the marginal-cost standard would negatively impact the production of information. This provision allows Member States to prevent cross-subsidisation of private re-use of PSI through other private parties under the marginal-cost standard.

4.3 On the Effect of Exclusive Rights on Competition

The general prohibition on the grant of exclusive rights in Article 11(1) of the PSI Directive is inspired by the non-discrimination principle according to which a public sector body that is the only source of

---

[31] This is also a concern expressed by the LAPSI Recommendations. See Ricolfi et al. (n. 24 above) 119 (arguing that, from an economic perspective, the standard should be of average costs and not marginal costs).

[32] As to this concern see Ricolfi et al. (n. 24 above) 113.

individual information should not grant privileges to individual private re-users and, thereby, distort competition.

Yet the grant of exclusive rights is not generally held to be anti-competitive under EU law. With regard to the licensing of intellectual property rights, the ECJ already held in the early *maize seeds* case that the grant of an open exclusive licence for a plant breeder's right does not constitute a restriction of competition in the sense of ex-Article 85(1) EEC Treaty (now Art. 101(1) TFEU).[33] The reason for this is that third parties will often only be willing to invest in the commercialisation of information, including the subject-matter of intellectual property protection, if they are protected against free-riding by competitors. Hence, quite often exclusivity is even required to open a market for new products.

The PSI Directive does not ignore this concern.[34] As explained above (at 3.5), Article 11(2) of the Directive allows for an exemption from the prohibition of the grant of exclusive rights where this is necessary for the provision of a service in the public interest. The special regulation of the grant of exclusive rights for the digitisation of cultural resources under Article 11(2a) of the Directive provides a major example for which exclusivity is needed to create sufficient incentives for investment by an individual re-user and to exclude free-riding on such investment by other re-users.

Conversely, it may even be argued that the PSI Directive does not go far enough to protect undistorted competition, namely, as regards who should be granted the exclusive right. Indeed, if one accepts that exclusivity is indeed required, competition concerns will then have to focus on the process of selecting the exclusive re-user. The PSI Directive fails to address this issue. A future revision of the Directive could take account of this concern by learning from the rules on government procurement that are also designed to guarantee a level playing field

[33] Case 258/78 *Nungesser and Eisele v Commission* ('*maize seeds*') [1982] ECR 2015, para. 58. An exclusive licence will be regarded as an open exclusive licence if it is granted to single licensees in different Member States without prohibiting these licensees from supplying the licensed product to customers in other Member States.

[34] This concern is even explicitly recognised by Recital 29 of Directive 2013/37/EU, which reasons that the grant of an exclusive right will be necessary if no commercial user would publish individual information without such an exclusive right.

between private competitors where they compete to enter into a contractual relationship with the state.[35]

4.4 Exempted Sectors

Since the PSI Directive pursues an approach that is largely in conformity with competition law principles, the remaining sector-specific exemptions in particular need to be critically reviewed.

While, in 2003, educational, research and cultural establishments were broadly exempted, the revision of 2013 has now brought libraries, museums and archives into the scope of application of the Directive. What still needs to be reconsidered is the decision to exempt libraries, museums and archives from the general obligation to grant re-use under Article 3 of the PSI Directive. This seems mostly inspired by the different degree to which such institutions in the Member States have meanwhile progressed with regard to the digitisation of their content. Indeed, one could argue that it should be for the Member States to decide whether such institutions should be confronted with claims to grant access to their documents in digitised format according to the rules set out in Article 5 of the Directive.

Beyond libraries, archives and museums, other educational, research and cultural institutions remain completely exempted from the application of the PSI Directive. This exemption applies in particular to schools and universities. Such exemption seems to be justified for the purpose of protecting such institutions against claims of private businesses to get broad access to educational material. In particular, from a competition policy perspective, it can be argued that many institutions compete with regard to school and university education and that hardly any educational material constitutes essential information similar to PSI in other sectors. Hence, future commercialisation of digital educational content, which is developing very quickly and for which especially many universities develop commercial strategies, not least for distance learning, is fully and with good reason left to competition in the market.

---

[35] See, in particular, Directive 2004/18/EC of the European Parliament and of the Council of 31 March 2004 on the coordination of procedures for the award of public works contracts, public supply contracts and public service contracts, [2004] OJ L 134, p. 114. This Directive has been amended several times. A consolidated version is available at: http://eur-lex.europa.eu/LexUriServ/LexUriServ.do?uri=CONSLEG:2004L0018:20120101:EN:PDF (accessed 30 December 2013).

More critical is the maintenance of the exception for public broadcasters in Article 1(2)(d) of the PSI Directive. Public broadcasters hold a large stock of often digitised data nowadays for which, if it does not already fall in the public domain, they often are able to grant copyright licences. With regard to the documentary audiovisual content of public broadcasters (news programmes, etc.) in particular, there is also a major public interest of an educational, cultural and historical nature in making this content broadly available to the public. On the other hand, there are certainly many reasons why individual principles of the Directive do not fully match the particular needs of public broadcasting. In particular, the imposition of the marginal-cost standard could have a negative impact on the financing of new content. Also, the financing of public broadcasting activities varies considerably between Member States. Yet such concerns could be better targeted by partial exemptions from individual provisions of the Directive and by leaving the decision of whether content of public broadcasters should be available for re-use to the national regime of the Member States according to the approach of the 2003 Directive. Still, public broadcasters may tend to defend the general exemption with the concern that they would otherwise have to share their programmes with their private competitors. Whether such concerns are legitimate is more than doubtful. As can be learned from the above-reported joint venture of the two major German public TV stations for the establishment of a digital online marketing platform,[36] the exemption enables public broadcasters to freely commercialise and economically exploit their archives in conflict with the policy considerations of the Directive. It is hard to see why public broadcasters should benefit from a more liberal regime than public libraries. At best, one could argue that public broadcasters should be able to act as freely with regard to the commercial exploitation of their archives as their private counterparts. This argument, however, ignores that the public broadcasts were produced within the scope of the broadcasters' public tasks and often financed by taxpayers' money or viewers' fees. In sum, these considerations show that the exemption for public broadcasters is in need of being more carefully reconsidered in the framework of the next review of the Directive.

---

36 See at n. 19 above.

4.5 On the Potentially Anti-competitive Nature of the Special Regime Applied to Public Sector Bodies

Indeed, subjecting a group of actors to a more interventionist regime of economic regulation than their competitors beyond the general rules of competition law usually has to be viewed as a particular form of interventionist industrial policy that violates competition policy principles.

Yet one also has to acknowledge that the PSI Directive does not regulate the conduct of private market participants as independent economic actors but of entities that belong to the public sector. Hence, by applying the principles of the PSI Directive, the state itself limits its own discretion when acting with regard to the re-use of PSI and not the economic freedom of a single group of independent market actors. In fact, a decision on how and according to which principles public sector bodies deal with the re-use of PSI has to be made anyhow and somewhere within public administration. Therefore, the PSI Directive does not distort competition by subjecting a single group of addressees to a more interventionist regime of economic regulation. Rather, what can be seen from the history of the PSI Directive is that the decision on how to deal with the re-use of PSI has gradually moved away from the individual public sector bodies to the national and finally the EU legislature. Hence, EU PSI legislation is not a case on state intervention in the competitive process but a case on the degree of European harmonisation regarding a particular kind of administrative decisions with economic impact on private parties' interests in the EU. Accordingly, the policy question is not whether there should be any intervention, but how much European harmonisation is needed and is appropriate for regulating the re-use of PSI. It seems that the 2013 revision of the Directive takes a very balanced approach in this regard by combining the national decision on the access regime with a European obligation to grant re-use to accessible information as well as taking into account the need of Member States to decide flexibly on the model of financing the performance of public tasks in the framework of regulating the charging regime.

4.6 Overall Evaluation

In sum, the PSI Directive establishes a regulatory regime that reacts to competitive concerns and that is by and large in conformity with generally accepted competition law principles. In particular, in 2013, the PSI Directive was improved from a competition law perspective by strengthening the regime with the introduction of a general obligation to grant re-use of PSI that is available under the access regimes of the Member States, by adjusting the charging policy and the rules on the grant of exclusive rights as well as by reducing the sector-specific exemptions. In the future, the PSI regime could be strengthened even more by regulating the process of selecting the private re-users to whom exclusive rights are granted and by further reducing the sector-specific exemptions especially with regard to public broadcasters.

The European PSI regime and EU competition law thereby establish two complementary elements of a more integrated system that can work in a mutually supportive way. The PSI Directive can particularly contribute to excluding refusals to grant access to PSI for re-use from the outset. If the public TV stations in the abovementioned *Magill* case (at 2 above) had been under an obligation to provide their programme listings as part of a PSI regime, the two stations would probably never have refused to cooperate with private publishers. And even where refusals still occur, the PSI regime has the potential of providing redress more effectively and much more quickly than competition law. Yet competition law also remains important in basically two regards: first, competition law adds a second layer of enforcement with its own remedies, including the possibility of imposing fines and acting through the European Commission as a European enforcement agency. Second, competition law can still fill gaps to the extent that the national access regime or exemptions preclude claims for re-use under the PSI Directive. Application of competition law, however, requires that public sector bodies that decide on commercial re-use can be regarded as 'undertakings'. This will be discussed in the following part of this chapter.

5. PUBLIC SECTOR BODIES AS UNDERTAKINGS

Whether the sector-specific regime of the PSI Directive and EU competition law indeed overlap depends on the definition of the addressees of both regimes. The PSI Directive applies to 'public sector bodies', EU competition law to 'undertakings'. Both concepts give rise to a number of uncertainties.[37] The issue of the overlap of the two regimes can be approached from the angle of the application of both regimes.

[37] This has been highlighted by previous research. See, for instance, K. Janssen, *The Availability of Spatial and Environmental Data in the European Union* (Kluwer Law International 2010) 434–438.

5.1 The Holder of PSI as an Undertaking in the Sense of Competition Law

The concept of an undertaking is used in Articles 101 and 102 TFEU without any explicit definition. Traditionally, the term is understood in European case-law in a broad and functional sense. According to the seminal *Höfner* judgment of the ECJ, an undertaking is defined as 'every entity engaged in an economic activity, regardless of its legal status and the way in which it is financed'.[38] From this definition, the Court concluded that even a public employment agency engaged with employment procurement may be classified as an undertaking.[39] In addition, the Court stated two things: first, the fact that employment procurement activities are entrusted to a public agency – as was the case in Germany, from where the *Höfner* case was referred to the ECJ – does not affect the economic nature of the activity since employment procurement is not necessarily carried out by public entities.[40] Thereby, the ECJ guaranteed that EU Member States do not foreclose the national market for private businesses by creating a national monopoly for a public entity without any control under EU competition rules.[41] Second, the Court also made clear that such a public entity is to be considered as an undertaking falling under EU competition rules even if it does not pursue any commercial objective. Hence, no provider/customer relationship involving a payment of the customer to the provider or any profit-making intent on the part of the public entity is required. Thus, EU competition law also controls Member States that withdraw certain economic activities from private businesses by creating a legal monopoly in the hands of a public entity that provides goods or services free of charge.

In the more recent *FENIN* judgment, however, the ECJ has recalled specific limitations of the functional definition of an 'undertaking' that are relevant for the application of the EU competition rules to public entities in particular.[42] The Court held that 'it is the activity consisting in offering goods and services on a given market that is the characteristic

---

[38] Case C-41/90 *Höfner and Elsner* [1994] ECR I-1979, para. 21.

[39] Ibid., para. 23.

[40] Ibid., para. 22.

[41] Note that Article 106(2) TFEU may create a limited exemption from Article 102 TFEU. But Article 106(2) TFEU is only applicable if there is an 'undertaking' vested with exclusive rights in the first place.

[42] Case C-205/04 P *FENIN v Commission* [2006] ECR I-6295.

feature of an economic activity'.[43] According to this understanding, the activity of a public entity that only consists in purchasing goods or services in a relevant market would not suffice to qualify as an economic activity as such. However, the purchasing activity in the upstream market is considered as commercial activity if the goods or services are purchased by the entity for the production of goods or the provision of services in another (downstream) relevant market.[44] Under these conditions, the (upstream) purchasing activity will also be controlled under EU competition rules.[45]

Both the *Höfner* and the *FENIN* judgments are relevant for the activities of holders of PSI. Since PSI constitutes an economically valuable commodity, public sector bodies seem to act as undertakings in the sense of the *Höfner* judgment. The fact that public sector bodies are not allowed to charge beyond the marginal-cost standard as a matter of the PSI Directive does not argue against commercial activity. Most notably, in this reading, it would be the PSI Directive itself that would lead to the applicability of competition law by triggering licensing activities of public sector bodies with regard to PSI re-use. In addition, the *FENIN* judgment could even bring contractual relationships in the upstream market for the generation of PSI into the ambit of competition law since this activity would be related to further economic activity in the downstream market for re-use of PSI.[46]

Yet, in its *Compass* judgment of 2012,[47] the CJEU finally took a much more restrictive approach to classifying a public sector body holding PSI as an undertaking in the sense of EU competition law. The case arose from a dispute before Austrian courts between Compass-Datenbank, an operator of a digital database and provider of added-value services regarding commercial data on companies, and the Republic of Austria. To operate its service, Compass-Datenbank sought acccss to data contained

[43] Ibid., para. 25 (citing Case 35/96 *Commission v Italy* [1998] ECR I-3851, para. 36).

[44] Ibid., para. 26.

[45] Arguably, the *FENIN* judgment creates loopholes for the protection of undistorted competition. Public entities are often important purchasers in markets and, therefore, can easily distort competition by their purchasing decisions. In this regard, EU law provides some protection under its public procurement rules, but cannot address, for instance, bundled purchasing activity of local governments in the form of a purchaser cartel.

[46] See also Lundqvist (n. 5 above) 87 et seq. (indicating that under *Höfner* and *FENIN*, both with regard to the production and transfer of PSI, public sector bodies could be regarded as undertakings).

[47] *Compass-Datenbank GmbH* (n. 6 above).

in the Austrian companies register for commercial re-use of that data. Under the Austrian law that implements the PSI Directive of 2003, the companies register was not classified as one of the public sector bodies under an obligation to grant re-use. Through an intermediary billing agency, the company register only provided information under conditions that excluded the use of such information in databases of the customers. While the Austrian courts held that Compass-Datenbank had no claim under Austrian PSI rules, the Austrian Supreme Court (*Oberster Gerichtshof*) finally referred the question of whether the Republic of Austria was under an obligation to allow re-use for commercial purposes as a matter of Article 102 TFEU to the CJEU. More concretely, the Court asked whether a public authority acts as an undertaking if it registers information provided by undertakings on the basis of a statutory reporting obligation and provides such information to third parties for payment, but prohibits any more extensive use.[48]

In its judgment, the CJEU confirmed that any activity consisting in offering goods or services in a given market constitutes an economic activity.[49] Yet the Court distinguished such activity from the exercise of public powers that are not of an economic nature.[50] In this regard, the Court confirmed previous case-law according to which a public entity can also be regarded as an undertaking in relation to only parts of its activities, if the activities that form that part are to be characterised as economic activities.[51] However, this type of distinction would require that such economic activity can be separated from the exercise of its public power, whereas the activity as a whole remains the exercise of public powers where such separation is not possible.[52] The CJEU concluded in the latter sense, namely that, based on the statutory provision of Austrian law, the data collection falls within the public powers of the entity[53] and that the provision of information based on a search of its own database cannot be considered a separable economic activity since the data are actually collected for the purpose of consultation by the public.[54] In a similar vein, the mere fact that Compass-Datenbank was charged for the supply of information, according to the Court, did not make this supply a separable economic activity since the fees to be charged were provided

---

48 Ibid., para. 33 (first of three questions referred to the CJEU).
49 Ibid., para. 35.
50 Ibid., para. 36.
51 Ibid., para. 37.
52 Ibid., para. 38.
53 Ibid., para. 40.
54 Ibid., para. 41.

for by the law of Austria.[55] Also, with regard to the restriction of the use of the information, the Court argued against economic activity. Thereby, the Court expressly pointed out that the register was 'not obliged to authorise free use of the data' and that it can legitimately consider that it was even mandatory as a matter of national law to prohibit the re-use of that data in the interests of the companies concerned.[56] Finally, the Court held the PSI Directive irrelevant for considering whether the refusal to allow the re-use constituted an abuse of a market-dominant undertaking, since the Directive did not contain any obligation to authorise such re-use.[57] Accordingly, the Court concluded that the Austrian companies register had not acted as an undertaking in the sense of Article 102 TFEU.[58]

The *Compass* judgment is very far-reaching and also problematic. It excludes EU competition-law control in cases in which such control is most needed, namely in instances in which the PSI Directive fails to provide for an obligation to allow re-use of publicly-held data. What matters more than this critique on the *Compass* decision is the question of what conclusions need to be drawn for the application of EU competition law after the revision of the PSI Directive, which now recognises an obligation to allow re-use in most instances based on the domestic access regime. The Court's reasoning in the *Compass* judgment rests on two elements that need to be distinguished. The first element relates to the classification of the collection of companies' data by the Austrian public entity as exercise of public power. The second element regards the inseparability of the provision of companies' data contained in the register to third parties from the collection of such data.

With regard to the first element, the CJEU does not only rely on the mere existence of statutory provisions that stipulate the tasks of the register. Rather, the CJEU refers to the statutory obligation of the companies to provide certain information and the enforcement power of

---

[55] Ibid., para. 42.

[56] Ibid., para. 47.

[57] Ibid., para. 50.

[58] Ibid., para. 51. Quite a different conclusion was reached earlier by the Italian Corte d'appello di Bologna, decision of 14 November 2008, *Ribes S.p.A. v Agenzia del Territorio*, available at: http://www.epsiplatform.eu/content/italian-public-sector-body-found-guilty-abuse-dominant-position (accessed 30 December 2013) (with English case summary). In this judgment, the Italian land registry was held to have violated both Italian and EU competition law for not providing information to a commercial re-user. The court confirmed that competition law and the PSI Directive are applicable in parallel.

the public entity responsible for the register to enforce these obligations.[59] This coincides with other cases in which the Court held that a public entity had acted in the exercise of public power. For instance, in *Diego Calì*, the Court held that the exercise of anti-pollution surveillance in an Italian oil port by a private entity that was vested with the right to provide such surveillance was to be considered the exercise of public power. Thereby the Court relied on two considerations. On the one hand, the anti-pollution surveillance was exercised in the public interest as part of the essential functions of the state.[60] Maybe more importantly in this decision, the Court also highlighted the enforcement powers of the entity by holding that such 'surveillance is connected by its nature, its aims and the rules to which it is subject with the exercise of powers relating to the protection of the environment which are typically those of a public authority'.[61] The *Diego Calì* judgment thereby confirms what was previously held in the *SAT* judgment in 1992.[62] In this case, the Court relied on the exercise of sovereign rights of the Member States to classify the supervision of air space of these states and the provision of air navigation control services through Eurocontrol as the exercise of public power.[63] The Court also pointed out that for the purpose of such control Eurocontrol is vested with powers of coercion to ensure compliance with international agreements and national rules on access, overflying and the territorial security of the contracting states.[64] This explains why the Court in *Compass* also had to rely on the enforcement powers vis-à-vis companies that were under a statutory obligation to inform the register, and could not rely on the provision of such information to third parties, to argue exercise of public power. In order to include the provision of such information to third parties as part of the exercise of public power, the Court had to rely on the inseparability argument.

This case-law can be generalised for the purpose of classifying the activities of entities holding PSI. The mere fact that the collection of the data falls within the scope of the performance of public tasks and that these tasks are defined by statutory provisions does not suffice to classify such activity as the exercise of public power as long as such activity is

---

59 This may be somewhat overlooked by Lundqvist (n. 5 above) 91 (strongly criticising the Court for equating acting on a statutory basis with exercise of public power).

60 Case C-343/95 *Diego Calì* [1997] ECR I-1547, para. 22.

61 Ibid., para. 23.

62 Case C-364/92 *SAT Fluggesellschaft* [1994] ECR I-43.

63 Ibid., para. 20.

64 Ibid., para. 24.

not linked with the exercise of public authority and enforcement powers.[65] This explains why in *Magill* the ECJ did not even question whether the public TV stations were to be regarded as undertakings. With regard to the programming activity, public broadcasters may well act based on statutory provisions and in performance of public tasks. But such activity is not linked to the exercise of enforcement powers against private parties. Accordingly, the newly created obligation of public sector bodies to grant access to PSI for re-use does not make the grant of such re-use, or its refusal, the exercise of public power, because public sector bodies do not enforce legal obligations of citizens and other actors but only act in performance of their own legal obligations vis-à-vis potential re-users of PSI. As in the *Höfner* case, the mere public law classification of a service provided by a public sector body and the absence of a profit-making intent did not exclude the classification of such service as the economic activity of an undertaking that is controlled by EU competition law.

Hence, the more critical aspect of the *Compass* judgment relates to the second element of the reasoning, namely, the inseparability of the provision of company information to third parties, such as Compass-Datenbank, from the exercise of public power. In this regard, the Court misses the point that, with regard to Compass-Datenbank, the Austrian public entity did not have to rely on powers to enforce statutory obligations of Compass-Datenbank. The fact that such enforcement powers exist with regard to the companies that have to provide information to the register cannot define the nature of the activity regarding third parties that claim access to such information. In arguing inseparability, the Court relied on two previous judgments in which the Court, quite on the contrary, had relied on separability in order to confirm the applicability of competition law at least to one part of the activities of a public entity.[66] In *Compass*, the CJEU changes its perspective by refusing to distinguish between different sectors of activity and, thereby, restricted the application of competition law.[67] In this regard, the CJEU is to be criticised for failing to apply competition law to a public entity that has,

---

[65] In a similar sense see Lundqvist (n. 5 above) 87 (arguing that public power activities should cover fewer activities than public task activities).

[66] Case C-82/01 P *Aéroports de Paris v Commission* [2002] ECR I-9297, para. 74; Case C-49/07 *MOTOE* [2008] ECR I-4863, para. 25.

[67] See also Lundqvist (n. 5 above) 87 (advocating a narrow interpretation of the 'public power exemption' to preserve the broadest application for EU competition law).

through control of essential information, the power to restrain competition in a downstream information market.[68] This latter argument was considered by the ECJ in the *Magill* case to confirm the existence of a market-dominant position of the public TV stations as well.[69] In contrast, the reasoning in *Compass* regarding inseparability remained very formalistic and without relevance for the application of competition law. Yet, what the Court nevertheless took into account with good reason is the possible legal obligation of the public entity to deny re-use as a matter of Austrian law in the interest of the companies to which the information related. However, this does not argue for the inseparability of the provision of the data to third parties from the exercise of public power. Nor does such legal obligation make the refusal to allow re-use the exercise of public power, since, also in this regard, the public entity does not have to rely on enforcement power vis-à-vis the claimants of re-use. Rather, such legal obligations should be considered in the framework of an abuse in the sense of Article 102 TFEU. This approach would have the additional advantage of empowering competition law enforcers to examine in detail whether there was a sufficient legal basis for refusing re-use in view of protecting the interests of the companies to which the relevant information refers.

The application of competition law to public sector bodies after *Compass* can be summarised as follows: the mere fact that the generation of PSI falls within the scope of performance of statutory public tasks does not argue against the application of competition law. Competition law is excluded from application if the generation of such data, by its very nature, is to be considered the exercise of public power. This requires the existence of enforcement powers related to obligations of private parties; such obligations will typically consist in obligations to provide specific information. Even if the generation of information cannot be considered as economic activity by undertakings but as the exercise of public power, the grant of re-use, or its refusal, can be considered economic activity to the extent that such activity can be separated from the exercise of public power available with regard to the collection of the information. Thereby, the approach of the CJEU to this separability test in *Compass* remains problematic. Yet, in future cases, recognition of an obligation to grant re-use as a matter of the PSI

---

68 In a similar vein see Lundqvist (n. 5 above) 93 (arguing that the Court should have taken some inspiration from the PSI Directive for distinguishing between upstream and downstream activity).

69 See at section 2 above.

Directive may also lead the CJEU to argue in the sense of separability.[70] More concretely, where a public sector body indeed grants re-use or even itself engages in commercial re-use of its own PSI beyond the scope of performance of its public tasks, such activity can more easily be classified as economic activity by an undertaking even in cases where the generation of the data falls within the realm of the exercise of public power.

5.2 The Application of the PSI Directive to Undertakings

Conversely, the application of the PSI Directive to undertakings in the sense of EU competition law also raises considerable uncertainties. Those uncertainties are caused by the definition of 'public sector bodies' in Article 2 of the Directive.[71] To the extent that Article 2(2)(a) requires that public bodies be established for the specific purpose of 'meeting needs in the general interest, not having an industrial and commercial character', the PSI Directive seems to choose a definition that is opposed to the general functional understanding of an 'undertaking' as economic activity in the sense of competition law. Yet, there are also competition law provisions that use wording similar to that of the PSI Directive. Article 106(2) TFEU relates to 'undertakings' that provide services in the 'general economic interest'. This provision demonstrates that the concept of an undertaking and that of 'general interest' are not necessarily mutually exclusive in EU law. This is possible because a general economic interest may also be pursued by economic activity. Hence, if the further qualification as to the 'non industrial or commercial character' only refers to the 'needs in the general interest', but not to the nature of the activity, also 'undertakings' in the sense of competition law especially those falling under Article 106(2) TFEU – would be covered by the PSI Directive. Parallel application of the two regimes to such entities also makes sense, since the Directive may bring more precision to the competition principles and even implement additional obligations regarding the commercialisation of PSI beyond what competition law can actually achieve.

Other uncertainties arise from Recital 10 of the Directive, according to which the definition of public sector bodies does not cover public

---

[70] See also Lundqvist (n. 5 above) 84 and 88 (arguing that the PSI Directive forces public sector bodies to become undertakings).

[71] See also at section 3.2 above.

undertakings.[72] The term 'public undertaking' is used in Article 106(1) TFEU and is further defined in the so-called Transparency Directive 2000/52[73] as an 'undertaking over which the public authorities may exercise directly or indirectly a dominant influence by virtue of their ownership of it, their financial participation therein, or the rules which govern it'.[74] Moreover, the Transparency Directive stipulates a presumption of 'dominant influence' in case the public authority holds the majority part of the undertaking's capital, controls the majority part of the votes attached to the shares or appoints more than half of the members of the undertaking's administrative, managerial or supervisory body.[75]

Covering such public undertakings by the PSI Directive is obviously needed against the backdrop of the ongoing trend to privatise state functions and the provision of public services in particular. Especially public-private partnerships for the digitisation of data may be implemented by joint venture companies established by public authorities and private undertakings. For achieving the goals of the PSI Directive, it does not matter whether PSI is generated by a state authority or a private company still under the 'dominant influence' of the state. However, the PSI Directive does not provide for a complete exemption of *all* public undertakings; and Recital 10 of the Directive should not be misunderstood in this sense. The scope of application of the Directive is clearly defined by its operational provisions of Article 2(1) and (2). Accordingly, a 'body governed by public law' in the sense of Article 2(2) may simultaneously fulfil the requirements of a 'public undertaking' in the sense of the Transparency Directive. Yet not all 'public undertakings' qualify as public sector bodies.[76] The bottom line remains that an entity

---

72 Recital 10 reads as follows: 'The definitions of "public sector body" and "body governed by public law" are taken from the public procurement Directives. ... Public undertakings are not covered by these definitions.'

73 Commission Directive 80/723/EEC of 29 July 1980 on the transparency of financial relations between Member States and public undertakings, [1980] OJ L 195, p. 35, as amended by Commission Directive 2000/52/EC of 26 July 2000, [2000] OJ L 193, p. 73.

74 Article 2(1)(b) of the Transparency Directive.

75 Article 2(2) of the Transparency Directive.

76 See also the critical position of the LAPSI network: Marco Ricolfi et al., 'The Exclusion of "Public Undertakings" from the Re-use of Public Sector Information Regime' in D. Tiscornia (ed.), *Open Data and Re-use of Public Sector Information* (Edizioni Scientifiche Italiane 2011) XX/1-2 *Informatica e diritto* 147, 151, also available at: http://papers.ssrn.com/sol3/papers.cfm?abstract_id=2218264 (31 December 2013) (arguing that public undertakings that

may only fall under the Directive if it is established for the specific purpose of meeting needs in the general interest, not having an industrial or commercial character.[77] The additional requirement that the entity is 'financed, for the most part by the State, or regional or local authorities, or other bodies governed by public law; or subject to management supervision by those bodies; or having an administrative, managerial or supervisory board, more than half of whose members are appointed by the State, regional or local authorities or by other bodies governed by public law',[78] proves that the PSI Directive takes account of the fact that privatised companies with less than complete control by public authorities increasingly fulfil tasks in the general interest. As can be seen, the concept of a 'body governed by public law' is even partially inspired by the concept of 'dominant influence' that characterises the definition of a public undertaking in the Transparency Directive.

It can therefore be concluded that some public undertakings are covered by the PSI Directive, namely, those that meet the definition of the 'public sector body'. The line drawn by the PSI Directive may be considered as appropriate for distinguishing those undertakings under state control for which the creation of additional obligations regarding re-use of PSI is justified and those that should benefit from the same scope of economic manoeuvre regarding the collection and dissemination of information as private competitors.

In sum, a more concrete analysis of the scope of application of the PSI Directive also leads to the conclusion that the PSI Directive and competition law overlap in many regards. But, still, identifying the precise overlap requires a thorough legal analysis of the legal conditions for an undertaking in the sense of competition law, on the one hand, and for a public sector body in the sense of PSI law, on the other hand.

6. FROM REFUSALS TO ALLOW RE-USE TO OPEN-DATA POLICIES

The history of PSI regulation in the EU has come a long way. In 2003, when the PSI Directive was adopted, the European legislature wanted to set a first incentive for Member States to convince their public sector institutions to become more open to requests of private businesses that

are necessarily exempted from public procurement rules are not necessarily exempted from the PSI Directive).

[77] Article 2(2)(a) of the PSI Directive.

[78] Article 2(2)(c) of the PSI Directive.

want to commercialise public sector information. The approach of the 2003 Directive was characterised by an industrial policy approach that recognised the commercial value of PSI and sought to promote the emergence of new markets for information services provided by private businesses that build on PSI. By 2013, many Member States and also public sector bodies have progressed even further. Whereas the 2003 Directive took account of the potential willingness of the public sector bodies themselves to commercialise their data by economic activity outside of the fulfilment of their public tasks to generate additional income, providing access of the larger public to PSI free of charge by building up open information platforms has gained support in many sectors, not least the cultural sector, all around the European Union as part of a new open-data policy. What characterises this policy is that states and their public bodies consider it their public duty to provide digitised information to the public free of charge.

This policy evolution is also of interest from a competition-policy perspective. Above all, the new open-data policy seems to collide with the interests of commercial re-users who have to convince consumers to pay for similar services. Hence, the open-data policy has the potential of excluding the suppliers of non-gratuitous information services from the market. If the Ministry of Justice of a given Member State provides an open and technically highly developed database platform with all court decisions to the public free of charge, private businesses will lose incentives to provide similar services in return for payment. Accordingly, the new open-data policy, from an economic and competition-oriented perspective, seems to conflict with the former economic rationale and industrial policy orientation of the PSI Directive.

Yet, from a more legal perspective, the conflict can be solved within the framework of the PSI Directive. The evolution to an open-data policy can be addressed through the concept of 'public task'. In other words, open-data policies widen the scope of the public tasks so as to integrate the making accessible of PSI to the public free of charge. While, in the past, libraries have concentrated their functions on allowing public access to books that are found on bookshelves, they now expand their mission to providing digital access through the establishment of platforms through which users can have access at least to public domain works for free. The PSI regime does not at all prevent the Member States and their public sector bodies from developing such open-data policies, although this reduces the economic potential of commercial added-value information services. Quite on the contrary, an open-data policy also produces benefits for private re-users. Digital data that are produced and made available to the public as part of an open-data policy fall within the scope of the re-use obligation of Article 3(1) of the PSI Directive and can therefore be integrated in distinct and more valuable digital platforms run by private re-users. Those re-users can aggregate data they receive from various PSI holders and other sources to larger databases and equip their digital services with more and refined utility functions.

This explains why, under the framework of the 2013 Directive, the EU legislature is able to combine the industrial-policy reasoning and the open-data reasoning as a dual justification for the PSI Directive without having to acknowledge an inherent conflict between the two. On the contrary, open-data policies make data more accessible for commercial re-users and create additional incentives for even more enhanced added-value information services. In this regard, Recital 6 of the 2013 Directive, in which the EU legislature reacts to the evolution of PSI policies, quite rightly states as follows:

> Member States have now established re-use policies under Directive 2003/98/EC and some of them have been adopting ambitious open data approaches to make re-use of accessible public data easier for citizens and companies beyond the minimum level set by that Directive. To prevent different rules in different Member States acting as a barrier to the cross-border offer of products and services, and to enable comparable public data sets to be re-usable for pan-European applications based on them, a minimum harmonisation is required to determine what public data are available for re-use in the internal information market, consistent with the relevant access regime.

Consequently, the emergence of open-data policies certainly marks a paradigm shift as far as data policies are concerned, namely, from ‘refusals to allow re-use’ to ‘providing digital data to the public for free’ as a new public task. This paradigm shift also creates additional competitive pressure on private re-users and may even drive some of them out of the market. But this does not provide sufficient reason to regard open-data policies as anti-competitive. Rather, such policies create new incentives for private businesses to develop their services even further for the benefit of consumers.

7. CONCLUSION

The analysis shows that, in 2003, the EU rules on the re-use of private sector information (PSI) took an industrial policy approach with a view to promoting the emergence of new added-value services and to enhancing economic growth.

Yet the rules of the PSI Directive by and large build on sound principles of competition policy. In particular, the Directive addresses the major competition concerns that arise in both cases of vertical integration – those where public sector bodies commercially exploit their PSI by also providing added-value services in downstream markets, and those where non-vertically integrated public sector bodies either refuse to grant access to PSI or try to exploit their market dominance through excessive pricing.

From a competition perspective, the 2013 revision of the PSI Directive has developed the regime in a positive sense. In particular, the creation of a European law obligation to allow re-use, by building on the national access regimes, will considerably increase the effectiveness of the system. In the framework of strengthening the charging regime, the EU legislature took into account the argument according to which public sector bodies should be allowed to achieve a reasonable return on investment – first, where the production of information is dependent on the revenue generated from re-use and, second, to the extent that the production of information is significantly financed through other third parties. With regard to the grant of exclusive re-use rights, the 2013 revision allowed for such rights where they are needed to create sufficient incentives for private businesses to invest in the provision of added-value services. Thereby, the Directive also established an appropriate balance between incentives for investment in the digitisation of cultural resources and the need to make digitised copies available to the public and other re-users after a certain period of time. By including archives, libraries and museums in the scope of application, the legislature of 2013 expanded the PSI regime into the cultural, research and educational sectors where open-data policies have been evolving enormously during the last decade.

Despite this overall positive assessment, the European PSI regime, also from a competition policy perspective, still has to evolve. Most importantly, the relevant markets and the business models of re-users have changed enormously. Some of the commercial re-users of PSI, such as Google in particular, have by now joined the group of the most powerful companies in the world. Private re-users of PSI have become large aggregators and, finally, even producers of data that could potentially substitute PSI. Thereby, public sector bodies and private businesses become competitors on the different levels of collecting, aggregating, processing, re-using and providing data to the public. The most important change regards the paradigm shift brought about by open-data policies.

These constant changes should convince the Commission to closely monitor how these markets evolve and to make adjustments to the PSI regime when needed. However, even against the backdrop of all these changes, which advocate a thorough review of the PSI regime, the principles already implemented in the 2003 Directive prove to be remarkably robust and can adequately address all the competition concerns. For the time being, only a few additional amendments can be recommended. These include, in particular, a regulation of the selection process for the grant of exclusive rights, for which the legislature could find some inspirations in the EU public procurement rules, and a reconsideration of the sectorial exemption granted to public broadcasters. In addition, the PSI Directive lacks legal certainty and takes a too cautious approach to third parties' intellectual property rights. With regard to intellectual property rights, the PSI Directive should clearly spell out that public sector bodies are under an obligation to grant licences for their original rights and to the extent that they are authorised to grant sub-licences for the rights of third parties.

The analysis also argues for parallel application of the PSI regime and EU competition law as two elements of an integrated regulatory competition framework for PSI-related markets. Unfortunately, the EU legislature has not managed to provide sufficient legal certainty regarding the application of the PSI Directive to undertakings in the sense of EU competition law, including public undertakings. Conversely, the CJEU's judgment in *Compass* is to be criticised for limiting the application of EU competition law too much in cases where the PSI Directive fails to provide for an obligation to allow re-use or where the Directive provides for exceptions from its general principles. Also against the backdrop of the *Compass* judgment, it is good to see that the 2013 revision of the PSI Directive has introduced an obligation to allow re-use as the rule and has extended the scope of application of the Directive.

PART 2

Pro-competitive regulation

5. Deepening the freedom of services through pro-competitive regulation: the case of the EU Services Directive

Maria Manuel Leitão Marques and Leonor Bettencourt Nunes

1. INTRODUCTION

In the European Union, the enforcement of competition law has had an underlying objective in addition to the guarantee of conditions of fair competition in the market: the establishment and maintenance of a European internal market. Therefore, the Union's policy for the establishment of the internal market and its competition policy are so intrinsically linked that they inevitably produce reciprocal effects. Removing obstacles to the free movement of goods, services, capital and persons guarantees wider access to the market, while the EU's competition policy prevents undertakings from reintroducing those obstacles through unilateral or bilateral behaviour.[1]

In the field of the fundamental freedoms, it has been demonstrated that the mere removal of barriers to free movement is not enough to achieve a cohesive single market. There is a need for positive integration through harmonisation and regulation of the internal market in order to create a 'level playing field'.

Nonetheless, regulation has commonly been considered as undesirable from the perspective of competition policy. Traditionally, deregulation and liberalisation were encouraged in order to promote free market access, remove distortions and assure the well-functioning of the market.

---

1 Commission Guidelines on Vertical Restraints, [2000] OJ C291, p. 1, para. 7.

However, regulation is not incompatible with competition; on the contrary, there are certain economic sectors in which regulation is the most adequate means to assure undistorted competition and free access to the market, namely in network sectors such as telecommunications and energy, among others. Modernisation of regulation, through its simplification and the use of information and communication technologies, may also have a pro-competitive impact when it removes bureaucratic barriers, increases transparency and thus facilitates access to the markets.

This considered, the aim of this chapter is to analyse the pro-competitive effects of regulation in the field of the fundamental freedoms by using the case of the Services Directive. First of all, focus will be given to the concepts of free access to the market as an essential facility for market integration and competition. The concept of regulation will also be explained in view of the anti-competitive and pro-competitive effects of regulation. Subsequently, the issue of regulating the fundamental freedoms and its relationship with the promotion of competition will be explored and then illustrated with the case of the Services Directive. Moreover, the final version of this Directive, and in particular its limited scope, will be discussed against the background of the conception and the objectives of the first Commission proposal. Special attention will be paid to the removal of administrative burdens considered as an important legal barrier to free movement of services. Administrative simplification is the main tool selected by the Services Directive to eliminate that barrier.

As we intend to demonstrate, if the goals of the Services Directive are achieved, specifically those concerning simplification, the path followed by the Directive can constitute a relevant case study of pro-competitive regulation not only at internal market level but also for each Member State of the EU and even for third countries.

2. FREE ACCESS TO THE MARKET: AN ESSENTIAL FACILITY FOR MARKET INTEGRATION AND COMPETITION

The establishment of a single European market, in which goods, persons, services and capital can circulate without barriers and under conditions of undistorted competition, is highly dependent on the guarantee of free market access through the elimination of restrictions or barriers.

In relation to the four freedoms, the ECJ (now CJEU) has demonstrated the relevance of the notion of market access from an early stage with the rulings in *Dassonville* and *Cassis de Dijon*,[2] under which any measure that directly or indirectly, actually or potentially hinders access to the market is to be considered a measure having equivalent effect to a restriction.[3] These decisions were the foundation of the market-access approach of the ECJ for free-movement cases, which has been developed in opposition to a discrimination approach, under which only discriminatory measures are considered restrictions or barriers to free movement. The Court has opted for a market-access approach on several occasions[4] and this has also been argued by the Advocates-General.[5] In his opinion in *Alfa Vita*, AG Poiares Maduro demonstrated the advantages of this approach in relation to the rationale of the establishment of the internal market and stated that 'the objectives of the internal market require not only combating discrimination based on nationality but also the opening-up of national markets to new products, services or economic operators'.[6]

The idea of market access is also central to competition law. If there are barriers to entry, the level of actual competitive constraints and potential constraints by new entrants is affected. Therefore, market shares alone cannot indicate market power, as 'a firm can exercise market power for a significant time only if barriers to entry exist'.[7] Considering this, the Commission has increasingly recognised the need to analyse barriers to entry, namely for the establishment of dominance and abuse under Article 102 and for merger assessment.[8]

---

[2] Case 8/74 *Dassonville* [1974] ECR 837 and Case 120/78 *Rewe* ('*Cassis de Dijon*') [1979] ECR 649.

[3] *Dassonville* (n. 2 above) para. 5.

[4] See, e.g., Case C-384/93 *Alpine Investments* [1995] ECR I-1141; Case C-415/93 *Bosman* [1995] ECR I-4921; Case C-190/98 *Graf* [2000] ECR I-493; Case C-405/98 *Gourmet* [2001] ECR I-1795; Case C-110/05 *Commission v Italy* ('*trailers*') [2009] ECR I-519.

[5] See, e.g., AG Jacobs in Case C-412/93 *Leclerc-Siplec* [1995] ECR I-179; AG Fennelly in *Graf* (n. 4 above); AG Tizzano in Case C-442/02 *Caixa-Bank France* [2004] ECR I-8961; AG Poiares Maduro in Joined Cases C-158/04 and C159/04 *Alfa Vita* [2006] ECR I-8135; AG Kokott in Case C-142/05 *Mickelsson and Roos* [2009] ECR I-4273.

[6] Opinion in *Alfa Vita* (n. 5 above) para. 38.

[7] A. Jones and B. Sufrin, *EU Competition Law: Text, Cases and Materials* (4th edn, OUP 2010) 84.

[8] Guidance on the Commission's enforcement priorities in applying Article 82 of the EC Treaty to abusive exclusionary conduct by dominant undertakings, [2009] OJ C 45, p. 7; Council Regulation (EC) No. 139/2004 on the control of concentrations between undertakings, [2004] OJ L 24, p. 1.

The Commission describes barriers to entry as 'factors which prevent or hinder companies from entering a specific market'.[9] As these factors may take many different forms, it is common to distinguish between legal barriers (e.g. regulation imposing licensing), economic barriers (i.e. advantages of the incumbent undertakings, such as sunk costs and economies of scale) and strategic or behavioural barriers (i.e. caused by the incumbent undertakings' exclusionary practices such as predation and margin squeeze).[10] In regard to economic and strategic barriers, several theories have been developed to provide a precise definition.[11] This theoretic discussion has an actual impact on competition policy, as the option for a very wide definition may produce false positives of market power and a narrower option may be too lenient and generate false negatives.[12] However, this discussion goes beyond the scope of this chapter, which will focus on regulation. Barriers imposed by regulation restrict trade and harm consumers; however, unlike, for instance, behavioural barriers, legal barriers are hardly caught under antitrust scrutiny, as the CJEU's state-action doctrine is very limited.[13]

Nonetheless, regulation may not always constitute a barrier. On the contrary, regulation can serve as a tool to eliminate existing barriers and restrictions and hence ensure market access and the promotion of

---

9 European Commission, Directorate-General for Competition, 'Glossary of Terms used in Competition Policy' (2002) 17.

10 O. Arowolo, 'Application of the concept of barriers to entry under Article 82 of the EC Treaty: is there a case for review?' (2005) 26 *ECLR* 249; R. Whish and D. Bailey, *Competition Law* (7th edn, OUP 2012), 365–366.

11 For an overview of the theories see, e.g., A. Jones and A. Sufrin (n. 7 above) 85 ff.; O. Arowolo (n. 10 above); R.P. McAfee, H.M. Mialon and M.A. Williams, 'What is a Barrier to Entry?' (2004) 94 *Am. Econ. Rev.* 461–465.

12 Jones and Sufrin (n. 7 above) 85.

13 The Court developed its 'state action doctrine' by reference to the jurisprudence of the US Supreme Court that orginated with the leading cases *Parker v. Brown*, 317 U.S. 341 (1943) and *California Liquor Dealers v. Midcal Aluminum*, 445 U.S. 97 (1980). In the EU case-law, this doctrine involves the application of Articles 101 and 102 to Member State action based on the principle of sincere cooperation contained in Article 4(3) TEU (formerly in Article 10 TEC), according to which Member States are responsible for assisting in the tasks of the Union and 'shall refrain from any measure which could jeopardise the attainment of the Union's objectives', for instance, anticompetitive measures. Some of the paradigmatic cases in the EU are: Case 13/77 *GB-Inno-BM v ATAB* [1977] ECR 2115; Case 229/83 *Leclerc* [1985] ECR 1; Case 231/83 *Cullet* [1985] ECR 305; Case 267/86 *Van Eycke v ASPA* [1988] ECR 4769; and more recently Case C-35/99 *Arduino* [2002] ECR I-1529 and Case C-94/04 *Cipolla* [2006] ECR I-1142.

competition, as will be demonstrated in the case study of the Services Directive. Before analysing this Directive, it is important to establish the notion and rationale of regulation.

3. WHAT IS REGULATION? WHY REGULATE?

Regulation refers to a binding set of rules to be applied by a body devoted to this purpose. It aims at restricting behaviour and prevents the occurrence of certain undesirable activities.[14]

We are taking into consideration both regulation imposed by a public body and also regulation carried out by other bodies (self-regulation), when these bodies are recognised by the state as regulators of certain economic activities or professions. The latter is called 'delegated regulation' to distinguish it from pure self-regulation.[15] Delegated regulation is especially relevant when analysing barriers to freedom of services. Frequently, these barriers are created by professional bodies, namely those that have the monopoly of profession representation at the national level, as is the case with the liberal professions (lawyers, doctors, engineers, architects, accountants, etc.).

Nowadays, regulation is becoming more multileveled. This means that for the same issue – for example, services – we need to consider regulation generated both by the state and other public bodies, above or below the state (for instance, international bodies, like WTO and the EU, or regional and local authorities).

Governments or other bodies may support regulation for several technical reasons. In a general approach, market failures, that is, the failures of market mechanisms to produce behaviour or results in accordance with public interest, and non-economic reasons (social and cultural reasons) are the rationale of regulation. Each piece of regulation can combine different justifications, joining economic and social justifications. In the decision-making process of enacting regulation, states may

---

[14] Our concept of regulation is restricted to regulation imposed by a public body, including delegated forms. A narrower approach has identified regulation with the rules applied to the regulated sectors by independent authorities, namely network industries and the financial sector. See M.-A. Frison-Roche, *Les 100 mots de la régulation* (PUF 2011) 114. Broader approaches to regulation enlarge the concept to all forms of social control, 'whether imposed by the state or other social institutions' (B. Morgan and K. Yeung, *An Introduction to Law and Regulation* (Cambridge University Press 2007) 4).

[15] See R. Baldwin, M. Cave and M. Lodge, *Understanding Regulation* (OUP 2012) 138.

also be influenced by other factors, such as the protection of certain groups of interests and, most commonly, national interests.

From a competition point of view, regulation can be neutral, thus without any relevant effects. That is the case, for instance, of some rules related to the protection of consumers or the protection of cultural patrimony, which are applied horizontally to several activities without discriminating any sector or provider. However, as previously mentioned, regulation can also impact competition either by anti-competitive effects, even if it is justified by overriding reasons relating to the public interest, or through pro-competitive effects, providing the legal framework for enabling market entrance and competition. These two possible effects will be further discussed and illustrated with examples.

4. COMPETITION AND REGULATION

4.1 Anti-competitive Regulation

Regulation, even if justified by other reasons, can produce anti-competitive effects by imposing barriers to entry of any kind, for instance by limiting the number of existent players in the market (through a *numerus clausus* or a system of quotas), delaying or deterring the entry of new players, or simply establishing disproportionate requirements in view of the interests it intends to protect.

There are limits to market access that can be technically indispensable, namely barriers related to the nature of the market itself (limits justified by the scarcity of available natural resources or technical capacity, as referred to in Article 12 of the Services Directive).[16] This is the case, for example, with radio channels, since radio spectrum licences are granted by public tender. In these cases, regulation of the public tender to grant the licences is the only way to guarantee some level of competition in that market.

However, regulatory barriers are not always natural or technically indispensable, but rather reflect economic policy options taken by the states, which are not always justified by the protection of general public interest. Sometimes states are lobbied by professional associations to protect the current professionals from new entrants.[17] Even if the expressed objectives of regulation are otherwise, the hidden objective is

---

[16] See J. Wolswinkel, 'The Allocation of a Limited Number of Authorisations' (2009) 2(2) *Rev. Eur. Adm. L.* 61.

[17] On the 'capture' in regulation, see Morgan and Yeung (n. 14 above), 61.

to limit competition in order to protect the established market players from new entrants, either national or from other Member States. In the last case, both new entrants who wish to establish themselves in that Member State, and those who want to provide goods or services from the Member State in which they are already established, are included.

There are several examples of these kinds of barriers in the field of services, of which we especially emphasise barriers concerning the liberal professions, which not only come from public regulation but also from professional associations (for instance, codes of conduct). In 2007, Paterson et al. performed a study for the European Commission which identified certain barriers concerning the liberal professions.[18] The study covered lawyers, notaries, accountants, architects, engineers and pharmacists' services. It was stated in its conclusions that 'the existence of certain types of restrictive anti-competitive regulation undoubtedly lends credence to the view that such regulatory structures can be used by professions to obtain economic results that are in their favour, but contrary to the needs of, and against the interest of consumers as a whole'.[19]

Besides liberal professions, in several European countries, the opening of markets in the case of pharmacies, taxi services and even large retailers (like hypermarkets) has also been subject to access restrictions that are aimed at controlling competition. These restrictions include quotas and/or minimum required distance between establishments, such as in the case of pharmacies in Portugal.

Sometimes there are no explicit regulatory barriers established, as exemplified above. Barriers can be 'invisible' when they result from excessive administrative burdens to comply with regulation, the lack of transparency of administrative procedures, the excess of discretionary power of administrative bodies, the difficulty to contact those bodies, and so on. These types of barriers make access to the market more difficult for all new entrants, regardless of their country of origin, and in that sense are not discriminatory. However, they are obviously more burdensome for new entrants coming from other Member States. This is true not only because foreign service providers may be obliged to comply with double burdens, but also because they are not as familiar with the requirements as are national providers. For this kind of situation, deregulation is not necessarily the only way to eliminate barriers, facilitate access to markets

[18] I. Paterson, M. Fink and A. Ogus, *Economic Impact of Regulation in the Field of Liberal Professions in Different Member States* (ENEPRI 2007), available at: http://www.enepri.org/ (accessed 31 December 2013).

[19] Ibid., p. 5.

and promote competition. Modernising regulation, simplifying, eliminating unnecessary and disproportionate requirements and making regulation easier to understand and to comply with are appropriate ways to get barriers removed without leaving relevant public values unprotected.

As shown below, this approach is dominant or at least very important in the Services Directive. It is one of the reasons why the Services Directive case study is not only unique and very relevant for the EU and the internal market but also at national level.[20] In section 6 below we will analyse how the Directive intends to eliminate the excess of administrative burdens and to solve difficulties in accessing information encountered by the services providers from other Member States.

4.2 Pro-competitive Regulation

Simpler regulation is our first example of a way to facilitate market access and to promote competition without deregulation. Therefore, markets can still be regulated, when regulation is needed to protect public interests. In the case of the EU, the effort to simplify and modernise must be greater, as regulation has to be easy to understand and comply with, not only by the nationals of the Member State in which the regulation is enacted, but also by nationals of all other Member States.

However, this is not the only example of convergence between regulation and competition aims. There are other examples of regulation which aim at promoting competition by granting access to markets. For that purpose regulation normally acts *ex ante*, while competition rules act *ex post*.[21]

An example of a situation in which only regulation can assure competition, in the sense of consumer welfare, is the case of natural monopolies, which can only comprise one player (such as transport and distribution of water, railways and sewage). These natural monopolies may be under public administration (or simply kept apart from the

---

[20] As is frequently demonstrated by the World Bank in its 'Doing Business' reports and also in several OECD reports, this is a problem for many undertakings of the world in terms of starting a business, getting a licence, etc.

[21] See N. Petit, 'The Proliferation of National Regulatory Authorities alongside Competition Authorities: a Source of Jurisdictional Conflict?' in D. Gerardin, N. Petit and R. Muñoz, *Regulation through Agencies in the EU* (Edward Elgar Publishing 2005) 180;. F. Cintioli, 'Integrazione e sovrapposizione tra regolazione e antitrust. Il caso dei servizi di interesse economico generale', in E. Bruti Liberati and F. Donati, *La regolazione dei servizi di interesse economico generale* (Giappichelli 2010) 93.

market) or under management by private entities, to which concessions are granted through a duly regulated public-tender process. In this case, competition is assured during the tendering stage and sometimes afterwards by performance comparison among market players (yardstick competition), if the market is fragmented on a territorial basis, for instance, as for water supply.

The liberalisation of network industries (railways, energy, telecommunications, water and transports) that were previously public monopolies, at the end of the 20th century and the beginning of the 21st, also originated pro-competitive regulation, both at the EU and the national level, especially through the creation of national independent regulatory authorities. This regulation intends to remove market failures, as well as to achieve non-economic objectives.[22] It is usually designated as market-friendly regulation that mimics a free market.[23]

Pro-competitive regulation has also been important at EU level as a way to implement fundamental freedoms. In fact, the fundamental freedoms provided for in the Treaties were not only established through deregulatory measures that removed existing national barriers and followed the path set by the case-law of the CJEU, which creatively interpreted the Treaty provisions. They were also significantly deepened by regulatory measures, such as regulations and directives, which either substituted national regulation for EU regulation or forced national regulation to change in order to comply with the Treaties. Therefore, national regulation became more market-friendly, which has benefited not only economic freedom and competition at EU level, but also within each Member State.

---

[22] Privatisation of public monopolies generated new regulation to protect the public interest, namely through the development of the concepts of 'universal service' and 'public service obligations'. This regulation has been cited as an example of how liberalisation does not always imply deregulation. See V. Aguado i Cudolà, 'Estudio preliminar. La incidencia del derecho de la Unión Europea y de la Directiva servicios en los diversos sectores de intervención administrativa: una panorámica general' in V. Aguado i Cudolà and B. Noguera de la Muela (eds), *Il Impacto de la Directiva de Servicios en las Administraciones Públicas: Aspectos Generales y Sectoriales* (Atelier 2012) 23.

[23] On regulation to promote competition in networked industries, see G. Ariño Ortíz, J.M. de la Cuétara Martínez and I. del Guayo Castiella, *Regulación Economica* (Aranzadi 2012), 112 and 215 ff.

5. REGULATION OF THE FUNDAMENTAL FREEDOMS AND PROMOTION OF COMPETITION: CONVERGENCE OF OBJECTIVES

The pro-competitive effect of regulation concerning the fundamental freedoms is provided by an intrinsic convergence of free movement and competition policy.[24] In fact, both have the same overarching goal of the establishment and maintenance of a single European market.[25]

It is well acknowledged that free movement and competition rules are fundamental provisions of the Treaties, which according to Baquero Cruz (among others), 'constitute, together with economic and monetary union and the common commercial policy, the basic layer of the economic constitutional law of the European Community'.[26] The core of the Treaties has always been the establishment of a common market between the Member States that assures 'free trade under conditions of fair competition'.[27]

Accordingly, a broad notion of the internal market comprises not only the fundamental freedoms, but also a system of undistorted competition as a means of protecting the well-functioning of the market. In fact, the Treaty of Lisbon emphasised that competition policy is an intrinsic and essential part of the internal market, by gathering the internal market and competition in one single protocol, and relocating the 'competition principle', previously enshrined in Article 2 TEC, to that same protocol.

The centrality of the concept of the internal market in the interpretation of Treaty provisions and its connection with competition is also evidenced by the existence of the 'single market imperative' in competition policy. This imperative is especially related to vertical agreements, such as export bans, territorial protection and geographic price discrimination, as these are more likely to divide the market along geographic lines. This is why such behaviour often leads to findings of violation of Article

---

[24] This section is based on the co-author's (Leonor Bettencourt Nunes) LL.M. dissertation at King's College of London, entitled 'Convergence Between Free Movement and Competition Rules' (not yet published).

[25] C. Semmelmann, 'The European Union's Economic Constitution under the Lisbon Treaty: Soul-searching among Lawyers Shifts the Focus to Procedure' (2010) 35 *E.L. Rev.* 522.

[26] J. Baquero Cruz, *Between Competition and Free Movement* (Hart Publishing 2002) 85.

[27] Commonly used expression since the Court's ruling in Case 32/65 *Ireland v Council and Commission* [1966] ECR 563.

101(1) TFEU and is, in practice, very unlikely to fulfil the conditions of Article 101(3) TFEU for an exemption.[28]

Furthermore, the Court's early rulings on both the fields of free movement and competition provide evidence of convergent approaches. In *Consten and Grundig* and *Dassonville*, the Court used nearly the same words to define the scope of application of Article 101 (agreements between undertakings) and Article 34 (free movement of goods).[29] Both the definitions of 'effect on trade' and 'measures having equivalent effect to quantitative restrictions' emphasised the non-hindering of trade between Member States and thus testified to a convergent inherent rationale of competition law with free movement rules.

Even though free movement and competition rules are directed, respectively, at barriers to the fundamental freedoms and anti-competitive conduct, these different application fields may overlap on several occasions. A very recent example of a case which raised questions on both free movement and competition law was *FAPL and Murphy*.[30] In this case the Court was confronted with a situation where the owner of a pub, Karen Murphy, was screening Premier League football matches using a decoder from Greece instead of a decoder from the licensed broadcaster in the UK.

From the point of view of convergence, it is interesting to see that the Court considered that the same facts were a violation of both free movement and competition rules. In relation to freedom of services, the Court circumvented a possible horizontal direct effect situation by stating that it was the national rules enforcing the broadcasting rights by prohibiting the import of foreign decoders that constituted a restriction to freedom to provide services.[31] The Court also considered the same grounds of justification, namely the protection of intellectual property rights, in order to deny the admissibility of both a justification for the

---

[28] P. Lindh, 'The Influence of Competition Law on Free Movement Rules' in H. Kanninen, N. Korjus and A. Rosas (eds), *EU Competition Law in Context: Essays in Honour of Virpi Tiili* (Hart Publishing 2009) 18. Recent examples of the single market imperative can be seen in Joined Cases C-501/06 P, C-513/06 P, C-515/06 P and C- 519/06 P *GlaxoSmithKline v. Commission* [2009] ECR I-9291; Case C-439/09 *Pierre Farbre* [2011] ECR I-9419 and Joined Cases C-403/08 and C-429/08 *Football Association Premier League (FAPL) and Murphy* [2011] ECR 9083.

[29] Joined Cases 56 and 58/64 *Consten and Grundig* [1966] ECR 299, 341 and Case 8/74 *Dassonville* [1974] ECR 837, para. 5.

[30] *FAPL and Murphy* (n. 28 above).

[31] *FAPL and Murphy* (n. 28 above), paras 88–89.

restriction to freedom to provide services and an exception to the ban on practices whose object is to restrict competition, under Article 101(3).

Convergence is not only present in the Treaties and in the Court's case-law. As we have stated, regulation and harmonisation measures regarding the internal market and the development of fundamental freedoms have a necessary pro-competitive effect by facilitating access to the market and levelling competition conditions. In regards to regulation, there are several directives that intend to promote market liberalisation and removal of barriers in the fields of goods, services, persons and capital.[32] Given the increasing relevance of services in the economy and the horizontal, ambitious and innovative character of the Services Directive, this has been chosen as our case study, forming as it does a good example of pro-competitive regulation.

6. THE SERVICES DIRECTIVE AND COMPETITION IN THE MARKET OF SERVICES

Services are a key area in the EU's economy, representing over 70 per cent of GDP and employment in the majority of the Member States.[33] This explains why the CJEU has been experiencing an increasing load of cases regarding free movement of services and developing a detailed jurisprudence. Nonetheless, as Hatzopoulos has pertinently pointed out, 'the limits inherent to negative integration and to the casuistic approach pursued by judiciary decisions have prompted the need for a general legislative text to be adopted for services in the internal market'.[34]

Considering this, the adoption of a directive on the freedom of establishment and freedom to provide services, which would create a true

---

[32] As Hatzopoulos states, the 'EU's approach in relation to service provision can be characterized as neither systematic nor coherent. ... Some regulatory blocks are sector specific (such as transport, the other network industries, financial services), while others are more horizontal (such as the mutual recognition of professional qualifications), typically with a relatively limited scope. It is only with the adoption of the Services Directive that a truly horizontal approach was adopted in the field of services.' See V. Hatzopoulos, *Regulating Services in the European Union* (OUP 2012) 223.

[33] Communication from the Commission to the Council and the European Parliament: 'An internal market strategy for services', COM (2000) 888.

[34] V. Hatzopoulos, 'Legal Aspects in Establishing the Internal Market for Services', College of Europe Research Papers in Law 6/2007, 2, available at: https://www.coleurope.eu/sites/default/files/research-paper/researchpaper_6_2007_hatzopoulos.pdf (accessed 31 December 2013).

internal market for services in Europe and codify the ECJ's case law in the field, was then put on the agenda of the Lisbon Strategy and the Services Directive itself entered into force in 2006.

The negotiation process of the Services Directive was one of the longest and most complex of the EU and led to the adoption of a version which considerably differs from the original proposition. Therefore, our analysis will start by considering the originally proposed draft and the controversy it generated, as well as the case law of the Court that served as inspiration for the Services Directive. Afterwards, the adopted text will be reviewed with regard to its scope of application and main goal. Finally, the provisions on administrative simplification and their impact on the achievement of the Services Directive goal, as well as on competition, will be explored.

6.1 The Original Version of the Directive

The original draft of the Services Directive generated a spiral of criticism and controversy that eventually resulted in a watered-down final text.[35] The discussion around the 'Bolkestein' Proposal of 2004 was centred on its proposals regarding free movement of services and, particularly, on the so-called country-of-origin principle. In fact, in regard to its provisions on freedom of establishment and on administrative simplification, the text was not significantly altered.

The 'Bolkestein' Proposal intended to provide the legal background for the deepening of the internal market for services by codifying the existing case-law and guaranteeing that host states would not be able to impose restrictions, for instance by requiring a domestic establishment for the provision of services (which was still the case in some Member

---

[35] The Services Directive has probably been the most controversial legal instrument of EU history. Nevertheless, sometimes the discussion was not really about the Commission Proposal. Other political goals of national political actors affected the discussion. See A. Crespy, *Qui a peur de Bolkstein – Conflits, resistences et democratie dans l'Union européenne* (Economica 2012); E. Grossman and C. Woll, 'The French Debate over the Bolkestein Directive' (2011) *Comp. Eur. Pol.* 344; E. Miklin, 'Government Positions on the EU Services Directive in the Council: National Interests or Individual Ideological Preferences?' (2009) 32 *West Eur. Pol.* (2009) 943; T. Rentrop, 'The Service Directive: What Is Actually New' (EIPASCOPE 2007), available at: http://www.eipa.eu/files/repository/eipascope/20071106123232_treSCOPE2007-2_internet-4.pdf (accessed 31 December 2013) 2; Aguado i Cudolà (n. 22 above) 22.

States).[36] The path followed by the Proposal was the adoption of the country-of-origin principle, which had already been the model used in other directives related to specific service sectors.[37]

The principle has its foundation in the *Cassis de Dijon* decision and in its principle of mutual recognition, under which a product lawfully marketed in one Member State is marketable in another, unless there are mandatory requirements of general interest that justifiably and proportionately impede this. Therefore, the legal standards of the home state are automatically recognised in the host state, excluding any dual regulatory burden that can only be justified by an open list of mandatory requirements established by case law.[38]

After *Cassis*, the Court began generally applying the principle of mutual recognition to free movement of services. In *Säger*, the Court stated that:

> the Treaty requires not only the elimination of all discrimination against a person providing services on the ground of his nationality but also the abolition of any restriction, even if it applies without distinction to national providers of services and to those of other member states, when it is liable to prohibit or otherwise impede the *activities of a provider of services established in another Member State where he lawfully provides similar services*.[39]

This line of case-law became, like *Cassis de Dijon* for free movement of goods, the general paradigm, being repeated on several occasions.

However, it can be argued that the 'Bolkestein' Proposal did not merely codify the case-law on this point. While the principle of mutual recognition is 'a rebuttable presumption of equivalence of the home state law, the [country-of-origin principle under the first version] is a rule of competence generally prescribing the inapplicability of the host state law'.[40] This would mean that the law of the host state is not applicable even if it does not have a restrictive effect. Hence, the controversy around

---

[36] C. Barnard, 'Unravelling the Services Directive' (2008) 45 *C.M.L. Rev.* 323.

[37] Ibid., 361.

[38] On the principle of mutual recognition see, e.g., C. Barnard, *The Substantive Law of the EU: The Four Freedoms* (3rd edn, Oxford University Press 2010) and R. Graham, 'Mutual Recognition and Country of Origin in the ECJ Case Law', in R. Blanpain (ed.), *Freedom of Services in the EU* (Kluwer Law International, 2006) 42.

[39] Case C-79/90 *Säger* [1991] ECR I-4221, para. 12 (emphasis added).

[40] N. Fichtner, 'The Rise and Fall of the Country of Origin Principle in the EU's Services Directive – Uncovering the Principle's Premises and Potential Implications' *Essays in Transnational Economic Law*, no. 54 (Martin Luther

the 'Bolkestein' Proposal was thus captured by the image of the 'Polish plumber' providing services in France as an encouragement for 'social dumping' and ultimately a compromise of the social dimension of the European internal market.[41]

Furthermore, the first Commission Proposal, while making access to the markets of other Member States much easier for service providers, would have caused distortions, in itself, as it would have led to distinct standards, according to the country of origin, to be applied to equal services and service providers within the same Member State.[42] Consequently, service providers from countries with less regulatory burden could have had a competitive advantage. It is possible that this also might have caused a race-to-the-bottom type of regulatory competition, in order to allow host countries to minimise these competitive advantages. However, such effects are difficult to predict.

Moreover, the country-of-origin principle, as first proposed by the Commission, also gave rise to some difficulties and doubts in regard to the effectiveness of the control of the implementation and compliance of service providers with the law of their country of origin, which was intended to be exercised by the home states.[43]

All this criticism led to the approval of a 'toned-down' final version. In addition to the several sectors that the Commission had already initially excluded from the scope of the directive, even more sectors were added to the exclusions list, and, most notoriously, the country of origin principle was retracted from Article 16, which now prescribes only that the host state 'shall ensure free access to and free exercise of a service activity within its territory'.

The final wording of Article 16 of the Services Directive is more closely related to Article 56 TFEU and to the interpretation that has been given to it by the case-law of the CJEU.

University Halle 2006), p. 16, available at: http://telc.jura.uni-halle.de/sites/default/files/altbestand/Heft54.pdf (accessed 31 December 2013).

41 Barnard (n. 36 above) 329.

42 G. Davies, 'The Services Directive: Extending the Country of Origin Principle, and Reforming Public Administration' (2007) 32 *E.L. Rev.* 233.

43 A. Hatje, 'Services Directive – a Legal Analysis' in F. Breuss, G. Fink and S. Griller (eds), *Services Liberalisation in the Internal Market* (Springer 2008) 15. On the retraction of the country-of-origin principle from the Services Directive see also M. Wathlet, 'La genèse de la Directive de Services', in Ch. Ferrari-Breeur (ed.), *La directive 'services': En principe(s) et en pratique* (Bruylant 2011) 27.

6.2 The Final Version

6.2.1 Inspiration from the case-law

As previously emphasised, the Services Directive intended to codify the case-law of the Court concerning the provision of services, making use of the freedom of establishment or free movement of services. However, as will be explained below, the Services Directive is clearly inspired by the case-law, but it also diverges from it in certain aspects.

First of all, the foundations of the freedom to provide services are drawn from the *van Binsbergen* decision, which concerned the imposition by Dutch law of an obligation imposed on all lawyers providing services in the Netherlands to be resident in the country.[44] Comparably to *Dassonville* and *Cassis de Dijon*, this ruling opted, even if less markedly, for a market-access approach, and opened the possibility for justifications under mandatory requirements based on public interest.

The possibility of justification is expressly established in the Services Directive by Article 15(3) (for establishment) and Article 16(1) and (3) (for free movement of services). This justification is subject to the principles of non-discrimination and proportionality, which had been long established by the case-law of the Court. In fact, in the case *Bond van Adverteeders*, the Court ruled that the mandatory requirements of general interest cannot be invoked to justify discriminatory measures.[45] Discriminatory measures are, nonetheless, justifiable through the express derogations provided by Article 52 TFEU and applicable to free movement of services under Article 62 TFEU. As primary law, these provisions are hierarchically superior and were thus not affected by the Services Directive.

In *Gouda*, the Court presented a preliminary list of the overriding reasons relating to the public interest already recognised by the case-law, amongst them the protection of service recipients, the protection of intellectual property, consumer protection and the conservation of the national historic and artistic heritage.[46] This list has been extended further by the Court's subsequent jurisprudence. Regarding freedom of establishment, the Services Directive refers to the concept of overriding reasons and thus expressly accepts the open-ended list of the Court. However, in relation to freedom of services, requirements can only be justified by reasons of public policy, public security, public health or

44 Case 33/74 *van Binsbergen* [1974] ECR 1299.
45 Case 352/85 *Bond van Adverteeders* [1988] ECR 2085, para. 32.
46 Case 288/89 *Gouda* [1991] ECR I-4007, para. 14.

protection of the environment. Clearly, the Services Directive did not intend to codify the case-law, but decided to limit the list of justifications to achieve the goal of deeper market integration by diminishing the state-imposed restrictions that can be considered justified.[47]

In regard to the principle of proportionality, this was recognised in the case-law on free movement as a way to balance the extensive scope of the freedoms and the possibility for justification of restrictions under public-interest requirements.[48] The proportionality test was fully enounced in terms of adequacy and necessity in the *Gebhard* decision and in relation to freedom of establishment but has been the paradigm approach for all of the fundamental freedoms.[49]

Finally, the Services Directive establishes a list of prohibited requirements for both freedom of establishment and free movement of services. These lists are clearly based on the Court's jurisprudence. For instance, the obligation on the provider to have an establishment in the host state was considered a violation of freedom to provide services by the *Commission v Denmark* decision of 1986.[50] The requirement to obtain an authorisation, such as registration with a professional body or association, was also considered contrary to Article 56 TFEU in *Corsten*.[51]

6.2.2 Scope of application

Services are defined as any self-employed economic activity, normally provided for remuneration (Article 4). Even though the Services Directive is a horizontal piece of regulation, there are many excluded services.

The material scope of the Directive was established negatively, through a series of exclusions and limitations. First of all, Article 1(2) to (7) submits that the Directive 'does not deal' with the liberalisation of services of general economic interest and privatisation of public entities, the abolition of monopolies providing services and the granting of state

---

47 J. van de Gronden and H. de Waele, 'All's Well that Bends Well? The Constitutional Dimension to the Services Directive' (2010) 6 *Eur. Const. L. Rev*, 397, 412.

48 N. Reich, 'How Proportionate is Proportionality? Some Critical Remarks on the Use and Methodology of the Proportionality Principle in the Internal Market Case Law of the ECJ' in H.-W. Micklitz and B. De Witte (eds), *The European Court of Justice and the Autonomy of the Member States* (Intersentia 2012) 83.

49 Case C-55/94 *Gebhard* [1995] ECR I-4165, para. 57.

50 Case 252/83 *Commission v. Denmark* [1986] ECR 3713, para. 18.

51 Case C-58/98 *Corsten* [2000] ECR I-1221.

aids, and 'does not affect' the promotion of culture, linguistic diversity or media pluralism, criminal law, labour law and fundamental rights.

More problematic in terms of competitive effects are the several sector-specific exclusions, which partly result from the long and controversial negotiation process of this directive.[52] The exclusions cover sectors which were related to public authority or maintained a public character even if already in the private sphere, sectors which were already comprised by sectorial directives and, finally, sectors which involved powerful lobbies or particularly sensitive fields. Therefore, the Directive does not apply to non-economic services of general interest, financial services, electronic communications services and networks, services in the field of transport, healthcare services (also comprising pharmaceutical services), audiovisual services, gambling services, activities connected with the exercise of official authority, social services, private security services, notary services or temporary work agencies (Article 2(2)).

Particularly unfortunate, for rather different reasons, are the exclusions regarding gambling and healthcare. An opportunity was lost to codify the confusing and detailed case-law of the Court, as the extensive jurisprudence in these sectors highlights the existence of important barriers to entry.

To the excluded sectors the case-law of the Court is still applicable, which leads to a fragmented regime, compromising legal certainty.[53]

Therefore, the main fields of the Directive's scope of application are: business services (managing consultancy, certification and testing, advertising, recruitment services); services provided to businesses and consumers (legal advice, construction, distributive trade, car rental, travel agencies etc.) and consumer services, including tourism.

---

[52] On the implications of the exclusions see L. Chabaud, 'La directive 2006/123/EC du Parlament Européen et du Conseil du 12 Décembre 2006 relative aux services dans le marché interieur. Les exclusions explicites: Article 2' in Ferrari-Breeur (ed.) (n. 43 above) 41; and V. Michel, 'Le champ d'application de la Directive de Services: entre cohérence et régression', in Ferrari-Breeur (ed.) (n. 43 above) 49; Barnard (n. 36 above) 323; House of Lords Report, *The Services Directive Revised* (2006) (which compared all the differences between the original version and the adopted one); Aguado i Cudolà (n. 22 above) 27.

[53] Barnard (n. 36 above) 344.

Even with all the aforementioned exclusions, the sectors covered by the Directive still represent 45 per cent of the EU's GDP.[54] In relation to these sectors, the Directive has been capable of actively reducing barriers to entry and, consequently, increasing competition. The legislature missed the opportunity to accomplish more by having more sectors covered and therefore there is still a 'free space' for some anti-competitive measures.[55]

6.2.3 The main goal of the Services Directive

The Services Directive's proclaimed goal was to create a true internal market for services and to remove barriers to freedom of establishment and freedom to provide services, based on the statement that growth in the economy is nowadays essentially driven by services.

The Services Directive intends to promote market access within the internal market and produce an overall more competitive service sector in the EU. In fact, market fragmentation 'has a negative impact on the entire European economy, in particular on the competitiveness of SMEs and the movement of workers, and prevents consumers from gaining access to a greater variety of competitively-priced products'.[56]

Several studies have presented preliminary assessments of the positive economic impact of the Directive, namely, concerning competitiveness and growth. For instance, Kox, Lejour and Montizaan estimated that the Directive would bring about an increase in bilateral trade in commercial services of 30 to 60 per cent.[57] Badinger et al. submitted that its trade-enhancing effects would increase competition in the sectors, thus creating a transmission channel to affect productivity, employment, investment and output.[58]

---

[54] Communication from the Commission to the European Parliament, the Council, the European Economic and Social Committee and the Committee of the Regions on the Implementation of the Services Directive: A partnership for new growth in services 2012–2015, 8 June 2012, COM(2012) 261 final, 2.

[55] J. Delgado, 'The Economics of the Services Directive' (2007) *Contratto e Impresa Europa* 959, 569. Anyway the rules and systems adopted to register or license the services covered by the Service Directive are probably going to infiltrate other sectors not covered by the Directive.

[56] Recital 4 of the Services Directive.

[57] H. Kox, A. Lejour and R. Montizaan, 'The Free Movement of Services within the EU', Document No. 69CPB (Centraal Planbureau – Netherlands Bureau for Economic Policy Analysis 2004/2005) 9.

[58] H. Badinger, F. Breuss, Ph. Schuster and R. Sellner, 'Macroeconomic Effects of the Services Directive', in Breuss, Fink and Griller (eds) (n. 43 above) 125.

A recent economic paper by the Commission has confirmed a positive macroeconomic impact of the Services Directive through trade and foreign direct investment. Moreover, the domestic impact of the reduction of barriers to entry, which has been overlooked by most of the studies, has also been a transmission channel with effects on labour productivity and on GDP. It is possible that this channel is responsible for an overall increase of between 0.4 and 1.8 per cent of GDP.[59]

6.2.4 Legal barriers to free movement of services

To achieve this goal and the associated positive economic impact, it is necessary to remove barriers which prevent providers from extending their operations beyond their national borders and from taking full advantage of the internal market. These barriers concern not only free movement of services but also freedom of establishment.

As has been frequently recognised, 'services are much more prone to Internal Market barriers than goods and are harder hit. … Whereas with goods only the goods themselves are exported, in the case of service provision it is often the provider himself, his staff, his equipment and material that cross national borders'.[60]

Barriers can occur throughout the cycle of service provision, from establishment (e.g. authorisation, registration and declaration requirements) and the use of the necessary inputs for the service provision, to promotion (e.g. rules of commercial communication), distribution (e.g. fixed and recommended prices), sales (e.g. differences in contract law) and after-sales activities (e.g. rules of repair and maintenance services).

The Services Directive takes into account difficulties perceived as obstacles by providers and recipients of services, whether or not they are compatible with EU law. Those kinds of barriers are not physical and technical. They are 'legal barriers' arising from national, regional and local regulation:

> The term 'legal barriers' covers all obstacles to the development of service activities between Member States deriving directly or indirectly from a legal

---

[59] J. Monteagudo, A. Rutkowski and D. Lorenzani, 'The Economic Impact of the Services Directive: A First Assessment Following Implementation', Commission Economic Paper 456 (June 2012) 36, available at: http://ec.europa.eu/economy_finance/publications/economic_paper/2012/pdf/ecp_456_en.pdf (accessed 31 December 2013).

[60] See Report from the Commission to the Council and the European Parliament on the state of the internal market for services presented under the first stage of the Internal Market Strategy for Services, Brussels (30 July 2002), COM(2002) 441 final, 6.

> constraint and which are liable to prohibit, impede or otherwise render less advantageous such activities. Such barriers … [are generated] by divergent national regulations, as well as from problems relating to the behaviour of national authorities, … including the use of discretionary powers … , unclear requirements applied on a case-by-case basis by national authorities, the result of which is often unpredictable.[61]

The legal barriers also include rules approved by professional associations and soft law, such as codes of conduct.

The Commission considered that, in order to effectively eliminate legal barriers, judicial review by the Court of Member States' infringement of the freedoms would not be enough; such a long procedure is not able to help achieve the economic goals envisaged for the service sector.

For Maydel, the main reason why these barriers are still present in the Member States is related to the suspicion between the Member States, the protection of national interests and resistance to modernisation of their own legal order.[62] For now, the objective of the Directive is mostly oriented towards this modernisation and towards the simplification of the law of the Member States, making it clearer and more accessible.[63]

7. ADMINISTRATIVE SIMPLIFICATION TO IMPROVE COMPETITION

7.1 Administrative Burdens as a Legal Barrier

Taking into account that administrative burdens have been identified as one of the most important barriers to freedom of services, the Services Directive aims at eliminating them, removing the legal uncertainty associated with cross-border activity and the lack of mutual trust between Member States. In order to cut administrative burdens, the Directive puts a special focus on simplification, unparalleled by any other directives or even informal initiatives of European institutions at the time.

Chapter II of the Services Directive is all about 'administrative simplification'. The large spectrum of procedures and formalities it

---

[61] Ibid., 13.

[62] N. Maydel, 'The Service Directive and Existing Community Law', in Breuss, Fink and Griller (eds) (n. 43 above) 21, 78.

[63] Simplification does not constitute the only contribution of the Services Directive to promoting competition. The Directive's rules in regard to advertisement of services of regulated professions (Article 24) and the exercise of multidisciplinary activities (Article 25) are equally relevant.

comprises, from access to the service activity to its exercise, shows the Directive's ambition as concerns simplification.[64] Chapters III and IV, on freedom of establishment and free movement of services, also pursue similar goals. Chapter VI on 'administrative cooperation' ensures that the Directive's aims are achieved as regards convergence of procedures.[65]

The objective of administrative simplification and burden reduction consists in the opening of national markets to service providers from other Member States. The elimination of the country-of-origin principle in favour of a 'country-of-destination' principle made the focus on simplification even more important.[66] The Directive could have chosen instead the path of harmonisation. However, harmonisation of the entire legislation concerning the several services included in the Directive would be an extremely long and complex process. Therefore, the adopted methodology is more decentralised and thus forces the Member States to modernise their own legal order. That effort can also result in a wider coherence or even convergence between the rules of each Member State. This kind of 'self-induced' harmonisation, in the words of Hatzopoulos, will result from the concentration of the administrative procedures for the access and exercise of an activity in a single point of contact, the reduction of documents, the quality and certification policies, and also from the promotion of European codes of conduct as a form of EU soft regulation (Article 37).[67] Further measures can also be taken at EU level, in case this expected convergence does not occur (Article 41).

Consequently, the Member States will be forced to revise their legal framework and administrative procedures which are relevant to the

---

[64] See European Commission, Handbook on Implementation of the Services Directive (2007) 17, available at: http://ec.europa.eu/internal_market/services/docs/services-dir/guides/handbook_en.pdf (accessed 31 December 2014): 'The concept of procedures and formalities is a broad one and includes any administrative step which businesses are required to take, such as submission of documents, filing a declaration or registration with a competent authority. It covers not only procedures and formalities which are a pre-condition for the exercise of the service activity but also those imposed at a later stage, in the course of the exercise of the activity, or even upon its completion (for example an obligation to report on a yearly basis the details of transactions carried out)'.

[65] On the different aspects of administrative simplification in the Services Directive, see Aldomà i Buixadé, 'La simplificaciòn en la Directiva de Servicios', in Aguado i Cudolà and Noguera de la Muela (eds) (n. 22 above) 147; M.M. Leitão Marques, F.P. Oliveira, A.C. Guedes and M.M. Rafeiro, *O Regime Jurídico do Licenciamento Zero* (Almedina 2012).

[66] In the same sense, see House of Lords Report (n. 52 above).

[67] See Hatzopoulos (n. 32 above) 260.

implementation of the Directive. This process has to be controlled by the Commission and it is the responsibility of the Member States to communicate the text of the new measures (Article 44).[68] This strict control is another sign of the importance of the simplification process for the success of the objectives of the Directive.

The screening of the relevant legislation requires changes to be made regarding the regulation of services that fall within the scope of the Directive. Judging from the Portuguese experience of the ongoing screening, this transformation can also result in a positive simplification of other economic activities not covered by the Directive. In Portugal, the concept of 'zero licensing', which replaced licences and authorisations by declarations for some kinds of services, was then extended to other activities outside the scope of the Directive.[69]

As will be analysed below, the Services Directive provides very specific rules and principles regarding legislation revision. These principles will be applied not only to the law itself, but also to the administrative procedures related to law implementation, including some technical features of information systems which support points of single contact.

7.2 Principles and Guidelines

Article 5(1) of the Services Directive imposes a general simplification obligation on Member States in relation to all procedures and formalities related to the access to and the exercise of service activities covered by the Directive. This general obligation encompasses all the principles

---

[68] It is quite an ambitious task, given that, for instance, in Portugal the Services Directive led to the revision of 68 pieces of legislation at the central administration level alone, and that local administrations have their own regulations of services within the scope of the Directive.

[69] See Decree-Law 48/2011, 1/04 and Decree-Law 196/2012, 1/08 on the simplification impact of 'Zero Licensing'; Leitão Marques et al. (n. 65 above); and M. Gorjão-Henriques 'The Implementation of the Services Directive in Portugal' in U. Stelkens, W. Wieb and M. Mirschberger, *The Implementation of the EU Services Directive, Transposition, Problems and Strategies* (TMC Asser Press and Springer 2012) 493. The 'zero licensing' is a simplified licensing regime for starting or modifying certain economic activities like retail, restaurants, hairdressers and flower shops, among many others. It replaces the existing burdensome and complex licensing procedures (required, for instance, to open a shop and/or install a canopy, a terrace, etc.) by a simple declaration through a single electronic point of contact.

regarding simplification, taking into account the experiences of the Member States and of the Commission.[70]

Some of these principles are expressly provided for by the Directive, namely, the principles of necessity and proportionality, the principle of points of single contact, the principle of plain language and the principles of swiftness, transparency and predictability.[71]

7.2.1 Necessity and proportionality

The principles of necessity and proportionality had long been established by the Court, as demonstrated above. In this context, necessity refers to the need for a justification by a reason of public interest. In the Services Directive, these two principles cover both freedom of establishment and free movement of services. The inclusion of these principles in the Directive provides them with a wider relevance and impact. It forces Member States to actively change, perhaps radically, their legislation in order to comply with these principles, instead of being only obliged to do so by ruling of the Court and in relation to concrete legislation.[72]

As concerns freedom of establishment, these principles apply to all 'administrative procedures for granting authorisations, licences, approvals or concessions, and also the obligation, in order to be eligible to exercise the activity, to be registered as a member of a profession or entered in a register, roll or database, to be officially appointed to a body or to obtain a card attesting to membership of a particular profession' (Recital 39). The Directive states that a Member State can only enact authorisation schemes in the case that 'a posteriori inspection would take place too late to be genuinely effective' (Article 9(1)(c)).

---

[70] Especially after the adoption of the Lisbon Strategy, the Commission engaged in a series of initiatives to increase quality, promote simplification and reduce administrative costs. From the documents produced, see Report from the Commission to the Council and the European Parliament, Minimizing regulatory burdens for SMEs – Adapting EU regulation to the needs of micro-enterprises, 23 November 2011, COM (2011) 803 final, and the Commission's Communications on Better Regulation, COM(2009) 15, COM(2008) 32, COM(2006) 689, Smart Regulation COM (2010)543, and recently on Regulatory Fitness, COM(2012) 746 final. Some of the initiatives in the field of information society (eGovernment) also contributed to this objective, namely, as concerns interoperability.

[71] On the principles of simplification see M.M. Leitão Marques, 'Simplex: A Quiet Revolution', in F. Barazzoni and F. Basilica (eds), *Verso la Smart Regulation in Europa* (Maggioli 2012) 361.

[72] See Hatzopoulos (n. 32 above) 173; Aguado i Cudolà (n. 22 above) 31.

Article 9 is not about harmonising administrative procedures and requirements for granting authorisations, but rather about removing overly burdensome authorisation schemes, procedures and formalities that hinder freedom of establishment and the creation of new service undertakings.[73]

It is not to be expected that many authorisation schemes and requirements will be totally eliminated and the establishment fully liberalised. While certain requirements are expressly prohibited, others should be subjected to prior evaluation in order to satisfy the principles of necessity and proportionality. In any case, the procedures will be significantly simplified.[74] A permit, often granted after a long and sometimes random procedure, can be substituted by a registry or declaration of opening of an establishment to the public authority, which may be controlled *a posteriori*.

This simplification of procedures and formalities does not necessary imply complete deregulation. The service provider may still have to comply with some requirements. For instance, in the case of installing an awning for a restaurant, the public authority in charge can still establish requirements in relation to size, width, inclination and colour that must be complied with, in order to protect town planning.

The Directive applies only to requirements that affect the access to or the exercise of a service activity. Therefore, requirements which do not specifically regulate or affect the service activity but have to be respected

---

[73] On the authorisation schemes in the Services Directive see Barnard (n. 36 above) 323–339. Specifically on the replacement of traditional authorisation schemes by declarations and registers, see Aguado i Cudolà (n. 22 above) 67; V. Parisio, 'Silencio positivo, denuncia de inicio de actividad y comunicación certificada de inicio de actividad en el procedimiento administrativo: la simplificación procedimental, entre el derecho interno e el derecho europeo, en Italia' in V. Aguado i Cudolà and Noguera de la Muela (eds) (n. 22 above) 91, 101; J.E. Pardo, 'La desconstrucción y previsible recomposición del modelo de autorización administrativa', in A. Noguera López, A. Arias Martínez and M.A Almeida Cerreda (eds), *La Termita Bolkestein: Mercado único vs. derechos cuidadanos* (Civitas 2012) 29; M. Rodríguez Font, 'Técnicas de controle en la transposición de la Directiva de Servicios: Comunicación previa y declaración responsable', ibid., 81. The Services Directive distinguishes between authorisations that are limited, because there is scarcity of available natural resources or technical capacity (Article 12), and authorisations that are limited by an overriding reason relating to public interest (Article 13). On this distinction see Wolswinkel (n. 16 above) 61.

[74] This is the case in Portugal, particularly through the new 'zero licensing' legal system referred to above.

by providers in the course of carrying out their economic activity, such as road traffic rules, rules concerning the development or use of land, town and country planning, and so on, do not need to be revised. The exclusion of these kinds of requirements limits the impact of the simplification effect promoted by the Directive and, consequently, its pro-competitive effect. Moreover, it is not always easy to distinguish which requirements do not specifically affect the access to or the exercise of a service activity. For instance, the imposition of quotas to access commercial activity for large retailers has been often connected with town planning.[75] Therefore, certain requirements which are excluded from the scope of the Directive may actually affect access to or exercise of a service activity.[76]

In spite of the exclusions and the practical difficulties they embody, the paradigm of the Directive is still radically different from the ones existent in some Member States. The traditional approach of a systematic mistrust of the administration vis-à-vis the citizens has been reversed. The main value is now deemed to be the trust in service providers, whether nationals or not, instead of an overwhelming administrative control, which is now only applicable to cases of greater risk and only if explicitly justified.[77]

7.2.2 Points of single contact

Even simplified procedures, such as registration or declaration, can be difficult for foreign operators to comply with. It is not obvious to foreign providers who the competent authority is to whom they must declare their activity in the host state, or which formalities and rules have to be complied with. For example, for the installation of a terrace on the

---

75 On the impact of the Services Directive on large commercial retailers see J.M. Pérez Fernández, 'La Directiva de Servicios y su impacto en la ordinación del gran equipamento commercial', in Noguera López, Arias Martínez and Almeida Cerreda (eds) (n. 73 above) 325.

76 The same happens with permits for the use of public domain, for instance to install a terrace. In Portugal, the screening of the legislation covered these situations, when associated with service activities. See M.M. Leitão Marques et al. (n. 65 above). See also M. Karpenschif 'La Directive de Services et les collectivités locales: entre contraintes nouvelles et espoirs déçus', in Ferrari-Breeur (n. 43 above) 109.

77 This approach keeps authorities from using resources to control low-risk situations, allowing them to use those resources for a more effective control of the cases which require careful and prior checks. See Leitão Marques (n. 71 above) 375. On the impact of the Services Directive in the Member States and the way it has been implemented, see the contributions to Stelkens, Wieb and Mirschberger (eds) (n. 69 above).

sidewalk, it would be necessary to know what part of the sidewalk can be used, what type of furniture can be installed, and so on. This is precisely why it is so important to concentrate the information in points of single contact.

The obligation of the Member States to create points of single contact is one of the greatest simplification tools of the Directive. Its importance is not only due to the user-friendly functionalities of the point of single contact (POSC) but also to its potential impact on cutting red tape, in view of the necessity to standardise procedures and eliminate dual controls, repeated documents, and so on.[78] The Commission is entitled to define all the common rules and standards of the POSC, in order to guarantee their interoperability at European level.[79]

Article 6 states that Member States shall ensure that it is possible for providers to complete all procedures and formalities needed to access service activities through points of single contact, in particular, all declarations, notifications or applications necessary for an authorisation from the competent authorities, including applications for inclusion in a register, a roll or a database, or for registration with a professional body or association, as well as any applications for authorisation needed to exercise their service activities.[80] Assistance from the competent authorities must also be available both for recipients and providers of services, particularly concerning the general interpretation and application of the requirements.

The Services Directive does not oblige Member States to set only one POSC in their territory, which was the option chosen by Portugal and Spain but not, for instance, by Germany.[81] Member States 'may choose to

---

78 On the functionalities and the impact of POSC, see E. Gamero Casado, 'El impacto de la Directiva de Servicios en la ventanilla única y la administración electronica', in Aguado i Cudolà and B. Noguera de la Muela (eds) (n. 22 above) 113, 116; Aldomà i Buixadé (n. 65 above) 159; S. Adalid, 'Mécanismes de simplification et de coopération administrative au niveau national: la notion de guiche unique' in Ferrari-Breeur (ed.) (n. 43 above) 168; Leitão Marques et al. (n. 65 above).

79 This is why the development of the points of single contact and their interoperability constitutes one of the objectives of the Digital Agenda for Europe. See http://ec.europa.eu/digital-agenda/. The Commission has promoted a large-scale pilot project on the matter named SPOCS (Single Procedure Online for Cross-border Services). On POSC interoperability see Gamero Casado (n. 78 above), 121.

80 It means that points of single contact are not only informational but also transactional.

81 The POSC in Portugal is named 'Balcão do Empreendedor' ('Entrepeneur POSC'). See Leitão Marques et al. (n. 65 above). On the Spanish case of

have different "points of single contact" for different sectors'.[82] This will surely hinder the impact of simplification by the POSC. It is also unfortunate that the European legislature decided to abandon the initial project of creating a European POSC, which would have had a far greater effect than the current regime.

The POSC must offer an electronic version, even if also available in physical points, in order to guarantee access for service providers from different Member States.[83] Taking into consideration that most of the competent authorities are local rather than central, this measure is also relevant for national service providers.

The implementation of the POSC is one of the greatest challenges of the Directive. The administrative cooperation required for that purpose does not mean that the national authorities involved have to change their competences and powers. Even if current powers are preserved, the functioning of the POSC system calls for intensive administrative cooperation between central and local authorities. To fully implement this horizontal cooperation, it is necessary to 'break down silos', in the sense of overcoming the vertical organisation of public administration. This has always been one of the major difficulties of administrative simplification.[84]

7.2.3 Plain language

The Services Directive lists all the information that must be made available in the POSC and how it should be presented (Article 7). Where appropriate, the POSC shall include a simple step-by-step guide and the

'ventanilla única', see J.J. Diez Sánchez and R. Martínez Gutiérrez, 'Directiva de Servicios y Administración Electrónica' in Noguera Lopez, Arias Martínez and Almeida Cerreda (eds) (n. 73 above) 153, 164; M.A. Arias Martínez, 'La ventanilla única como instrumento para la simplificación procedimental exigida por la Directiva 2006/123/CE relativa a los servicios en el mercado interior', in Noguera López, Arias Martínez and Almeida Cerreda (eds) (n. 73 above) 179; Gamero Casado (n. 78 above) 126.

[82] See European Commission, Handbook on Implementation of the Services Directive (n. 64 above) 20.

[83] Electronic points of single contact should cover all the following aspects: electronic authentication of the applicant; electronic automatic filling out of forms; electronic submission of declarations and requests; submission of complementary information; electronic payment; electronic receipt of declarations; notification of final decision by the relevant authority.

[84] On simplification and administrative cooperation, see J.-L. Sauron, 'Les mécanismes de simplification et de coopération administratives entre administrations nationales', in Ferrari-Breeur (ed.) (n. 43 above), 143.

information must be provided in plain and intelligible language, which is currently defined as 'writing that is clear, concise, well-organized, and follows other best practices appropriate to the subject or field and intended audience'.[85]

The Directive focuses on the quality and clarity of information in order to guarantee effective accessibility by all users. Article 7(3) also stipulates that 'Member States shall ensure that the information and assistance ... are provided in a clear and unambiguous manner, that they are easily accessible at a distance and by electronic means and that they are kept up to date'. Article 13(1) provides that 'authorisation procedures and formalities shall be clear'.

Accordingly, it is not sufficient that information is made available in an electronic single point. It is necessary that this information is simple and intelligible, in order not to replace physical bureaucracy by electronic bureaucracy.

7.2.4 Swiftness, transparency and predictability

Simplification also requires administrative procedures to be more swift, transparent and predictable. Each one of these principles is a corollary of the previous ones. The elimination of licences and authorisation for establishment shortens the time it takes to conclude procedures. Even if a requirement or an authorisation scheme is imposed or maintained, Article 13(3) establishes that 'authorisation procedures and formalities shall provide applicants with a guarantee that their application will be processed as quickly as possible and, in any event, within a reasonable period which is fixed and made public in advance'. Article 13(3) of the Directive limits excessive delays by the administration, by providing that only 'when justified by the complexity of the issue, the time period may be extended once, by the competent authority, for a limited time. The

---

[85] See the U.S. Plain Language Act, Public Law 111-274 of 13 October 2010, sec. 3(3). Originally from the US, the plain language movement in administrative information has several European expressions today. See M. Cutts, 'Clarifying Eurolaw – How European Community directives could be written more clearly so that citizens of Member States, including lawyers, would understand them better' (2001), available at: http://s3-eu-west-1.amazonaws.com/plcdev/app/public/system/files/5/original/ClarifyingEurolawNOCOVERS.pdf (accessed 31 December 2013); Ministry of Justice Sweden, 'Plain Legal Language: Sweden's Approach to Clearly Written Laws', 27 November 2006, available at: http://www.oecd.org/dataoecd/51/18/37788778.pdf (accessed 31 December 2013); and M.M. Leitão Marques and M. Domingues, 'Simplificar com Linguagem Clara' in R. do Carmo (ed.), *Linguagem, Argumentação e Decisão Judiciária* (Coimbra Editora 2012) 75–96.

extension and its duration shall be duly motivated and shall be notified to the applicant before the original period has expired'.

Furthermore, authorisations may be granted not only by a formal decision, as quickly as possible, but also by silent consent.[86] Therefore, when the deadline expires, the authority can no longer refuse, as failing to respond within the set time period leads to a tacit grant of an authorisation (Article 13(4)).

Electronic access to information in a single point also induces swiftness in the administrative procedures. Member States must ensure that the points of single contact and the competent authorities respond as quickly as possible to any request for information or assistance (Article 7(4)).

An electronic procedure also improves transparency if service providers can follow and monitor the various stages of their application. Moreover, online simulators, if available, can enable applicants to know in advance the waiting times for a permit or authorisation, making administrative procedures more predictable. This is very important for simplification purposes, especially in more extensive procedures.

8. CONCLUSION

As has been firmly established throughout this chapter, regulation is not always harmful to competition and the perfect illustration of this is regulation directed at the development of the single European market.

In fact, market access is an essential precondition to both the enhancement of competition and market integration. EU-level measures intended to deepen the freedoms and reduce or remove national barriers not only promote the establishment and maintenance of an internal market but also promote competition, by opening the markets to free economic initiative.

Therefore, by aiming at creating a true internal market for services and eliminating important barriers to free movement, the Services Directive is an example of pro-competitive regulation. The relevance of the Directive, and thus one of the reasons it was chosen as our case study, is its

[86] On authorisation by default by public authorities, when these do not decide within the time period, see Aguado i Cudolà (n. 22 above) 79; Parisio (n. 73 above) 94; D. Santiago Iglesias, 'La incidencia de La Directiva de Servivios y de sus normas de transposición en el régimen jurídico del silencio administrativo', in Noguera López, Arias Martínez and Almeida Cerreda (eds) (n. 73 above) 129.

horizontal character, which was intended to comprise a large range of sectors in order to promote market access, competitiveness and economic growth. Even though the scope of application was narrowed significantly for numerous reasons and the Directive was watered down due to the controversy it generated, its macroeconomic impact will still be substantial.

As legal barriers are pointed out as the most obvious obstacles to market access and exercise of service activities, the Services Directive focused on removing administrative burdens. In fact, even in the form of indistinctly applicable measures, administrative burdens create an obvious disadvantage for the establishment and the provision of services by persons and undertakings from other countries and, frequently, impose a dual burden. Therefore, the Services Directive provides for several measures of administrative simplification in order to modernise the legal orders of Member States.

The implementation of the Services Directive has not been an easy task in regards to simplification in a broad sense. There is still a long way to go until the expected goals are achieved all over the EU. As we have shown above, success depends basically on the capacity of the Member States, under the control of the Commission, to reform regulation by making it smart, less bureaucratic and disproportionate, less discretionary, more transparent and predictable and easier to understand and to comply with. This will be done through the use of information and communication technologies to implement interoperable points of single contact. All these tasks require intensive administrative cooperation within the Member States and between them and the European Commission.

In spite of the difficulties that simplification implies, the Communication on the implementation of the Services Directive of August 2012 emphasises that:

> Hundreds of national laws have been modernised and thousands of discriminatory, unjustified or disproportionate requirements have been eliminated throughout the EU. The tools which have been created ('Points of Single Contact') to support implementation of the Directive are now operational in most Member States and are helping to reduce significantly administrative burdens in this area.[87]

Even though it is still too early to assess the overall effects of the Directive in the whole of the EU, the positive impact on competition and

[87] Commission Communication (n. 54 above).

growth of legal modernisation and simplification can actually be wider than the scope of the Directive itself. It will inevitably remove unnecessary and disproportionate requirements to service activities, which are intrinsically related to those found in the Directive. It is clear that it will benefit not only foreign providers but also national providers in the countries where simplification is successful.

The removal of these burdens is not the only contribution of the Services Directive to the promotion of competition in the field of services. The Directive has also eliminated other obstacles that are harmful to competition, such as the prohibition to exercise multidisciplinary activities or advertise the services of regulated professions. Nonetheless, the reduction of administrative burdens through simplification is certainly one of the most important and original paths that has been chosen for the construction of an internal market in which the fundamental freedoms and competition are effectively protected and guaranteed.

6. Abuse of administrative monopoly in China

Thomas K. Cheng

1. INTRODUCTION

After 14 years of gestation, the Anti-Monopoly Law, China's first comprehensive competition law, was finally passed in August 2007 and came into effect on 1 August 2008. One of the reasons for the delay was the issue of abuse of administrative monopoly, one of the most controversial competition issues in China. Some commentators believe that abuse of administrative monopoly, which refers to administrative measures or conduct that impede internal trade and restrict competition, is the most serious competition problem facing China, and the Anti-Monopoly Law would not be complete without provisions addressing it. Other commentators argue that abuse of administrative monopoly is not a genuine competition law issue and should be dealt with under administrative law or other areas of law. In fact, in the US and the European Union (EU), the equivalent of abuse of administrative monopoly is not dealt with under competition law. In the US, the issue is a constitutional matter regulated under the dormant commerce clause of the US Constitution. In the EU, the issue falls within the rubric of the articles of the Treaty on the Functioning of the European Union (TFEU) concerning the free movement principles. In fact, some other commentators believe that abuse of administrative monopoly is a systemic issue that requires a political, not a legal, solution. In the end, the first group of commentators won out and the Anti-Monopoly Law incorporates provisions that prohibit the abuse of administrative monopoly.

Despite the disagreement among commentators on the appropriate vehicle for tackling the issue, there is a consensus that abuse of administrative monopoly is a serious problem in China. If left unaddressed, it will threaten to undermine the success of the economic reforms in the country. This chapter will examine this serious competition issue facing China. Section 2 defines abuse of administrative monopoly and provides some examples of the phenomenon. Section 3 reviews the history of legislation pertaining to and enforcement against abuse of administrative monopoly, including some early regulations and circulars, the Anti-Unfair Competition Law, and finally, the Anti-Monopoly Law. A detailed review is provided of the provisions in the Anti-Monopoly Law related to abuse of administrative monopoly, the implementation of rules and regulations issued by the enforcement authorities, and recent cases. Section 4 delves into the question of how the Chinese enforcement authorities should tackle non-discriminatory administrative measures that nonetheless impede internal trade and restrict competition. After a brief survey of the prevailing approaches in the US and the EU, some suggestions are offered to the Chinese authorities on how to determine the legality of these measures. Section 5 concludes the chapter.

2. AN OVERVIEW OF ABUSE OF ADMINISTRATIVE MONOPOLY

Abuse of administrative monopoly refers to administrative measures or conduct adopted by government agencies to distort competition or to erect barriers to market entry. It has been said that given the pervasiveness of government intervention in the Chinese economy, abuse of administrative monopoly poses a much more serious threat to free competition in China than does anti-competitive conduct by private enterprises.[1] Despite the term being widely used in Chinese academic and legal circles, it has been pointed out that the term 'abuse of administrative monopoly' has never been recognized in official Chinese legal documents.[2] The expression used in Chinese laws and regulations is 'abuse of administrative power to exclude or restrict competition'.[3] Consistent with general academic usage, this chapter will continue to use the term 'abuse of administrative monopoly'.

Abuse of administrative monopoly is common in China. Examples have included discriminatory license fees, discriminatory inspection and technical standards, compulsory purchase of locally produced goods, and even outright road blockades. For instance, in 1996, the Shanghai

---

[1] B. Owen, S. Sun and W. Zheng, 'Antitrust in China: The Problem of Incentive Compatibility' (2005) *J. Comp. L. & Econ.* 123, 134.

[2] Y. Huang, 'Administrative Monopoly in China – Background Information' (on file with author), 1.

[3] Ibid.

municipal government issued regulations prohibiting taxi companies from buying cars with engines smaller than 1.6 liters in capacity, which effectively blocked the import of the popular Shali taxi model produced in Tianjin, the main competitor of locally produced taxi cars.[4] In the same year, the Beijing municipal government ordered that cars with engines over 1.0 liter in capacity could only be used every other day, but exempted vehicles produced by Beijing Jeep Corp from the order.[5] In 1999, Hubei Province, which produces Citroën cars, imposed an RMB 70,000 fee on the purchase of Shanghai-produced Santana cars. This measure was a reaction to the Shanghai municipal government's discriminatory licensing policy, which imposed an RMB 20,000 license fee for Santana cars and an RMB 80,000 fee for other cars. In 2001, the Guangzhou government stopped issuing licenses to cars with 1.0 liter or smaller engines, effectively preventing smaller cars produced in Sichuan Province and Tianjin from competing with the larger Accord cars produced locally.[6] In the same year, the Shanghai municipal government banned cars over a certain weight from using major roads, which effectively excluded larger cars produced in Sichuan from the local market.[7] These incidents vividly illustrate how local governments make use of administrative measures to protect local companies from outside competition.

In fact, there have been even more egregious examples of abuse of administrative monopoly. Some local governments compel government sub-units, businesses, and consumers to purchase local goods. A good example is Shuchen County in Anhui Province, whose protective measures have been widely reported, including by the official national TV network CCTV.[8] The county government adopted the Shuchen County Commercial Reorganization, Management, and Examination Proposal, which set out market share targets for local products, such as wine and

---

[4] P. Sun, K. Mellahi and E. Thun, 'The Dynamic Value of MNE Political Embeddedness: The Case of the Chinese Automobile Industry', 41(7) *Journal of International Business Studies* 1161, 1168 (2010).

[5] Ibid.

[6] 'City Slaps License Ban on Smaller Vehicles', *South China Morning Post* (20 August 2001).

[7] 'Players Ranks to Thin as Car Sector Surges', *South China Morning Post* (8 September 2001).

[8] 'Small Protection, Big Harm – Understanding Regional Protectionism', CCTV.com, available at: http://www.cctv.com/lm/365/-1/32949.html (accessed 31 December 2013).

cement.[9] In addition, the government set up a special unit to protect local businesses, and used a wide range of administrative measures to ensure that market share targets were reached. The measures included: (1) requiring government employees to purchase local products – in 2000, county teachers were paid three bottles of local wine in lieu of RMB 60 as part of their salary; (2) requiring consumers to use local products – civilians who wanted to build a house were required to use locally produced cement, or their construction permit applications would not be processed; (3) requiring government units to purchase local products – under the Regulations on Government Purchase of Alcohol, county government units must use local wine for official functions; and (4) requiring manufacturers to purchase locally produced inputs – under a number of county regulations on cement use in construction projects, construction materials manufacturers must purchase locally produced cement.

The measures adopted by the local governments in Chongqing City, a city in southwestern China, to promote Eagle mineral water, a locally produced brand are another example. The Longbao Party Labor Committee Office adopted a number of measures to promote the brand.[10] First, the Office issued a Notice on the Use of Eagle Mineral Water as the Official Drinking Water for Longbao, which required residents in Longbao to consume Eagle mineral water only.[11] An inspection unit was set up to ensure compliance with the Notice.[12] The local government further required all primary and secondary school students in the Longbao area to drink Eagle mineral water only.[13] The Wuqiao Party Labor Committee Office similarly issued a Notice on Supporting the Sales of Eagle Mineral Water and compelled all the administrative units under its jurisdiction to consume Eagle mineral water only.[14] Most egregious of them all, some local governments have set up check points at regional borders to obstruct entry of commodities, such as fertilizers, from other regions.

---

[9] Ibid.

[10] B.Y. Guan, F. Huang and J. Cao, *Xing Zheng Long Duan Zhi Xing Zheng Fa Gui Zhi* (China University of Politics and Law 2008) 51 et seq. (work in Chinese).

[11] Ibid.

[12] Ibid.

[13] Ibid.

[14] Ibid.

Examples include the governments of the City of Liangping and Nanchuan County in Sichuan Province, which in 2002 set up roadblocks on highways to prevent entry of fertilizers from outside their respective regions.[15]

The harm of such protectionist measures and conduct on the Chinese economy is obvious. It has been estimated that the internal tariff between the various provinces in China in 1997 was roughly at 46 percent, which had increased by 11 percent from a decade earlier.[16] The internal trade barriers within China were estimated to be at the same level as those between the various Member States of the European Union and those between the US and Canada.[17] It has been further ascertained that in 1997, Chinese consumers purchased 21 times as many goods produced by their native province as goods produced by other provinces.[18] Protectionist measures adopted by local governments which are outlawed under the Anti-Monopoly Law hindered the development of a fully integrated national market in China.

However, it is worth pointing out that economists have found that abuse of administrative monopoly has been in decline in China. Using sophisticated statistical analysis, Yu and Yu concluded that '[f]rom 1985 to 2006, China's regional administrative monopoly degree has seen a decreasing trend; particularly from 1992 to 2002 China experienced the most obvious fall in the degree of regional administrative monopoly'.[19] The authors further predicted that 'it is foreseeable that within the next few years the degree of administrative monopoly in China would decrease further'.[20] This is consistent with the finding of the State Council of the PRC, which noted in 2004 that regional protectionism had improved in China.[21] The authors also found an interesting fact about abuse of administrative monopoly that is of relevance to this chapter. The

---

[15] W. Zheng, 'Beware Picket Fences are Re-erected – in Some Places, Tangible Regional Protectionism has Decreased, but Intangible Regional Protectionism has Increased', *People's Daily* (15 April 2002) 1.

[16] Guan, Huang and Cao (n. 10 above) 156 et seq.

[17] Ibid.

[18] Ibid.

[19] L. Yu and D. Yu, 'The Measure of Regional Administrative Monopoly in China' in M. Faure and X. Zhang (eds), *Competition Policy and Regulation: Recent Developments in China, the US and Europe* (Edward Elgar Publishing 2011) 93 et seq.

[20] Ibid.

[21] 'Regional Protectionism is Decreasing in Our Country', People.com.cn, available at: http://www.people.com.cn/BIG5/jingji/1045/2301853.html (accessed 31 December 2013) (original in Chinese).

authors noted that there has been a rise in soft regional protectionism since 2002. This is to be expected because as the laws that prohibit outright discriminatory measures are more vigorously enforced, provincial and local governments intent on pursuing protectionist ends will have to turn to more subtle means. These measures may not have an obvious protectionist purpose or may be ostensibly justified by other valid policy objectives. The adjudication of the validity of these measures will require a more nuanced approach than that currently supplied by the provisions in the Anti-Monopoly Law.

3. LAWS PERTAINING TO ABUSE OF ADMINISTRATIVE MONOPOLY

3.1 Early (pre-Anti-Monopoly Law) Laws and Regulations

To combat these abuses of administrative power, the Chinese government has adopted a number of laws and regulations. Given the long-standing history of abuse of administrative monopoly in the country, these laws and regulations have been adopted since the early days of China's economic reform. These have included Article 6 of the Temporary Stipulation of the State Council on the Promotion and Protection of Socialist Competition in 1980, the Circular Concerning the Prohibition of Blockages in Purchasing and Marketing Industrial Products in 1982, the Circular Concerning Breaking Down Inter-Regional Market Blockages and Further Invigorating Commodity Circulation in 1990, the Anti-Unfair Competition Law in 1993, and the Regulations on Prohibiting Local Blockades in Market Economic Activities in 2001. There are also myriad local regulations such as the Chengdu City Anti-Unfair Competition Regulation. The Temporary Stipulation of the State Council on the Promotion and Protection of Socialist Competition states that '[i]ntroduction of competition requires eradication of regional protectionism and departmental division. Any region or department must not blockade the local market, and must not prohibit the sale of non-local goods in the local market'.[22] This language suggests that regional protectionism is not a recent phenomenon and has been in existence for almost as long as economic reform has been on-going in China. The Anti-Unfair Competition Law represented another serious attempt by the Chinese government to put an end to abuse of administrative monopoly. This time, the

22 Guan, Huang and Cao (n. 10 above) 37.

government resorted to a national law as opposed to State Council circulars or regulations to prohibit such practices. The key provision in the Anti-Unfair Competition Law is Article 7, which provides that:

> The government and its organ shall not abuse its authority to force others to purchase commodities from an appointed seller or prohibit fair competition from other sellers. The government and its organs shall not abuse its authority to prohibit outside commodities from entering the local market, or prohibit domestic commodities from reaching outside markets.

There are a number of inadequacies in the Anti-Unfair Competition Law's prohibition of abuse of administrative monopoly. First, the prohibition is not sufficiently comprehensive. Article 7 essentially prohibits three types of conduct: (1) local government compelling purchase from a designated seller; (2) local government prohibiting non-local goods from sale in the local market; and (3) local government prohibiting export of local goods. The final two types of conduct only encompass outright prohibition and not indirect measures that erect barriers to keep non-local goods from entering the local market. These measures include discriminatory fees or discriminatory inspection standards, which do not directly prohibit the entry of non-local goods, but nonetheless obstruct the free movement of goods within China. The second, and the bigger, problem is that the penalty is not severe enough to achieve any deterrent effect. Article 30, which provides the penalty for violation of Article 7, states:

> If the government or its departments violate Article 7 of this Law to force others to purchase commodities from an appointed seller, obstruct other sellers from engaging in fair competition, or limit transfer of commodities between regions, the superior government shall order the offending government to rectify these measures; If the violation is serious, the same level government organ or the superior government organ shall administratively punish the person who bears direct responsibility. If the designated seller takes advantage of its position to charge a high price or charge unnecessary fees, the enforcement authority shall confiscate the illegal income, and may impose a fine in the amount of from more than one to less than three times of the illegal income.

In reality, it is a bit of a misnomer to call this the penalty provision, because it prescribes no penalty for the offending official at all. In non-serious cases, all that will happen to the offending official is that he will be told by a superior official to stop. It is perhaps too obvious to point out that such a remedy will create no deterrent effect on the officials. The penalty for the more serious cases, of course, carries a more substantial deterrent effect. But it is not clear what case constitutes a serious one. In any case, this administrative punishment mechanism has been rarely invoked. As will be explained below, this deficiency also plagues the Anti-Monopoly Law.

3.2 The Anti-Monopoly Law

For a variety of reasons, such as inadequate penalty or insufficient enforcement, these early laws and regulations failed to eradicate abuse of administrative monopoly. When China contemplated adopting a competition law, it was suggested that the law should include provisions that prohibit abuse of administrative monopoly. Despite the prevalence of abuse of administrative monopoly and its negative impact on the Chinese economy, Chinese scholars were split on whether abuse of administrative monopoly should be dealt with in the Anti-Monopoly Law. Professor Xiaoye Wang, one of the leading competition law scholars in China, asserts that the Anti-Monopoly Law should reflect the Chinese economic reality, which features abuse of administrative monopoly as the most pernicious distortion of competition.[23] This dictates that abuse of administrative monopoly be included in the Anti-Monopoly Law. A contrary view was propounded by Professor Jichun Shi of Renmin University, who argues that abuse of administrative monopoly is ultimately a political problem that can only be dealt with through political reforms, and not competition law enforcement.[24] This division of opinions was reflected during the drafting process of the Anti-Monopoly Law, during which the chapter proscribing abuse of administrative monopoly was taken out and then reinstated.[25] In fact, the treatment of abuse of administrative monopoly was highly controversial and resulted in delay of the overall legislation. Professor Wang's view eventually prevailed. The provisions that were eventually adopted, however, were detailed in their proscription but lacking in teeth. The inclusion of abuse of administrative monopoly in China's first comprehensive competition law is consistent with the experience of other transitional economies, which have also given a prominent place to regulation of public restraints in

---

[23] As cited by Y. Huang, 'The Role of State in Shaping China's Competition Policy – An Analysis in Chinese Context' (on file with author) 23.

[24] Ibid.

[25] H.S. Harris, Jr., P. Wang, Y. Zhang, M.A. Cohen and S.J. Evrard, *Anti-Monopoly Law and Practice in China* (OUP 2011) 179–180.

their competition laws.[26] The provisions pertaining to abuse of administrative monopoly are contained in Chapter Five of the Anti-Monopoly Law. There are six articles in this chapter:

Article 32 prohibits government bodies from compelling purchases of goods or services from designated undertakings, which was fairly common during the heyday of abuse of administrative monopoly. In fact, as will be explained below, such practices have not disappeared since the promulgation of the Anti-Monopoly Law. One of the first cases on abuse of administrative monopoly after the entry into force of the Anti-Monopoly Law involved precisely this kind of conduct. In the AQSIQ case, the AQSIQ, the Chinese quality assurance regulator, required companies to use the service provided by a company in which it had a stake.

Article 33 proscribes administrative measures that impede the free movement of goods, including discriminatory charges, discriminatory technical or inspection standards, discriminatory licensing procedures, and roadblocks. Article 34 ensures equal treatment of non-local firms in public procurement exercises. Article 35 bans discrimination against non-local investments and discrimination against non-local firms setting up branches in the locality, which is crucial to a company's operation in a particular locality in China. Article 36 prevents government bodies from compelling undertakings to engage in anti-competitive conduct otherwise proscribed by the Anti-Monopoly Law. And Article 37, which may be considered as a catch-all provision, instructs government bodies not to issue regulations that eliminate or restrict competition. It can be applied to protectionist measures that do not directly fall within the previous five provisions. As will be explained later, this provision serves a crucial function in the control of soft regional protectionism, that is, administrative measures that are not outright discriminatory but nonetheless impede the free movement of goods across provinces and localities, and non-discriminatory measures that nonetheless hinder internal trade or restrict competition.

Penalties for violating Chapter Five of the Anti-Monopoly Law are stipulated in Article 51, which states that:

> Where any administrative organ or an organization empowered by a law or administrative regulation to administer public affairs abuses its administrative power to eliminate or restrict competition, the superior authority thereof shall order it to make correction and impose punishments on the directly liable

[26] R.A. Boner, 'Antitrust and State Action in Transition Economies', [1998] *Antitrust Bull* 84.

> person(s)-in-charge and other directly liable persons. The anti-monopoly authority may put forward suggestions on handling according to law to the relevant superior authority.

The penalty imposed by the Anti-Monopoly Law for abuse of administrative monopoly is quite similar to that under the Anti-Unfair Competition Law. In both instances, the enforcement authority is supposed to approach the superior authority of the offending government organ and ask that superior authority to order the offending organ to cease the violation. Article 51 also provides for the imposition of punishment on directly liable persons-in-charge. However, what type of punishment is not specified. Article 51 certainly does not provide for the imposition of fines or allow the recovery of damages by private parties. Therefore, it seems that the provisions of the Anti-Monopoly Law dealing with abuse of administrative monopoly suffer from the same deficiencies as those in the Anti-Unfair Competition Law.

3.3 Implementation of the Anti-Monopoly Law

3.3.1 Implementing rules and regulations

Implementation and enforcement of Chapter Five of the Anti-Monopoly Law has not been particularly active since the Law came into effect in August 2008. On 31 December 2010, the State Administration for Industry and Commerce (SAIC) issued the Rules on Prohibition of Abuse of Administrative Power for the Purposes of Eliminating or Restricting Competition. These Rules are largely a reiteration of the provisions in Chapter Five of the Anti-Monopoly Law. For example, Article 3 of the Rules enumerates the types of measures and conduct prohibited by the Rules. These include compelling purchases from a designated seller, imposing discriminatory technical requirements or inspection standards, adopting discriminatory administrative licensing requirements or practices, imposing blockades against non-local goods, adopting discriminatory bidding standards or procedures, restricting investment in or establishment of local branches by non-local undertakings, and compelling undertakings to enter into monopolistic agreements or commit abuse of dominance in violation of the Anti-Monopoly Law. This is largely conduct that is proscribed by Articles 32 to 36 of the Anti-Monopoly Law. Article 6 of the Rules provides for the same penalty as Article 51 of the Anti-Monopoly Law for violation. Perhaps what sets these Rules apart from Chapter Five of the Anti-Monopoly Law is Article 5, which stipulates that undertakings may not enter into monopolistic agreements or commit abuse of dominance on the grounds that they were compelled or authorized to do so by administrative agencies, or permitted to do so by administrative regulations adopted by such agencies. Article 8 of the Rules provides for the same penalties on undertakings for entering into monopolistic agreements and committing abuse of dominance as those provided for by the Anti-Monopoly Law. Article 5 clarifies that undertakings cannot use administrative permission, authorization, or compulsion as an excuse for violating the Anti-Monopoly Law. From Article 8, one can surmise that China has not followed the lead of the US in adopting the state action doctrine as a defense for violation of the Sherman Act. Under the US Supreme Court case of *Parker v. Brown*, anti-competitive conduct (1) in furtherance of a clearly articulated state policy and (2) actively supervised by the state is exempted from federal antitrust scrutiny.[27] Under the Anti-Monopoly Law, at least as interpreted by the SAIC, provincial (or more generally, governmental) authorization of the conduct is not a defense against an Anti-Monopoly Law enforcement action.

The SAIC is only responsible for enforcement against non-price related anti-competitive conduct; price-related monopolistic agreements, abuses of dominance, and abuse of administrative monopoly fall under the jurisdiction of the National Development and Reform Commission (NDRC). On 29 December 2010, the NDRC issued the Regulation on Monopolistic Pricing Practices, which contains a few provisions on price-related abuses of administrative monopoly. Article 20 of the Regulation prohibits administrative organs from adopting the following conduct to obstruct the free flow of goods across provinces: (1) imposition of discriminatory fees on non-local goods; (2) imposition of discriminatory fee standards on non-local goods; (3) stipulation of discriminatory pricing on non-local goods; and (4) other price- or fee-related conduct that obstructs the free flow of goods across provinces. Article 21 further prohibits administrative organs from compelling undertakings to engage in price-related monopolistic conduct. Lastly, Article 22 proscribes administrative organs from adopting rules and regulations that eliminate or restrict price competition. Article 24 provides that the penalty for abuse of administrative monopoly is that stipulated in Article 51 of the Anti-Monopoly Law, that is, an order by a superior authority to cease the infringing conduct.

---

27 *Parker v. Brown*, 317 U.S. 341, 63 S. Ct. 307 (1943).

3.3.2 Cases

Enforcement against abuse of administrative monopoly by the SAIC and the NDRC has not been particularly active. The author is aware of only one case brought by these two enforcement authorities and two court cases. In what is generally known as the first enforcement action under the Anti-Monopoly Law against abuse of administrative monopoly, the Guangdong Provincial Administration for Industry and Commerce (AIC) proposed to the Guangdong provincial government that the Heyuan municipal government rectify an alleged abuse of administrative monopoly.[28] In that case, the Heyuan municipal government held a government affairs meeting on the promotion of GPS usage to enhance public transportation safety. At the meeting, the GPS tracking and monitoring platform of New Space-Time Navigation Technology (NST) was chosen as the only approved municipal tracking and monitoring platform. All the other GPS operators were required to upload their monitoring data onto NST's platform. NST was allowed to charge the other GPS operators a data upload service fee of no more than RMB 30 per vehicle. The decision at the meeting was subsequently confirmed by the Working Plans for Promoting GPS Vehicle Data Recorder, which expressly set out the requirement that real-time monitoring data of specified types of vehicles in Heyuan must be uploaded to the monitoring platform designated by the local government. In order to ensure compliance with the Working Plan, the Heyuan government later asked its traffic management bureau to fail the annual review of vehicles whose monitoring data were not uploaded onto NST's platform. The Guangdong AIC was of the view that appointing NST's platform as the designated platform and allowing NST to charge its competitors a service fee stifled competition in the GPS operator market. This was further augmented by the measure adopted by the traffic management bureau of failing the annual review of vehicles not using NST's services. The Guangdong AIC officially proposed to the Guangdong provincial government that the Heyuan government revoke the abusive measure. In response to Guangdong AIC's suggestion, on 12 June 2011, the Guangdong government issued an administrative review decision finding that the Heyuan government violated the Anti-Monopoly Law and ordering the cessation of the abusive conduct.

---

[28] S. Ning and J. Huang, 'First Enforcement Action under Anti-Monopoly Law against Administrative Monopoly', *Westlaw China* IP 1 (13 September 2011) 1.

A number of interesting observations can be made about this case. First, this incident vividly illustrates the toothless penalty provisions of the Anti-Monopoly Law. According to the media reports, the only consequence suffered by the Heyuan government was cessation of the offending measure. No officials were sanctioned. This can hardly serve to deter future officials contemplating implementing abusive administrative measures. Second, there is no question that the measure adopted by the Heyuan government violated the language of Article 32 of the Anti-Monopoly Law. The Heyuan government clearly compelled the other GPS operators to use the platform service provided by NST. What is not clear is whether the Heyuan government pled any defense for its conduct and, if so, how the Guangdong AIC treated those defenses. The Heyuan government presumably could argue that centralizing the monitoring data was for a public safety reason, perhaps because NST has a proven track record of superior service, and appointing one platform would allow the Heyuan government to monitor the quality of service more easily. Details about this case by and large came from the Chinese media.[29] As far as this author is aware, the Guangdong AIC did not issue a formal decision explaining its reasoning. Therefore, it is impossible to know whether the Heyuan government put forward any defenses and how these defenses were treated by the Guangdong AIC.

A more fundamental question is whether the Guangdong AIC could have entertained a public-safety defense at all under the language of the Anti-Monopoly Law. The provisions in Chapter Five do not provide for any defenses or justifications for conduct that would otherwise be deemed to be abuse of administrative monopoly. The public-safety justification that could have been put forward by the Heyuan government is admittedly slightly flimsy. The media reports do not clarify the relationship between the Heyuan government and NST. If it turns out that the Heyuan government has an ownership interest in NST, the administrative measure would be even more suspicious and the defense more likely to be pretextual. But one can easily imagine situations where a local government has adopted a measure or a regulation for a legitimate public-policy purpose which nonetheless burdens internal trade or restricts competition within China. The Anti-Monopoly Law does not offer any guidance on how these competing considerations will be balanced, if at all. Nor do the rules and regulations issued by the SAIC

---

[29] S. Ning and J. Huang, 'First Enforcement Action under Anti-Monopoly Law against Administrative Monopoly', *Westlaw China* IP 1 (13 September 2011) 1.

and NDRC. As enforcement authorities manage to root out overtly discriminatory or protectionist measures, they will be increasingly faced with trade-restrictive administrative measures that could be justified on public-policy grounds. If the Anti-Monopoly Law is interpreted literally to permit no justifications for trade-restrictive measures, the Anti-Monopoly Law would strike down many legitimate government measures. This author believes that a better approach is to allow the enforcement authorities and the courts to consider legitimate justifications, which means that the authorities will need to fashion an approach for balancing trade-restrictive effects and public policy justifications.

As far as this author is aware, the Chinese media have reported two other Anti-Monopoly Law cases involving abuse of administrative monopoly. One of them was resolved and one of them is still ongoing. The ongoing one concerns Shanxi Joint Transport Group and the Taiyuan Railway Bureau. On 7 September 2011, Shanxi Joint Transport Group brought suit against the Taiyuan Railway Bureau in the Taiyuan Xinghualing District People's Court over the latter's alleged inaction over the former's application to open more ticket outlets in Taiyuan.[30] The court accepted the case on 13 September 2011. The defendant is a local authority of China's Ministry of Railway in Taiyuan.[31] The Ministry of Railway is responsible for the provision of railway passenger and freight services, the regulation of the railway industry, and the development of the railway infrastructure in China.[32] The Taiyuan Railway Bureau is responsible for approving the establishment of railway ticket outlets in Taiyuan.[33] Prior to May 2006, Shanxi Joint Transport owned 13 of the 40 railway ticket outlets in Taiyuan. Since then, a total of 74 new outlets have been approved by the Bureau, all of which were operated by the Bureau's subsidiaries. Since 2007, Shanxi Joint Transport has submitted annual applications to the Bureau to establish more ticket outlets, but to no avail. On 25 January 2011, Shanxi Joint Transport submitted two applications to establish ticket outlets and telephone booking services, but had yet to hear from the Bureau. Shanxi Joint Transport claimed that with its ticket outlets severely restricted, its service quality was significantly affected and hence competition for railway services was restricted as a result of the Bureau's administrative inaction. The case is yet to be resolved.

---

30 A. Fels, X. Wang and J. Su, 'Taiyuan Railway Bureau Sued for Monopoly' (2011) *China Competition Bulletin* 1, 3.

31 Ibid.

32 Ibid.

33 Ibid.

On 1 August 2008, the day the Anti-Monopoly Law came into effect, eight Chinese companies involved in electronic anti-counterfeiting technologies brought a suit against the Administration of Quality Supervision, Inspection and Quarantine (AQSIQ) for abuse of administrative monopoly in the Beijing First Intermediate People's Court. In particular, it was alleged that since 2005, AQSIQ required companies using the electronic quality control online system PIATS to pay a registration fee in order to ascertain the authenticity of the product.[34] On the face of the allegation, it is quite likely that AQSIQ has violated Article 32 of the Anti-Monopoly Law, which prohibits administrative organs from compelling undertakings to purchase commodities or services from a designated seller. The case is all the more suspicious because AQSIQ owned a 30 percent stake in the company that operates PIATS. The court handed down a decision on 8 September 2008, dismissing the plaintiffs' case on statute-of-limitation grounds.[35] However, while the suit was pending, the AQSIQ voluntarily removed the restriction.

A number of interesting issues are presented by these two cases. First, it is not entirely clear from the language of the Anti-Monopoly Law that the courts can hear a private abuse-of-administrative-monopoly case. Article 50 expressly provides for the right of private parties to seek redress for monopolistic agreements and abuse of dominance, but it is silent on whether the right extends to abuse of administrative monopoly. Article 51, which is the only article concerned with the remedies for abuse of administrative monopoly, makes no mention of private suits. In the draft comments of the Regulation on the Relevant Issues Concerning the Application of Law in the Trial of Civil Monopoly Dispute Cases of the Supreme People's Court, Article 6 mentions the right of private parties to sue the seller designated by an administrative organ with which the parties are compelled to deal to recover damages.[36] However, this language was taken out in the final version of the Regulation, which, therefore, remains entirely silent on the right of private parties to sue over

---

34 A. Potter, M. Han and F. Toh, 'China's Anti-Monopoly Law – Six Months On', Asialaw.com (March 2009), available at: http://www.asialaw.com/Article/2121760/Channel/16707/Chinas-Anti-monopoly-Law-six-months-on.html (accessed 31 December 2013).

35 Ibid.

36 Consultation draft for Supreme People's Court's Regulation on the Relevant Issues Concerning the Application of Law in the Trial of Civil Monopoly Dispute Cases of the Supreme People's Court, available at: http://www.court.gov.cn/gzhd/zqyj/201104/t20110425_19850.htm (accessed 31 December 2013).

abuse of administrative monopoly.[37] In light of the uncertain status of the private right of action over abuse of administrative monopoly, it is somewhat of a surprise that the two courts accepted these cases.

The second issue is whether administrative inaction or omission falls within the scope of the Anti-Monopoly Law. The Law does not specifically address administrative inaction as an abuse of administrative monopoly. One may perhaps characterize the Taiyuan Railway Bureau case as involving discriminatory approval standards. The facts are certainly suspicious that the only undertakings which have been able to obtain approval since 2007 have all been the bureau's own subsidiaries. The most applicable provision in Chapter Five to this case would probably be Article 33(3), which prohibits 'imposing administrative licensing specially on commodities from outside the locality so as to restrict them from entering the local market'. There are a number of problems with applying this provision to the case, however. First, it is not clear whether the approval process constitutes administrative licensing for the purpose of the Anti-Monopoly Law. More importantly, the provision is concerned with commodities from outside the locality. The Taiyuan Railway Bureau case does not concern importation of non-local commodities. In fact, the undertaking being discriminated against is a local undertaking. This case does not present the usual scenario of abuse of administrative monopoly whereby protectionist administrative measures are adopted to erect barriers to non-local undertakings or goods. Hence, it does not involve regional protectionism, but is concerned with an administrative organ favoring its own enterprises.

In fact, this case highlights one of the drawbacks of Chapter Five, which is its focus on regional protectionist measures. Articles 33 to 35 all make express references to non-local goods or undertakings, suggesting that these provisions may not apply when it is local goods or a local undertaking that is being discriminated against. However, as the *Taiyuan Railway Bureau* case aptly illustrates, abuse of administrative monopoly need not necessarily target non-local goods or undertakings. The only provision in Chapter Five that may cover this case is the catch-all Article 37, which states that '[a]ny administrative organ may not abuse its administrative power to adopt provisions that eliminate or restrict competition'. Again, the obstacle to applying this provision is that the Taiyuan Railway Bureau did not adopt any anti-competitive provisions. It

---

[37] Official draft for Supreme People's Court's Regulation on the Relevant Issues Concerning the Application of Law in the Trial of Civil Monopoly Dispute Cases of the Supreme People's Court, available at: http://jwlaw.blog.163.com/blog/static/56363587201241504631404/ (accessed 31 December 2013).

simply failed to act. One must wait and see how the Shanxi court will resolve this case eventually to find out which provision of the Anti-Monopoly Law applies to this case, if at all.

4. THE SEARCH FOR A BALANCING APPROACH

4.1 Should the Anti-Monopoly Law Apply to Non-discriminatory Administrative Measures that Hinder Internal Trade?

As shown in the preceding section, Chapter Five of the Anti-Monopoly Law focuses on administrative measures that are outright discriminatory and that directly restrict the free flow of goods across provinces. Most of the measures in the contemplation of the drafters of the Law are naked restraints of trade that serve no useful purpose other than protecting the local market or local undertakings. Most of these measures, such as regional blockades and outright discriminatory fees or quality standards, can be easily identified. Once identified, the protectionist tendencies and hence the legality of these measures are usually beyond dispute. There are two reasons why the enforcement authorities will increasingly be faced with measures that may require more sophisticated and subtle analyses. First, as noted by Yu and Yu, soft regional protectionism has been on the rise in China since 2002. It seems that provincial and local governments are becoming increasingly adept at disguising their protectionist measures as legitimate government regulation. To ferret out protectionist measures, the enforcement authorities must be able to distinguish between disguised protectionist measures and legitimate government regulation and to balance the trade-restrictive effect against the legitimate policy objective. This is aptly illustrated by the Heyuan GPS platform case.

Second, a more fundamental question facing the enforcement authorities and the courts is whether the provisions on abuse of administrative monopoly in the Anti-Monopoly Law only apply to outright discriminatory measures or whether they also apply to non-discriminatory administrative measures that nonetheless hinder internal trade or restrict competition in China. Most of the provisions in Chapter Five seem to focus on outright discriminatory measures. However, Article 37, with its more open-ended language, could potentially be applied to non-discriminatory measures that nonetheless burden inter-provincial trade or restrict competition. Article 37 proscribes any administrative measures that eliminate or restrict competition. If competition is interpreted to mean competition between local and non-local goods or undertakings, then Article 37 can be invoked to strike down any administrative measure that hinders regional trade in China, regardless of its overtly discriminatory character. This, however, only addresses the question of whether the Anti-Monopoly Law could be applied to non-discriminatory measures that burden internal trade or restrict competition. It does not indicate whether the Anti-Monopoly Law should be applied to such measures.

This is indeed a difficult question to answer. There are many reasons why the Anti-Monopoly Law should not be applied to such administrative measures. The experience of the US and the EU is that determining the legality of such government measures requires careful balancing of trade-restrictive effects and the importance of the government policy objective. Such balancing is often difficult for the courts, which adjudicate disputes involving these measures in the US and the EU, to undertake. In China, this task is not even undertaken by the courts (given that it is not entirely clear whether courts can hear suits involving abuse of administrative monopoly), but by officials in NDRC and SAIC who enforce the abuse-of-administrative-monopoly provisions of the Anti-Monopoly Law. These officials, lacking both adjudicatory experience and the body of case-law that exists in the US and the EU as guidance (these enforcement authorities have not been issuing detailed decisions explaining their reasoning in Anti-Monopoly cases, nor are they likely to in the future), will be even more hard-pressed to perform the balancing exercise. However, the experience of the EU also shows that to achieve a truly integrated national or regional market, scrutiny of trade-restrictive measures cannot stop at outright discriminatory measures but must extend to non-discriminatory measures that nonetheless hinder internal trade. Given China's status, albeit somewhat notional, as a unitary country, and its aspiration to unlock all the economic benefits of a truly integrated national market, the Anti-Monopoly Law should be applied to non-discriminatory measures that hinder internal trade.

The remaining question to be answered is how. What kind of balancing approach should the enforcers apply? How much deference should they give to the legitimate regulatory objectives of provincial or local governments? Lessons can be drawn from the experiences of the US and the EU in this respect.

4.2 The US Experience

Unlike China, the United States did not choose to address regional protectionism and market fragmentation issues in its antitrust law, the Sherman Act, the Clayton Act, and the Federal Trade Commission Act. In fact, long before there was any contemplation of a competition law, the founders of the United States and the drafters of its Constitution were aware of the perils of regional protectionism. After the US became independent in 1776, the nation remained a collection of highly autonomous states with a weak federal government. Protectionism quickly emerged, with the various states imposing internal tariffs and other trade barriers. The situation became so dire that the various states reached a consensus that a strong federal government and elimination of internal protectionism were necessary to preserve the cohesion of the new nation. It was under such circumstances that the founders of the new republic decided to meet in Philadelphia in 1787 to draft the US Constitution.

The drafters of the Constitution agreed that there should be a greater centralization of powers to regulate and to facilitate commerce among the various states. This was enshrined in Article I, § 8, of the US Constitution, which succinctly states that 'The Congress shall have Power [to] regulate commerce [among] the several States'. However, and perhaps somewhat surprisingly, given that the main impetus for the Constitution Convention was the elimination of regional protectionism, the Constitution did not contain any express provision prohibiting the states from imposing restrictions on interstate commerce. Therefore, strictly speaking, there is no equivalent in the US Constitution to Chapter Five of the Anti-Monopoly Law.

This glaring omission was rectified by the US Supreme Court, which interpreted Article I, § 8, of the US Constitution, which is generally known as the interstate commerce clause, to impose judicially enforceable limits on state legislation and measures that excessively burden interstate commerce. This was done in the famous case of *Gibbons v. Ogden*[38] in 1824. The issue in that case was whether the state of New York could grant a statutory monopoly for the operation of steamboats in New York waters and prevent steamboats with a federal license from operating in the state. The Court invalidated the grant of monopoly by drawing a distinction between the police powers and commerce powers exercised by the various states. Police powers refer to the power of the states to enact legislation in the realm of public health, public safety and other matters the powers over which the states did not surrender to the federal government under the Constitution. The Court cited inspection laws and quarantine laws as examples of laws that the states could lawfully enact under the US Constitution even though these laws may affect interstate commerce. However, the states may not exercise commerce powers to legislate in matters that were implicitly reserved for

38 *Gibbons v. Ogden*, 22 U.S. 1 (1824) (Wheat).

Congress under the interstate commerce clause even though Congress has not acted on the matter. This means that not only does the interstate commerce clause expressly empower Congress to regulate matters related to interstate commerce, it also creates negative restrictions on the ability of the states to interfere with such commerce. This inference of a negative restriction on the states under the interstate commerce clause has come to be known as the dormant commerce clause.

The modern approach to the dormant commerce clause, which is largely predicated on a balancing exercise, can be said to have begun in *Southern Pacific Co. v. Arizona*.[39] In striking down an Arizona law that limited the length of trains operating in the state, the Court articulated a balancing test as follows: 'Hence the matters for ultimate determination here are the nature and extent of the burden which the state regulation of interstate trains, adopted as a safety measure, imposes on interstate commerce, and whether the relative weights of the state and national interests involved are such as to' render the state regulation impermissible. The current formulation of the balancing test came from *Pike v. Bruce Church, Inc.*:[40]

> Where the statute regulates even-handedly to effectuate a legitimate local interest, and its effects on interstate commerce are only incidental, it will be upheld unless the burden is clearly excessive in relation to the putative local benefits. [If] a legitimate local purpose is found, then the question becomes one of degree. And the extent of the burden that will be tolerated will of course depend on the nature of the local interest involved, and on whether it could be promoted as well with a lesser impact in interstate activities.

As Professor Chemerinsky succinctly concludes, 'the central issue in dormant commerce clause cases is whether the benefits of the state law outweigh its burden on interstate commerce'.[41]

As the jurisprudence currently stands, the Court approaches a dormant commerce clause case by first placing it in one of the following three categories: facially discriminatory laws against out-of-state interests, facially neutral laws with a protectionist purpose or effect, and finally, non-discriminatory laws with a disproportionate effect on interstate commerce. The Court has declared that the first two categories of state

---

39 *Southern Pacific Co. v. Arizona*, 325 US 761, 65 S Ct 1515, 1521 (1945).

40 *Pike v. Bruce Church, Inc.*, 397 US 137, 90 S Ct 844, 847 (1970).

41 E. Chemerinsky, *Constitutional Law: Principles and Policies* (4th edn, Wolters Kluwer 2011) 439.

laws are subject to a virtual *per se* rule of illegality. It is only the third category of state laws that will be evaluated under the *Pike* balancing test.

Most of the cases in which state law was found to be discriminatory resulted in invalidation of the law. One notable exception was *Maine v. Taylor*.[42] That case involved an outright ban on the importation of out-of-state baitfish into the state of Maine. The discriminatory effect of the law was beyond dispute; the only issue was whether the state regulatory interest at issue justified the discrimination. The Court held that Maine's interest in protecting its native species from parasites and adverse interaction with non-native species of baitfish justified this law. The Court further noted that this objective could not have been achieved by a less restrictive means. This Maine law was reminiscent of quarantine laws, for which the Court has professed a more lenient attitude since *Gibbons v. Ogden*.

Most non-discriminatory state laws have survived the Court's scrutiny under the dormant commerce clause and been upheld. Cases producing adverse results for non-discriminatory state laws have involved unconvincing justifications or unsubstantiated public benefits. In *Minnesota v. Clover Leaf Creamery*, after finding, perhaps less than persuasively, that the state law at issue was non-discriminatory, the Court proceeded to uphold it on environmental grounds. The Court asserted that the burden on interstate commerce was 'not clearly excessive in light of the substantial interest in promoting conservation of energy and other natural resources and easing solid waste disposal problems'.[43] In *CTS Corp. v. Dynamics Corp. of America*,[44] the Court upheld an Indiana law that required approval by a majority of the pre-existing disinterested shareholders before an acquirer of 'control shares' of an Indiana corporation could acquire voting rights. The Court found the law non-discriminatory, as it affected in-state and out-of-state acquirers alike. Furthermore, the Court was persuaded by the state's regulatory objectives. It noted that the state of Indiana had a legitimate interest in promoting the stability of share ownership of domestic corporations and ensuring an adequate voice for existing shareholders of these corporations.

This is not to suggest that the US Supreme Court has upheld every non-discriminatory state law under the balancing approach. In *Bibb v.*

---

42 *Maine v. Taylor*, 477 U.S. 131, 106 S. Ct. 2440 (1986).

43 *Minnesota v. Clover Leaf Creamery Co.,* 449 U.S. 456, 101 S. Ct. 715 (1981).

44 *CTS Corp. v. Dynamics Corp. of America*, 481 U.S. 69, 107 S. Ct. 1637 (1987).

Navajo Freight Lines,[45] the Court invalidated a state law that required all trucks travelling through or in the state to use curved mudguards to prevent spatter and increase road safety. The two main reasons given by the Court for the decision were: first, the law deviated from that prevailing in a vast majority of states – straight mudguards were legal in 45 states – and second, the District Court not only found curved mudguards to produce no safety benefits, it found them to be more dangerous than straight ones. In other words, the Court was unconvinced by the public-policy justification for the law.

One of the most difficult questions under the balancing approach is how the courts should compare two unequal qualities: the burden on interstate commerce and a legitimate state regulatory objective. Justice Scalia has long criticized the inadministrability of the balancing test. A glance at the cases suggests that the US Supreme Court seldom engages in meaningful balancing. It seems that once a regulatory purpose is found to be legitimate and substantiated by evidence, and the state law at issue is found to be non-discriminatory, the law will be upheld in most cases. *Bibb* can be explained on the ground that the Court found the regulatory purpose unsubstantiated by the facts. One may justify this deference to the states' prerogative to pursue legitimate regulatory goals on the ground that the individual states are regarded as sovereigns under the US federal system. This argument does not apply in the Chinese context and hence the Chinese enforcement authorities or courts may justifiably attach less weight to provincial and local regulatory goals.

One final comment is that while the US Supreme Court has often noted the existence of a less restrictive alternative when striking down discriminatory state laws, this has not been a mandatory requirement for non-discriminatory state laws. In fact, according to Professor Chemerinsky, the Court has never invalidated a non-discriminatory state law on the ground that the same regulatory objective could be achieved by a less restrictive means.[46]

4.3 The EU Experience

Again, similar to the US, the EU did not choose to tackle the equivalent of abuse of administrative monopoly under its competition law, Articles 101 and 102 TFEU. Instead, the issue is dealt with under the internal trade provisions of the TFEU. The TFEU guarantees four freedoms to

45 *Bibb v. Navajo Freight Lines*, 359 U.S. 520, 79 S. Ct. 962 (1959).
46 Chemerinsky (n. 41 above) 451.

ensure the development of an open internal market: the free movement of goods (Articles 28–37 TFEU), the free movement of persons (Articles 45–55 TFEU), the freedom of establishment and to provide services (56–62 TFEU), and the free movement of capital (Articles 63–66 TFEU). These four freedoms are more extensive than those enjoyed by Chinese citizens under the current Chinese political-legal system. Chinese citizens do not enjoy the free movement of persons under the 'hukou' system, for example. Most of the measures and conduct regulated by Chapter Five of the Anti-Monopoly Law fall under the rubric of free movement of goods, especially Article 34 TFEU, which prohibits the imposition of quantitative restrictions on imports and measures having equivalent effect on trade between Member States. The only exception is Article 35 of the Anti-Monopoly Law, which is concerned with investment in and setting up of local branches by non-local undertakings, activities that fall under the free movement of capital and the freedom of establishment under EU law. The following exposition will therefore focus on the development of the law under Article 34 TFEU.

Unlike the Anti-Monopoly Law, which resorts to specific enumeration of proscribed measures and conduct, the language in Article 34 TFEU is very general. It refers to quantitative restrictions on imports and measures having equivalent effect (MEQR). The first question the European courts faced when applying Article 34 TFEU was what exactly the phrase means. In *Dassonville*,[47] the former European Court of Justice (ECJ, now CJEU) gave the phrase the broadest interpretation when it declared that '[a]ll trading rules enacted by Member States which are capable of hindering, directly or indirectly, actually or potentially, intra-Community trade are to be considered as measures having an effect equivalent to quantitative restrictions'.[48]

It was clear from the early case-law that Article 34 TFEU applies to distinctly applicable rules – national measures which directly or indirectly discriminate against imported goods. The ECJ has consistently struck down such rules. These cases have included *Commission v Italy*,[49] in which the ECJ annulled Italy's import restrictions for cars, *Commission v Ireland*,[50] in which the ECJ expressed its disapproval of a promotional campaign for Irish goods funded by the Irish government, *Commission v United Kingdom*,[51] in which the Court ruled against

47 Case 8/74 *Dassonville* [1974] ECR 837.
48 Ibid., para. 5.
49 Case 154/85 *Commission v. Italy* [1987] ECR 2717.
50 Case 249/81 *Commission v. Ireland* [1982] ECR 4005.
51 Case 207/83 *Commission v. United Kingdom* [1985] ECR 1201.

country-of-origin labeling requirements imposed by the British government, and *Commission v Ireland*,[52] in which the Court ruled against discriminatory public tender requirements that favored national products. What was perhaps less clear was whether the Article also applied to indistinctly applicable rules that nonetheless impede trade between the Member States.

The ECJ settled this question once and for all in the seminal *Cassis de Dijon* case.[53] As Professors Craig and de Burca argue:

> [T]he removal of discriminatory trade barriers is undoubtedly a necessary condition for the attainment of single-market integration. It is not, however, sufficient. There are many rules that do not discriminate between goods dependent upon the country of origin, but which nevertheless create real barriers to the passage of products between Member States.[54]

In fact, the result in *Cassis de Dijon* had been foreshadowed in *Dassonville*, in which the ECJ did not require discriminatory effect to be an ingredient of an MEQR under Article 34 TFEU. In *Cassis de Dijon*, the ECJ declared that:

> Obstacles to movement within the Community resulting from disparities between national laws relating to the marketing of the products in question must be accepted in so far as those provisions may be recognized as being necessary in order to satisfy mandatory requirements relating in particular to the effectiveness of fiscal supervision, the protection of public health, the fairness of commercial transactions and the defence of the consumer.[55]

In such sweeping language, the ECJ declared that Article 34 TFEU applies to indistinctly applicable rules that nonetheless impede trade between the Member States. The case concerned a German law that prescribed the minimum alcoholic content for alcoholic beverages at 25 percent. The liqueur Cassis de Dijon, which only had an alcoholic content of between 15 and 20 per cent, was hence barred from the German market. The German law at issue made no distinction between imported and domestic alcoholic beverages. It applied to them both alike. The ECJ concluded that the German law, which imposed a requirement above and beyond what was imposed by French domestic law, constituted

52 Case 45/87 *Commission v. Ireland* [1988] ECR 4929.

53 Case 120/78 *Rewe-Zentrale AG* ('*Cassis de Dijon*') [1979] ECR 649.

54 P. Craig and G. de Burca, *EU Law: Text, Cases and Materials* (4th edn, OUP 2008) 677.

55 *Cassis de Dijon* (n. 53 above) para. 8.

an MEQR under Article 34 TFEU and required justifications. The German government attempted to justify the German law on public health and consumer protection grounds, both of which were rejected by the ECJ. The ECJ hence struck down the German law at issue as an MEQR. The most relevant aspect of this case for our purpose is the ECJ's pronouncement that an MEQR would only be upheld if it was justified by one of the mandatory requirements.

One of the greatest difficulties facing the ECJ after *Cassis de Dijon* is how to limit the reach of its very expansive ruling. Under the reasoning in *Cassis*, many national economic regulations can be said to affect the free movement of goods. As expected, private parties have increasingly resorted to Article 34 TFEU to challenge unfavorable national economic regulations. The most notorious saga involved the Sunday trading law cases, in which the Sunday trading laws especially of the United Kingdom were challenged as an MEQR under Article 34 TFEU.[56] The Court held that Sunday trading laws were in principle caught by Article 34 TFEU, but could be validated if they were justified by some mandatory requirements and the effects of the rule were proportionate. The application of the proportionality test was to be handled by the national courts, which encountered considerable difficulty in doing so.[57] Eventually, the ECJ provided first guidance by ruling that the effects of Sunday trading laws were proportionate to the purpose to be achieved.[58]

Under continuous pressure from challenges brought by traders against national economic regulation, the ECJ attempted to clarify the state of the law in *Keck and Mithouard*,[59] in which the ECJ drew distinctions between national rules that regulate the nature of the good itself and rules that are concerned with selling arrangements. The ECJ declared:

> [c]ontrary to what has been previously decided, the application from other Member States of national provisions restricting or prohibiting certain selling arrangements is not such as to hinder directly or indirectly, actually or

---

56 Case 145/88 *Torfaen* [1989] ECR 3851; Case C-169/91 *Council of the City of Stoke-on-Trent* [1992] ECR I-6635.

57 Case C-169/91 *Stoke City Council v. B & Q plc* [1990] 3 CMLR 31; *Wellingborough BC v. Payless* [1990] 1 CMLR 773; *B & Q plc v. Shrewsbury BC* [1990] 3 CMLR 535.

58 Case C-332/89 *Marchandise* [1991] ECR I-1027; Cases C-306/88 *Rochdale Borough Council* [1992] ECR I-6457, C-304/90 *Reading Borough Council* [1992] ECR I-6493; and *Council of the City of Stoke-on-Trent* (n. 56 above).

59 Joined Cases C-267/91 and 268/91 *Keck and Mithouard* [1993] ECR I-6097.

> potentially, trade between Member States within the meaning of the *Dassonville* judgment ... provided that those provisions apply to all affected traders operating within the national territory and provided that they affect in the same manner, in law and fact, the marketing of domestic products and of those from other Member States.[60]

The rationale for drawing this distinction is that rules regulating the nature of the goods will have to be satisfied by the importer in addition to the rules of the same nature applicable in its own national territory. The burden of dual compliance is very likely to impede market access for imported goods. In contrast, rules regulating selling arrangements impose equal burdens on all those seeking access to the market in a particular Member State. They do not impose extra costs on the importers and hence do not constitute an MEQR under Article 34 TFEU. In the light of this more recent case-law, it is much clearer now that, in the above-mentioned Sunday trading cases, Article 34 TFEU was not violated.

The jurisprudence on Article 34 TFEU continued to evolve over time. The ECJ attempted to apply the distinction drawn in *Keck and Mithouard*, but the line between rules regulating selling arrangements and those concerned with product characteristics is not always as stark as one would hope. Occasionally, the ECJ reclassified rules regulating selling arrangements as rules that governed product characteristics and put them within the ambit of Article 34 TFEU.[61] Starting in the late 1990s, the ECJ began to focus more on whether a particular national law impedes the market access of imported goods.[62] Market access has been given an even greater emphasis in some recent cases.[63] The idea is that if a national rule significantly impedes the market access of imported goods, it will fall within the ambit of Article 34 TFEU.

The most relevant part of the EU jurisprudence on free movement of goods for our purpose is what justifications are accepted for a trade-restrictive measure and what type of scrutiny the European courts apply in determining whether to accept the justification. The first observation to make is that the European courts have been less deferential than the US courts to non-discriminatory measures. Recall that under the prevailing US Supreme Court jurisprudence, most non-discriminatory state measures are upheld. Only when the proffered state regulatory objective is not

[60] Ibid., para 16.

[61] Case C-368/95 *Vereinigte Familiapress* [1997] ECR I-3689.

[62] Cases C-34-36/95 *De Agostini* [1997] ECR I-3843; Case C-254/98 *TK-Heimdienst Sass* [2000] ECR I-151.

[63] Case C-110/05 *Commission v. Italy (Trailers)* [2009] ECR I-519; Case C-142/05 *Mickelsson* [2009] ECR I-4273.

supported by evidence would the court strike down the state law at issue. The European courts take a more restrictive approach. First, they do not simply accept any state regulatory objectives. The ECJ has formulated a list of accepted regulatory objectives, which will be elaborated in detail below. Moreover, unlike in the US (recall that the US courts do not ask whether the same regulatory objective can be achieved by a less restrictive means for non-discriminatory laws), the European courts have imposed a proportionality requirement. The courts often ask whether the same regulatory objective can be attained by less restrictive means.

The EU jurisprudence on justifications for trade-restrictive national measures is slightly complicated because there in fact exist two forms of justifications. The first one arises from Article 36 TFEU, and includes public morality, public policy or public security, the protection of health and life of humans, animal or plants, the protection of national treasures possessing artistic, historic or archaeological value, and the protection of industrial or commercial property as reasons for justification. The justifications under Article 36 TFEU are also available to discriminatory national measures, which, in order to avail themselves of the justification, must be the least restrictive means possible to attain the regulatory objective. These defenses are strictly construed and the courts scrutinize closely whether a particular national measure is truly justified by one of the grounds listed in Article 36 TFEU. There is a second form of justification for indistinctly applicable rules, which are known as mandatory requirements under *Cassis de Dijon*. The original mandatory requirements include the effectiveness of fiscal supervision, the protection of public health, the fairness of commercial transactions and consumer protection. Subsequent case-law has extended the list to include environmental protection, plurality of the media, and the encouragement of cinematic arts as well.[64] The application of the mandatory requirements is subject to the principle of proportionality. The courts will assess whether there are less restrictive means to attain the same regulatory objective. For example, it is common for the courts to challenge the invocation of consumer protection as a justification by arguing that the same purpose can be achieved by labeling rules.[65]

---

[64] Case 302/86 *Commission v. Denmark* [1988] ECR 4607; *Vereinigte Familiapress* (n. 61 above); Joined Cases 60 and 61/84 *Cinéthèque* [1985] ECR 2605.

[65] Case 178/84 *Commission v. Germany* [1987] ECR 1227.

4.4 Lessons for China

The US and EU experiences hold a number of lessons for China in applying the Anti-Monopoly Law to non-discriminatory administrative measures that nonetheless impede internal trade or restrict competition.

As mentioned earlier, the provision in the Anti-Monopoly Law that can most likely be applied to non-discriminatory administrative measures that nonetheless impede internal trade or restrict competition is Article 37, which is triggered when an administrative measure eliminates or restricts competition. The question is what the scope of Article 37 is. What kind of administrative measures are caught by it? Any administrative measures that affect trade within China? This would arguably be too broad. The jurisdictional trigger of Article 37 is that the administrative measure must eliminate or restrict competition. Any measure that restricts the market access of non-local goods by definition restricts competition in the market in which those non-local goods compete. Recent EU jurisprudence under Article 34 TFEU emphasizes market access. Therefore, China can look to this body of case-law for guidance on what should be regulated under Article 37. To avoid the difficulty the ECJ has faced in its jurisprudence, China would do well to avoid a rigid distinction between rules regulating product characteristics and those governing selling arrangements, and focus on impediment of market access instead. Any administrative measure that prevents or directly and substantially hinders access to the local market will be caught under Article 37 of the Anti-Monopoly Law.

In terms of the justifiability of a trade-restrictive measure, the US and the EU present China with two options. Under the *Pike* balancing formula, the US approach is one that demonstrates a high degree of deference to the regulatory prerogatives of the states. As suggested earlier, once a state regulatory purpose is found to be legitimate and substantiated by evidence, and the state law at issue is found to be non-discriminatory, the law will be upheld in most cases. The US courts also generally do not apply a proportionality requirement to non-discriminatory state laws. The EU approach is one which applies a much more intensive scrutiny of the regulatory justifications offered by the Member States. First, not every state regulatory objective is accepted by the European courts as legitimate. The objective must fall under one of the mandatory requirements for an indistinctly applicable rule or one of the enumerated exceptions in Article 36 TFEU for a distinctly applicable rule. Second, the European courts also apply a proportionality test and require the national law to be proportionate to the objective to be attained. This means that the objective cannot be achieved by a less restrictive means.

Which approach should China adopt? Should it adopt the permissive attitude of the US courts to provincial or local regulatory objectives? There are perhaps two reasons for the deferential attitude shown by the US courts to state regulatory prerogative. First, the various states in the US are recognized as sovereigns with a whole range of regulatory powers guaranteed by the US Constitution. Therefore, one could argue that the various states deserve substantial deference. Second, as Justice Scalia points out, the *Pike* balancing formula is very difficult to apply. Under that formula, the courts are in fact asked to compare the trade restrictive effects of a state law with the importance of a state regulatory objective, which are arguably incomparable. The sovereign justification relevant to the US is clearly inapplicable to China, as individual provinces and localities are not sovereigns. China is a unitary state where individual provinces are sub-units of the central state. The non-recognition of a state action doctrine by the SAIC is consistent with this view.

As to the inadministrability of the *Pike* balancing formula, Justice Scalia may have overstated his case. What the US courts are asked to do under the *Pike* balancing formula is largely similar to what the European courts have done under Article 34 TFEU. In both cases, the courts are asked to evaluate the legitimacy of the regulatory objective and the proportionality of the means to the end. The European courts have handled this task admirably in the Article 34 cases. The ECJ has simplified its task by announcing in advance a list of accepted regulatory objectives under the rubric of mandatory requirements. This obviates the need to evaluate the legitimacy of the regulatory objective in every instance. And the ECJ has applied the proportionality test with rigor, accepting the justification when the means fit the end and rejecting it when the means are excessive. Its examination of national laws that purportedly protect consumers and comparison with the alternative of labeling rules is an apt illustration of this. Moreover, the EU approach also obviates the need for balancing. The European courts have structured the analysis slightly differently from the US courts. Under prevailing EU jurisprudence, the threshold issue is whether a national law constitutes an MEQR, and there is a variety of approaches to determine that under EU law. Once a national law is determined as an MEQR, the remaining question is justification and proportionality. Meanwhile, the *Pike* balancing formula does in fact invite the courts to balance trade-restrictive effects against the importance of state regulatory objectives, which is arguably very difficult to do. The Chinese enforcement authorities can avoid this task by adopting the EU-structured two-step approach.

Given China's professed desire to create a truly integrated national market, and the unitary nature of its political system, China probably should not opt for the deferential attitude of the US approach and should apply a more searching scrutiny as under EU law. A proportionality test would seem appropriate as it helps to ensure that internal trade or competition is not being unnecessarily restricted. Whether the enforcement authorities should compile a list of acceptable regulatory objectives, as in the case of mandatory requirements, requires some consideration. On the one hand, compiling a list the way the ECJ has reduces flexibility. It is probably impossible to enumerate in advance all the possible legitimate regulatory objectives. In the EU, this concern is alleviated by the fact that the ECJ can add to the list of mandatory requirements as it sees fit in new cases. On the other hand, given the multitude of enforcement agencies, the provincial and local AICs and Pricing Bureaus involved in the enforcement of Chapter Five, some control over the scope of legitimate regulatory objectives will help to prevent arbitrary enforcement and local favoritism. On balance, given the current state of the political system, the Chinese enforcement authorities probably should create a list of acceptable regulatory objectives in advance.

Lastly, it is important to remember that Article 37 of the Anti-Monopoly Law extends beyond the reach of the US dormant-commerce-clause jurisprudence and the EU law on free movement of goods because Article 37 is not predicated on national or regional protectionism. It is triggered if a provincial or local measure restricts or eliminates competition. Therefore, it should potentially apply to the scenario in the *Taiyuan Railway Bureau* case whereby a local administrative organ abuses its administrative power to favor its own undertakings at the expense of other local ones. In other words, impediment of the market access of other local undertakings could also trigger Article 37. Although the overwhelming focus of Chapter Five of the Anti-Monopoly Law is on regional protectionist measures, Article 37 is drafted in such a way that it could offer protection to local enterprises against abuses by local administrative bodies. This problem is likely to be particularly serious in China, given the heft of the state sector in the economy. Governments at various levels in China control state-owned enterprises. These governments are likely to be tempted to make use of administrative measures to assist or favor their own enterprises to the detriment of private enterprises. It is thus important that Article 37 not be limited to regional protectionist measures, but also apply to abuse of administrative monopoly that harms local enterprises.

5. CONCLUSION

Despite its comprehensive nature, the Anti-Monopoly Law has not addressed what has plagued enforcement in the area of abuse of administrative monopoly thus far: the lack of effective sanctions. As suggested above, the previous laws and regulations failed to stamp out abuse of administrative monopoly largely because of ineffective enforcement and deficient penalties. The Anti-Monopoly Law suffers from the same inadequacy, as Article 51 only provides for admonition by the superior authority for an offending government body and disciplinary measures for the responsible individuals. The superior authority is unlikely to have the incentive to be vigilant against abuse of administrative monopoly, as any measure or conduct that benefits a lower level government body may indirectly benefit its superior authority. Scholars have suggested that there should be civil liability for government agencies in violation of the abuse of administrative monopoly provisions.[66]

An enhancement of penalties on its own, however, is unlikely to provide a fundamental solution to the lack of effective enforcement of these provisions. The fact remains that the Anti-Monopoly Law expects one part of the Chinese bureaucracy to bring enforcement actions against another part of the bureaucracy, an event which is highly unlikely to happen in the current Chinese political system. An enforcement mechanism that utilizes a third-party adjudication system would sidestep this problem, which is in fact what is done in most other jurisdictions, such as the US and the EU. This option, however, is unavailable in China as the judiciary lacks independence and is very much under the control of the executive. It is highly unlikely that the judiciary would rule against the executive of the same level of government in an abuse of administrative monopoly case. Absent an impartial enforcement agency, the abuse of administrative monopoly provisions of the Anti-Monopoly Law are likely to remain sporadically enforced and unlikely to serve as an effective antidote to the widespread abuse of administrative monopoly in China.

---

66 E.M. Fox, 'An Anti-Monopoly Law for China – Scaling the Walls of Government Restraints' (2008) 75 *Antitrust L.J.* 178, 191; B. Song, 'Competition Policy in a Transitional Economy: The Case of China' (1995) 31 *Stanford J. Int'l L.* 387, 410.

7. The competition policy dimension of the regulation of water and sanitation services in Brazil

Gesner Oliveira

1. INTRODUCTION

The objective of this chapter is to discuss the competition policy dimension of the water and sanitation services in Brazil. It presents the basic sanitation situation in Brazil, with an emphasis on the sector's regulation. It estimates the timeline of the universalization of water supply and sanitation in Brazil, explaining the need to increase investment and productivity. It is argued that good regulation could stimulate competition within the sector. This article indicates that the elimination of the enormous infrastructure bottlenecks in the emerging countries depends on a pro-competition regulation and not on the elimination of competition under the pretext of the existence of a natural monopoly.

Regulation is essential in the water and sanitation sector due to the natural monopoly characteristics, high unrecoverable costs (sunk costs) and positive externalities on health and the natural environment, among other factors. This does not mean however that there is no competition in the sector. The presence of a pro-competitive regulation is paramount for the quality of the services supplied.

This study is organized in six sections. Besides this introduction, Section 2 presents the basic sanitation situation in Brazil. Section 3 contains an estimation of the investment needs for different universalization goals. Section 4 touches upon sanitation regulation aspects in Brazil. Section 5 contextualizes sanitation service regulation, highlighting the competitive dimension that exists in this sector. A final section contains the major conclusions.

2. THE BASIC SANITATION SITUATION IN BRAZIL

The Brazilian water and sanitation situation is tragic. Figure 7.1 shows that in 2011 only 56 per cent of the Brazilian population had access to the sanitation network and 84 per cent had access to clean treated water. In regard to waste treatment, data from the last National Basic Sanitation Survey (PNSB, 2009) inform us that only 29.4 per cent of sewage is treated.

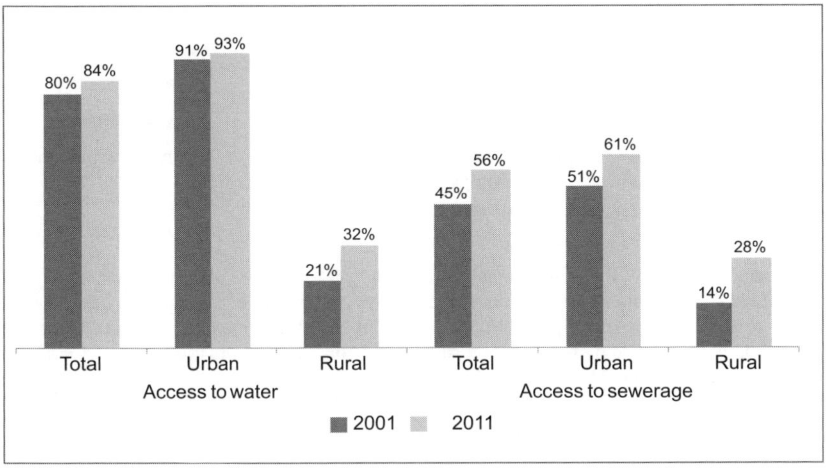

Sources: PNAD/IBGE Annual surveys (2001 and 2011) and PNSB (2009). Access to water: percentage of residents living in housing integrated into the general water supply network. Access to sewerage: percentage of residents in urban housing with sewage collecting network and percentage of rural residents in housing with sewage collecting network or septic tank.

Figure 7.1 Proportion (%) of the Brazilian population with access to clean treated water and sewerage

Figure 7.2 shows that 32 million Brazilians do not have proper access to running water (general supply networks), 85 million Brazilians do not have proper access to a sewerage sanitary network (collecting networks in the urban areas and collecting networks or septic tanks in the rural areas), 134 million do not have their homes' waste treated and more than six million do not even have a bathroom.

The spread of sanitation coverage is very slow. According to the 2011 National Housing Sample Survey (PNAD 2011),[1] from 2001 to 2011

[1] PNAD (*Pesquisa Nacional por Amostra de Domicílios* – National Survey by Household Sample, published by Instituto Brasileiro de Geografia e

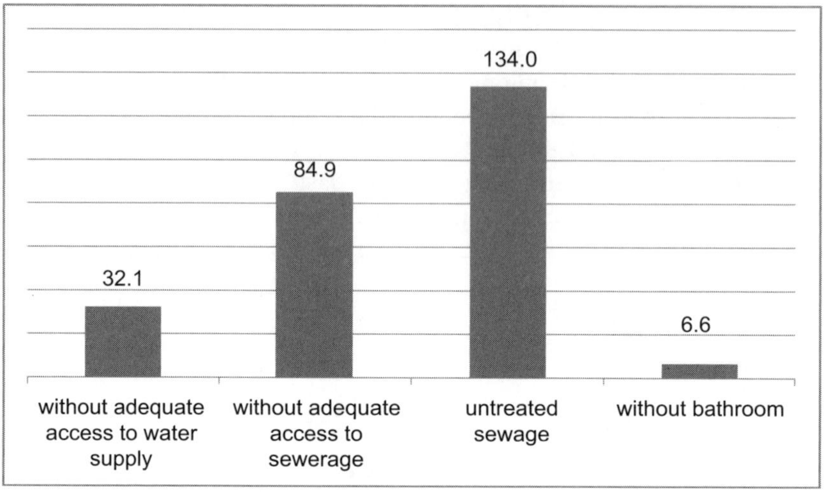

Sources: PNAD/IBGE Annual survey (2011) and PNSB (2008). Adequate access to water: percentage of residents in housing connected to the general water supply network. Adequate access to sanitation system: percentage of residents of urban housing connected to sewage collecting network and percentage of rural residents of housing connected to collecting network or with septic tank.

Figure 7.2 Brazilians without access to water, sewerage and bathrooms (in millions of people)

sewage collection increased only 11 percentage points. This pace is slower than the growth of other public utilities within that same period such as telephony, which rose from 58 per cent in 2001 to 91 per cent in 2011. In a similar period, electric power supply coverage, which was at 95.5 per cent of houses in 1991, grew to a virtually universal level (99.3 per cent according to the 2011 PNAD).

The sanitation coverage is very heterogeneous in Brazil. According to the National Information System on Sanitation (SNIS) data for 2012 the few states of the Federation in which more than 70 per cent of urban housing has access to a sewage collecting service are Distrito Federal,

Estatística) is an annual survey that obtains information on demographic and socioeconomic characteristics of the population such as gender, age, education, work and income, and characteristics of households, and with variable frequency, information on migration, fertility, marriage, among others, as having collection unit households. Specific topics covering demographic, social and economic aspects are also investigated.

São Paulo and Minas Gerais. The smallest rates of coverage are found in Amapá, Pará, Rondônia and Piauí.

The sanitation situation in Brazil's rural areas is even more critical. According to the PNAD 2011, 72 per cent of the rural population does not have access to a proper sanitation system.

Operationally speaking, the sanitation services situation in the country is not encouraging either. Non revenue water (NRW), that is, the rate of water in the sanitation system that does not generate revenue due to physical losses (e.g., leakages) or commercial losses (e.g., fraud) is very high; although it is possible to note a slight downtrend, this rate has been close to 40 per cent for the last 12 years. Figure 7.3 shows the path of distribution losses in recent years.

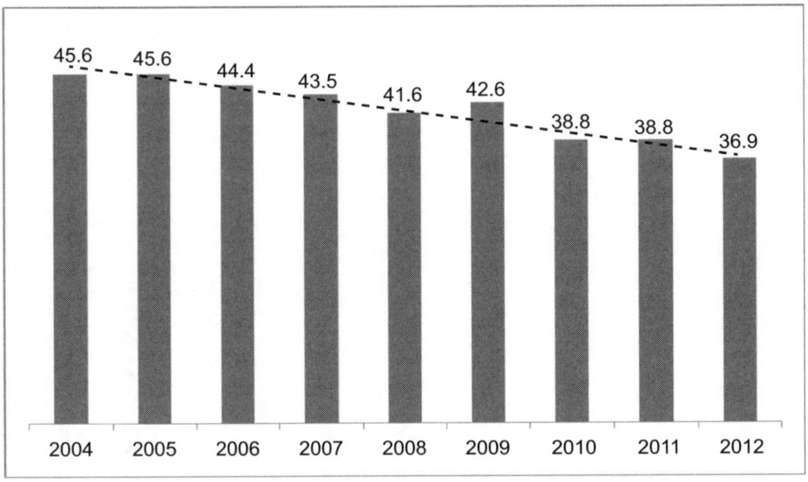

Source: SNIS (2012). SNIS (*Sistema Nacional de Informações sobre Saneamento* – National Information System on Sanitation) is a database administered at the federal level, which contains information on institutional, administrative, operational, managerial, economic, financial and quality on the provision of water services, sewerage and solid waste management. For water services and sewerage, the data have been updated annually since the reference year 1995. Regarding solid waste management services, data are also updated annually since the reference year 2002.

Figure 7.3 Distribution losses over time (%)

The water loss level in Brazil went from 45.6 per cent in 2004 to 36.9 per cent in 2012, a reduction of 8.7 percentage points within the period. And yet the scenario remains very worrying considering that the majority of companies do not measure their water losses in a consistent manner.

When comparing Brazil with developed countries, it becomes clear just how great the room for improvement is. Towns in Germany and Japan show distribution losses of 11 per cent, while some in Australia show 16 per cent. Brazil would have to reduce its water losses by a minimum of 10 percentage points to even become comparable with those countries.[2]

3. INVESTMENT ESTIMATE FOR DIFFERENT UNIVERSALIZATION SCENARIOS

The slow development of sanitation statistics reflects persistently low investments in the sector. Figure 7.4 shows that sanitation investments were between R$ 3.8 billion and R$ 4.7 billion until 2007. There was a slight uptrend from 2008 to 2010, although investments fell again in 2011.

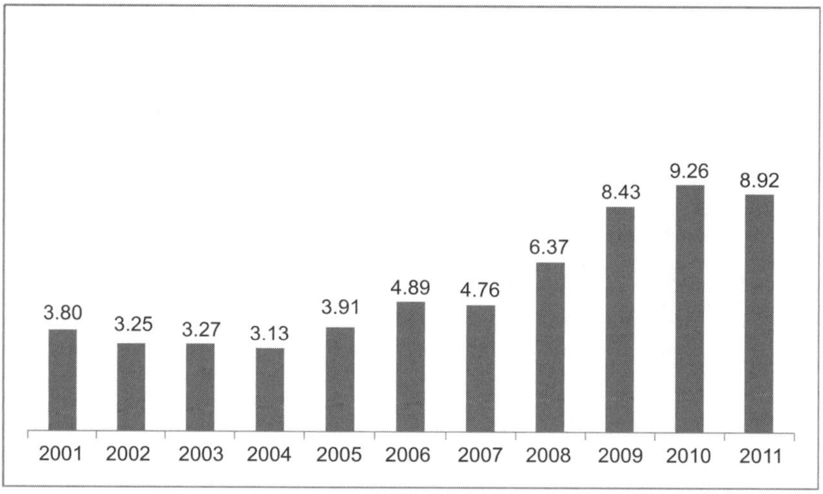

Source: Chart by author based on SNIS data as of January 2012 – aggregate investments made by service suppliers, municipalities and states.

Figure 7.4 Sanitation investments in Brazil in R$ billions (constant value, 2001–2011)

[2] However, the International Water Association (IWA) draws attention to the fact that although rates of loss are easily understood by all, such numbers are too tenuous for comparing losses between companies or towns.

The organization of the water and sanitation sector in Brazil relies upon three types of service providers:[3]

(1) state companies, which hold circa 75 per cent of the water and sanitation services, encompassing 25 companies;
(2) municipal public services, which could be autarchies or mixed-economy companies, which add up to circa 1,600 institutions in the whole country; and
(3) private companies, which constitute a group of 70 entities that obtained concessions in the 1990s. Some of the larger cities with private concessionaires are Manaus (AM), Campo Grande (MS) and Niterói (RJ).

One of the factors that explain the low investment level is the fact that among the 25 state companies, the majority do not have adequate conditions to access long-term financing. The recent investments of sanitation companies, on comparison, show a disparate situation. Two of the companies known for their good performance raised their joint yearly average investment from R$ 1.3 billion in the period 2003–2006 to R$ 2.3 billion in the period 2007–2008, a growth rate of 73 per cent. If these two companies are excluded from the calculation, the yearly average investment in Brazil moves from R$ 3.16 billion in the period 2003–2006 to R$ 3.11 billion in the period 2007–2008, a reduction of 1.7 per cent.

On top of being scarce, investment in sanitation shows low efficiency. One representative indicator of this low efficiency is the Brazilian average water losses index, calculated by the SNIS at 37.4 per cent, a number which is probably underestimated. Less efficient companies have loss indexes of more than 60 per cent, that is, the company loses more than half of its production.[4] The sector's low investment in maintenance leads to situations in which companies invest in new water systems and, at the same time, lose more water than this new system's capacity.

---

[3] More information about the segment can be found in the document 'Saneamento Básico – Estrutura – Perspectivas – Perfis de Empresas do Valor Econômico' (2006), available at: http://www2.al.rs.gov.br/forumdemocratico/LinkClick.aspx?fileticket=rNeetJhmeT0%3D&tabid=3230&mid=4650 (accessed 31 December 2013).

[4] Planning and Integrated Investments Secretary (SPI), Planning Ministry. Content was available on the Ministry portal and later withdrawn.

According to the Planning Ministry,[5] the sanitation enterprises in Brazil are characterized by difficulties in project preparation and deficiencies in works and services management (lack of technical or institutional capacity). The difficulties in the execution of projects and enterprises make work more expensive and of lower quality.

Another worrying aspect is the low investment in research and development, the consequence of which is the use of old technologies that from an operational viewpoint are less efficient.

In the next section it is shown how an increase in investment and the improvement of efficiency could influence the sanitation universalization scenarios in Brazil.

The goal of universal sanitation in Brazil demands action on two fronts. The first is to increase the investment level, which is very low, as demonstrated in section 2. The second is to increase efficiency, reducing the marginal incremental capacity cost of providing water and sewerage.

This section contains an exercise with four supply development scenarios for water and sanitation in Brazil. Within the four scenarios, the following premises were used:

- PNSB 2009 supply rates: (i) water – supplied to 78.6 per cent of homes; (ii) sewerage – supplied to 44 per cent of homes; (iii) sewage treatment – supplied to 29.4 per cent of homes;
- population growth defined by IBGE[6] (Brazilian population of 215 million inhabitants by 2050);
- average investment between 2002 and 2009, according to SNIS (2009), of R$ 5 billion;[7]
- necessary sanitation investment in order to reach and maintain universal water and sewerage supply by 2060:[8]
  - without productivity increase (scenarios 1 and 2): R$ 255 billion total investment;
  - with 30 per cent productivity increase (scenarios 3 and 4): R$ 168 billion total investment.

---

[5] Ibid.

[6] IBGE stands for Instituto Brasileiro de Geografia e Estatística which is the most important public entity in Brazil for the collection of the major socioeconomic indicators, including the National Accounts.

[7] The 2009 and 2010 data are not yet available at SNIS. Projected values were considered.

[8] The scenario was built on the hypothesis that all collected waste will be treated, i.e., the collection cost is included in the treatment cost.

Table 7.1 summarizes four scenarios regarding the time it will take to achieve universal water and sewerage supply, the necessary investment to achieve that universal supply and the total investment until 2060. The exercise shows that the increase of the investment level and the increase of productivity are equally important to reduce the time necessary to achieve universalization.

Table 7.1 Sanitation universalization scenarios

Scenarios	Year of the universalization		Investments	
	Water	Sewage	Universal	Until 2060
(1) Current level of investment is maintained	2039	2060	R$ 255 bn	R$ 255 bn
(2) Investment is doubled	2021	2031	R$ 220 bn	R$ 255 bn
(3) Current level of investment is maintained and productivity is increased by 30%	2028	2042	R$ 165 bn	R$ 186 bn
(4) Investment is doubled and productivity increased by 30%	2017	2024	R$ 150 bn	R$ 186 bn

In the worst-case scenario, in which the current investment level and productivity level are maintained, sanitation universalization does not occur until 2060 and water universalization only in 2039. In the best-case scenario, which doubles the current investment level and increases productivity by 30 per cent, universal sanitation is reached by 2024, and water supply by 2017.

4. SANITATION REGULATION ASPECTS

The insufficient regulation today constitutes one of the many challenges that, for decades, has inhibited investments in the water and sanitation infrastructure. The Sanitation Law (11.445/07) in combination with the Public Consortium Law (11.107/05) offers, although in a generic form, parameters of a sectoral regulatory framework. The law establishes criteria for regulation decisions aiming to create economic incentives, and it has as its general principles the independence, transparency, form, speed and objectivity of the decisions.

Figure 7.5 presents the evolution of the sectoral legal framework since enactment of the National Sanitation Plan (Planasa) in the seventies, organized by a financing system with a relevant role for the Habitation National Bank (BNH) and the creation of the State Company for Basic Sanitation (CESBs).

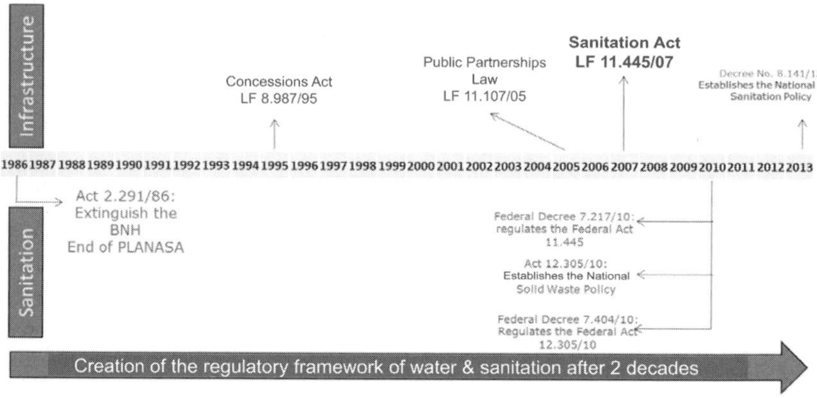

Figure 7.5 Development of the sector's legal framework

Throughout the 1990s, the effects of the ongoing international crisis with its strong repercussions on the emerging economies affected Brazil and had, as a consequence, the reduction of federal funds in the field of sanitation. The average yearly investment, which was R$ 1.3 billion in the 1995–1998 period, fell to R$ 263 million in 1999 and circa R$ 21 million in 2000. In the current decade, the uncertainties surrounding regulation have represented investment-limiting factors. Furthermore, uncertainty regarding, for example, the excessive bureaucracy in granting funding and the absence of a more solid jurisprudence on which level of government – municipal or state – holds the granting power in metropolitan regions persisted.

The Law No 11.445/07 brought several modifications to the Brazilian sanitation regulation scenario. This law highlighted the importance of consumer affairs and the focus on the client. Besides that, it also brought new general guidelines for establishing technical norms, rules to regulate the relationship between more than one service provider acting in the same town, and legal structures and guarantees that bring greater stability to the sector. Table 7.2 shows a schematic comparison between the sanitation sector characteristics in the 'Planasa era' and the new configuration since enactment of the Sanitation Law and the Consortium Law.

Table 7.2 Comparison of Planasa with new regulation

Basic National Sanitation Plan (PLANASA)	Law No 11.445/2007
Planning by the operator	Planning by the conceding power
Contracts without solid legal support	Programme or concession contract
Self-regulation	Regulatory agency
Public financing	Market financing
Focus on supply	Focus on client
Natural monopoly	Competitive environment
Water as a free good	Scarcity of hydric resources and greater concern with the price of water

Source: Author's analysis.

Other fundamental changes were the obligation to subject contracts for provision of public sanitation services to regulation by an independent regulatory body (increasing the need for transparency and for service quality standards) as well as the withdrawal of the responsibility for planning investments in water and sewerage from the operators, transferring it to the granting authority. Along the same lines, it became necessary to demand formal contracts between the granting authority and the operator, be it through a concession contract or a programme contract, derived from the federative arrangement between state and municipality in the terms of the Law No. 11.107/05.

Within the new legal-framework model of sanitation regulation, there was, therefore, a migration from a self-regulating system with service provider companies performing internal controls to a concept of independent planning and regulation. In this context, the sanitation service operators became responsible for reaching the goals established by independent bodies and not linked to the operators themselves.

5. COMPETITIVE ASPECTS OF SANITATION SERVICES REGULATION

The conventional notion of the sanitation sector as being characterized by a typical natural monopoly needs to be put into perspective. At least three types of competition can be observed here:

(1) intermunicipality competition for concessions;
(2) competition at municipality level between the service providers and providers of alternative water sources;
(3) competition for service provision induced by regulation mechanisms.

In the specific case of competition for service provision, the incentive mechanisms designed into the regulation in the sanitation sector are especially relevant. Such stimulus may occur in two formats: *individual incentives* or *yardstick competition*.

In the individual incentives format[9] the regulating body will tend to take into consideration parameters that are observable by the monopolist. Meanwhile, under the benchmark or yardstick competition[10] formats, the regulation design will be determined by the monopolist's behaviour towards its peers. The two schemes aim at increasing monopoly efficiency. However, the system based on absolute measures may arrive at very different results than the one based on relative measures.

The regulating body, the principal, faces a moral risk when it doesn't succeed in observing or monitoring the agent's regulated actions. The latter might not have an interest in adopting the level of effort considered by the former to be adequate. This way, the principal will need to provide incentives for the agent to reach the level of effort considered adequate.

The optimal contract, when the principal is concerned with only one agent, depends especially on the agent's attitude towards risks. The

[9] The economic analysis regarding regulation in the individual-incentives format is one in which the regulator induces the regulated to reveal its private information that will be the basis for the regulation to be developed. This regulation of an individual nature was described in the analysis of J.-J. Laffont and J. Tirole, 'Using Cost Observation to Regulate Firms' (1986) 94 *J. Pol. Econ.* 614; J.-J. Laffont and J. Tirole, *A Theory of Incentives in Procurement and Regulation* (MIT Press 1993); J.-J. Laffont, 'The New Economics of Regulation Ten Years After' (1994) 62 *Econometrica* 507.

[10] The regulation based on *yardstick competition* was suggested by A. Shleifer, 'A Theory of Yardstick Competition' (1985) 16 *RAND J. Econ.* 319.

literature shows that if the agent is averse to risk, the principal will face the conflict (*trade-off*) between sharing the risks and providing incentives. On the other hand, when the agent is neutral regarding risk and the complete information is observable there is no conflict between incentives and certainty.[11]

In general, a yardstick-competition model is preferable to individual-incentives schemes providing that:

(1) there are common uncertainties among the companies operating in the market;
(2) the companies' actions mutually impact their performance and the companies are able to observe each other's actions without the knowledge of the regulator.

Generally, the agents' problem does not consist only of the non-observance of the effort or of the agents' actions, but also comes from the fact that they have private information. Such information asymmetry leads to the adverse-selection problem.

The Shleifer approach (1985)[12] shows that when the regulator stops using its own company-regulation parameters and starts to base its evaluation on other companies' performance, this creates mechanisms similar to those operating within competition among locally monopolist companies. The author suggests building *benchmarks* of the participant companies from econometric methods as a basis for choosing the policy on pricing and transfers. This requires that the company's payoff becomes based on its counterparts' actions, generating competition among them. In the sanitation sector, there would be a sector initially formed by local self-regulated monopolies and, as soon as regulation is enacted, companies incited to compete due to the yardstick competition mechanism.

The regulation by yardstick competition is one of the key concepts of the Water Act that defined economic regulation of the water industry in the United Kingdom.[13] As a consequence, in England and Wales the companies' costs were reduced and a better service was provided to the

---

[11] More information on the discussion regarding the agent-principal model can be found in P. Bolton and M. Dewatripont, *Contract Theory* (MIT Press 2005); and J.-J. Laffont and D. Martimort, *The Theory of Incentives – The Principal-Agent Model* (Princeton University Press 2002).

[12] Shleifer (n. 10 above).

[13] J.W. Sawkins, 'Yardstick Competition in the English and Welsh Water Industry: Fiction or Reality?' (1995) 5 *Utilities Pol'y* 27.

consumer. The dissemination of the appropriate indicators serve to show, to all agents involved, the companies' relative positions. Based on this information, consumers, the government, suppliers and other agents started to demand explanations regarding the distortions in the companies' performance. Facing this situation, the companies mobilized in such way that disparities went down over time.[14]

There are other relevant aspects related to competition among water and sanitation companies. One of these aspects is unfair competition. Unfair competition in the area of public-service concessions appears in two forms. First, there is that associated with the illegality of alternative sources. Some consumers collect water from their own sources, for example an artesian well. The problem here is that those consumers, frequently do not have the necessary grantee licences to use these wells. This can cause environmental impacts such as over-exploration, phreatic water contamination and ground instability, as well as generating public health problems.

Second, the establishments that use alternative sources do not always declare the correct sewage volume dumped into the public network. This implies an extra expenditure for the sanitation service providers that need to measure these volumes in order to avoid the underestimation of sewage services and consequent revenue loss. Besides that, it affords unequal competition on markets with similar clients duly connected to the public network. Notice that the Sanitation Law obliges the establishments to become connected to the public network. In this regard, Article 45 of the Sanitation Law 11.445/07 states:

> Exempting the contrary dispositions of the titular norms, of the regulation body and of the environment, all permanent urban building will be connected to the available public network of water supply and of sanitary waste and subject to the tariff payment and other public prices resulting from the connection and the use of these services.

In contrast to lower consumption segments, the segment of big clients is characterized by low fixed costs, individualized solutions and, consequently, greater demand elasticity and the existence of an effectively competitive regime. There are two regulation aspects that distort competition in this segment:

---

14 J.W. Sawkins, 'The Development of Competition in the English and Welsh Water and Sewerage Industry' (2001) 22(2) *Fiscal Studies* 189. In this same work, the author reflects that the progress on extending competition in England and Wales was slow and that it did not succeed in stimulating potential competitors to enter the market.

(1) economic: represented by the current tax structure rigidity that concessionaires must comply with; and
(2) technical: represented by the asymmetric and sometimes informal price monitoring of official concessionaires vis-à-vis other market agents.

However, there is evidence that this tax structure rigidity leads to four inefficiencies:[15]

(1) the *consumer is damaged* once less rivalry among the market players drives prices up;
(2) there is *network subutilization* when the big client opts for an alternative supply source, making the capital applied to the infrastructure less efficient;
(3) *economic-financial sustainability is compromised* when the concessionaire is prevented from accessing several markets; this stability is essential for the company to fulfil its promises with regard to public sanitation policy; and
(4) *inefficiency* in resource allocation occurs once companies access markets where the concessionaire is more competitive.

6. CONCLUSIONS

To summarize the main points of this article, I have laid out a panorama of sanitation in Brazil, as well as investment scenarios for the universalization of this service in the country.

I conclude that the Brazilian sanitation situation is tragic. The comparison among the country's regions, as well as with other developed and developing countries, shows that the sanitation services lag considerably behind demand and international benchmarks.

The reduction of the delay in universalizing the sanitation system is a difficult challenge, but possible to overcome. The slow growth of sanitation rates reflects persistently low investments in the sector. It is estimated that, if the current levels of investment and productivity were maintained, universal sewerage would occur only in 2060 and universal

---

[15] This evidence is empirically presented by D.C.O. Alves, P.C. Pereda, D.S. Grimaldi and A. Fraga, 'Concorrência no fornecimento de água em São Paulo: evidências e impactos na elasticidade da demanda dos grandes clientes da Sabesp' in G. Oliveira and P. Scazufca (eds), *A economia de saneamento no Brasil* (Editora Singular 2009) 89.

water supply only in 2039. However, it is demonstrated that under the necessary conditions, it is possible for universal sewerage to be achieved by 2024 and universal water supply by 2017. To achieve this goal, it is vital to increase investments and improve the sector's productivity.

The insufficiency of regulation today constitutes one of many challenges that for decades have inhibited water and sewage infrastructure investments. The model of the new regulatory framework in the sanitation sector, therefore, has provided for a migration from a system of practically self-regulated companies and departments to a system of external regulation.

Finally, the aspects defining competitiveness in the sanitation sector were demonstrated, refuting the notion that there is no space for competition in this segment. The conditions that differentiate regulation by *yardstick competition* or by *individual incentives* were revealed. In addition, other competitiveness aspects, such as negotiations with big clients and unfair competition in the public service concession areas, were discussed.

This discussion suggests that the elimination of the enormous infrastructural shortfalls in emerging countries depends on pro-competitive regulation and not on the elimination of competition under the pretext of the existence of a natural monopoly.

8. Pro-competitive regulation of personal data protection in the EU

Simonetta Vezzoso

1. INTRODUCTION

Globally, the regulation of personal data protection is likely to become increasingly significant in the coming years. Much as there is a distinct trend towards promoting an ever more incisive use of personal data with a view to achieving not only economic, but also social benefits, consensus is growing that a high level of protection is needed.[1] The regulatory approach to personal data protection is already well established in the EU. Worldwide, the first data protection law was enacted by the German federal state of Hesse in 1970,[2] while Sweden passed the first national law in 1973, followed by Germany in 1977 and France in 1978.[3] The EU

[1] V. Reding (European Commission Vice President and Commissioner for Justice, Fundamental Rights and Citizenship) and J. Bryson (US Secretary of Commerce), 'EU-U.S. Joint Statement on Data Protection', European Commission MEMO12/192 (19 March 2012), available at: http://europa.eu/rapid/pressReleasesAction.do?reference=MEMO/12/192&format=HTML&aged=0&language=EN&guiLanguage=en (accessed 31 December 2013) ('[t]his is a defining moment for global personal data protection and privacy policy and for further interoperability of our systems on a high level of protection').

[2] The Hesse Data Protection Act ('*Hessisches Datenschutzgesetz*'); in Europe, the original German expression referring to 'data protection' is still employed, despite the fact that, strictly speaking, it is not the data that are protected, but the rights of individuals whose data are handled.

[3] Forerunner to those legislative initiatives was the 1968 Council of Europe's Recommendation 509 on human rights and modern scientific and technological developments, stating that 'newly developed techniques such as phone-tapping, eavesdropping, surreptitious observation, the illegitimate use of official statistical and similar surveys to obtain private information, and subliminal advertising and propaganda are a threat to the rights and freedoms of individuals and, in particular, to the right to privacy'.

Data Protection Directive still in force today was adopted in 1995[4] and its influence on the development of data protection legislation extends well beyond Europe.[5]

Recently, the European Commission has decided to propose substantial changes (a reform package) to the current legal framework.[6] Even in the market-friendly US landscape, the Federal Trade Commission (FTC)[7] and the White House[8] do not ignore the pressing need to make the protection covering personal data more effective. It is not hard to anticipate that competition among comprehensive data protection systems, at present mitigated by the EU's dominance, will likely intensify in the near future.

Seemingly, legal provisions impinging on the commercial gathering and use of personal data have a significant impact on a variety of economic activities. In particular, personal data have become an essential element of many entrepreneurial activities characterizing the so-called Internet economy. The OECD in 2008 described personal data as the basic currency of the information economy,[9] contributing in a significant way to competitiveness and economic growth. Thus, for instance, while consumers browse the web, data are generated and then used for boosting online advertising, and the latter in turn supports an ever-expanding array of services available to users; moreover, those data are used with the purpose of optimizing products and services.[10] It follows that regulation

---

4 However, it should be remembered that the European Parliament has been calling on the Commission to work on a legislative instrument since 1975.

5 G. Greenleaf, 'The Influence of European Data Privacy Standards Outside Europe: Implications for Globalisation of Convention 108' (2012) 2 *Int'l Data Priv. L.* 68.

6 See at section 2 below.

7 See FTC, 'Protecting Consumer Privacy in an Era of Rapid Change: Recommendations for Businesses and Policymakers' (2012), available at: http://www.ftc.gov/os/2012/03/120326privacyreport.pdf (accessed 31 December 2013).

8 In particular, the Obama Administration called on Congress to pass the Consumer Privacy Bill of Rights, see The White House, 'Consumer Data Privacy in a Networked World: A Framework for Protecting Privacy and Promoting Innovation in the Global Digital Economy' (2012), available at: http://www.whitehouse.gov/sites/default/files/privacy-final.pdf (accessed 31 December 2013).

9 A. Gurría (Secretary-General of OECD), 'On the Future of the Internet Economy', Closing remarks to the 2008 OECD Ministerial Meeting (18 June 2008), available at: http://www.oecd.org/document/8/0,3343,en_2649_34487_40863240_1_1_1_1,00.html (31 December 2013).

10 C. Tucker, 'The Economic Value of Online Customer Data', Background Document to the Joint WPISP-WPIE Roundtable 'The Economics of Personal

stalling the use of personal data in advertising-supported Internet platforms is likely to negatively affect a series of current web-related economic activities. Ideally, a satisfactory level of data protection should not ultimately result in less dynamic markets and less competition. Still, the regulatory approach to privacy considers consumers to be much more fragile, and markets considerably more prone to failure, than the ecumenical competition policy approach. Whereas companies compromising consumers' privacy might at times encounter bad publicity affecting their businesses, consumers, generally, trade away their privacy with much less compunction than is necessary for a predominantly market-based solution to data protection issues.

While *ad hoc* regulation plays the primary role in ensuring the protection of privacy, at least in the EU, a few market practices involving personal data could attract the earnest attention of competition authorities. Recently, EU Competition Commissioner Joaquin Almunia, while acknowledging that '[w]hen unfair or manipulative commercial practices become pervasive in a market to the detriment of consumers and users the matter is best resolved with regulation', remarked that 'competition policy should … be vigilant *vis-à-vis* the implications of the use of commercial data', such as a single dominant company infringing 'privacy laws to gain an advantage over its competitors'. Commissioner Almunia further stressed the necessity to 'strike the right balance between regulation and competition policy enforcement' and called for 'a proper governance of privacy rights and of the commercial use of personal data'.[11]

Almunia's short remarks contain a significant reference to the more general issue of the interface between competition law and regulation. In the EU Commissioner's own words, the pervasiveness of the commercial practices damaging consumers' privacy prove the need for an *ad hoc* regulatory intervention, addressing market failures/problems more effectively than by way of *ex post* competition rules. In this respect, the reach of competition policy on issues involving consumer privacy occupies a somewhat residual area. Thus, for instance, as illustrated by Commissioner Almunia himself, when firms, in order to gain a competitive

---

Data and Privacy: 30 Years after the OECD Privacy Guidelines' (1 December 2010), available at: http://www.oecd.org/internet/interneteconomy/46968839.pdf (accessed 31 December 2013).

[11] J. Almunia, 'Competition and Personal Data Protection', Remarks to the meeting of the Privacy Platform Initiative (26 November 2012), available at: http://europa.eu/rapid/press-release_SPEECH-12-860_en.htm?locale=en (accessed 31 December 2013).

advantage, do not abide by those privacy provisions, there would be room for intervention also by competition authorities.

The interface between competition law and data protection regulation, however, could prove to be slightly more elusive than the previous example would seem to suggest. If there is a significant level of promising complementarity between the two policy areas, there is also some room for potential conflict. Thus, for instance, overly strict privacy provisions might pose serious restraints on the firms' commercial operations, thus causing markets to perform less competitively. Still, in spite of its relevance, the assessment of data protection regulation from a pro-competition perspective is comparatively underdeveloped.[12] The already mentioned reform package announced by the Commission in January 2012 contains just a few provisions that have attracted some attention from competition policy scholars.[13] Moreover, if competition policy might be effective in sanctioning private practices not adequately controlled by *ad hoc* regulation, the relevant question would be whether the mere exercise of the regulatory oversight on the questionable practice, or even its requirement under specific privacy obligations, could suffice to make that conduct immune from competition scrutiny.[14]

The remainder of the chapter proceeds as follows. Section 2 briefly illustrates the evolution of data protection regulation in the EU and highlights the most significant provisions of the January 2012 reform proposals. Section 3 makes the central point that the impact of data protection regulation on competition and market processes needs to be carefully scrutinized, and continues by analysing a few specific elements of the reform package from a pro-competition perspective. Section 4 reflects in particular on the scope of general competition policy at the intersection with data protection regulation.

---

[12] See, however, for an early exception R.C. Picker, 'Competition and Privacy in Web 2.0 and the Cloud' (2008) 103 *Nw. U. L. Rev. Colloquy* 1, 10–11, available at: http://www.law.northwestern.edu/lawreview/colloquy/2008/25/LRColl2008n25Picker.pdf (accessed 31 December 2013).

[13] See at section 3 below.

[14] See at section 4 below.

2. THE EVOLUTION OF THE DATA PROTECTION LEGAL FRAMEWORK IN THE EU

2.1 The 1995 Data Protection Directive

If the public and private record keeping of individual data is a very old phenomenon, well-known advancements in computer science dating back to the mid-1960s have made it a much more cost-effective, pervasive, and potentially rewarding activity. Since its emergence in Europe in the 1970s, data protection regulation has been perceived as an integral element of consumer protection. In some jurisdictions, the missions of protecting consumers and protecting markets are assigned to a single authority. However, on the European side of the Atlantic,[15] data protection authorities must be separate entities enjoying 'complete independence',[16] as they are 'an essential component of the protection of individuals with regard to the processing of personal data'.[17]

Most importantly, according to EU legislation, the right to protection of personal data is a fundamental human right. Article 8 of the Charter of Fundamental Rights of the European Union, to which the Lisbon Treaty conferred treaty status, states that '[e]veryone has the right to the protection of personal data concerning him or her'. Moreover, Article 16 of the Treaty on the Functioning of the European Union (the previous Treaty Establishing the European Community), reiterates and reinforces

---

[15] The situation is different for instance in the US, where there is no independent data protection authority; see FTC Commissioner J. Brill, 'Privacy, Consumer Protection, and Competition', Keynote speech at the 12th Annual Loyola Antitrust Colloquium (27 April 2012) 3, available at: http://www.ftc.gov/speeches/brill/120427loyolasymposium.pdf (accessed January 2013). If a stand-alone US data protection authority develops in the future, this will likely be a spin-off from the FTC's present activities; see also W.E. Kovacic, 'The Institutions of Antitrust Law: How Structure Shapes Substance' (2012) 110 *Mich. L. Rev.* 1019, 1031.

[16] Article 28(1) of Directive 95/46/EC of the European Parliament and of the Council of 24 October 1995 on the protection of individuals with regard to the processing of personal data and on the free movement of such data, [1995] OJ L 281, p. 31.

[17] Case C-518/07 *Commission v. Germany* [2010] ECR I-1885, para. 23. More recently, the Court of Justice ruled that the Austrian Data Protection Authority did not fulfil the requirements of independence as outlined in the European Data Protection Directive; see C-614/10 *Commission v. Austria* [2012] ECR I-0000 (not yet published).

that right by stating that '[e]veryone has the right to the protection of personal data concerning them'.[18]

The core of data protection regulation in the EU lies in Directive 95/46/EC (Data Protection Directive).[19] The EU Directive, following in the footsteps of the Council of Europe[20] Convention 108 for the Protection of Individuals with regard to Automatic Processing of Personal Data,[21] introduces a general legal framework for data protection for EU Member States, though it excludes from its scope the processing of data by justice and home affairs authorities. The 1995 Directive was conceived also as an instrument to lift obstacles to the development of the internal market (the 'first pillar'). In fact, it was feared that episodes of data blocking from high to low protection countries, due to a lack of harmonization between Member States' legislation on data protection, could have hampered cross-border trade within Europe. Based on the Data Protection Directive, a substantial layer of common principles and derived legal concepts are in place throughout the EU, referring, among other matters, to the activity of data gathering and processing, to the rights of the 'data subjects', and to sanctions.

The Directive broadly defines 'personal data' as all information relating to an identified or identifiable natural person, either directly or indirectly.[22] Recital 26 of the Directive adds that 'the principles of protection shall not apply to data rendered anonymous in such a way that the data subject is no longer identifiable'.

---

[18] In pre-Lisbon times, fundamental rights in EU law found protection in particular in an indirect way, by way of reference to general principles of EU law. General principles of EU law derive from constitutional traditions common to Member States, e.g. the right to pursue a commercial activity, rights to defence, privacy, proportionality, etc. The Charter of Fundamental Rights of the EU, signed and 'proclaimed' by the Presidents of the Parliament, Council and Commission in Nice on 7 December 2000, was addressed to EU institutions and Member States. In a 2005 Communication, the Commission committed to be bound by the Charter. Still, the Court of Justice in 2006 affirmed that the Charter was an auxiliary source of EU law, not a legally binding instrument; see C-540/03 *Parliament v. Council* [2006] ECR I-5769, para. 38.

[19] Directive 95/46/EC (n. 16 above).

[20] Founded in 1949, the Council of Europe is a separate body from the European Union, comprising 47 members and 800 million Europeans. Its priorities are the respect of human rights, democracy and the rule of law.

[21] Convention 108 for the Protection of individuals with regard to automatic processing of personal data of 28 January 1981, available at: http://conventions.coe.int/Treaty/en/Treaties/Html/108.htm (accessed 31 December 2013).

[22] Article 2(a) Data Protection Directive.

With regard specifically to the collection and processing of personal data, Article 18 imposes a general obligation to notify all data processing operations to the data protection authorities. However, Member States were given ample room for determining broad exemptions from the notification requirement, for instance in the case that the 'data controller'[23] should ensure internal control of data processing operations by appointing a data protection officer. Article 6 sets out a list of principles 'relating to data quality', among others that personal data must be 'not excessive' in relation to the purposes for which they are collected and/or further processed. Article 7, also in list form, indicates the conditions under which personal data can be processed, such as on the basis of informed and meaningful consent to data processing by the data subject, and on the basis of a legal obligation. Moreover, processing is permitted after having conducted a balance of interest between 'the purposes of the legitimate interests pursued by the controller or by the third party or parties to whom the data are disclosed' and 'the interests for fundamental rights and freedoms of the data subject which require protection under Article 1(1)'.

Additional protection is afforded to the categories of sensitive personal data, defined in Article 8(1), as 'personal data revealing racial or ethnic origin, political opinions, religious or philosophical beliefs, trade-union membership, and the processing of data concerning health or sex life', which may be processed by private and public bodies only for specific purposes and under special conditions and safeguards.[24] Articles 10 and 11 provide for the obligation of the data controller or his representative to inform that data subject as to the identity of the controller, the purposes of the processing and to provide any further information 'in so far as such further information is necessary, having regard to the specific circumstances in which the data are collected, to guarantee fair processing in respect of the data subject'.

As to the specific rights of the data subject *vis-à-vis* those processing her personal data, the Directive provides in particular for the right to access, rectify, block and delete one's own data. With regard to the

---

[23] The 'data controller' refers to the natural or legal person or body which – alone or jointly with others – determines the purposes and means of processing; see Article 2(d) Data Protection Directive. Thus, for instance, social network providers are in principle considered data controllers according to the Directive.

[24] Article 8(2), specifies some exceptions to the rule, such as where '(a) the data subject has given his explicit consent to the processing of those data, except where the laws of the Member State provide that the prohibition referred to in paragraph 1 may not be lifted by the data subject's giving his consent'.

enforcement in the case of infringement of the provisions adopted pursuant to the Directive, data protection authorities hear and review claims or complaints and are charged with investigating possible infringements.[25] Moreover, data subjects are entitled by ordinary administrative or civil law to go to court and seek redress and corrective action.

2.2 The 2012 'Reform Package'

As mentioned above, the 1995 Directive was specifically tailored to respond to the needs of data protection as they were emerging at the beginning of the 1990s. Since then, technologies, markets and user behaviour have changed in ways very difficult to predict before. For instance, cloud computing and social networks could hardly have been anticipated in 1995. Among the most significant developments of the last two decades are the increased capacities to store vast quantities of digital information, the significant improvements in methods of so-called data mining or analysis, the new possibilities to connect devices, and the employment of Web 2.0 technologies in the marketing of products and services, such as behavioural advertising. The networked society we live in, in which personal data are continuously collected, enriched, amended, exchanged, and reused, presents much higher risks but also somehow very different risks of abuse than the ones anticipated at the end of the last millennium. Moreover, in our globalized society, state borders play even less of a role today than they did 18 years ago. In particular, cross-border data processing and international transfers have significantly increased since the Data Protection Directive was enacted. As stated by the OECD in 2011, the challenges for privacy regulations are 'to reflect the broader scale of today's uses of personal data with a view to more effectively protecting a fundamental value and to foster both individual trust and the economic and social benefits associated with responsible and innovative uses of personal data'.[26] Finally, behind the Commission's decision to propose a new legal framework, there were also the results of

---

[25] Member States have the obligation to lay down the sanctions provided for in cases of infringement. Apart from administrative fines, in some countries also criminal sanctions are imposed.

[26] OECD, 'Terms of Reference for the Review of the OECD Guidelines Governing the Protection of Privacy and Transborder Data Flows of Personal Data' (2011) 4, available at: http://www.oecd.org/sti/ieconomy/48975226.pdf (accessed 31 December 2013).

two successive implementation reports[27] of the Directive, which pointed to a wide array of unresolved problems, especially with regard to significant differences in the level of data protection afforded in the Member States, which hampered the internal market policy objective.

On 25 January 2012, the European Commission adopted a comprehensive package aimed at reforming the EU rules on data protection, including a proposal for a Regulation containing the general rules on data protection[28] and a proposal for a Directive on data protection in the law enforcement sector. The Commission's stated aim was to provide a consistent and high level of data protection in the EU. The proposed Regulation is supposed to replace the current Directive 95/46/EC and, being directly applicable in the Member States, it would create a single source for legal provisions on data protection throughout the EU, without the usual country-by-country variation normally following the adoption of a Directive.[29] One of the main aims of the regulation is in fact to remove some of the costs due to so-called legal fragmentation, that is, the costs of having to comply with the data protection laws of other Member States.[30] Since the Regulation would have clear priority over any national

---

[27] Report from the Commission – First Report on the implementation of the Data Protection Directive (95/46/EC) (15 May 2003), COM (2003) 265 final; Communication from the Commission to the European Parliament and the Council on the follow-up of the Work Programme for better implementation of the Data Protection Directive, [2007] OJ C 255, p. 1.

[28] Proposal for a regulation of the European Parliament and of the Council on the protection of individuals with regard to the processing of personal data and on the free movement of such data (General Data Protection Regulation): COM (2012) 11 final (25 January 2012).

[29] If referring to a Regulation would create a one-stop shop, there is, however, some space for reconciling uniform data protection rules with national specificities, such as possible exemptions and derogations stated in specific national rules that relate to freedom of expression, health, employment, professional secrecy and churches and religious associations. Moreover, Article 21 would permit Member State law to restrict the scope of certain provisions in the Regulation to protect public interests, such as those linked to criminal offences, regulated professions and important economic or financial matters. To this (hopefully limited) extent, there will still be the need to refer to the legislation in different Member States.

[30] The costs of legal fragmentation are basically made up of translation costs, legal assessment works, and clerical work. Under the current Data Protection Directive, data controllers are affected by the data protection legislation of another Member State if they are established in that other Member State and processing is done in the context of that other establishment. According to the

law not compatible with it,[31] in a few instances the level of protection currently enjoyed in some Member States could well be reduced.[32]

However, the way towards the approval of the reform package is a long and tortuous one. The tabled proposals are currently subject to analysis by the European Parliament and will be subject to further negotiations in the Council. The Commission has indicated 2014 as a possible time for enactment, and, in any case, Member States will have two more years to amend their national legislation before the Regulation comes into force.

If the Commission considers that 'there is general agreement that the current framework remains sound as far as its objectives and principles are concerned',[33] the Regulation Proposal would nevertheless firmly reinforce the position of the data subjects. Thus, Article 7 strengthens the exercise and the necessity of consent, which will have to be explicit, and a company will have the burden of proving that every subject has given consent for the processing of their data for specified purposes. The law defines consent as 'any freely given specific, informed and explicit indication of will'. Moreover, the Commission intends to strengthen some of the individual rights already foreseen by the Directive, in particular regulating the right to the portability of data[34] and the right to be forgotten.

As for enforcement, the proposed Regulation aims at making remedies and sanctions more effective. It would introduce a right for organizations or associations defending data subjects' rights and interests to lodge a complaint before a supervisory authority or to bring an action to court.[35] Importantly, a fine of up to 2 per cent of the violator's worldwide annual

---

Commission, 'established' means having a retail outlet or subsidiary in another Member State.

[31] See Article 288 TFEU.

[32] See P. Blume, 'Will It Be a Better World? The Proposed EU Data Protection Regulation' (2012) 2 *Int'l Data Priv. L.* 130, 131 ff. for the example based on Danish law, providing for a special protection with respect to personal identity numbers (PINs), whereas within the framework of the proposed Regulation they would be considered as 'ordinary' personal data.

[33] Impact Assessment accompanying the proposed reform package, Commission Staff Working Paper (25 January 2012), SEC(2012) 72 final, 7, available at: http://ec.europa.eu/justice/data-protection/document/review2012/sec_2012_72_en.pdf (accessed 31 December 2013).

[34] At section 3.3 below.

[35] So far the European Commission has abstained from proposing mandatory collective redress mechanisms and, more recently, opted for a non-binding Recommendation. See Commission Recommendation of 11 June 2013 on common principles for injunctive and compensatory redress mechanisms in the

turnover could be imposed (up to €1 million). Furthermore, EU law would be applicable to undertakings established outside the EU but offering goods and services to people in the EU or monitoring the behaviour of 'data subjects' in the Union, that is, individuals who can reasonably be identified from the data in question.

From a more institutional perspective, it is particularly noteworthy that the Regulation would significantly reinforce the role and powers of national supervisory authorities, both alone and jointly. As already mentioned, the Regulation would establish a one-stop shop for individuals and organizations. The data protection authority of the Member State where a controller has its main establishment or residence is deemed the authority competent for the supervision of processing activities in all Member States. Cooperation among the supervisory authorities is also reinforced, and obligations to exchange information or organize joint investigations are introduced. In situations where there is no establishment in the EU and where the processing activities are related to the offering of goods and services to data subjects in the Union or the monitoring of their behaviour, however, any data protection authority whose Member State is affected by processing operations is competent according to Article 51(1), but the Regulation lacks rules on which authority in these cases should take the lead.

The Regulation also clarifies and structures the role of the European Data Protection Board, ensuring its independence through the provision of a secretariat independent from the Commission. In particular, any authority can request that any matter be dealt with by the Board. Moreover, according to the draft Regulation, the authorities may, acting on the request of their respective nationals, challenge another authority's decision. In this way, the institutional setting foresees a certain level of competition between the national supervisory authorities.

However, the reinforced role of the supervisory authorities does not deprive the Commission of significant powers. In particular, the Commission can trigger the so-called 'consistency mechanism' by seizing the Board, but it may also adopt an opinion and a suspending decision according to the conditions of Articles 58 and 59, and even overrule a decision of a national supervisory authority in a specific matter by way of adopting an implementing act.

Member States concerning violations of rights granted under Union Law, [2013] OJ L 201, p. 60.

3. THE EU REGULATORY APPROACH: CLOSE-UP FROM A PRO-COMPETITION PERSPECTIVE

3.1 The Current Debate Surrounding the Proposed Reform Package

The reform package put forth by the Commission in January 2012 has attracted much attention. This is unsurprising, particularly considering that the proposed regulatory complex is likely to have a significant impact on a wide range of organizations, both from the private and the public sector, comprising those organizations established outside the EU that process the personal data of data subjects residing in the EU when offering them goods or services or monitoring their behaviour.

The harmonization of data protection rules by means of regulation is likely to lead to a reduction in administrative burdens for businesses operating in more than one Member State. However, the proposed Regulation aims also at inducing organizations to take a more pro-active approach to data protection, and this necessarily would imply some extra costs of compliance with European data protection provisions. Thus, in particular, businesses need to demonstrate compliance with the regulation,[36] notify data protection breaches to the supervisory authority,[37] employ data protection officers pursuant to Article 35(1), and carry out data protection impact assessments. In this respect, some have expressed the view that the proposed data protection regulation would impose more burdens on organizations than benefits.[38]

Others have pointed out that some of the new obligations imposed on data controllers such as the above-mentioned 'right to be forgotten' are

---

[36] The proposed Regulation imposes a general obligation on data controllers to demonstrate compliance with data protection obligations. Article 28 also requires that each processor and controller keep up all administration of processing activities unless they employ fewer than 250 people and process personal data only as an activity ancillary to their main activities; thus it applies to large organizations and smaller businesses classified as carrying out risky processing. Article 35 of the proposed Regulation states that the data protection officer must be designated when certain requirements are fulfilled, namely, the processing is carried out by a public authority or by a business employing 250 people or more, or the core activities of the controller or the processor require regular and systematic monitoring of the data subjects.

[37] At section 3.2 below.

[38] See the UK Ministry of Justice's Impact Assessment of the Proposal for an EU Data Protection Regulation, November 2012, stating that the EU Commission has overestimated the savings that less legal fragmentation could bring to businesses, and underestimated the extra costs arising from having to comply

neither reasonable nor feasible.[39] Further criticism has been attracted in particular regarding the system of mandatory administrative sanctions for intentional or negligent infringements of the Regulation, which is considered to some extent excessive. In place of this it has been suggested that wider provision should be made for warnings or reprimands, as well as for mitigating factors in determining the level of pecuniary sanctions.[40]

Perhaps the most serious argument put forward against the Regulation, though, is that its 'overly prescriptive' nature is likely to stifle competition, innovation and therefore growth.[41] It should be recalled, however, that roughly the same argument was made around the year 1995, when the European Directive was passed, but the undeniable successes harvested by the so-called digital economy since that period would seem to give this argument little support *ex post*.[42] Still, we cannot be sure that, had the European legislation been somewhat less restrictive, in the period since its introduction *fiercer* competition and even *higher* levels of innovation would not have been experienced in Europe.

Despite their relevance, in-depth reflections concerning the likely impact of data protection regulation on competition processes are rather scarce, and the competition dimension of privacy plays only a marginal role in the framework of the current discussions concerning the revision

---

with the new requirements, available at: https://consult.justice.gov.uk/digital-communications/data-protection-proposals-cfe/results/eu-data-protection-reg-impact-assessment.pdf (accessed 31 December 2013).

[39] See J. Rosen, 'The Right to be Forgotten' (2012) 64 *Stan. L. Rev. Online* 88, available at http://www.stanfordlawreview.org/sites/default/files/online/topics/64-SLRO-88.pdf (accessed 31 December 2013).

[40] See Irish Presidency of the Council of the European Union, Discussion Paper prepared for the Informal Justice and Home Affairs Ministers' Meeting, Dublin 17–18 January 2013, available at http://www.eu2013.ie/media/eupresidency/content/documents/FINAL-Discussion-paper-on-data-protection-for-Informal-JHA-Council.doc (accessed 31 December 2013)

[41] C. Timburg, 'U.S. Firms, Officials Resisting Europe's Push for Stronger Digital Privacy Rules' *Washington Post* (25 January 2013), available at: http://www.washingtonpost.com/business/economy/us-firms-officials-resisting-europes-push-for-stronger-digital-privacy-rules/2013/01/24/1ae712e6-61ab-11e2-b05a-605528f6b712_story.html (accessed 31 December 2013) ('officials from the Commerce Department and the U.S. Mission to the European Union have largely echoed industry concerns that the bill could hinder innovation and economic growth worldwide').

[42] See C. Bennett, 'The Geo-Politics of Personal Data' *Harv. Int'l Rev.* (14 December 2012), available at: http://hir.harvard.edu/the-geo-politics-of-personal-data (accessed 31 December 2013).

of the reform package in the context of the different EU institutions.[43] Even though personal data protection as a human right can hardly be seen as the potential victim of some obscure blend of economic trade-offs, broad competition policy considerations could at a minimum enrich the current, at times rather muddled policy debate. In particular, the argument that privacy has increasingly become a competitive dimension should be carefully considered.[44] In this vein, the following part of this section is devoted to a brief analysis of two elements of the reform package that would seem particularly significant from a pro-competition perspective.[45]

3.2 Requirement to Notify Personal Data Breaches

Article 31(1) of the draft Regulation requires 'data controllers' to notify the supervisory authority of personal data breaches without undue delay and, where feasible, within 24 hours. Under the current 1995 Directive, there is no general obligation on data controllers to report breaches of security which result in loss, release or corruption of personal data.[46] Businesses are solely required to notify the supervisory authority of their processing activities, unless exemptions apply.[47] Presently, when personal

---

[43] For an 'early' understanding of the influence of the regulation of 'data streams' both on privacy and competition processes see Picker (n. 12 above) 3.

[44] See FTC, 'On the Need for Privacy Protections: Perspectives From the Administration and the Federal Trade Commission', Statement Before the Committee on Commerce, Science, and Transportation, U.S. Senate (9 May 2012) 4, available at: http://ftc.gov/os/testimony/120509privacyprotections.pdf (accessed 31 December 2013) ('Companies should improve their privacy disclosures and work toward standardizing them so that consumers, advocacy groups, regulators, and others can compare data practices and choices across companies, thus promoting competition among companies').

[45] As required by the 2009 European Commission Impact Assessment Guidelines, an *ex ante* analysis of the impact on effective competition forms part of the 'reform package'; see Annex 10 of the Impact Assessment (n. 33 above). The analysis is merely focused on the overall 'cost and price competitiveness', hence it does not offer any detailed analysis of core provisions.

[46] There is however a general obligation to notify national data protection authorities of the automatic processing of personal data, pursuant to Article 18 of the Data Protection Directive, an obligation that the reform package aims at abolishing.

[47] Several data protection authorities charge for notifications, their fee ranging from €23 to €599; see Impact Assessment 14 (n. 33 above).

data are for instance lost, altered, accessed by or disclosed to unauthorized persons, such breaches can be reported voluntarily to the data protection authority.[48]

Moreover, Article 32(1) of the draft Regulation provides for the obligation of the data controller to notify the personal data breach to the data subject without undue delay '[w]hen the personal data breach is likely to adversely affect the protection of the personal data or privacy of the data subject'.

The new requirement is likely to impose on data controllers additional costs that could be significant, especially for small and medium-sized businesses.[49] From the viewpoint of a pro-competitive approach to data protection, however, the requirement introduced by the Directive appears very important. Valuable information about on-going breaches is a precondition for competition in privacy to work properly. If users react to those personal data breaches for instance by switching to a different social network or health insurance, the company involved will likely suffer a financial loss that might work as a powerful stimulus towards a more effective approach to data protection.

The choice of the appropriate threshold for notification to data subjects is critical in this respect, especially in order to avoid so-called notification fatigue and de-sensitization.[50] Thus, it seems appropriate to limit the scope of the notification obligation to 'serious' events, as the draft Regulation proposes. Article 32(5) states that the Commission can provide guidance concerning circumstances in which a personal data breach is likely to adversely affect the personal data as referred to in Paragraph 1. However, it would have seemed more appropriate to clarify those circumstances within the text of the Regulation itself.

---

[48] The revised e-Privacy Directive already introduced such a requirement for providers of publicly available electronic communications services, e.g. providers of Internet access; see Article 29 Data Protection Working Party, 'Working Document 01/2011 on the current EU personal data breach framework and recommendations for future policy developments' (5 April 2011), available at: http://ec.europa.eu/justice/policies/privacy/docs/wpdocs/2011/wp184_en.pdf (accessed 31 December 2013). Still, some countries, like Germany, had already enacted legal provisions setting forth a personal data breach framework applicable across sectors.

[49] See the EU Commission's Impact Assessment (n. 33 above).

[50] See BEUC, 'Position Paper on Data Protection – Proposal for a Regulation' (27 July 2012), available at: http://epic.org/privacy/BEUC-Position-Paper.pdf (accessed 31 December 2013).

3.3 Data Portability

Another much-debated element of the reform package is the proposal to introduce a right to data portability, as put forward in Article 18 of the draft Regulation.[51] Article 8(2) of the EU Charter of Fundamental Rights states that 'everyone has the right of access to data which has been collected concerning him or her, and the right to have it rectified'. Pursuant to Article 12 of the Data Protection Directive, individuals already have the right to access their personal data, and in particular to obtain from the data controller communication 'in an intelligible form of the data undergoing processing', but the form of the communication is not specified, the way in which that right can be exercised varies considerably from country to country within the EU, and that access has become particularly challenging in connection with the online environment.[52]

Pursuant to the proposed Article 18 of the Regulation, data subjects could, first, obtain a copy of their personal data 'processed by electronic means and in a structured[53] and commonly used format'. The copy itself must be 'an electronic and structured format which is commonly used and allows for further use by the data subject'. Furthermore, individuals would be granted the explicit right to transfer 'personal data and any other information provided by the data subject and retained by an automated processing system' into another automated processing system 'where the data subject has provided the personal data and the processing is based on consent or on a contract'. The transfer should be 'without hindrance by the controller', and data should be 'in an electronic format which is commonly used'. Article 18(3) gives the Commission the power

---

[51] The right of number portability is already well known from the telecoms sector. See Article 30 Directive 2002/22/EC on universal service and users' rights relating to electronic communications networks and services, [2002] OJ L 108, p. 51, as amended by Directive 2009/136/EC, [2009] OJ L 337 p. 11; consolidated version available at: http://eur-lex.europa.eu/legal-content/EN/TXT/?uri=CELEX:02009L0136-20091219 (accessed 31 December 2013).

[52] See the EU Commission's Impact Assessment (n. 33 above), 27 ('individuals can access their own data more easily in some Member States than in others').

[53] The Draft Regulation does not specify, however, what a 'structured' format is. Commonly, unstructured data do not reside in a fixed location, like for instance pdf files, e-mail messages or blogs. Examples of structured data would be, for instance, spreadsheets.

to specify the electronic format and the 'technical standards, modalities and procedures for the transmission of personal data'.[54]

Article 18 should be read against the background of Article 15 of the draft Regulation, which provides for the 'general' right of access for the data subject. Article 15 states that the data subject has the right to obtain communication of the personal data undergoing processing from the controller, but the main difference is that Article 18 specifically deals with the condition for reuse of the data, by the data subject herself and/or by another automated processing system.

As seen above, Article 18(2) introduces the right to export personal data and other information provided by a data subject to another service 'without hindrance' by the controller. It is not clear, however, if this would involve an affirmative obligation on the part of the controller to transfer data directly to another service, that is, to provide for some degree of interoperability between electronic processing systems.[55] The data that the individual has the right to transfer should be in electronic form. As mentioned before, the Regulation would give the Commission the power to specify the electronic format and the further technical requirements for allowing the transmission of personal data.

The new requirement would apply across sectors, whenever automated processing systems of personal data are involved, affecting, among other things, the above-mentioned cloud computing services and smartphone applications. The exercise of this new right would imply, for instance, that a user may decide that data placed in one cloud computing environment should be moved to a different cloud computing environment.

This provision is likely to be costly for data controllers to implement. For instance, cloud computing providers currently do not employ standard data formats and service interfaces allowing for portability between competing providers.[56] Moreover, the exercise of the right to data

---

[54] Moreover, in compliance with legislation, a copy of the data must remain with the original controller for a given period in order to comply with specific accounting, tax and similar regulations.

[55] See P. Swire and Y. Lagos, 'Why the Right to Data Portability Likely Reduces Consumer Welfare: Antitrust and Privacy Critique' (2013) 72 *Md. L. Rev.* 335, 339, also available at: http://digitalcommons.law.umaryland.edu/cgi/viewcontent.cgi?article=3550&context=mlr (accessed 31 December 2013).

[56] See Article 29 Data Protection Working Party, 'Opinion 05/2012 on Cloud Computing' (1 July 2012) 16, available at: http://ec.europa.eu/justice/data-protection/article-29/documentation/opinion-recommendation/files/2012/wp196_en.pdf (accessed 31 December 2013).

portability could have a negative impact on currently successful business models based on the gathering, exclusive control and monetization of consumers' data.[57] Still, and more generally, it could be of substantial benefit to consumers and competition, not only in terms of price but also regarding privacy-enhancing characteristics. For instance, if a data subject can access and retrieve precise information from the controller concerning her usage of a specific paid-for service, like mobile telecommunication, she can use those data to search for the most suitable market tariff, and avoid the less attractive contracts. The benefit to consumers will be seen especially in terms of the reduced costs of searching for better deals. Additionally, by being able to access all of their usage data, consumers can more easily put pressure on firms to compete to offer them the most attractive price and other conditions. This not only leads to increased competition but also to the development of new services and perhaps even new intermediary firms set up to enable consumers to find the most suitable offer.[58] Moreover, the right of data portability would enable data subjects whose data is locked into a specific service to move to a better service, stimulating quality competition in the market.[59] Whilst the right to data portability can arguably increase competition among data controllers operating in the same market,[60] more competition among data controllers could transform into incentives to adequately take care of the data subjects' increasing privacy concerns.[61] Individuals should be given the effective right to freely choose and freely change the best privacy environments for their personal

---

[57] Placing restrictions on behavioural advertising would also limit the ability of businesses to charge higher prices by targeting those customers with a higher marginal willingness to pay.

[58] See 'Know Thyself: Data Lockers Promise to Help People Profit from their Personal Information', *The Economist* (15 December 2012), available at: http://www.economist.com/news/business/21568438-data-lockers-promise-help-people-profit-their-personal-information-know-thyself (accessed 31 December 2013).

[59] See Directorate General for Internal Policies, 'Reforming the Data Protection Package' (2012) 61, available at: http://www.europarl.europa.eu/document/activities/cont/201209/20120928ATT52488/20120928ATT52488EN.pdf (accessed 31 December 2013).

[60] See P.J. Harbour and T.I. Koslov, 'Section 2 in a Web 2.0 World: An Expanded Vision of Relevant Product Markets' (2010), 76, *Antitrust L.J.* 749, 780.

[61] According to a recent survey, 70 per cent of Europeans are concerned that their personal data may be misused: see Special Eurobarometer 359, 'Attitudes on Data Protection and Electronic Identity in the European Union' (June 2011)

data. In this respect, a certain level of competition could help ensure that the fundamental right to privacy and data protection is sufficiently protected and respected by controllers.

The contours of the data portability right as provided for by Article 18 of the draft Regulation are not totally clear, though, in particular because most of the critical 'technicalities' (that is, electronic format and the technical standards, modalities and procedures for the transmission of personal data) are left to later clarifications by the Commission. Of course, standardization of data formats and other compatibility measures put forward by the Commission in a later phase should be conceived so as not to hamper those services from expressing their full functionalities. Furthermore, in the rather remote event that the language of Article 18 remains largely unaffected by the various negotiation phases the draft Regulation is currently going through, the effectiveness of the new right will critically depend on the interpretation of rather vague legal concepts like 'without hindrance'.[62]

146, available at: http://ec.europa.eu/public_opinion/archives/ebs/ebs_359_en.pdf (accessed 31 December 2013).

[62] See Swire and Lagos (n. 55 above) 344 ('Interpretation of "without hindrance" will substantially determine the reach of Article 18'). Even more uncertainty could be the result of the negotiations surrounding the reform package, though. A good example of this is the amendment proposal put forth by the J.P. Albrecht, Rapporteur for the European Parliament's Civil Liberties, Justice and Home Affairs Committee Draft Report on the Proposal for a General Data Protection Regulation, available at: http://www.europarl.europa.eu/meetdocs/2009_2014/documents/libe/pr/922/922387/922387en.pdf (accessed 31 December 2013). According to the proposal, Article 18 should be merged with Article 15. The Albrecht Draft Report, however, blurs the legal contours of the right to export personal data and other information to another service even further, in so far as it provides that the right should be exercised 'where technically feasible and appropriate'. The critical change in the text appears at least partially in line with the amendments suggested by the US Chamber of Commerce, 'Comments and Proposed Amendments to the General Data Protection Regulation' (September 2012), available at: http://www.uschamber.com/sites/default/files/grc/US%20Chamber%20comments%20on%20EU%20Data%20Protection %20Regulation%20Sept%202012.pdf (accessed 31 December 2013), and already contained in S. Kelly (Rapporteur), Draft Opinion of the Committee on Industry, Research and Energy for the Committee on Civil Liberties, Justice and Home Affairs (8 November 2012), available at: http://www.europarl.europa.eu/sides/getDoc.do?pubRef=-%2f%2fEP%2f%2fNONSGML%2bCOMPARL%2bPE-496.562%2b01%2bDOC%2bPDF%2bV0%2f%2fEN (accessed 31 December 2013).

4. THE INTERFACE WITH EU COMPETITION POLICY

4.1 On the Competition Dimension of Personal Data

As we have seen above, the protection of personal data in Europe has traditionally been a regulatory issue. So far, the European Commission has not handled any case involving data-driven anticompetitive practices under Article 102 TFEU.[63] In the context of merger control, at the time Google made public its plan to acquire DoubleClick, an online advertising company specializing in delivering ads to websites and tracking their performance, the question as to whether merger review should consider the implications of a single entity entrusted with vast amounts of personal information of web users was raised.[64] While paying due attention to those arguments, the competition authorities on both sides of the Atlantic were convinced that the merger review should consider the combination of the parties' databases solely from the perspective of negative effects on competition, and, following that analysis, the acquisition was unconditionally cleared.[65] The majority opinion of the US Federal Trade Commission approving the merger explained that it considered the argument that the combination of Google's and DoubleClick's 'data sets of consumer information could be exploited in a way that threatens consumers' privacy' to be unrelated to antitrust concerns in

[63] See Almunia (n. 11 above). The same lack of experience with data-driven practices also characterizes the antitrust enforcement on the other side of the Atlantic; see Harbour and Koslov (n. 60 above) 787.

[64] Commission Decision of 11 March 2008, Case COMP/M.4731 – *Google/DoubleClick*, [2008] OJ C 187, p. 10. See also E. Edwards, 'Stepping Up to the Plate: The Google-DoubleClick Merger and the Role of the Federal Trade Commission in Protecting Online Data Privacy' (2008), available at: http://ssrn.com/abstract=1370734 (accessed 31 December 2013); J. Brockhoff, B. Jehanno, V. Pozzato, C.-C. Buhr, P. Eberl and P. Papandropoulos, 'Google/DoubleClick: The First Test for the Commission's Non-horizontal Merger Guidelines' (2008) No. 2 *Competition Policy Newsletter* 53.

[65] Instead, according for instance to the Data Protection Commissioner for Schleswig-Holstein, the merger should have been approved only subject to the condition that transfer of consumer data between Google and DoubleClick be prohibited; see T. Weichert, 'Letter to Competition Commissioner Neelie Kroes' (26 September 2007), available at: https://www.datenschutzzentrum.de/suchmaschinen/20070926-doubleclick-google.html (accessed 31 December 2013).

merger analysis.[66] Nevertheless, the Federal Trade Commission investigated whether the proposed merger would adversely affect consumer privacy as a non-price attribute of competition and determined that this was not the case.[67] Similarly, the European Commission concluded that Google and DoubleClick were not direct competitors, and that the vertical dimension of the merger did not raise concerns about potential non-horizontal anticompetitive effects.[68]

The competition authorities' stance in *Google/DoubleClick* is not surprising. In fact, most competition scholars and practitioners would likely agree that privacy as such is not a competition issue.[69] However, given the increased economic importance of the 'asset' in question, competition authorities both in the US and the EU are increasingly aware that practices involving the accumulation, particular uses of, or dealings with personal data in the future could also become a matter of considerable interest to them.[70]

Undeniably, the concentration of user information can represent a significant competitive advantage. For instance, large platform providers may have the ability to track most of their users' online activities and monetize such information in the form of advertising and revenues from application developers.[71] It is well known that one core characteristic of

---

66 FTC, 'Statement of the Federal Trade Commission Concerning Google/DoubleClick', FTC File No. 071-0170 (20 December 2007) 2, available at: http://www.ftc.gov/system/files/documents/public_statements/418081/071220googledc-commstmt.pdf (accessed 31 December 2013).

67 Ibid., 12.

68 Case COMP/M.4731 – *Google/DoubleClick* (n. 64 above).

69 Indeed, some would even hold that a high level of data protection could ultimately result in less competition. See J.D. Campbell, A. Goldfarb and C. Tucker, 'Privacy Regulation and Market Structure' (2011), available at: http://ssrn.com/abstract=1729405 (accessed 31 December 2013). The authors hold that data protection could contain a bias in favour of incumbents and thereby disfavour start-ups; roughly the same point was recently made by FTC Commissioner M. Ohlhausen. See 'FTC Official Skeptical of Privacy Legislation', *National Journal* (16 October 2012), available at: http://techdailydose.nationaljournal.com/2012/10/ftc-official-skeptical-of-priv.php (accessed 31 December 2013).

70 See Almunia (n. 11 above).

71 J.T. Rosch, 'Intel, Apple, Google and Facebook: Observations on Antitrust and the High-Tech Sector', Remarks before the ABA Antitrust Section Fall Forum 18 (18 November 2010), available at: http://www.ftc.gov/speeches/rosch/101118fallforum.pdf (accessed 31 December 2013).

so-called Web 2.0[72] companies is their proficiency in dealing with the personal and additional data they control, on which they could possibly base their market dominance in Internet-related industries and also more traditional ones. In this context, it is not very difficult to see that, for instance, the refusal to facilitate data compatibility among competing services could under certain circumstances produce anti-competitive foreclosure effects.

The next question would then be how to adequately address personal data-related issues in the context of competition policy. In order to be demonstrated, alleged abuses of dominant position involving specific dealings with personal data will have to be based on convincing theories of harm. In this respect, it is worth noticing at the start that some characteristics of the markets for the control of personal data are not uncommon to other Internet-related industries.

In particular, business success in these markets critically depends on the creation and exploitation of network effects. Thus, for instance, a user joining a social network benefits from accessing and sharing personal data and different types of information with others, and the value to her is likely to increase with larger numbers of users. Positive network effects inherent in the market, however, could hamper entry by a rival social networking service and thereby help a firm achieve and maintain dominance in that market.

Several Internet-related markets share the further crucial characteristic that their services are not monetized directly, but by way of trading the data accumulated in interactions with their users. The most common revenue stream in this respect comes from behavioural advertising, but there are also other types of more or less specialized data usages and trading. In the remaining part of this section we briefly deal with the core Article 102 TFEU enforcement notions of market definition and assessment of abusive conduct when applied in the context of data markets (at 4.2 below); the last part is dedicated in particular to the issue of data protection obligations as possible defences against allegations of anti-competitive conduct (at 4.3 below).

---

[72] T. O'Reilly, 'What Is Web 2.0 – Design Patterns and Business Models for the Next Generation of Software' (1st quarter 2007) No. 65 *Communications & Strategies* 17, also available at: http://www.unige.ch/ses/socio/pdrs/programme/20072008/collectifsmorges/Communicationsstrategies.pdf (accessed 31 December 2013).

4.2 Article 102 TFEU and Data-driven Practices

Under the current Article 102 TFEU enforcement approach, the definition of the relevant markets is likely to be a delicate issue in assessing data-driven practices.[73] Under appropriate circumstances, it could even make sense to focus directly on the market for personal and related data in order to assess possible anti-competitive practices,[74] instead of on the various markets for the services offered in order to gather those personal data (such as social networks[75] and search engines), especially if we consider that the difficult exercise of market definition should aim at understanding how the different market players interact in the real world. Interestingly, different services could produce different types of 'knowledge' about users. Thus, users' data gathered via search could arguably be different from users' data gathered via social interactions. The relevant question here should be whether different types of knowledge sets could form separate markets for the sake of competition analysis.[76] Furthermore, the market for personal data gathered via online search and useful

---

[73] See OECD, 'Market Definition', Policy Roundtables (2012), 22, available at: http://www.oecd.org/daf/competition/Marketdefinition2012.pdf (accessed 31 December 2013) ('Traditionally, the first steps in every competition analysis are the definition of the relevant market, the identification of relevant competitors, the computation and assignment of market shares').

[74] See C. Butts, 'The Microsoft Case 10 Years Later: Antitrust and New Leading "New Economy" Firms' (2010) 8 *Nw. J. Tech. & Intell. Prop.* 275, 290 ('The true product Facebook brings to the "market" is not its technology, but the social information about, and access to, its vast user base').

[75] For a thorough discussion of social networks under competition law see S.W. Waller, 'Social Networks and the Law: Antitrust and Social Networking' (2011–2012) 90 *N.C. L. Rev.* 1771. The author speculates at length about the possibility of identifying a market for social networking sites, but also notes that 'the enforcement agencies and the courts examine multiple relevant markets in the same case or investigation, often from multiple perspectives', at 1779. 'Data markets' are considered in order to calculate actual market shares, together with 'user markets' (total page views/registered users) and 'advertising markets' (online display advertising/online and offline advertising markets). According to the author, social networking sites compete in a market for information that 'users post to their social networking sites or reveal through their communications with others', at 1784.

[76] For instance, former FTC Commissioner P.J. Harbour wrote in her dissenting statement on the *Google/DoubleClick* merger that the Commission could have defined 'a putative relevant product market comprising data that may be useful to advertisers and publishers who wish to engage in behavioral targeting'. See FTC File No. 071-0170, available at: http://www.ftc.gov/os/caselist/0710170/071220harbour.pdf (accessed 31 December 2013).

to those wanting to engage in targeted advertising could be different from the market for aggregated and anonymized data about users' preferences and Internet behaviour, gathered for instance by online advertisers using cookie-enabled tracking technologies.[77] However that may be, to the extent to which refined technologies are able to 'de-anonymize' data, that difference could significantly vanish.

If a market for personal data could be defined in the abstract, the next decisive step would be the delineation of the exact boundaries of this market and by that the identification of the relevant players in terms of significant competitive interactions. In the case of personal data gathered by way of online social interactions, it can be debated whether Facebook offers the same 'networking experience', and therefore engenders the same type of personal data 'disclosure', as LinkedIn, Twitter, or more specialized social networking sites like TripAdvisor. Furthermore, sites like Amazon are increasingly developing web-based tools enabling a few forms of social interaction, among book readers for instance, and the data gathered in this way are likely to be highly valuable not only to Amazon itself, but also to other players, in particular book publishers.

Beyond delicate issues pertaining to the definition of the relevant market, competition interventions in markets dealing with personal data will critically depend on the assessment of actual consumer harm. On the one hand, if the market is defined by the service offered to consumers, like for instance Internet search, users could be considered as 'paying more' for a specific service in case of a likely deterioration in the privacy conditions of use, that is, the quality of the service is reduced. According to a comprehensive Eurobarometer survey referring to the November–December 2010 period and published as part of the reform package, 70 per cent of Europeans are concerned that their personal data may be misused.[78] Assessing this particular sort of quality reduction under specific circumstances can prove to be particularly complex, though. Even if the dominant position of a particular undertaking on a specific data market is conclusively established, not every unilateral modification of the users' privacy conditions, such as modifications allowing for a more intensive tracking of users' behaviour by the controller (that is, the search engine), or the treatment of already uploaded personal data in a less private way, could be considered an abuse under Article 102 TFEU.

[77] The disaggregated data instead normally belongs to the individual clients of the online advertising company.

[78] Special Eurobarometer 359 (n. 61 above) 146.

Furthermore, there could be efficiencies to be taken into account, such as a more personalized online experience.[79]

On the other hand, practices like the refusal to allow for data portability and compatibility could be considered for their supposed foreclosure effects. In this respect, if an undertaking holds a dominant position on the market for personal data generated by way of social interactions, specific strategies aimed at making it more difficult for consumers to switch to a competing service could require the attention of competition authorities. For instance, Facebook in a couple of instances blocked tools making it easier to export data stored on its website to Google+.[80]

4.3 Potential Conflicts between Data Protection and Competition Policies?

It should be remembered, however, that under Article 102 TFEU the dominant undertaking could prove to have an objective business justification for its allegedly exclusionary conduct involving data-driven practices. Moreover, undertakings accused of anticompetitive conduct under EU law could invoke the implicit 'regulated conduct defence'.[81] Thus, for instance, competition authorities eager to address complaints put forward by app developers and involving data-related practices pointing to a possible abuse of dominant position under Article 102 TFEU could be

---

79 P. Swire, 'Submitted Testimony to the FTC Behavioral Advertising Town Hall' (18 October 2007), available at: http://www.europarl.europa.eu/meetdocs/2004_2009/documents/dv/testimony_peterswire_/Testimony_peterswire_en.pdf (accessed 31 December 2013).

80 See C.S. Yoo, 'When Antitrust Met Facebook' (2012) 19 *Geo. Mason L. Rev.* 1147, 1155.

81 See OECD, 'Regulated Conduct Defence', Policy Roundtables (2011), available at: http://www.oecd.org/daf/competition/mergers/48606639.pdf (accessed 31 December 2013); International Competition Network, Antitrust Enforcement in Regulated Sectors Working Group, 'General Introduction – Report to the Third Annual Conference in Seoul' (April 2004) 4 available at: http://www.internationalcompetitionnetwork.org/uploads/library/doc377.pdf (accessed 31 December 2013) ('Antitrust enforcement, unless there is a specific exemption, is always possible when there is a restriction of competition which falls under the prohibition of the antitrust law and this restriction may be attributed to an autonomous firm decision, i.e. it is not mandated by regulation').

confronted with the platform owner's justification that she was acting under the obligation to protect personal data.[82]

In this respect, it is not very difficult to anticipate that privacy-related concerns could easily become one of the likely business justifications put forward by Web 2.0 undertakings accused of anticompetitive conduct.[83] As former FTC Commissioner Rosch put it, 'an issue we will likely face on the horizon is what to do when high tech firms start using the need to protect consumers' privacy as a defence to an antitrust claim', and he frankly admitted that he did not know what the answer was.[84]

For the broader picture of this and other potential issues at the interface between data protection and competition policies in the framework of EU law, it should once more be acknowledged that data protection has a distinct human-rights dimension. The constitutional nature of the commitment to undistorted competition is, however, also beyond dispute.[85] The commitment to 'undistorted competition' was previously embedded in the so-called principles portion of the European

---

[82] The platform's privacy conditions are in fact a key element of the relationship between the platform owner and apps developers. When Facebook in 2007 launched the Facebook Platform, apps approved by Facebook were given access to a considerable amount of information concerning Facebook users. The ensuing Facebook saga, involving extensive investigations conducted by data protection authorities on both sides of the Atlantic, shows that the data and platform controller might have a strong interest in providing data to apps developers, especially at the platform's launch. However, especially in a more mature phase of business development, intra-platform relationships could become rather tense, and this might raise the legitimate question of whether any of the allegedly privacy-related practices put forward by the platform owner could have an anti-competitive nature. See also OECD, 'The Digital Economy', Issue Note by the Secretariat of the Competition Committee (2001) 24, available at: http://www.oecd.org/daf/competition/The-Digital-Economy-2012.pdf (accessed 31 December 2013) ('The app developers used the platforms' technology, sometimes at no charge, and a symbiotic, virtuous circle between the platforms' rising popularity/network effects and the app developers' innovations worked to everyone's advantage. But both Twitter and Facebook can quickly change from being an upstream partner to being a downstream rival').

[83] Yoo (n. 80 above) 1155.

[84] Rosch (n. 71 above).

[85] The TFEU, which incorporates the competition provisions, is the constitutional Charter of the EU: see Case C-294/83 *Les Verts v. European Parliament* [1986] ECR 1339, para. 23. On the constitutional dimension of EU competition see also J. Drexl, 'Competition Law as Part of the European Constitution' in A. von Bogdandy and J. Bast (eds), *Principles of European Constitutional Law* (2nd edn, Hart Publishing 2010) 659.

Community Treaty, Article 3(1)(g) EC. The Treaty on European Union (TEU), the Lisbon Treaty, moved the commitment to 'undistorted competition' to Protocol No. 27 annexed to the Treaties, stating that 'the internal market as set out in Article 3 of the Treaty on European Union includes a system ensuring that competition is not distorted'. The legally binding nature of the protocols is guaranteed by Article 51 TEU. Article 3 TEU, setting out the EU objectives, states that the Union 'shall work for the sustainable development of Europe based' among other things on 'a highly competitive social market economy'.

Fundamental rights, of course, play a relevant role also in the enforcement of the competition provisions of EU treaties, in particular with regard to the rights of defence, the presumption of innocence and the principle of legal certainty in competition proceedings. It can however be argued that the clear recognition of fundamental rights by the Lisbon Treaty such as the right to personal data protection, in conjunction with the at least partial downgrading of the requirement of undistorted competition, could encourage a more holistic approach to the interpretation of competition law. In particular, as is already the case as regards the reconciliation of competition law with collective fundamental rights,[86] EU courts could increasingly employ a balancing metaphor for the reconciliation of competition law with individual fundamental rights,[87] arguably beyond those having a clear social characterization.

Besides future and hard-to-predict balancing exercises possibly taking place before European courts, the current legal framework already offers some valuable guidance concerning the core question of whether requirements under the data protection law regime could represent plausible justifications against serious allegations of anti-competitive behaviour.

The Court of Justice of the European Union has clearly stated that Member States (legislative, executive, regulatory authorities), pursuant to the loyalty clause of the Treaty on European Union,[88] cannot adopt

---

[86] Case C-438/05 *International Transport Workers' Federation and Finnish Seamen's Union* [2007] ECR I-10779, para. 79 ('Since the Community has thus not only an economic but also social purpose, the rights under the provisions of the Treaty on the free movement of goods, persons, services and capital must be balanced against the objectives pursued by social policy').

[87] I. Lianos, 'Competition law in the European Union after the Treaty of Lisbon' in D. Ashiagbor, N. Countouris and I. Lianos (eds), *Competition law in the European Union after the Treaty of Lisbon* (Cambridge University Press 2012) 252, 275.

[88] Article 4(3) TEU.

regulations that would deprive EU competition rules of their effectiveness, such as those encouraging undertakings to violate EU competition law, or making those violations inevitable by undertakings. And if they do, those regulations should be dis-applied by all Member States authorities, including courts. Already in 1977, the Court in *GB-Inno* concluded that: 'while it is true that Article 82 [now Article 102 TFEU] is directed at undertakings, nonetheless it is also true that the Treaty imposes a duty on Member States not to adopt or maintain in force any measure which could deprive that provision of its effectiveness'. Likewise, continued the Court, 'Member States may not enact measures enabling private undertakings to escape from the constraints imposed by Articles 81 [now Article 101 TFEU] to 89 [now Article 109 TFEU] of the Treaty'.[89] In *Van Eycke* the Court re-stated the principle previously established in *GB-Inno* that the EU legal framework requires the Member States not to introduce or maintain in force measures, even of a legislative nature, which may render ineffective the competition rules, and clarified that:

> such would be the case … if a Member State were to require or favour the adoption of agreements, decisions or concerted practices contrary to Article 81 [now Article 101 TFEU] or to reinforce their effects, or to deprive its own legislation of its official character by delegating to private traders responsibility for taking decisions affecting the economic sphere.[90]

However, competition liability of private entities under the EU competition rules is distinct from the Member States' obligations under the Treaty.[91] If a Member State does not fulfil its obligations under EU law and adopts a regulation compelling undertakings to engage in anti-competitive behaviour that cannot be justified to ensure the provision of a service of general economic interest, an undertaking involved in competition proceedings may avoid sanctions by evoking a regulated-conduct defence. As the Court of Justice recently recalled in the *Deutsche Telekom* case, this applies, however, only 'if anti-competitive conduct is required of undertakings by national legislation, or if the latter creates a legal framework which itself eliminates any possibility of competitive activity on their part'.[92] The regulated-conduct defence is not permitted if

[89] Case 13/77 *GB-Inno* [1977] ECR 2115, para. 31.

[90] Case 267/86 *Van Eycke* [1988] ECR 4769, para. 16.

[91] Case C-198/01 *Consorzio Industrie Fiammiferi* [2003] ECR I-8055, para. 51.

[92] Case C-280/08P *Deutsche Telekom v. Commission* [2010] ECR I-9555, para. 81.

a national law merely encourages or makes it easier for undertakings to engage in autonomous anti-competitive conduct.[93] In such cases, the presence of a regulation is merely a mitigating factor when setting the sanction.[94] Moreover, the Court of Justice recalled in this context that dominant undertakings have a special responsibility not to allow their conduct to impair genuine undistorted competition on the common market,[95] possibly legitimating particularly strict interpretations of the regulated conduct defence when invoked in the context of Article 102 TFEU.[96]

Going back to personal data-related issues, two relevant questions should be asked in order to assess whether the undertaking's conduct is to be considered legitimate under EU law. First, whether the alleged anti-competitive practice put forth by the dominant undertaking was covered by any existing obligations under data protection regulation. Second, whether despite obligations under data protection regulation, there was still room for autonomous conduct by the dominant undertaking. It should be recalled at this point that the data protection regime in the EU often leaves undertakings significant room to manoeuvre in choosing how to proactively pursue the privacy objective. In this respect, the allegedly anti-competitive practice might have been one amongst an array of other available ways of achieving a high level of protection of personal data as required by EU law.[97]

Finally, and conversely, it seems very unlikely that pro-competition arguments could ever be called upon in order to fully justify breaches of data-protection rules. For instance, when Google launched the highly controversial Buzz feature, it clearly aimed at competing directly with Facebook's dominant social network. Without prior notice or the opportunity to consent, Gmail users were automatically set with followers

---

93 Ibid., para. 82.

94 European Commission, Guidelines on the method of setting fines imposed pursuant to Article 23(2a) of Regulation No 1/2003, [2006] OJ C 210, p. 5, 29.

95 Case C-280/08P *Deutsche Telekom v. Commission* [2010] ECR I-9555, para. 83.

96 On the strict interpretation of the requirements to be fulfilled for a valid regulated-conduct defence under Article 101 TFEU see also *Consorzio Industrie Fiammiferi* (n. 91 above) para. 67.

97 A possible difference to the *Deutsche Telekom* case, however, is that the national regulatory authority in that case was operating under national law. In our scenario, data protection obligations would directly derive from secondary EU legislation. In so far as this could make a difference, it should be asked, however, whether the national law applied by the German authority in the *Deutsche Telekom* case had in fact been essentially implementing European law.

derived from the list of their most frequent contacts; moreover, that information was publicly accessible to anyone viewing a user's profile. Google's move, which, possibly, would have fostered competition and lowered barriers to entry in a market negatively affected by the presence of strong network effects, raised very serious and legitimate data-protection concerns.[98]

5. CONCLUSION

In Europe, personal data protection is an issue mainly dealt with by regulation. The first comprehensive data protection legislation at state level was enacted by Sweden. Since 1995, the EU has undertaken important harmonization efforts of national data protection legislations. Last year, the Commission tabled a complex and ambitious proposal to overhaul the 1995 Data Protection Directive. From a pro-competition perspective, the draft Regulation, which is part of the reform package put forward by the Commission, contains some interesting elements, such as the right to data portability that, if suitably implemented, might help promote competition.

Beyond the stringent regulatory approach to data protection possibly to be confirmed in the EU, the European Commission and the national competition authorities in the EU are likely to become increasingly involved with allegations of anticompetitive conduct in connection with data-driven practices. Some difficult issues on the horizon will likely involve the definition of the relevant markets, as well as theories of harm especially related to alleged abuses under Article 102 TFEU. Finally, in the interest of consumers, the interface between competition and data protection enforcement will need to be carefully worked out, at both the substantive and the institutional level.

---

[98] Google then settled with the FTC – see *In Re Google Inc.* – Agreement containing consent order, File No. 102 3136, available at: http://www.ftc.gov/sites/default/files/documents/cases/2011/03/110330googlebuzzagreeorder.pdf (accessed 31 December 2013) – and with the parties behind a derivative class-action lawsuit. Moreover, Google publicly apologized about Buzz, which was eventually replaced by Google+ in the course of 2011.

PART 3

Anti-competitive market intervention and regulation

9. The suppression of the competition policy agenda in the context of an over-regulated economy: the case of Venezuela

Claudia Curiel Leidenz

1. INTRODUCTION

Competition policy in Venezuela has been actively and progressively developing since 1991, when the special law regulating competition was enacted. However, the institutional framework developed in Venezuela during the political leadership of Hugo Chávez suppressed the possibility of the free market model to subsist. During the last ten years the state has introduced more than 300 norms and regulations that affect the market conditions, the scope of economic freedom and the principle of private property. The purpose of increasing the state's participation in and control over the economy has been to besiege private economic activity.

The core goal of this article is to explain that as a consequence of this siege, which will be thoroughly analysed, competition policy has no applicability in Venezuela.

2. BACKGROUND

The enactment of the Law for the Promotion and Protection of Free Competition took place within the framework of a process of adjusting and opening the Venezuelan economy, as part of second-generation reforms.[1] In this context, it was decided to suppress direct and centralized state control, which previously had affected a large portion of the

[1] The second-generation reforms followed a first wave of reforms, or 'first-generation reforms' whose main characteristics were structural reforms such as the liberalization of the financial system, the privatization of public

economy. At the same time, Venezuelan society was in the middle of a transition towards commercial opening and institutional and regulatory modernization.

When the competition law was enacted, the country was not prepared culturally or formally to adopt competitive dynamics, since the combination of state control schemes and protectionism did not foresee that type of free decision and performance by economic actors.

It must also be remembered that in the Latin American context, such reforms were not only taking place in Venezuela, but simultaneously in many other Latin American countries that were aiming at modernizing and adopting schemes to defend competition.

The creation of a competition policy was hence accompanied by the political will to enhance a general process of economic reform. To depart from the previous prevailing paradigm of strong state interventionism raised the need to concentrate efforts in competition advocacy. In any case, there was a clear understanding of the need to create an institutional framework that would accommodate a new way of thinking and of managing economic matters.

Hence, the Venezuelan antitrust system was built on two main pillars. The first pillar was the Law for the Promotion and Protection of Free Competition and its Regulations. This instrument followed the model of European competition law and constituted a true innovation for Venezuela. The second pillar was the creation of an autonomous agency, the Superintendence for the Promotion and Protection of Free Competition, which was vested with the authority to implement this brand new legal instrument.

From the moment of its creation, the Superintendence for the Promotion and Protection of Free Competition was very active in both promoting the competition advocacy agenda and guaranteeing competition law enforcement.

The competition advocacy agenda had its focus on such issues as:

(1) *Promotion and education on competition policy principles*: The Venezuelan law is called Law to Promote and Protect the Exercise of Free Competition. Both its name and its provisions reflect the intention of the legislature to create room for a process of cultural change in Venezuelan society, to incorporate incentive schemes for better market performance, and to replace the system of state

---

enterprises, trade liberalization and deregulation of controls. The second-generation reforms then focused on the institutional framework.

control and supervision with autonomous decision-making by the market participants. The promotion of such competition principles also required the instruction of judicial bodies, which never before had to review decisions related to the proper functioning of the market, on the enforcement of competition law. In addition, there was no academic infrastructure, with no chairs for competition law and no research in the field.

(2) *Inter-institutional consultation regarding the design of different public policies*: The new law refrained from providing powers to the competition authority to issue binding opinions regarding different public policies that could interfere with the objectives of institutionalizing a free market economy. However, in its first years the Superintendence played a very active part, for instance, in dismantling established price-control schemes in the economy. In particular, it placed special emphasis on the agricultural sector. Moreover, the administration of the Superintendence, over time, detected a large array of anticompetitive conducts that was supported by the Executive.

(3) *Advisory function of the Superintendence in the privatization of state-owned monopolies*: While competition law enforcement is largely concerned about investigating antitrust cases such as cartels, abuse of dominant position, exclusionary practices and unfair competition, the Superintendence also participated in the technical-economic analysis in the process of privatization of state-owned enterprises that took place in different sectors of the economy. In these cases, the Superintendence had the power to issue prior and binding opinions regarding the effects of each privatization case on the relevant markets.

During the first ten years of enforcement of the competition law, the implementation activity was intense and Venezuela was in the advantageous position of receiving training and technical support from agencies of countries with greater tradition and experience. This support was reflected in the learning curve of the Superintendence in applying the prohibitions provided for by competition law in practice, the design of the competition advocacy agenda and the level of technical management that was reached by the staff of the agency.

In any case, an important learning process took place in the institutional framework established to support the economy based on healthy competition. In 1999, another important political decision was made in the country with the adoption of a new National Constitution. This new Constitution introduced guidelines and guarantees that correspond to a free market economy. Yet, no major changes occurred during the first years of validity of the Constitution; quite on the contrary the practice of competition law as well as the rest of the economic laws started to enter into some kind of inertia, in the sense that the impetus of the competition advocacy disappeared and the number of relevant cases went down.

However, in 2001, a completely new political model started to be incorporated that again modified the model of economic arrangement of the Venezuelan society. Those changes also found a concrete expression in the institutional context. In the following, this chapter aims at documenting and analysing how these transformations affected the two fundamental elements of any free market system. On one hand, a progressive and substantial transformation of the principle of private property has been implemented. On the other hand, the control schemes of the state and the agenda of a direct and greater participation in the economy have substantially corroded the right of economic freedom.[2]

3. THE 'SIEGE OF PRIVATE PRODUCTIVE ACTIVITY'

Since the entry into force of the 1999 Constitution, more than 300 regulations (of legal or subsidiary rank) and decisions have been introduced that affect the operation of private productive activity. Of that total, more than 280 correspond to – ordinary or organic – laws. Moreover, President Chávez had four 'Enabling Laws' enacted during his periods in office (in 1999, 2000, 2007 and 2010), under which many regulations critical to the economy have been adopted.[3]

The gradual appearance since 2004 of laws and public policies that affect the economy, and therefore can be termed as a 'siege of private economic activity', can be examined using an analytical tool that was developed by the author during her tenure as Chief Economist in the National Confederation of Industrial Chambers (2002–2006). This chapter uses an updated version of this tool under the conceptual assumptions described below.

In the following, the analysis of the institutional framework is laid out in terms of the identification of regulations and actions that have been applied and inhibit the appropriate functioning of the market, or suppress

[2] This chapter is based on the talk given by C. Curiel Leidenz, 'Estado, propiedad y organizaciones socioproductivas' in Encuentro de Organizaciones Sociales 2012 (Universidad Católica Andrés Bello, Caracas 2013) 103.

[3] It has been estimated that more than 70 per cent of the laws affecting the economy, created since 1999, have been approved through the Enabling Law.

the validity of the right to the free exercise of economic activity.[4] The core of the 'siege' is constituted by those rules that imply greater current and future restrictions on entrepreneurial activity.

The inventory of regulations that are part of the 'siege' has been classified in three dimensions, according to the nature of its effects on the activity of companies in the short and long term, and on the market dynamics.

3.1 Institutional Components

The rules that have been adopted as part of the 'siege' affect the guaranty of private property and the right to the free exercise of economic activity. All of these legal instruments have in common the type of effects they have on entrepreneurial activity, among which the following several aspects are to be pointed out:

First, institutional risks[5] are increased to the extent that citizens and businesses cannot foresee the parameters for decision-making by the agency in charge of administrating a certain public policy. That effect can vary in response to several elements, such as changes in the Ministries; the proliferation of laws; the absence of information mechanisms and accountability; or the establishment of 'revolutionary justice' as the criterion for the society to make decisions.[6] Second, transaction costs ensue. When it comes to making decisions in the operation of a business

---

[4] The viewpoint used in this document simplifies the criterion used between 2003 and 2006 in the first versions of the analysis of the 'siege'. That approximation was used by the author for the analysis of the version of the 'Industrial Siege' presented at the 2006 International Congress of Conindustria, which included a total of 124 items of public policies that constituted a real or potential threat to the development of the industrial activity, grouped in six categories. See E. Gómez Sigala (President of Conindustria), Situación de la Industria en Venezuela (PowerPoint 26 July 2006), available at: http://w3old.conindustria.org/web2005/rrcc/congreso2006/gomezsigala_p.pdf (accessed 31 December 2013).

[5] The term of institutional risks refers to the probability that a new internal or external event affects positively or negatively the organizational ability to accomplish legally, effectively, efficiently and economically the objectives and the public policies established within a regulatory framework. The term of institutional risks also includes regulatory risks that private parties face once a decision is made in a given regulatory context.

[6] 'Revolutionary justice' is defined by a text entitled as 'Participative Democracy of the Simon Bolivar National Project 2007–2013'. In this text it is established that 'justice is above rights and the law, even though it presupposes them'. In this sense, when it is stated that economic activity cannot seek profit

a number of contingencies must be foreseen that increase the costs of receiving information, maintaining a constant update of the interpretations of the regulations or preparing contracts related with the activity of that business. Additionally, companies are subject to cumbersome procedures that entail very narrow time windows in order to materialize the access to foreign exchange and other vital elements for their operation.[7]

Third, firms are much more likely to be exposed to sanctions, as the discretion of the officials managing any given public policy increases. This element has intensified in view of the incorporation of precautionary measures for immediate execution in important laws. For example, the Law for the Defence of the Consumer in the Access to Goods and Services enables government officials to apply precautionary measures like confiscation, temporary closure or administrative intervention when evidence is found that a company has incurred any fault provided for in that Law. Fourth, the operation costs of firms increases, with a bias in favour of large companies: Numerous regulations demand operational changes and adaptations of internal processes in companies which creates entry barriers for medium and small enterprises, while large companies can deal which such administrative burdens more easily. This is a bias in

---

but has to serve the general interest, it will be understood that state agencies will focus on that objective for which private parties are 'co-'responsible.

[7] Initially transaction costs were defined as those costs incurred by executing a transaction in a market. When Ronald Coase stated this definition he pointed out that the use of the market requires finding the other contracting party, provision of information, establishment of contract conditions, negotiation and establishment of a control structure regarding the parties' compliance with the obligations. See R.H. Coase, 'The Nature of the Firm' (1937) 4(16) *Economica*, New Series 386. He also stated that companies, when coordinating their decisions and optimizing the use of resources, try to minimize these transaction costs. However, when the analysis of public policies is considered, it is no longer a question of the costs of using the market, but also about the costs that are incurred to ensure that the contractual objectives are met. See O.E. Williamson, *The Economic Institutions of Capitalism – Firms, Markets, Relational Contracting* (The Free Press 1985). Such considerations allow a broader and pertinent definition that conceives transaction costs as those required to establish and maintain property rights. See D.W. Allen, 'Transaction Costs' in B. Bouckaert and G. de Geest (eds), *Encyclopedia of Law and Economics, Volume One: The History and Methodology of Law and Economics* (Edward Elgar Publishing 2000) ch. 0740. Changes in the regulatory framework can modify contractual relationships with third parties, or can modify property rights, as long as such rights include all sets of rules and government and organization structures. Therefore, families, companies, governments, non-profit institutions and contracts are all seen jointly or as property rights.

favour of market concentration, which contradicts the government's official position against monopolies. Fifth, the government's policy destroys trust[8] in society and thus weakens the current and future social capital. Within this classification state actions that pretend to modify the ability to build fundamental agreements for proper productive activity are of most concern in this regard. Concerning the regulation of the labour relationships, a most prominent and emblematic example to be named in this respect involves the government initiative to create several parallel unions within the same economic sector. This leads to precarious labour relationships, derived from the weakening of contractual mechanisms and the undermining of the presumption of good faith and mutual trust. This approach distorts the role of the workers, as, based on ideological propaganda and training, workers are deployed in positions and functions with a political agenda beyond the strictly productive and economic goals. The trust issue is of extreme importance, as it constitutes a necessary though not sufficient condition for progress in a society. This reaches a clear expression in the relationship that Kliksberg explains when he states that the elements that make up social capital trigger wealth and the strength of the social fabric of a society, features that allow the acquisition of individual benefits and benefits for all.[9]

---

8 Trust is the expectation that rises within a community with normal, honest and cooperative behaviour, based on common rules shared by all the members of said community. According to Francis Fukuyama, when this element is not present in society, people who do not trust one another cooperate just under a scheme of rules and regulations that have to be negotiated, agreed upon, litigated and implemented, sometimes forcefully. In this way, the legal apparatus and its effective implementation, as well as hierarchies, serve as substitutes for trust. See F. Fukuyama, *Trust: The Social Virtues and the Creation of Prosperity* (Simon & Schuster 1996). Each society settles on a number of distinctive features and internalizes reciprocal moral obligations for each member of the group, and, complementarily, by explicit rules and regulations. These habits and rules confer on the members of the community the necessary reasons for mutual trust. As long as trust exists, the individuals are not inhibited to exploit the available economic opportunities. These elements are linked with the concept of social capital developed by Coleman as the ability of individuals to work together with others in groups or organizations to reach common goals. See C.S. Coleman, 'Social Capital in the Creation of Human Capital' (1988) 94 (Supplement) *Am. J. Sociology* 95. The ability for association depends on the degree in which the members of one community share rules and values, and the ease with which they subordinate individual goals to those of the group.

9 See B. Kliksberg, 'Capital Social y Cultura. Claves Olvidadas del Desarrollo' in Corporación Andina de Fomento Capital Social (ed.), *Clave para una agenda integral de desarrollo* (Norma Color 2003).

Figure 9.1 summarizes these analytical criteria that constitute the first dimension of the 'siege of private productive activity'. A common element of the criteria presented in this figure is that they have caused a deterioration in the conditions for markets to function, and therefore, intentionally or not, imply a tremendous setback in the fundamental conditions that should be ensured for market operation to reach efficiency levels that will enable the benefits of the market economy to be transferred to consumers and end users. In other words, these policies that introduce conditions and restrictions for the operation of the private economy directly and inevitably harm the majority of the citizens, in particular consumers. On an institutional level, control and planning mechanisms substitute free decision-making in the market.

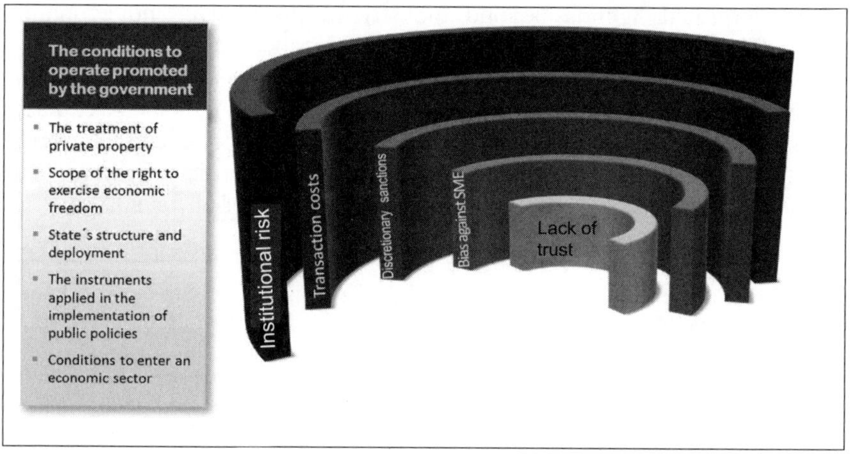

Figure 9.1 Institutional components

This situation is aggravated by a further factor. Instead of commercial rivalry still operating within those limited spaces confined by interventionist policies, a second layer of public policies has been introduced. These policies express two fundamental characteristics: first, they suppress individual autonomy of the economic agents through control and distortions by the direct participation of the state in the economy. Second, the introduction of privileges for political reasons produce market effects similar to those arising from dumping or unfair competition. It is hard to quantify the long-term costs and the market distortions that are generated by this approach regarding the efficiency and the number of participants and quality of performance (in terms of diversity and quality of products as well as choices for consumers).

Due to lack of space, we will not comment on each of the elements presented in this part of the analysis. Yet, in the following, this chapter classifies and prioritizes the different initiatives, laws or public policies which are part of the siege into five categories based on the effects described above and according to their relevance for assessing their overall economic impact.

Table 9.1 presents the policy initiatives, laws or public policies on a scale from 0 to 5, with the following impact factors: 0: inexistent; 1: very low; 2: low; 3: medium; 4: high; 5: very high.

From the total of 37 initiatives, laws or public policies considered, the designated qualifications show that the elements with the greatest consequences regarding the institutional character of private companies are expropriations, the Law of Costs and Fair Prices and the proliferation of control agencies. No individual considerations were made for each case. It is only stated that these initiatives increase transaction costs and undermine trust among economic agents. Emphasis has been placed on the relevance of the Law of Costs and Fair Prices, which constitutes an accelerator regarding the new form of the role of the private sector that is under way in the government's agenda. In any case, this new institution, more focused in exerting social and political control, has an agenda that does not favour the existence and operation of the market, nor does it aim at preserving the principle of private property or the prevalence of free competition.

Issues that have higher points are precisely institutional risks and trust deterioration. Hence, as a result of the economic policy advocated by the Bolivarian political revolution in Venezuela, uncertainty and distrust have emerged as characteristic elements. Beyond the impact this may have on investment decisions by private enterprises, these features also undermine sustainable growth and challenge the very existence of the market.

3.2 Displacement of Economic Agents and Imposition of Restrictions

The second dimension of our analysis of the siege is presented in a figure that gathers specific components that imply displacement and imposition of restrictions on private economic actors. The nature of the effects these components have in common is different from the institutional conditions reviewed above. In the first place, the public policies considered interfere with the market by generating barriers to the entry of businesses and their ability to stay in the market for reasons other than transactional costs. In the second place, within this group direct interventions of the state by means of companies and productive units are considered, as well as the quality of the competitive process as such.

Table 9.1 The institutional components

Policy initiative, law or public policy	Increases institutional risk	Generates transaction costs	Increases the exposure to discretionary sanctions	Increases the cost of operating enterprises	Destroys trust	Total
Expropriations	5	5	5	5	5	25
Law on Fair Costs and Prices (regulation of margins at all levels of the chain of production, distribution and commercialization)	5	5	5	4	5	24
Law that Promotes and Regulates the New Means of Joint Associations between the State, Community Initiative and Private Initiative	5	5	4	5	5	24
Expansion of the number of Supervision and Control entities (a food industry could be monitored by at least 35 different government agencies, military units or by community organizations)	5	4	5	4	5	23
Law for the Defence of the People's Access to Goods and Services (includes drastic sanctions that can be applied immediately in the framework of consumer protection)	5	4	4	4	5	22
Enforcement of the principle of Social Control	5	3	5	4	5	22
Direct allocations in state procurement and contracting	5	4	5	3	5	22
Implementation of Land's Law (suppression of property deed)	5	5	5	2	5	22
Absence of any Anti-Inflationary Policy	5	5	1	5	5	21
Unified labour inspections	5	3	5	3	5	21
Withdrawal from the CAN and Mercosur incorporation	4	5	5	3	4	21
Inspections and requirements duplicated and uncoordinated	5	4	5	3	4	21
Removing labour relations and collective bargaining agreements	5	3	4	4	5	21

Application of Social Ethic Commitments	4	4	4	4	4	20
Reform of the Law of Electricity Services	3	5	4	4	4	20
Organic Law of Alimentary Security and Sovereignty	4	3	5	4	3	19
Barriers of access to public facilities	4	4	3	3	5	19
Project of New Antimonopoly Law (before the National Assembly)	5	3	4	2	4	18
Reform of corporate law	4	4	4	2	4	18
Law of Banking Sector Institutions	4	4	3	4	3	18
Organic Law on the Environment	4	2	5	3	4	18
Suppression of tripartism (concerted decisions on labour issues between representatives of the private, public and labour sector)	5	3	4	2	4	18
Rationales for expropriation and intervention of enterprises	5	1	5	1	5	17
Procedure followed for the adoption of laws and regulations	5	2	5	0	5	17
Bilateral agreements (over 1,300 cooperation agreements signed between the Venezuelan state and other countries)	3	3	3	4	4	17
Absence of channels of relationship between private companies and the government	3	3	4	3	3	16
Anti-business and anti-capitalism speeches (matrix of opinion that criminalizes employers)	4	1	5	1	5	16
Law of illegal currency exchange (penalization of purchasing foreign currency outside the official market)	4	2	4	2	4	16
Application of the concept of 'relative private property'	5	1	4	1	4	15
Criminalization and severe penalization of economic faults	4	2	4	2	3	15
Lack of accountability mechanisms regarding governmental activities	4	0	5	1	5	15
Activation of the instances for central planning system	4	2	4	2	2	14
Reform of the Law of Armed Force	4	1	4	1	4	14
Organic Law on Security and National Defence	5	0	5	1	2	13
Organic Law on Communes	4	0	3	0	4	11

Policy initiative, law or public policy	Increases institutional risk	Generates transaction costs	Increases the exposure to discretionary sanctions	Increases the cost of operating enterprises	Destroys trust	Total
Reform of the Central Bank Law	5	0	0	0	5	10
Borrowing strategy of the central government	5	0	0	0	5	10
Total	165	105	149	96	158	

This classification includes the policy initiatives that fulfil any of the following conditions:

- Some economic agents are granted privileged conditions in the private sector, by exempting them from requirements that apply to competing agents in the same markets;
- Space for autonomous decision-making of firms is reduced, especially through limitations to their decision-making spheres.
- Resources that are key to productive activity, such as foreign currency and imports, are displaced, as new constraints and cumbersome processes apply to companies seeking access to such resources.
- Access to public infrastructures or assets (such as technical training) that can hardly be provided by the private sector is suppressed.
- Barriers or obfuscation hinder entry to the purchase markets of the state, especially to the supply of intermediate goods for the basic industries.
- Labour costs increase due to significant incorporation of asymmetries against employers and explicit increases in the contributions they are required to make.[10]
- Another type of distortion occurs in international trade negotiations. The government has not used any opportunity to negotiate the opening of new markets for Venezuelan exports. It has only signed cooperation agreements under which goods are imported from other countries.

Figure 9.2 summarizes the criteria considered within this dimension of the 'siege of private productive activity'.

In the following, the different initiatives, laws and policies are assessed and prioritized. In Table 9.2 each of these different initiatives, laws and public policies is evaluated on a scale from 0 to 5, with the following impact factors: 0: inexistent; 1: very low; 2: low; 3: medium; 4: high; 5: very high. The inventory is organized according to its relevance for the aggregate formed by the seven categories of this component of the analysis.

---

[10] The application of the methodological tool to the siege that the author applied until 2006 had the labour issue as an additional and separate component. However, the version of this instrument presented in this document grants prevalence to the concepts that have been discussed, so that the labour cost is incorporated into the second group of components.

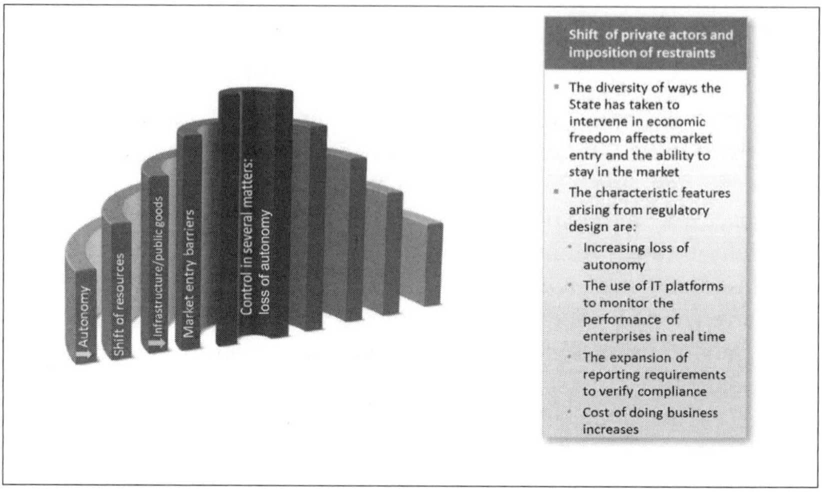

Figure 9.2 Shift of private actors and imposition of restraints

Of the 24 initiatives that make up this category, the measures related to 'labour solvency'[11] and job security have the greatest impact on the loss of room for manoeuvre of the private sector, regarding its autonomy in decision-making, the increase in labour costs (especially by increasing exit barriers) and the introduction of asymmetries putting private companies at a disadvantage compared to other actors, particularly public bureaucracy and state enterprises. The third place is occupied by the growing role of the state as an importer displacing private companies from their natural markets and using practically all available infrastructure.

The three features that have the greatest impact in this part is the creation of privileges for some market participants, thereby distorting competition, the suppression of autonomy in decision-making and the ability to obscure, and raise barriers to, market access, especially those linked to the public procurement. The latter, in an economy where oil exploitation has so much weight, has a special relevance.

[11] 'Labour solvency' (solvencia laboral) stands for a confirmed status of compliance with all labour laws and standards (to date, more than fifty rules and regulations contain obligations that affect the labour matters). Without that 'solvency', companies cannot access foreign currencies for imports, or enter into contractual transactions with the state. The currency exchange regime applied in Venezuela implies that all foreign exchange is provided by an administrative agency. It is the only way to access imports. Every company that needs to import inputs or raw materials has to show its status regarding labour solvency.

Table 9.2 Distortion of competition to the prejudice of private actors

Initiative, law or public policy	Privileged treatment of some market actors	Reducing space for autonomous decision-making	Blocking access to resources that are key to doing business	Blocking access to infrastructure or public goods	Raising market entry barriers	Increases labour cost	Loss of export markets	Total
Labour solvency	5	5	4	3	5	3	0	25
Labour mobility forbidden (since 2003)	5	5	3	0	5	5	0	23
State as a major importer	5	3	2	4	4	0	4	22
Politicization of the labour inspectorates	5	4	3	0	4	4	0	20
Non Domestic Production Certificate[a]	4	3	2	0	4	0	5	18
Parafiscal charges. In specific sectors this charge takes up a minimum of 3% of the companies' earnings	4	3	4	0	4	3	0	18
Price control regime (since 2003, applied to a specific group of products classified as essential)	4	5	4	0	4	0	0	17
Criteria applied to determine fair profits, and regulation of profit margins in specific goods	5	5	3	0	4	0	0	17
Foreign exchange controls	4	5	4	0	4	0	0	17
Raw material supply agreements	5	4	3	2	3	0	0	17
Intervention in the portfolio of products in regulated sectors[b]	5	5	2	0	5	0	0	17
Mandatory increase in the national minimum salary	4	4	0	0	4	5	0	17
Proposal of state intervention in consumer patterns	5	4	3	1	3	0	0	16
Imposition of welfare obligations on the private sector	5	5	5	0	1	0	0	16

Initiative, law or public policy	Privileged treatment of some market actors	Reducing space for autonomous decision-making	Blocking access to resources that are key to doing business	Blocking access to infrastructure or public goods	Raising market entry barriers	Increases labour cost	Loss of export markets	Total
Platforms for monitoring business activities in real time	4	5	4	0	3	0	0	16
Over 350 state-owned enterprises and over 200 social property units	5	3	3	0	5	0	0	16
Barter of merchandises with oil exports	5	0	0	2	4	0	5	16
Discretion in issuing solvencies and permissions	3	4	4	0	4	0	0	15
Replacement of professional training centres by centres for socialistic formation	0	2	4	4	3	2	0	15
Deployment of the idea on necessary consumption[c]	3	5	3	0	3	0	0	14
Deterioration of the country's general infrastructure	0	0	3	4	4	2	0	13
Duties to disclose information	0	4	3	1	4	0	0	12
Merchandising Mobility's Control Systems[d]	0	5	4	0	0	0	0	9
Total	85	88	70	21	84	24	14	

Notes:

[a] This Certificate is another requisite imposed to access foreign currency and imports. Firms must show that there is no local production of the item for which import they are requesting administrative authorization.

[b] When firms have some product within the price control regime, restrictions are imposed to dedicate its productive capacity to categories or varieties of products that are not covered by this regulation.

[c] This mandate has been primarily advanced by Jorge Giordani, who was Minister of Planning during virtually the entire stay in power. In accordance with this mandate, people should be guaranteed access to goods they really need. Beyond this set, goods are not necessary and only respond to consumerism. Society could do without the availability of those goods.

[d] In 2008, an online platform was established. Each food business must enter into an online system load of each truck and volumes of goods intended for their customers in each office. The system emits a guide, without which the trucks cannot move, under penalty of being retained and sanctioned.

3.3 Subjecting Economic Activity to a System of Parallel Control through Social Organizations

According to the National Constitution, Venezuelan society is organized around a system of participatory and direct democracy. This norm of participation is intended to replace the representative democracy. The implicit abandonment of the latter would, by definition, require the dismantling of the different structures of political intermediation and the displacement of the elites. Through laws that support the construction of the new political model, new institutions, namely the Presidential Commission of the Communal Power, the Security and Defence Council and the Central Planning Commission have emerged. These new institutions play new state roles and alternate in exercising certain powers and/or sharing competencies.

Within the constitutional reform proposed in 2001, but then rejected in a referendum, the Communal Power was included as an agency to articulate all forms of political and social organization called on to provide the basis for a participative democracy and the empowerment of the people. The National Assembly established this structure through the enactment of a group of laws in 2010.

This is of fundamental relevance for private enterprises, since the recognition of that group of social organizations (hereinafter referred to by the term 'Community Power') as stakeholders is necessary for two reasons. First, the National Assembly has progressively conferred competencies to those entities in parallel with state functions attributed to the traditional – executive, legislative and judicial – powers. Second, these agencies have the power to exercise control functions, and to intervene in the activities of firms if these firms' activity affects common or collective interests, provided that the requirements and conditions stated by law are met.[12]

This form of state intervention operates in parallel with the traditional exercise of administrative powers of the state. On top of this bodies and committees of the socialist state also exercise control functions and may intervene in economic activity. This includes, for example, joint actions of control committees and the Bolivarian militia to supervise food

[12] Those powers apply in economic emergency situations, in strategic sectors and any other situation that could be qualified as extraordinary and where the general interest prevails over individual rights.

distribution; or the intervention by Farm Workers' Councils in the processes of land expropriation.[13]

The appearance of these actors occurs at the same time as the regulatory system on the economy has intensified its sanctioning activity and much economic activity has been criminalized. In this sense, control and supervision modalities over production have increased. This implies that the number of control mechanisms and situations has increased, and these include information requests, visits to plants and business establishments. In addition, supervision over productive units has progressively come to entail more acts of confiscation and criminal components. This policy of economic control has also resulted in a significant increase in the number of actors involved in fiscal supervision. For example, while there were a total of 13 regulating and/or supervising agencies in the year 2000, currently there can be more than thirty institutions scrutinizing a firm. In addition to the number, the frequency and intensity of these fiscal supervisions are very high, and the growth of public bureaucracy is causing frictions and significant transaction costs for operating firms.

This subject is very new and is closely related to the design of the parallel progression of political control over society, while this chapter will only focus on the impact of this development on the ability of private parties to do business.

These impacts are substantial. A clear example is provided by the Law of Costs and Fair Prices (LCFP), which is designed based on the communal state, in that it designates competencies and faculties to defined entities based on these laws of the parallel state. Specific examples are the Communal Councils (whose special Law was reformulated in December, 2009) and the Socialist Workers' Councils (created by the Law of Communes). The LCFP defines these as entities for social control, as they constitute an organized body of popular power. These bodies are legitimately constituted as long as they are registered with the ministry that is competent for social organization matters, and their source of legitimacy does not depend on the legalization of an assembly or any electoral process. In assigning to these entities the role of auxiliaries for the surveillance of the compliance with its provisions, the Law of Costs and Fair Prices is attributing to the Communal Councils a

---

[13] The Land Law enacted in 2002 establishes the possibility of intervention or disrupts the property rights over the land when it is shown that it is affecting the public interest, or that it is not dedicated to their most productive use. The Farm Workers Councils can activate the so-called land intervention processes, culminating with the expropriation of large and medium extensions that become occupied by these new organizations.

profile with no precedent for these organizations. Meanwhile, the Communal Councils, through the Committees of Supply and Speculation, are widely empowered to initiate control activities aimed at verifying compliance with the Law of Costs and Fair Prices. Communal Councils are of even wider importance for economic activity because, beyond this special Law, they have gained increasing control powers in all matters related to the general interest.

Regarding this last aspect, it is worth noting that the functions of the Communal Councils are wide and that they can become active, investigating also in the field of fiscal supervision and other diverse areas. The intensity of this function is relevant for all activities carried out in the Councils' geographical area. Any plant, distribution centre, customer service office or any other productive facility must be able to explain all the aspects regulated by the Law of Costs and Fair Prices to the Communal Councils of its area. This also includes the formation of the prices at the specific level of the production or distribution chain on which the individual firms operate.

In addition to this, there has even been the very ideology-inspired proposal that the Communal Council should be responsible for reverting surpluses made by firms back to the local community.

The elements considered above allow us to develop a set of critical features of the second dimension of the 'siege of economic productive activity':

(1) Increase of the number of bodies with supervisory powers over enterprises. These powers have been gradually developed in a significant number of regulatory instruments.
(2) Lack of expertise, but large discretionary power of the representatives of the Communal Councils and other forms of social organization regarding enterprises.
(3) The imposition of the new institutional structure generates new sources of uncertainty and delay in the preparation of businesses to be in full compliance with the law.

For the two dimensions of the 'siege of economic productive activity', the different initiatives, laws and public policies were assessed and prioritized above. Table 9.3 gathers the inventory of the initiatives, laws or public policies, placing each one on a scale from 0 to 5 with the following impact factors: 0: inexistent; 1: very low; 2: low; 3: medium; 4: high; 5: very high. The inventory is organized according to its relevance for the aggregate formed by the three categories of this component of the tool.

Table 9.3 Subjecting economic activity to a system of parallel control through social organizations

Initiative, law or public policy	Social organizations with supervisory powers	Lack of expertise, but large discretionary power	Imposition of a new institutional framework	Total
Deployment of the principle of social control	5	5	5	15
Assignment of functions to the Socialist Workers' Councils	5	5	5	15
Executive powers assigned to the State Community	5	5	5	15
Incorporation of militia actions Councils and Committees	4	5	4	13
Creating patrols[a] on the activities of the companies	4	5	4	13
Conditioning of investment to communities	3	5	5	13
Recognition of a single Central Organization of Workers	3	4	5	12
Federal Council of Government Act and its Regulations[b]	3	3	4	10
Total	32	37	37	

Notes:

[a] Patrols are political vigilance bodies that have been established in state enterprises and public bodies, and that in principle are responsible for the organization and political formation of workers.

[b] The Federal Government Council is a body created by the Constitution that deals with the funding of projects and the transfer of resources between different levels of government and community powers.

This table draws attention to the close relationship between the empowerment of organizations with territorial scope and proposals related to the construction of a new socio-productive model. This therefore indicates a very different underlying approach whereby the communities or their organized representation happen to have powers to define the type of business ownership (private or social), the nature of the activity and the scope of the decisions that a company may adopt in the future.

3.4 Corrosion of the Guarantee of Private Property

From the vast amount of regulatory instruments that were generated during successive government terms led by President Chávez, there has been a progressing corrosion of both private property and economic freedom. An example of the growing restriction in these areas is the subordination of corporate actions to elements of national interest.

President Chávez pointed out this matter on several occasions. For example, in his speech of 10 March 2009, when analysing the sense of direction that enterprises should have in their productive activity, he stated:

> Besides which, prices are not to make money. This is one of the differences with capitalism, which seeks only to accumulate money. We are socialists, the Revolutionary Government makes houses to assure the attention of the needs of the people, not to make money … Enterprises have to subordinate themselves to the national interest.

When giving houses to the people President Chávez said: 'All the life I have left will be used serving the weak'.[14]

This subordination of private property to the general interest has found a clear expression in the recognition of the concept of 'relative private property' as provided as part of the so-called 'Salto Delante' of 2004,[15] and developed in the proposal for Constitutional Reform of 2007. Within this analysis it is not assumed that the characterization of property as 'relative' is related to the definition of social property. In fact, the component related to general interest offers a much closer link with a hegemonic control over the decisions of individuals than with the

---

[14] Venezolana de Televisión, National News, 11 March 2009.

[15] See Ministerio para la Comunicación y la Información de la República Bolivariana de Venezuela (MINCI), Taller de Alto Nivel 'El Nuevo Mapa Estratégico' (12/13 November 2004), available at: http://www.minci.gob.ve/wp-content/uploads/downloads/2013/01/nuevomapaestrategico.pdf (accessed 31 December 2013).

promotion of forms of ownership other than private from an ideological perspective.

The majority of the initiatives, regulations and public policies considered here have two additional connotations: (1) they undermine the scope of the right to the free exercise of economic activity; and (2) they help to corrode the guarantee of private property under the Constitution.

Private property is defined in Article 115 of the National Constitution. It is indicated there that the state ensures private property as a way in which every person is entitled to the use, enjoyment and disposal of his or her assets. Additionally, it is pointed out that property will be subject to the contributions, restrictions and obligations established by law with purposes of public or general interest, and only for reasons of public utility or social interest by final judgment and prompt payment of just compensation may the expropriation of any kind of assets be declared.

As has been pointed out, economic freedom is a dimension that is affected concurrently by the interpretation that in effect is applied to the principle of property. Therefore, as situations have been building up in which the principle of property has been adjusted to the needs of the New Model, the principle of property established in the 1999 Constitution has progressively been corroded.

While there is a list of situations that illustrate this matter, in this document the focus is on the decrees of expropriation of enterprises that have been issued since 2004. Since 2002, the government has taken over more than 1,000 means of production through expropriations, interventions or nationalizations. This figure includes the taking over of agricultural land, waging a war against large estates, taking over paralysed enterprises, and the deployment of control over sectors that were declared as strategic. According to the figures offered by the Venezuelan Industrial Confederation, between 2002 and the end of August 2012, the National Executive had taken over 1,168 companies, 41 per cent of which correspond to the construction area; 24 per cent, agro-industrial; 19 per cent, oil; 6 per cent, commercial; and 3 per cent, food, among others such as pharmaceuticals, containers and electricity.[16]

This matter is highly indicative of the siege, and it illustrates the reach that the state currently has over private enterprises.

It must be pointed out that the Venezuelan law of consumer defence, known as INDEPABIS, provides for expropriation as a sanction for

---

[16] See '1,168 empresas intervenidas en 10 años', *El Nacional* (9 October 2012), available at: http://www.el-nacional.com/economia/Expropiacion-Economia-Venezuela_0_59394258.html (accessed 31 December 2013).

economic offences, which were traditionally treated as administrative offences. Moreover, the arguments for expropriation are not entirely predictable. They include the need of the state to reinforce its ability to attend to a particular provision, for safety reasons and food sovereignty. In other words, the motivations to expropriate are so broad that, in the end, they encompass practically the country's whole private production sector.

Neither national utility nor economic sovereignty is defined within the current legal framework in Venezuela. The drastic actions of expropriation that have taken place since 2002 allude to these and other categories, but do not invoke public interest, which is the cause that the Constitution requires as justification to seize private property. Consequently, the decisions for these interventions are based on extra-constitutional reasons.

Table 9.4 Expropriation motivations of analysed cases

Motivation of the expropriation decisions	Number of cases	Distribution (per cent)
Expansion of state operative capacity; the development of a particular government project; strategic sector	73	23.6
Development of tourism	1	0.3
Expropriation of buildings and urban spaces for building homes	82	26.5
Procedures to rescue lands, cancellation of property titles, execution of state property rights, or public lands	36	11.7
Economic reactivation and workers' protection	6	1.9
Make an activity an exclusive state activity	88	28.5
Food security and sovereignty	23	7.4
Total	309	

Source: Official Gazette (several years) and author's calculations

Table 9.4 summarizes the motivations found to have been involved in expropriation decrees in 309 cases studied that were issued between 2002 and 2012. Beyond these numbers, some analytical considerations emerge.

First, the fundamental reasons to expropriate or to apply similar measures to companies or production facilities are related to reserving an activity or exploitation for the state. Second, guaranteeing efficient operation, activation of a strategic plan or implementation of a sector policy are not among the justifications for such measures. Third, seen as isolated cases, the right to housing is relied upon for many of the acts of expropriation. Fourth, if the specific cases of the taking of land and the suspension of licences to distribute fuel were to be added, the distribution would change dramatically. However, it is assumed that the central conclusion regarding the government's motivation in expropriation cases generally would not be altered by modifications of these figures.

An additional point to be made regarding the issue of expropriations is that the decrees containing these measures rarely invoke the Law of Expropriations as their only basis. The regular process relies on other instruments, especially the Law on Food Security and Sovereignty; the Law on Land and Agriculture Development; the Law on the Defence of the People in the Access of Goods and Services; the Special Law of Popular Defence against Hoarding, Speculation and Boycott, and any other conduct that affects the consumption of food or products subject to price controls; and the Organic Law on the State's Reserve of Assets and Services related to primary activities of hydrocarbons, among others.

In sum, this analysis shows that expropriations take place against the economic rationale. They are ordered for other purposes in addition to declaring certain activities to be a public utility.

The first version of this article was completed in April 2012. Yet before final publication the most important elements that constitute the substantive analysis have worsened. First, in May 2012 the labour law reform was enacted, which introduced major changes in contractual relations and inventive schemes for private companies. Second, in January 2014 the Law of Fair Prices, which reiterates the public amenity value for all assets in all economic activities taking place in the country, was passed. According to this law, all profit rates and final prices of all goods and services that are produced, provided or sold in the country are subject to a control scheme. Furthermore, in October 2013 the High Authority for the People's Defence Economy was created, which has become the highest supervisory body for private production. This body exercises discretion over state agencies and the armed forces in matters that concern the relationship of the individual to the state, in a context in which the prevalence of all types of checks and surveillance threatens to take away what has still remained of individual initiative.

4. CONCLUSION

Conclusions from this analysis can be drawn in two directions. In the first place, this chapter attempted to explain what happened with competition policy in Venezuela, and secondly, the objective was to identify the conditions necessary in order for markets and private initiative to exist.

The institutional framework that has been developed in Venezuela since 1999 suppressed the possibility of the free market model to subsist. Venezuelan competition policy has declined and finally disappeared.

The continued implementation of the strategies that have been applied in relation to economic activities has completely neutralized any competition policy agenda in Venezuela, for several reasons:

- There is increasingly less opportunity for the market to function.
- The state is building up a bureaucratic and technological platform to support its intention to monitor all areas of businesses' decision-making processes.
- The guarantee of private property is seriously compromised.
- Markets are distorted through concentration, the nature and extent of barriers to entry and the low number of participants.
- A further distortion arises from the increasing involvement of the state as employer, with significant advantages over private employers.
- Intensive control of economic activities through supervisory bodies and the criminalization of such activities significantly erode the performance of the private economic sector and restrict the functioning of markets.
- The standardization of consumption may compromise the survival of the dimensions of competition related to diversity and choice.

The Venezuelan competition agency as an institution has been practically dismantled. The private sector does not really advocate for a revival of competition policy, because the possible outcomes of competition law intervention would have much less significance than those expected to arise from the government's control agenda.

During the last ten years the state has introduced more than 300 laws and regulations that affect the market conditions, the scope of economic freedom and the guarantee of private property in Venezuela. The purpose of increasing the state's participation in and control over the economy has been to besiege private economic activity. The present analysis of that new universe of laws, regulations and public policy initiatives shows their ability to affect the market's very existence, and the dynamics that may occur in it.

In addition to the regulatory field, the government has developed a strategic guideline to reduce the importance of the private sector in the economy and expand both the role and the importance of the public sector, as well as the presence of a 'social' dimension. One scheme that has been implemented in terms of that strategy has been the expropriation and nationalization of enterprises in various sectors.

In short, both components of the siege, in the sense of the interpretations that have been applied to the principle of private property, render the Venezuelan economy devoid of conditions for the market to operate in and for firms to grow.

The factors that have been analysed above involve a significant institutional regression. The cost of returning to the path of economic development in these circumstances will be much greater than that incurred by the Venezuelan society when it took its first steps in the field of competition policy.

10. Competition and imposition of investment targets in the Brazilian pay-TV market

Arthur Barrionuevo and Pedro Dutra

1. INTRODUCTION

This chapter deals with the legal and economic aspects of the proposal contained in the Questionnaire about the Imposition of Commitments on Conditional Access Service (SeAC) Providers, annexed to Public Consultation No. 65 of 19 December 2011 (Appendix II), drafted by ANATEL, the Brazilian National Communication Agency. The commitments are intended to boost competition and growth in the market for pay-TV services by means of the imposition of coverage targets (number of households) that the operators of these services in the cable-TV sector will be obliged to fulfil, so as to receive a licence to operate in each municipality.

2. THE 'QUESTIONNAIRE'

2.1 The Public Consultation

On 19 December 2011, ANATEL published Public Consultation No. 65, which defines its objective as preparing 'Regulations for Conditional Access Services (SeAC) and the rules that will govern the provision of cable TV services (TVC), multichannel multipoint distribution services (MMDS), direct-to-home television and audio distribution service (DTH) as well as Special Pay TV Services (TVA)'.

However, according to its Point 2.5, the Consultation is based on the following considerations:

> The opportunity to obtain feedback from society with regard to the feasibility of imposing commitments on the companies that have been granted a licence

> to operate SeAC to stimulate investment in land-based telecommunication networks, which contribute to the growth of broadband access in Brazil, as presented in the case files under examination.

This opportunity materializes in a 'Questionnaire about the Imposition of Commitments on SeAC providers', annexed to the Consultation (Appendix II), the text of which reads as follows:

> (1) How should one define the commitments for SeAC providers which belong to major economic groups, so as to make them economically feasible and maximize investments in the expansion of fixed telecommunication networks?
> (2) In this sense:
> (2.1) What types of commitments in terms of provision of SeAC by means of fixed telecommunication networks would be most appropriate?
> Geographical coverage within the service provision area, in the form of service to groups which include more and less attractive municipalities;
> Coverage within a service coverage area, in the form of a percentage of households being able to obtain the service;
> Service provided to public sector establishments or public utilities within the service coverage area.
> (2.2) What are the criteria for determining the major economic groups to be affected by these commitments?
> (2.3) What would be the appropriate level of these commitments?
> (2.4) What would be the appropriate timeframe for meeting these commitments?
> (2.5) What would be the advantages and disadvantages of imposing these commitments?
> (2.6) What would be effective mechanisms for monitoring and supervising the compliance with these commitments?

2.2 The Power Asserted by ANATEL

The purpose of the Consultation was to submit to the public a proposal for regulating conditional access services (SeAC), which is governed by Law 12485/11. However, Point 2.5, which is quoted above, addresses an issue related to broadband services, which is not covered by this SeAC Law.

Surely this is not the appropriate way for ANATEL to carry out its regulatory function: it relied on legal authority the aim of which is to develop rules that deal exclusively with the SeAC, while pay TV constitutes a subject relating to broadband, which, indeed, is not covered by the SeAC Law.

Of course, within the strict limits of its legal authority, ANATEL may adopt rules that are duly motivated and necessary for the control of telecommunication services. However, in the present case, we should rule out any potential argument that SeAC providers, using their land-based networks, offer both pay-TV as well as broadband services.

The approach taken by ANATEL to address a subject that falls outside the realm of the SeAC Law collides with the legal objectives of the Consultation and causes legal uncertainty. ANATEL tends to assert absolute discretion to draft a consultation of the public without paying due regard to the limits of the legal basis that governs it, as we shall see further on.

2.3 An Inappropriate Consultation

The reasons for the creation of the regulatory agencies in the 19th century in the United States, which have also been recognized in Brazil ever since the first decades of the 20th century,[1] lie in the greater technical expertise of these State agencies, which specialize in intervening in the economy, in relation to the judiciary, where many of the disputes resulting from the action of these agencies are finally decided. In addition to their technical expertise, by using their power to regulate the market, the regulatory agencies try to produce more immediate results and benefits for the companies and consumers concerned.

Both characteristics of this form of regulation confer unique flexibility upon the regulatory agency, which neither the judiciary nor the legislature has, namely, when it decides questions of a regulatory nature and adopts rules that regulate the market, it is normally able to achieve its aims.

The technical expertise of the regulatory bodies explains why their power is not limited to enforcing the law, by also encompassing, within the limits of its authority, a rule-making power.

Therefore, the regulatory agency is expected to provide adequate technical responses to questions that arise within its jurisdiction by also adopting and publishing generally applicable rules that take into account the interests of all stakeholders.

Public consultation is not only the most effective instrument for identifying those interests; it is also the appropriate procedure for democratic regimes to take and has its roots in the ordinary legislative process. Representation of society's different interests is not limited to formal parliamentarian representation of the citizens but, in certain

---

1 See P. Dutra, 'Regulação Econômica: Trajetória e Perspectivas' in M.L. Padua Lima (ed.), *Direito e Economica – 30 Anos de Brasil* (Editora Saraiva 2012) 326.

specific situations, should be extended and improved through public consultation in order to identify all relevant interests prior to the adoption of generally applicable rules.

All of these rules, whether they emanate from the legislature or regulatory agencies, should serve the interests of the relevant stakeholders. Of course, the questions that need to be resolved vary in their complexity, as do the interests that the rule-maker has to take account of.

This explains why rules in many fields of market regulation can only reach satisfactory results if the proposals for such rules, on which the public is consulted, are based on technical expertise and if they are drafted in accurate and clear language. The arguments for such rules need to be well exposed, so that the public that is being consulted is able to make useful comments regarding the project.

Quite rightly, Article 42 of the General Telecommunications Law (LGT) establishes that the drafts for regulatory rules must be submitted to the public for consultation.[2] In other words, ANATEL, whenever it intends to adopt new regulatory rules, has to consult the public on the draft for such rules.

Yet the 'Questionnaire' does not comply with these requirements set by the LGT, since – contrary to the proposed regulation of the SeAC Law to which it is annexed – it does not consist of a draft of regulatory rules, but rather a list of extremely complex questions couched in incomprehensible language. In addition, ANATEL did not present any further explanations that would be necessary for a correct understanding of these questions. Indeed, reading the Questionnaire, the question arises of who would be capable of 'defining commitments … so as to make them economically viable and maximizing investments in the amplification of land-based telecommunication networks', owned by 'SeAC providers which belong to major economic groups'?

In the Questionnaire, even ANATEL asks 'what the criteria are for determining the major economic groups that will be affected by these commitments'. In other words, already the first and most important question of the Questionnaire raises serious doubts as to whether it can produce good answers. Also the authors of this chapter do not feel capable of providing such an answer.

Listening directly to society in the way that the Questionnaire does gives the regulatory action a distorted plebiscitary nature. The negative

---

[2] Article 42 reads as follows: 'The drafts of legislative measures will be submitted to public consultation, formalized by publication in the Official Gazette of the Federal Executive, with criticisms and suggestions meriting examination and remaining available to the public in the Library.'

effects of this measure are not only due to its obvious, both formal as well as substantive, impropriety, but also due to the fact that it adds to the regulatory uncertainty from the point of view of society.

If this way of consulting the public were accepted, ANATEL could adopt an approach that is less in accordance with the legal principles that govern market regulation, and ANATEL itself suggest that it should consult society regarding the prices of the telecommunications services regulated by ANATEL.

The legislature wanted to avoid this risk, along with others that challenge ANATEL's regulatory action, by limiting the principle of consulting the public on its original idea, namely, to consult the public on draft rules that are formulated by the agency. After all, the regulation of markets is clearly a technical function and, for this reason, the rule-making power conferred upon the agencies should perform this function, without however getting too detached from the interests of the stake-holders.

2.4 The Questionnaire in More Detail

2.4.1 The proposal contained in the Questionnaire

The 'Questionnaire's' first question is not clear. Its wording conceals its purpose, which is exposed however by its title, namely, to define the way of obliging an SeAC provider, which is a member of an economic group, whose economic activity in the market was supposedly authorized by ANATEL, to invest in its land-based network, in the way and to the extent that ANATEL determines, so as to contribute to the growth of broadband access in Brazil.

In other words, the 'Questionnaire' asks how ANATEL, by means of the rule that it itself has issued, can impose upon a SeAC provider, which operates under the rules of private law and which is owned by private shareholders, the obligation to invest in and amplify their already existing land-based network, so that this provider can be forced to offer broad-band services, all in accordance with the terms and conditions that ANATEL decides.

In the light of Point 2 of the 'Questionnaire' (see at 2.1 above), there is no doubt as to this purpose.

Point 2.1, which relates to the coverage of fixed telecommunication networks, can be summed up in the following way: SeAC providers that belong to major economic groups that already have land-based networks would be obliged:

- to offer broadband access in municipalities that are 'less economically attractive' – that is, to offer the service in municipalities in which there is insufficient demand to recoup the investment;
- to offer broadband access to a number of households that would be fixed by the regulator – that is, to offer the service in municipalities whose income does not allow its inhabitants to contract broadband services at the market's competitive price;
- to offer broadband access to public sector establishments or public utilities, indicated by the regulator.

2.4.2 Economic effects of the proposal contained in the questionnaire

If the purpose pursued by the 'Questionnaire' were implemented, beyond the conflict with its legal basis, the economic effects would be negative: there would be less investment, there would be a decrease in the number of municipalities served by cable networks and, as a result, there would be a drop in the number of subscribers and the level of competition in these municipalities.

An initial analysis of the obligations anticipated by the 'Questionnaire' shows that the burden of imposing commitments to 'maximize investments in the amplification of land-based telecommunications networks' on the 'major groups' would fall on operators acting in competitive open markets, as they are the ones operating under private law, whereby the providers do not have any guarantees of financial stability and, therefore, depend on the profitability of their investments in order to be able to continue investing.

On the occasion of a public hearing that took place on 24 January 2012, ANATEL, listed two main guiding principles of the SeAC's regulations: (i) technological neutrality; and (ii) incentives for investment.

However, the proposal anticipated in the 'Questionnaire' of imposing an obligation to supply under the terms of coverage indices fixed by the agency – and consequently indirectly charging the providers' private shareholders – is contrary to these two principles stated by ANATEL.

The SeAC encompasses the provision of pay-TV services that were previously provided by TVC, MMDS and DTH, without any discrimination whatsoever. By only imposing commitments on those providers that already have 'land-based telecommunications networks' (a euphemism for cable TV, TVC), the 'Questionnaire' seems to revive the technological differentiation that was abolished by the SeAC Law. So, the principle of technological neutrality would be compromised.

Likewise, the incentives for investment would also be compromised. The imposition of commitments to comply with certain coverage indices means exactly the opposite, in other words, part of the investments that the TVC provider would be obliged to make would provide no return. It has to be noted that the entire network would only be paid for by those users who are able and willing to enter into a respective service contract, while that part of the network which it compulsorily extended to households whose residents have no interest in or are not in a financial position to contract the said service would not generate a sufficient return to cover the cost of the additional investment made.

Even in municipalities, where investment projects would be attractive for new entrants by having a positive net present value (NPV),[3] such projects would turn into negative NPV projects, in which it would not be worth investing, since the venture would be unable to cover either the resources invested or its weighted average cost of capital (WACC as it is usually referred to in corporate finance).

This line of reasoning is not merely a theoretical possibility. Using data relating to Brazilian municipalities and operating figures for the sector we can show the negative effects on the making of investments caused by the imposition of targets by means of a simple exercise, which is carried out in two stages.

At the first stage, in 2010, Barrionuevo and Lucinda,[4] in applying a model regarding entry into the TVC sector, identified municipalities where the entry of at least one new provider would be profitable. At the second stage, using data, which was provided by NET Serviços de Comunicação, on average revenue per user by income bracket, operating expenditure and investment expenditure as well as amortization and depreciation terms, it was possible to calculate, taking into account different levels of compulsory investment made in the municipalities listed (measured as coverage in terms of the percentage of households) to examine whether the net gain would be positive (attracting investments) or negative (discouraging the carrying out of investments).

However, prior to this it should be made clear that we start from the assumption that the service is provided under private law and that,

---

3 Net present value (NPV) is the present value of the mathematical sum of future payments and receipts discounted at an appropriate interest rate, minus the cost of the initial investment. The rate at which the NPV is equal to zero is the Internal Rate of Return (IRR) which indicates the profitability of a given investment. In order for an investment to be made, the IRR has to be greater than, or at least equal to, the company's cost of capital.

4 A. Barrionuevo and C. Ribeiro de Lucinda, *Análise das Condições de Entrada no Mercado Brasileiro de TV a Cabo* (Associação Brasileira de TV por Assinatura 2010).

therefore, there are no restraints on the entry of new providers and prices are determined by the competition between them.

If the market operated under a monopolistic regime of exclusivity, such as the TVC service did in the USA prior to the introduction of MMDS and DTH, the price could be fixed at a level that would allow the setting of coverage targets (and hence of investments) previously agreed with the providers. For instance, holding a public tender between possible interested parties for the provision of pay-TV services in a given municipality would make it possible for each of the bidders, by taking into account their efficiency and the expected return, to make an offer to extend the coverage in their area of operation.

This possibility is explained by the fact that the companies would compete 'for' the market and not 'in' the market. Thus, monopolistic prices would make it possible to undertake investments that would not be profitable in competitive markets.

In contrast, where there is competition, monopolistic prices and margins are not feasible, which makes it impossible to reward investment (and as a result extending coverage) in this way. Under a competitive regime, it is competition between the established companies and potential new entrants that reduces prices and stimulates growth in the market and in investments and not compulsory coverage or investment indices.

Thus, there is yet another insurmountable contradiction between the proposal contained in the 'Questionnaire', which simultaneously intends to oblige the providers to furnish coverage in groups of more and less attractive municipalities, instead of allowing the entry of any interested party that has the capacity to bear the administrative costs, providing such parties with an authorization and thus guaranteeing that there would be competition in the SeAC market.[5]

The contradiction in the proposal contained in the 'Questionnaire' is clear. The first set of measures presumes the existence of monopoly power[6] (albeit restricted) in order to finance compulsory investments in areas that are known not to be profitable, while the second combination promotes competition and reduces monopoly power, thwarting the very objective pursued by the previous set of measures.

---

[5] It is of little importance as to whether the 'economic groups' are big, medium or small; the logic in terms of the search for profitability is the same, and the factor that defines this profitability, among others, is the degree of competition in the market, rather than the size of the economic group.

[6] Monopoly power in economic language is the capacity to set prices and, in addition, to avoid competition.

Therefore, bearing in mind the current reality of the pay-TV market in Brazil, where there is intense competition, rapid growth, and in which DTH already accounts for more than 50 per cent of the subscribers, it is wishful thinking to believe that one can impose coverage indices – and the respective non-profitable investments – on either new or old TVC operators.

Other instruments – such as subsidies for users or the reduction of taxes – should be considered by ANATEL for expanding the land-based network and as a result boosting the subscriber base.

2.4.3 Parameters for identifying economically attractive municipalities

In the following, we list the parameters that defined the municipalities that should be economically attractive to new providers.

2.4.3.1 Entry into the pay-TV market The purpose of Barrionuevo and Lucinda's study of 2010 was to understand how the easing of requirements necessary to obtain cable TV licences could contribute to the amplification of the land-based network.

In a competitive market, such as this is, it was examined whether, given the easing of the requirements necessary to obtain cable TV licences, new cable companies would enter those markets where no service is currently available, and, if so, in which markets this would take place.

These questions were evaluated using Bresnahan and Reiss' methodology,[7] whereby the dependent variable is the number of companies offering a specific type of service – cable TV, broadband or a combination of the two, the so-called combo – within a given market. For its part, this number of companies depends upon variables that would determine both the company's variable profit per user and the number of users in a determined city, as well as variables related to the fixed costs of entry in the said area. Based on this it is possible to determine whether, in a given region, the entry of a particular number of companies would or would not be profitable.

Taking into account the figures collected by the Brazilian Telecommunications Atlas and the Brazilian Institute of Geography and Statistics (IBGE), the model was applied to a sample consisting of 1,289 Brazilian municipalities (2007), corresponding to roughly 143 million inhabitants, which is a significant percentage (around 75 per cent) of the country's population (190 million).

---

7 T.F. Bresnahan and P.C. Reiss, 'Entry and Competition in Concentrated Markets' (1991) 99 *J. Pol. Econ.* 977.

The results of this study showed that, in the first place, the majority of Brazilian municipalities that do not have any type of pay-TV or broadband services, or a combination thereof, will remain without any access to these services.

Approximately 3 million inhabitants (15 per cent), out of a total of 21 million who are currently without service, would gain access to some of the services offered by the providers that use cable. The other 85 per cent – corresponding to the remaining 18 million inhabitants – would remain without any access to these services.

It is also important to bear in mind that in addition to these 18 million inhabitants there are another 45 million who live in cities with a population of less than 20,000 inhabitants, for which no figures were collected in the original sample.

The group of municipalities that are home to the 3 million inhabitants where a company would enter with one of the services provided by the cable companies (pay-TV, broadband or a combination thereof) with authorization to enter, in other words, where the market itself creates incentives to entry, are examined below.

2.4.3.2 Entry of new operators with compulsory coverage in the pay-TV market In order to understand how the existence of compulsory coverage affects investment, we used information in relation to revenues, costs and investments that was provided by NET Serviços de Comunicação in the municipalities where the abovementioned study pointed to the entry of a new operator, under the condition that there was no obligation to make any further investments.

The exercise that was carried out was very simple, and involved the simulation of a profit and loss (P&L) statement for the fiscal year, which on the expenses side included the weighted average cost of capital (WACC), which rewards shareholders and creditors, and where the result was a final net margin from the provision of the pay-TV service to households of different income brackets.

In order to determine the impact of compulsory coverage, we start off with the following simplified assumption: when investments are made in a new municipality, the said investments are made in a certain order: the first ones served are the households in the A income class, then those in the B income class, then the C income class and so on down to class E.[8] Below, we calculate the operating margin by the income class A, B and

8 Putting it simply it is also assumed that each household represents either no or only one subscriber. Therefore, there is not more than one subscriber per household.

C, using the average revenue per user, net of indirect taxes, by income bracket, deducting operating expenditure, also by income bracket (in the same way that the average type of package bought by each income bracket varies, so too does the programming cost associated with it). This calculation takes into account all the services offered by a TVC company, namely pay-TV, broadband and fixed-line telephony.

Given the insignificant participation by the D and E income classes in the subscriber base, a value of zero was attributed both for the revenues and for the operating expenditure resulting from the households in these income brackets.

With regard to expenses with investments, capital expenditure (CAPEX) was divided into two categories, CAPEX I and CAPEX II. The main components of CAPEX I are expenses with sales, installation of the service in the user household and the set-top box equipment. The value of CAPEX I is amortized over a period equivalent to the average number of years that a client remains with the TVC company.

The main components of CAPEX II are the expenses of network construction, which were calculated by municipality and by unit of equipment. Although the ideal thing would be to work with the long-term marginal-cost coefficient, where all the costs are variable, some investments are of a 'semi-variable' nature. Thus, a value was calculated for a company that could provide the service to 60,000 households and, based on this, an investment value per household was calculated. The CAPEX II per-household value is depreciated over a period corresponding to the average figure for depreciation regarding this equipment, according to NET Serviços de Comunicação.

So that the economic cost is calculated in its entirety, we need to include the WACC. This value was calculated in the study performed by Baldez de Almeida (2011) in relation to the cost of capital of the pay-TV sector in Brazil,[9] which exhibits different nominal WACC values, calculated according to different CAPM specifications. The following models are utilized: (1) Local; (2) Global; (3) Goldman Sachs; (4) Solnik and (5) Adjusted USA. The different estimates are due to use of different sources of capital: the company's own or that of third parties, and domestic or international.

---

[9] L. Baldez de Almeida, *Custo de Capital do Setor de TV por Assinatura* (Masters thesis, Centro de Estudos em Regulação de Mercados, Universidade de Brasília, Brasília 2011), available at: http://repositorio.unb.br/bitstream/10482/9849/1/2011_LucianaBaldezAlmeida.pdf (accessed 31 December 2013).

In the authors' assessment, the Goldman Sachs estimate of 8.23 per cent p.a. is the most appropriate one to represent this cost in the long term, and for this reason this was the estimate used.

The results of these studies show that the net margin is positive for the A, B and C income brackets, and negative under the assumption of compulsory coverage for the D and E income brackets.

It should be noted that the methodology of calculating the P&L for the period presented here is actually a sophisticated one. For instance, one could calculate the NPV, where depreciation and amortization come in with a positive value, and the fact that it covers a broad timeframe makes it possible to cope with the growth of the business over the years.

However, this would mean assuming a set of additional hypotheses, which are subject to controversy. What would the rate of migration from the D and E classes to the C class be? And from the C class to the B class? How would competition from DTH affect the evolution of the average revenue per user of the different classes? These are just a few examples out of so many other questions, and the underlying assumptions would have to be explained. Since the current calculation is an example, and not a precise estimate, it was decided to keep things simple, with the results being presented below.

Summing up, the procedures used to estimate the likely effects of coverage demands coupled with the access of new operators in the domestic cable TV markets include the following.

Initially, a model was estimated to determine which cities were most likely for companies to enter the local markets, given the profitability incentives. For each of the various different cities, a calculation was made of the number of households in each social class, as per the classifications given by the Brazilian Association of Advertising Companies (ABEP). At the same time, average revenue per user, as well as average cost per user (household) was also calculated. Based on these values, the contribution margin per user in each of the social classes – from A to E – was calculated. Based on these margins, simulations were made of the effects on the profitability of the companies resulting from different levels of coverage demanded from the operators.

Since the coverage commitment makes it compulsory to invest in households with a negative margin, the higher the level of coverage demanded, the less incentive there is for the companies to enter these cities.

Table 10.1 Effects of the compulsory coverage index on investments

Coverage demanded (%)	Cities with profit > 0	Cities with profit < 0	Sum of positive profits (R$)	Sum of negative profits (R$)
10	180	0	218,647,276.13	0.00
20	180	0	218,647,276.13	0.00
30	180	0	218,647,276.13	(606,107.40)
40	178	2	218,647,276.13	(8,634,781.89)
50	164	16	218,647,276.13	(25,737,031.56)
60	126	54	218,647,276.13	(48,328,862.84)
70	90	90	218,647,276.13	(75,832,714.10)
80	71	109	218,647,276.13	(107,516,550.82)
90	53	127	218,647,276.13	(145,009,533.06)
100	15	165	218,647,276.13	(302,035,309.30)

Source: Produced by the authors based on information from the IBGE, NET Communications Services and Baldez de Almeida (2011).

In Table 10.1, one can observe the effects on the incentive to entry resulting from different levels of household coverage demanded.

Although the calculation is merely an example, bearing in mind the substantial number of D and E class households by comparison with that of A and B class households, it can be observed that the compulsory coverage index anticipated in the 'Questionnaire' will have a very pronounced negative effect on the investment decision. The number of cities where there will be an incentive to invest shows an inverse correlation with the coverage index. If ANATEL's objective is, as it claims, to maximize the number of municipalities with TVC providers, the market is itself capable of stimulating providers to enter the 180 municipalities mentioned here. However, if a coverage index is imposed, and if it exceeds 30 per cent of the households, it would have the opposite effect, that is, it would reduce the number of entrants and consequently hamper the expansion of the land-based network.

2.4.4 The Questionnaire's lack of conformity with the law

2.4.4.1 Insurmountable contradictions In its very title, the Questionnaire demonstrates an insurmountable contradiction to the law and, more importantly, a marked violation of the law.

The contradiction lies in the fact that ANATEL is asserting the legal authority to impose commitments and conditions. However, ANATEL is not in a legal position to impose them.

The term 'commitment' presumes the free manifestation of intent, agreement between parties, promisor and promisee. In contrast, any imposition constitutes a unilateral act of a coercive nature that compels someone to comply with the demand or order that is being imposed upon him.

Is ANATEL, by means of resolutions made by its Supervisory Board, authorized to impose commitments on SeAC providers, which have 'land-based telecommunications' networks, and which operate under the private law regime laid down by the LGT?

The answer is negative, not just because of the logical impossibility indicated above, that a 'commitment' cannot be 'imposed', but more importantly because it would be contrary to the law for ANATEL to impose a commitment such as that anticipated in the 'Questionnaire', on any provider of telecommunications services.

2.4.4.2 Violation of the law Under the public law regime on the provision of telecommunications services laid out in the LGT, ANATEL has no power to make investment of private resources compulsory in view of extending the land-based networks used to provide telecommunications services. The Brazilian legal system does not allow for imposing an obligation on a private party to provide a particular service, no matter who this party is.

Public law can only provide for a universal service obligation in the telecommunication sector, if the service provider is identified through a public tender. Indeed, here, the bidder who won the tender will be obliged to increase supply by enlarging the land-based network. Yet, in this case, the universal service obligation is not unilaterally imposed on him, but is included from the start in the tender and the subsequent concession contract. Later, the public authorities may decide that it is necessary to alter the scope of the universal service obligation, but it can only do this by means of renegotiation, never by unilaterally imposing additional obligations.

If under the public law regime laid out in the LGT only the renegotiation of the clauses that govern the provision of the services is allowed, under the private law regime one cannot even contemplate the idea of imposing commitment on providers operating in their area of activity.

The private law regime is one of free initiative. This is a founding principle of the constitutional order, which covers the entire legal system. No legal norm and no public agency – such as ANATEL – is allowed to oppose, restrict, ignore or distort free initiative without legal authorization. The LGT itself acknowledges the constitutional principle of free initiative by establishing that ANATEL as the competent state agency has to respect its Article 126 according to which 'the right to operate telecommunications services under the private law regime will be based on the constitutional principles of economic activity'.

Indeed, the most important constitutional principle of economic activity is precisely that of free initiative, that is, the freedom of the economic agent to initiate its lawful venture in the best way by freely deciding how to invest its capital and what risks to take.

Article 128 of the LGT, which order is also directed at ANATEL, reads that ANATEL 'when imposing administrative constraints upon the right to operate the various service modalities under the private law regime ... will respect the demand of minimum intervention in private life, ensuring that freedom will be the rule, with the prohibitions and restrictions of the public authorities being the exception'.

Therefore, in addition to the requirement for ANATEL to rigorously comply with the law, there is also the obligation placed upon ANATEL to intervene as little as possible in the private legal system, because the legislature understands, and rightly so, that freedom of initiative is the predominant rule for services provided under the private legal system. Furthermore, and without any doubt, administrative constraints do not include the 'imposition of commitments' on SeAC providers as owners of land-based networks, which would indirectly affect also the interests of the shareholders.

The imposition of service obligations anticipated in the 'Questionnaire' would hence result in a shift of decision-making power over the investment of private capital: decisions would no longer be made according to criteria and risks set and assessed by the owners of these resources, but exclusively according to the criteria set by ANATEL, which in this way would extend its jurisdiction to include the resources of telecommunication companies and finally their shareholders.

The shareholders of operators of land-based networks, though operating under a private law regime, would no longer decide how, when and where to invest their resources: under the terms of the 'Questionnaire', by an act issued by ANATEL, this entity itself would decide where to invest these resources.

2.5 ANATEL's Regulatory Power

With regard to the limit to the regulatory powers granted to the regulatory agencies, legal doctrine and jurisprudence have for a long time and to a very copious degree dealt with this subject, and both are unanimous in their view that this power must be restricted under the terms of the law in order to curb the expansionist ambitions of these administrative agencies.

For sure, the tasks that these agencies are entrusted with in terms of regulating markets are complex ones. These entities must be able to rely on legislative instruments that enable them to effectively intervene in dynamic markets, such as is the case with the telecommunications market, which is driven by major technological innovations that come one after the other at great speed.

The collection of answers to public consultations that ANATEL has amassed relies on various legal and economic opinions, the object of which is precisely the limit of ANATEL's regulatory power. For its part, the legal culture developed within ANATEL by its in-house consultants in relation to this and other disputed themes is one of acknowledged technical quality. Therefore, there is a significant body of doctrine regarding this subject, and there is no need here to cover this once again by providing an extensive list of doctrinal and case-law arguments and quotes.

On the other hand, it would not appear inappropriate to inquire what the reasons are, in fact and in law, that induced ANATEL to propose the rules that the 'Questionnaire' anticipates.

Would it be admissible for ANATEL to impose upon providers, who are operating under a private law regime, a duty to make investments in accordance with its commands? Would it be admissible for ANATEL to take away from the shareholders of these providers the right to freely decide in relation to the investment of their resources? Would it be admissible for ANATEL to impose the amplification index of land-based networks and the geographical areas in which they should be amplified? Would it be admissible for ANATEL to determine the criteria for defining major economic groups? And what market reality would be the basis for the proposal contained in the 'Questionnaire'?

It would be reasonable to expect ANATEL, when it took it upon itself to impose commitments, a course of action that is totally foreign to the LGT, to provide a study that could demonstrate the sustainability of the investment in land-based networks to be imposed by it upon SeAC providers. This market study would have revealed geographical areas where there was sustainable demand for broadband services provided by land-based networks which had not yet been developed by private enterprise, despite the fact that the offer of this service has registered pronounced rates of growth over the last few years.

However, ANATEL did not publish any study that would enable it to assume that the investments which it intends to oblige SeAC providers to make, in the manner anticipated in the 'Questionnaire', would be sufficiently profitable to compensate for carrying them out.

Now, if ANATEL itself, which is the regulatory body for the telecommunications sector, and which has more than fifteen years of experience in this capacity, is unaware of any such numbers – or did not disclose them to the stakeholders that it is consulting – how can the stakeholders be expected to know them, analyse them and then reply to the 'Questionnaire'? In addition, this 'Questionnaire' has not presented any properly developed proposal in relation to the form of resolution, such as that regarding the SeAC Law, to which the 'Questionnaire' was attached.

Both the broadband market and the pay-TV market, or the so-called SeAC market as the new law calls it, have been registering significant rates of growth. And this growth is due to the foresight of the drafters of the LGT, who established the rule that these services should be provided under private law and thus facilitated the creation of a competitive regime that is directly responsible for the allocation of investments in the networks that has enabled the expansion in the supply of these services that has been observed.

The desire to have broadband and pay-TV services at one's disposal is the wish of all consumers, in the same way that having a mobile phone was in the past – a wish that, to a large extent, has been satisfied, as can be observed from the figures in connection with this service, which continue to grow, as do the figures for broadband and pay-TV.

It should be noted that the growth in the supply of telecommunications services has been sustainable, in other words, capable of rewarding the investments that make it possible. It is the competitive pressure in these markets that is behind the expansion in the supply that has been observed over the last few years, and this expansion continues because the prices of these services are falling, with the providers of these observing the rule that only competition can increase supply, improve quality and reduce prices of goods and services.

3. THE LAW ON CONDITIONAL ACCESS SERVICES (SEAC) AND THE CABLE LAW

The Law on Conditional Access Services (SeAC Law) totally redefined the regulatory framework of pay-TV in Brazil by revoking and amending previous regulations. Among the most significant aspects of the new regime that was established by the SeAC Law is the deliberate abandonment of the division that previously characterized the provision of these services by the different technologies by means of which the services could be provided. Before the adoption of the SeAC Law, there were multiple regulations governing this service according to the different technologies for providing them.

One of these regimes, related to the provision of cable TV (TVC) services, stipulated an obligation to provide such cable TV services in designated geographical areas, and a duty on the provider, by means of a determined index, to extend its network to the previously designated area. In current terms, it set coverage indices (ICs).

The universal services obligation, where the exclusive right to operate is granted to a private party by the public authorities, is not foreign to the law. The adoption of such a policy makes it possible to increase supply when it is not feasible under a competitive regime, and in this context the provider is the only one who is authorized to provide the service in the designated area.

The opposite occurs under a regime of free competition based on private law, under which, as is well known, all telecommunications services are provided with the exception of the fixed line telephone services. In this case, the supply – the 'coverage' of the market – is dictated by the competitive dynamics of the market, which forces the providers to decide on the amount of investment, and the risk to run, that is needed in order to meet the demand for their services. Under this regime, the regulator is especially called upon to suppress and prevent any abuse of economic power that restricts or may restrict competition.

The SeAC Law radically changed the regulatory structure of pay-TV services in response to the experiences made in this market, and completely opened it up to free competition, according to the law governing it. All SeAC providers will compete for the preferences of the users of their services, being governed by the same legal rule. And thus they have to decide how, where and when to invest. A provider's success will depend on its getting this decision right, as it will be in direct competition with the other providers, all of whom are seeking the preference of SeAC users.

However, migration to the regime established by the new SeAC Law is not compulsory. That is to say, the TVC provider is not obliged to migrate to the SeAC regime. Article 37(2) SeAC Law states that

> the current providers of TVC, MMDS, DTH and TVA, as long as they meet the necessary objective and subjective conditions, may ask ANATEL to adapt their respective licences to the terms of authorization for the provision of the conditional access service.

Therefore, there is no obligation for providers to migrate from the previous regime to the one created by the SeAC Law. However, those providers who migrate to the new regime will be subject to it in full, while the previous law will cease to apply to them.

The aforementioned Article 37(2), of the SeAC Law improperly provides for the 'adaptation of the respective licences to the terms of authorization'. In other words, the licences that were granted for the provision of services (TVC) under the regime that preceded the SeAC Law would be 'updated' and thus transformed into authorizations to provide services of conditional access. This wording contradicts the meaning of the SeAC Law.

As has already been seen, the regime for the provision of services of conditional access is radically different to that under which pay-TV services were provided. The new regime has its own instruments, and its first one, as the enabler of the SeAC provider, is the authorization granted to it by ANATEL. The authorization grants the right to provide services of conditional access in the way that the SeAC Law establishes. There is no such thing as a conversion, or an adaptation of legal regimes: there was the previous regime, which was revoked – it left the legal world – and now the new legal regime is in force. Likewise, there is no way to convert licences, which were instruments of the regime that has expired, to authorization, which belongs to the new regime that has taken the place of the previous one.

In our opinion, the aforementioned Article 37(2) SeAC Law should be read in the following way: 'the current providers of TVC, MMDS, DTH and TVA, as long as they meet the necessary objective and subjective conditions, may request from ANATEL … the authorization to provide conditional access services'. This wording corresponds to the sense of the SeAC Law. One cannot imagine two classes of authorization pursuant to the SeAC Law, one in the form of an adapted authorization and the other as an original authorization granted under the SeAC Law.

The provider who migrates to the regime of the new law will obviously no longer be subject to the legal regulations that were previously applicable to it. The licences and the contracts of those providers who did not migrate to the SeAC regime will remain in force, that is to say those who opted to continue under the previous regime.

One cannot imagine that any providers will migrate, and take up this option that the SeAC guarantees them, while at the same time remaining under obligations that were in force under the previous legal regime. The opposite assumption would be absurd, by requiring recognizing a special class of provider that carries a double list of obligations: those established under the regime that has expired and those established by the regime that is in force. This double regime would force the provider to comply with previous demands in relation to the coverage of areas, although the SeAC Law has already entered into force. The targets set at that time are obligations of the previous regime, not the current one, and therefore can no longer apply.

The SeAC regulations cannot establish such double obligations. Although Article 89(11) of the Consultation No. 65 may suggest it, a close examination does not confirm this suspicion; on the contrary, it disproves it:

> (11) Providers of TVC, MMDS, DTH and TVA Services who adapt their consent instruments should undertake to comply with the obligations assumed under their current licences, in each Service Provision Area, within the timeframes established in the respective licence instruments, *as long as this does not conflict with the SeAC Law*. [Emphasis added]

Without specific authorization, regulations cannot stipulate what conflicts with the intent of the legislature; therefore, it is not possible for ANATEL to add things to the SeAC Law that are not compliant with what was stipulated by the legislature.

The duty to comply with obligations established by law or by previous contracts should be resolved in that context. However, Article 89(11), of the Consultation as quoted above, eliminates any doubt by establishing at its end that the command contained in the provision may not conflict with the SeAC Law.

As has been shown, the SeAC Law does not establish, nor does it confer the power to establish compulsory coverage of geographical areas. This obligation, which was agreed under the previous regime and at that time was applicable to TVC, has no place in a fully competitive regime such as that established by the SeAC Law. Therefore, in respect of the provision of conditional access services, the law does not provide any legal basis according to which a provider of such services carries the obligation to cover certain geographical areas.

The authorization to provide conditional access services initiates a new era for those providers who are already operating in the pay-TV market, of competition not just among each other, but also in relation to the new entrants, to the authorized providers who are starting off in this field of activity.

As is well known, in competitive markets, competitive pressure is the key factor behind the investments that are made by competing undertakings. And these investments are aimed at meeting the demand from users, which increases because competitive pressure results in a continuous drop in the prices of the services provided.

Because of this fact, in competitive markets, maintenance of a universal service obligation of universalization is simply out of the question. Such obligation – which is always agreed, but never imposed – loses its meaning in markets where the regime is one of free competition. For this reason, under a private law regime, the very essence of which is free competition, there is no room for obligations in terms of area coverage, of universal service, of any obligations whatsoever being stipulated by the regulatory agency in terms of the enlargement of the network.

Once the SeAC Law is in force, how could it set obligations in terms of coverage, which is a concept that was inherited from the previous regime that has now been revoked? Undoubtedly, in this new era, with the coming into force of the SeAC Law, competition should be much more intense. This is why it is so important that the SeAC Law should unify the market that is being inaugurated, under a single set of rules.

4. CONCLUSION

First, the imposition of commitments in terms of investments that is anticipated in the Questionnaire, equal to an instrument of a state-run economy, would contradict the economic order as defined in the Constitution. The Brazilian constitutional legislature rejected coercive intervention in the same way Italian legal scholars argued that the state should not command private economic activity. Brazil's political experience has been that coercive intervention produces harmful results – in the telecommunications market as well – and for this reason, that regime was eliminated by the present Constitution, which granted to the state the task of regulating and monitoring economic activity, always in accordance with the law.

Second, the imposition of commitments in terms of investments – the imposition of coverage – on SeAC providers would not only damage the legal system, it would also derail the entire competitive structure of the broadband and pay-TV market, which would result in a decrease in the supply of pay-TV and broadband services, contrary to that which might be assumed from an initial examination of the proposal contained in the Questionnaire.

Third, the economic effect of the implementation of the measures anticipated in the Questionnaire would be negative. Contrary to ANATEL's intention, the imposition of coverage would prevent investments in municipalities that are economically attractive to a new entrant.

Instead of increasing investments, it would reduce new investments in networks by TVC companies, consequently reducing the number of households that could be reached by means of the ordinary expansion process. Table 10.1 shows the significant impact in this sense, and also reveals that the higher the coverage index, the greater the negative impact on investment. Therefore, if it were ANATEL's objective to increase the number of municipalities where there is investment, the market would be capable of encouraging the expansion of services to include a further 180 municipalities. However, if this purpose were admissible and ANATEL were to impose a coverage index that exceeded 30 per cent of the households, the effect of this measure would be the opposite of what was intended: entry of providers and the expansion of Brazil's cable network would be severely hampered.

Fourth, the SeAC Law explicitly prohibits obligations in terms of coverage of geographical areas in the form of coverage indices. On the contrary, it arrives as vigorous stimulus to free competition. The legislator has been advised that this regime is the regime provided for in the Federal Constitution and therefore established in the LGT. But what is more, the SeAC Law clearly allows the profitable allocation of resources, which stimulates competition, thus boosting supply, as can be seen from the marked indices in the growth of supply that have been observed in the pay-TV market. Previous obligations in terms of coverage indices have to be abandoned within the framework of the law and, it should be noted, of the conditions imposed in the framework of its implementation.

11. Intellectual property rights: from state-initiated restraints of competition to state-initiated competition

Rudolph J.R. Peritz

1. INTRODUCTION: TWO QUESTIONS AND A DEEP CONFLICT

This chapter addresses two questions about US intellectual property rights as state-initiated restraints of competition. First, what explains the reversal of fortunes, the decline of antitrust, the elevation of IPRs to primary importance, and, in consequence, a weakened commitment to free competition? Second, how can the benefits of free competition be re-introduced into the policy debates over IPRs, debates concerning the public interests in advancing economic growth and promoting fair distribution of its benefits?

After discussing the decline of antitrust, this chapter offers a surprising source for re-introducing competition policy and, with it, an entirely new approach to resolving a long-standing tension between IPRs and antitrust at its breaking point – the deep conflict between a patent holder's fundamental right to exclude and the antitrust prohibition against a monopolist's refusal to deal.

2. THE CONTEXT

Intellectual property ownership has become a critical issue in current debates concerning not only national competition policies but also international trade and development, whether about the availability of generic pharmaceuticals, the impact of TRIPS on developing countries, the adoption of the controversial Anti-Counterfeit Trade Agreement (ACTA), or corporate acquisitions of large patent portfolios.

Why have intellectual property rights (IPRs) become the overriding issue in these intertwined debates? Simply put, because all three – competition, trade, development – call for attempts to mediate between stronger rights to encourage innovation on the one side and, on the other, better access to increase its dispersion; all three involve questions about the relationship between economics and politics; and all three provoke rhetorical swordplay between those defending free markets and those defending industrial and trade policies. Of course, things are never so simple as the dueling rhetorics portray, especially because *laissez-faire* as well as trade and industrial policies are all economic programs shaped and enforced by political institutions.

This chapter focuses on national competition policy and the status of IPRs in the US debates.

In the United States, the dominant view holds that stronger IP protection leads naturally to more innovation, more competition, and more economic growth. Given the dominant view, it is easy to forget that there is nothing natural about IPRs and that they are state-initiated restraints of competition.

But IPRs have not always been held in high regard. When the US Congress passed the first national patent and copyright acts in 1790, many viewed the statutes as necessary evils, as state-created monopolies to be minimized. This attitude still prevailed a century later, when the Sherman Anti-Trust Act, the national competition statute, was passed. Through the early 1900s, progressive-minded legislators and political activists were intent on controlling the power of all monopolies, including those attributable to IP ownership. Even that era's *laissez-faire* Supreme Court shared the progressive view of IPRs despite their conservative view of general property rights. This broadly held antipathy toward monopoly was expressed in decisions involving intellectual property rights when, for example, the Supreme Court rejected arguments that copyright or trademark ownership should allow manufacturers to set resale prices, or that patent ownership should justify forced bundling provisions in sales contracts.[1] For most of the 20th century, the antitrust statute's national competition policy trumped IPRs, with the result that they were strictly confined. Conduct such as setting resale prices or

1 *Dr. Miles Medical Co. v. John D. Park & Sons Co.*, 220 U.S. 373 (1911); *Motion Picture Patents Co. v. Universal Film Co.*, 243 U.S. 502 (1917). On resale price maintenance, see R.J.R. Peritz '"Nervine" and Knavery: The Life and Times of Dr. Miles Medical Company' in E. Fox and D. Crane (eds), *Antitrust Stories* (West Publishing, 2007), also available at: http://ssrn.com/abstract=959425 (accessed 31 December 2013).

forced bundling was prohibited because it fell outside the strict scope of specific statutory rights granted by patent, copyright, or trademark laws.

More recently, however, the relationship between IPRs and antitrust has been turned on its head. Since the 1980s, not only have IPRs been strengthened but antitrust enforcement has been diluted; now, IP ownership shields much anti-competitive conduct from antitrust scrutiny. Thus, for example, antitrust courts no longer prohibit trademark owners from setting resale prices for branded goods they sell to independent retailers; nor do courts prohibit patent owners from requiring customers to buy complementary products bundled with their inventions.[2]

3. WHY THE REVERSAL OF FORTUNES?

And so the first question: given the long-standing commitment to free competition, what can explain the 30-year decline of antitrust and, at the same time, the expansion of IPRs despite their clear character as state-initiated restraints of competition?

The place to begin is the commitment to 'free competition'.[3] What exactly do we mean by 'free competition'? The answer becomes clear once we restate the question as follows: What is it we want to free competition from?

In the United States, this question has long elicited two sharply different responses. First, we want to free competition from political control, from oppressive government intervention. In this sense, free competition expresses a commitment to entrepreneurial liberty, and antitrust is seen as a market-based alternative to government industrial policy. Second, we want to free competition from private economic control, from the oppressive power of accumulated private capital. In this second sense, free competition expresses a commitment to rough equality and, here, antitrust is seen as a market-based mechanism to limit private economic power. In sum, free competition reflects commitments to both liberty and equality, and concerns about oppressive power, both political and economic.

---

[2] In both examples, the doctrinal analysis is not quite so simple. The approach is a rule of reason, which calls for a fact-intensive analysis to determine legality. But the practical effect is *de facto* legality, given the high cost of litigation and the low probability of success. See also the Patent Act, 35 U.S.C. § 271(d)(5) regarding bundling of patented inventions.

[3] This framework was introduced in R.J.R. Peritz, *Competition Policy in America: History, Rhetoric, Law* (rev. edn, OUP 2001).

But these commitments to equality and liberty can produce a fundamental tension in the idea of free competition. When free competition's commitment to economic equality calls for government intervention to curb private economic power, that very government intervention infringes on free competition's commitment to liberty. As suspicion of government intervention has deepened since the era defined by the Nixon Administration's Watergate scandal in the United States, a *laissez-faire* inflected distrust of government intervention has surpassed progressive concerns about economic and commercial inequality. In consequence, the dominant ideology in the US now favors free markets in the belief that they are better left alone than monitored or regulated by distrusted government.

Understanding the forces driving antitrust's decline provides the background for inquiry into the coincident rise of intellectual property rights. Aren't IPRs too the products of intervention by distrusted government? Yes, they are. Even more deeply than antitrust regulation, aren't IPRs state-initiated restraints of free competition? The answer again is: Yes, IPRs infringe on commitments to both liberty and equality. First, IPRs infringe on free competition's commitment to liberty since they result from direct government intervention. Second, IPRs also infringe on free competition's commitment to equality insofar as they grant IP owners direct government support of private power to pursue economic monopoly.

So, what has led US policy makers to expand IPRs despite their conflict with free competition's commitments to both liberty and equality, particularly their conflict with the liberty interest driven by distrust of government intervention?

Two different conceptions of IPRs have justified their expansion notwithstanding their doubled restraint of free competition. First, some have viewed IPRs as natural rights. Second, others have viewed patent and copyright in particular as constitutional entitlements, as pre-governmental rights to encourage innovation. In both views, the government's animating role has slipped out of the picture.

First, IPRs are broadly understood as an especially compelling form of natural property rights. Their moral foundation is especially compelling because they not only satisfy John Locke's labor theory of value but also reward the Romantic genius of individual imagination. This image of inventorship has tied innovation to individual effort; this inventorship is associated more with Steven Jobs' persona than with his battalions of employees, more with Nobel Prizes awarded to individuals in biology and medicine than with the international networks of high-priced laboratories supporting the named winners. In this view, the government is not seen as the source but rather the protector of ex-ante IPRs. What emerges is a powerful ideology of IPRs as the just deserts of individual genius, as commercial reward for success in intellectual competition on the merits. Thus any expansion of IPRs is seen as fuller protection of perfectly natural rights, while any narrowing of IPRs is seen as oppressive government restraint of the natural workings of competitive markets.

Second, there is the dominant scholarly view of patent and copyright as constitutional rights, rights enacted but not created by government. Indeed, the US Constitution does empower Congress to enact patent and copyright protection for the specific purpose of advancing knowledge and industrial technology.[4] And so patent and copyright can be understood as constitutionally drawn incentives to encourage inventive activity, incentives to encourage research and development. This view is consistent with the intuitively attractive economic tenet that IPRs provide the financial incentive needed for inventors to invent and for investors to invest in research and development. And when they do, all of society benefits from the economic progress that results. In economic terms, without the incentive of patent and copyright protection, new ideas and their embodiments are too quickly and too easily copied, imitated, and reproduced. Inventors and their investors will not gain enough profit to undertake the risky enterprise of research and development. In this economic translation of constitutional imperative, government intervention is justified by the market failure of unfettered competition.

So patent and copyright, whether viewed as natural or constitutional rights, have been expanded in the belief that more is better, that maximizing the means maximizes the ends, whether the ends are protection of natural rights or encouragement of inventive activity to promote economic progress.

Though the natural rights view is popular, it is the constitutional rights view that has always informed scholarly and policy debates in the US, the view that patent and copyright are the private means to promote the public benefits of innovation and economic growth. So it is worthwhile to interrogate the economic incentive logic that has come to dominate the constitutional rights view of patent and copyright as the private means to produce the public benefits of economic progress.

Although the economic incentive rationale for patents and copyrights is intuitively attractive, the fact is that it simply does not hold because there are deep problems with the logic, problems that have been recognized by

---

[4] 'To promote the Progress of Science and useful Arts, by securing for limited Times, to Authors and Inventors, the exclusive Right to their respective Writings and Discoveries', US Constitution, Article I, § 8, cl. 8.

economists and policy makers for almost a hundred years: though the incentive rationale for IP rights makes common sense, the fact is that it does not stand up to close scrutiny.[5]

First, there are theoretical critiques that go back almost a century. As a general matter, there is no logical basis for assuming that increasing the means increases the end. To equate them is a logical category error. Then there is the more focused economic criticism that incentive theory does not take into account opportunity costs; that is, it does not account for the lost benefits of alternative investments, benefits that would have resulted from investment in, for example, more production or better employee training.

Second, in addition to theoretical critiques, over 50 years of economic studies have failed to find empirical support for the benefit side of incentive theory. Let me be clear about this: despite fifty years of trying, there is no empirical evidence to support the view that the economic benefits of intellectual property rights are superior to free competition in the production of innovation or the advancement of economic growth. In sum, the private benefits of patents and copyrights to inventors and investors can tell us nothing about their effects on the public good.

Though the economic incentive story provides no justification for IPRs as state-initiated restraints of free competition, the story remains dominant for several reasons. Not only is the Romantic image of individual inventorship enthralling, but the ideology of natural property rights is commanding, as is the financial and political power of those whose business models depend on protection of IPRs. And supporting these forces is an anxious neo-mercantilist insistence that IP protection must be maximized because it represents the United States' last competitive advantage in global markets. Finally, there is the jurisprudence, whose persistent category error equates means with ends, and private profit with public benefit. Despite a century of scholarly criticism, too many scholars and judges in the United States still proceed as if maximizing patent rights serves to maximize innovation and, with it, economic progress. These forces have entrenched the dominance of IPRs in the United States despite long-held antipathy toward state-initiated restraints of competition.

[5] For references, see R.J.R. Peritz, 'Competition *Within* Intellectual Property Regimes – The Instance of Patent Rights' in A. Ezrahi and S.D. Anderman (eds), *Intellectual Property and Competition Law: New Frontiers* (OUP 2011) 27.

4. THE RE-INTRODUCTION OF FREE COMPETITION

Although IP debates in the US have only begun to recognize the equality and access-based arguments voiced by the human rights community, economic criticisms of the incentive story have gained traction in mainstream IP literature.[6]

These developments open the door to my second question: How can the benefits of free competition be re-introduced into the policy debates concerning IPRs, debates addressing the twin public interests of advancing economic growth and promoting fair distribution of its benefits? There are competition policies waiting to be applied, neglected competition policies already at hand.

The surprising source for these new arguments to re-invigorate free competition policy lies not within the boundaries of antitrust but rather within the IP domain itself.

This essay concludes with an example of the patent regime's baseline commitment to free competition. The example serves two purposes. First, it illustrates one fundamental way in which competition policy governs and limits patent rights. Second, this instance of patent competition policy is so powerful that if it were properly understood by antitrust courts, it would radically change their view of patent rights and, with it, their antitrust tolerance of anti-competitive conduct by patent owners. You might say I am taking antitrust to patent school to teach something about free competition.

My example proceeds in two steps. First, I describe the competition logic supporting a recent and influential Supreme Court patent decision that limits the owner's right to stop competitors from using its patented invention. Second, I apply the Court's limiting patent logic to a landmark antitrust decision in order to correct the court's overly deferential view that patent ownership automatically provides a shield of antitrust immunity.[7]

Antitrust courts have consistently and mistakenly concluded that as a general matter, patent ownership automatically justifies a dominant firm's refusal to deal so long as the refusal lies within the scope of a valid

---

[6] Peritz (n. 5 above); W.M. Landes and R.A. Posner, *The Economic Structure of Intellectual Property Law* (Harvard University Press 2003) 9–10 and 294–333.

[7] *Independent Service Organizations Antitrust Litigation*, 203 F.3d 1322 (Fed. Cir. 2000), *cert. denied*, 531 U.S. 1143 (2001) (hereinafter *Xerox*). See n. 8 below for discussion of its continuing landmark status.

patent. Why? Because the courts view it as the patent owner's fundamental right to deny access to the patented invention.

But these antitrust decisions have failed to separate the question of a patent's validity from its power to exclude. It is this very distinction between right and remedy that provides the basis for the Supreme Court's patent decision in the landmark *eBay* case, which tightened the requirements for a patent holder to obtain an injunction against an infringer.

In its *eBay* decision, the Supreme Court pointed to the patent statute, which explicitly instructs judges to apply traditional equity principles to balance private and public interests in determining whether an injunction should be issued. Since the *eBay* decision, patent holders have found it much more difficult to persuade courts to restrain infringing competitors from selling their patented inventions. As a result, more infringers are permitted to compete against the patent owner with the owner's patented invention. Of course infringers do not get away scot free; they must pay damages and reasonable royalties. But they are permitted to compete.[8]

Although the Supreme Court's *eBay* opinion has widely influenced lower courts to limit the power of patent owners to restrain competitors, this patent law decision has not been understood in competition terms and, in consequence, has had no influence on antitrust decisions involving the competitive effects of patent ownership.

Yet it makes perfect sense that patent law's approach to injunctions should be imported into the antitrust analysis of refusals to deal by dominant firms because the legal questions and economic stakes are precisely the same. In both, patent owners seek judicial authorization to restrain competition on the logic of patent rights to exclude.

So, what would patent law's competition logic look like in an antitrust case involving a dominant firm's refusal to deal?

5. RESOLVING THE DEEP CONFLICT

In a well-known pair of antitrust decisions, the *Kodak* case in California and the *Xerox* case in Washington, DC, two influential Federal Courts of

---

[8] *eBay Inc. v. MercExchange, L.L.C.*, 547 U.S. 388, 126 S.Ct. 1837 (2006). According to the Court, an injunction is only issued if the following requirements are fulfilled: '(1) the right-holder has suffered an irreparable injury; (2) remedies available at law, such as monetary damages, are inadequate to compensate for that injury; (3) considering the balance of hardships between the plaintiff and defendant, a remedy in equity is warranted; and (4) the public interest would not be disserved by a permanent injunction', 126 S.Ct., 1839.

Appeal concluded that as a general matter, patent ownership justifies a dominant firm's refusal to deal, a refusal to do business with competitors, so long as the refusal is within the scope of a valid patent since the essence of a patent is the right to refuse others access to the invention.[9]

But these antitrust decisions have failed to recognize that all litigation, including antitrust and patent litigation, involves two separate issues. The first is liability: Was there an infringement of patent rights? If the answer to the liability question is yes, then there is the second issue of remedy. Is the dominant firm always justified in refusing to sell a rival replacement parts that are patented? Does patent infringement automatically justify an injunction? Recognition of that simple distinction between liability and remedy is the framework for the Supreme Court's landmark patent decision in *eBay*: Just because patents are statutory property rights they do not require the automatic finding that their infringement calls for the property remedy of injunction. Injunctions are equitable remedies; what that means in the Anglo-American tradition is that courts are called upon to balance the public and private impact of keeping a patent infringer off the market. In other words, patent courts are called upon to do a particular kind of competitive impact analysis.

The competition logic suffusing the *eBay* decision is not new. Indeed, in a somewhat neglected opinion, the Supreme Court declared over 25 years ago that there is a 'baseline of free competition upon which the patent system ... depends'.[10] Since the turn of the 21st century, *eBay* is but one in a series of Supreme Court decisions that has limited IP rights, especially patent rights, in ways that restrain their effects on free competition.[11]

So what would patent law's competition logic of equitable balancing look like in the two influential antitrust cases mentioned above, both

---

[9] *Xerox* (n. 7 above); *Image Technical Services, Inc. v. Eastman Kodak Co.*, 125 F.3d 1195 (9th Cir. 1997), *cert. denied*, 523 U.S. 1094 (1998). The two courts agreed on the principle that patent ownership provides a legitimate business justification for a dominant firm's refusal to deal with competitors, though they did disagree in other respects. There have been no circuit court decisions directly on point since this pair. Since the Supreme Court later curtailed the Federal Circuit's jurisdiction over antitrust claims in *Holmes Group, Inc. v. Vornado Air Circulation Systems, Inc.*, 535 U.S. 826, 829-30 (2002), *Xerox* no longer has precedential value but retains persuasive value, particularly given its agreement with the approach earlier taken in *Data General Corp. v. Grumman Systems Support Corp.*, 36 F.3d 1147 (1st Cir. 1994).

[10] *Bonito Boats, Inc. v. Thunder Craft Boats, Inc.*, 489 U.S. 141, 145–7 (1989). See Peritz (n. 5 above).

[11] Peritz (n. 5 above).

involving a monopolist's refusal to deal?[12] I will apply the logic to the facts in one of them – the *Xerox* case.[13]

Xerox persuaded the Federal Circuit Court of Appeals that patent ownership provided the reasonable business justification necessary to immunize from antitrust liability its refusals to sell patented replacement parts to competitors who service and repair Xerox copiers. If the equitable approach taken in the Supreme Court's *eBay* decision were imported into this antitrust case, then patent ownership would not automatically excuse the refusal. Rather, Xerox would have the more substantial burden of persuading the court that its refusal to sell replacement parts to independent service companies should be permitted in the circumstances. To determine whether the refusal should be permitted, the court would apply *eBay*'s competition logic of equitable balancing. This traditional equity approach would require the court to evaluate and then balance four factors to determine whether the restraint would be fair in the circumstances.[14]

First, Xerox would have to prove that it would suffer irreparable harm if required to sell patented replacement parts to a competitor. Here, irreparable harm is not likely. To begin with, there would be no harm to Xerox's reputation. What of loss of market share? That would occur only if the services offered by Xerox were inferior or if its prices were higher. And that harm would result from competition on the merits, not from competitors' free riding on Xerox's accomplishments.

Second, what of Xerox's lost profits? According to the second factor, which overlaps the first to a significant extent,[15] the refusal is not justified if damages would provide adequate compensation. Generally, damages are viewed as adequate compensation for lost profits. And here profits would be lost only if Xerox sold replacement parts to independents at wholesale, something they would not be required to do. Moreover, profits from replacement parts might actually increase if better quality service brought more customers into the market.

---

[12] The Federal Circuit has recently recognized competition as the public policy factor in applying *eBay*'s injunction test. *Bard Peripheral Vascular, Inc. v. Gore & Assoc.*, 670 F.3d 1171, 1192 (Fed. Cir. 2012).

[13] *Xerox* (n. 7 above).

[14] The four factors are listed supra (n. 9 above).

[15] This observation appears in an extensive critique of *eBay*'s injunction jurisprudence. M.P. Gergen, J.M. Golden and H.E. Smith, 'The Supreme Court's Accidental Revolution? The Test for Permanent Injunctions' (2012) 112 *Colum. L. Rev.* 203.

Third, would a requirement to deal impose greater hardships on Xerox than a refusal to deal imposes on independent competitors? Here, a requirement to deal would impose hardship on Xerox only if production of parts could not meet demand, an unlikely event especially if parts manufacture was outsourced, as it usually was. On the other hand, given the typical lack of interoperability between functional substitutes – for example, Xerox machines will not take Kodak or IBM replacement parts – Xerox's refusal to deal would cause great hardship to the independent service companies and to competition more generally in the repair market for Xerox copiers.

Fourth and finally, what is the effect of the court's permitting Xerox's refusal to deal on the public interest? Given US antitrust's identification of public interest with consumers, the inquiry would address the more narrow question of the impact on consumers. In the short run, antitrust's traditional static efficiency analysis would conclude that permitting the refusal to deal would restrain competition and, as a result, likely lead to higher prices.

In the long run, the dynamic efficiency analysis associated with patent policy and more recent antitrust policy would inquire into the impact on innovation. The traditional answer is that a loss of monopoly profits would lower Xerox's incentive to innovate and, in consequence, social welfare would be harmed. But as described above, current economic analysis has shown the traditional incentive theory to be unsupported in fact or theory. So, even if Xerox were worse off, that does not mean less innovation or less progress overall. Indeed, society might be better off. Why? There are numerous reasons, including the following two. First, any funds not invested in research and development might be better off spent, at least in part, in other activities, including more production or more research that yields invention whose value does not call for patent protection. These are termed opportunity costs. Second, competition provides its own incentive to innovate, but without the social costs of monopoly profits and thus greater dispersion to users, both consumers and follow-on inventors.

Taking the Supreme Court's patent jurisprudence seriously calls for antitrust courts to perform an equitable balancing of the four factors driving the *eBay* decision's competition policy. Applying this teaching of patent law to the antitrust trial of Xerox's refusal to deal would impose a burden on Xerox to show that the equity test clearly points in favor of restraining competition. But it doesn't: There is no harm to its reputation. Lost profits are compensable by damages. Here, additional competition in the repair market could increase profits in the market for the patented replacement parts; lost profits, if any, would result from competition in the repair market and thus would not merit damages. The balance of hardships clearly falls on the independent service companies, not Xerox. And finally, the public interest, here defined in terms of consumer benefits of lower prices, better service, and more choice following more follow-on innovation, all weigh on the side of requiring Xerox to sell its patented repair parts to independent competitors.

To conclude, recall that the Federal Circuit in the *Xerox* case viewed patent ownership as an automatic business justification for a dominant firm's refusal to sell replacement parts to independent repair companies. The result was no competition on the market. Correcting this mistaken view of patent rights and their relationship to antitrust policy marks the importance of taking antitrust to the patent school of free competition.

We started with a patent, a state-initiated restraint on competition, and then applied its logic to an antitrust case, with the effect being state-initiated, involuntary cooperation between a dominant firm and its rivals, and with the forced cooperation's ultimate result being state-initiated competition.

6. AN AFTERWORD

The public interest in promoting competition and nourishing its rich environment for innovation is particularly vulnerable when a patent-holder's refusal to deal involves a standards-essential-patent (SEP) – a patented component that firms must use with their own products and services to interoperate with industry-wide standard technologies.[16] In these SEP cases, the patent holder typically seeks an injunction against firms negotiating licenses at royalty rates the holder rejects as too low. Most cases arise in the context of industry standard setting organizations that have adopted the SEP holder's technology in exchange for the holder's agreements to license the SEPs to everyone on fair, reasonable and non-discriminatory (FRAND) terms. The common question in these cases is whether the SEP holder can obtain an injunction and thereby refuse to deal with the would-be licensees unless royalty rates increase.

US and European agencies and courts increasingly tend to agree that FRAND terms provide adequate remedies at law and, thus, that injunctions are unavailable. But unlike the refusal to deal cases such as *Xerox* discussed in this essay, the compulsion to cooperate in SEP cases comes

---

[16] My thanks to Josef Drexl for bringing these cases to my attention and for clarifying their significance, and to Peter Picht for providing several European references.

not from the state and its public policy to promote competition. Rather, the compulsion to cooperate comes from private agreements forged in the negotiations of industry standard setting organizations. The state is simply holding the SEP holder to its bargain contract – its promise to license at FRAND rates in exchange for designating its patent the industry standard.

While there is growing trans-Atlantic consensus that injunctions should be denied in SEP cases if certain requirements are fulfilled, doctrinal authority diverges. In the US, courts and agencies have explicitly applied the Supreme Court's patent logic from *eBay*,[17] while continental European courts and the European Commission mostly discuss competition law as a defense to the claim for the injunction, expressing particular concern about abuse of dominant positions derived from holding SEPs.[18]

---

[17] See, e.g., *Apple, Inc. v. Motorola, Inc.*, 869 F. Supp. 2d 901 (N.D. Il. 2012) (Posner, Circuit J., sitting by designation), available at: http://publicaa.ansi.org/sites/apdl/Documents/Standards%20Activities/Critical%20Issues/Judge%20Posner%20Opinion%20in%20Apple%20v.%20Motorola,%20June%2022,%202012.pdf (accessed 31 December 2013); *reversed in part, vacated in part, affirmed in part, remanded*, – F.3d – , 2014 WL 1646435 (Fed. Cir. 2013), available at: http://cafc.uscourts.gov/images/stories/opinions-orders/12-1548.Opinion.4-23-2014.1.PDF (accessed 31 December 2013). See also U.S. DOJ/USPTO, 'Policy Statement on Remedies for Standards-Essential Patents Subject to Voluntary F/RAND (8 January 2013), available at: http://www.justice.gov/atr/public/guidelines/290994.pdf (accessed 31 December 2013) (citing *eBay* and expressing competition concerns). This approach also made it back to England where courts in SEP cases have now decided that an injunction will not be issued under the general English law principle when damages provide an adequate remedy at law. See *Nokia OYJ v. IPCom GmbH*, [2012] EWHC 1446 (Ch.)

[18] See, e.g., District Court The Hague of 14 March 2012, Dkt. Nos. 400367/HA ZA 11-2212, 400376/ HA ZA 11-2213, 400385 / HA ZA 11-2215 (*Samsung Elecs. Co. Ltd/Apple Inc.*) (applying both competition and contract analyses). In the two SEP cases against *Samsung* and *Motorola Mobility* (Case COMP/39.985), the European Commission expressed its view that the owner of an SEP that has entered into a FRAND commitment abuses their market dominant position if they claim injunctive relief against a user who has shown their willingness to negotiate a FRAND license. On 29 April 2014, the Commission terminated proceedings in both cases, on the one hand, by accepting binding commitments by Samsung to refrain from seeking injunctions in Europe based on its SEPs against producers of smart phones and tablet PCs, and, on the other hand, by rendering a prohibition decision against Motorola Mobility that had refused to enter into similar commitments. See European Commission of 29 April 2014, Case AT.39939 – *Samsung – Enforcement of UMTS Standard Essential Patents*, C(2014) 2891 final, available at: http://ec.europa.eu/competition/antitrust/cases/dec_docs/39939/39939_1501_5.pdf (accessed 31 May

Nonetheless, the two bodies of law, patent law in the US and competition law in Europe, both point in the same direction: the public interest in competition that spurs innovation and improves consumer choice. This contrast in approach provides a telling example of how US patent law's fundamental commitment to free competition can provide a powerful antidote to US antitrust doctrine that misguidedly restrains competition when allowing dominant firms to monopolize markets by refusing to deal with competitors.

2014); European Commission, 'Antitrust: Commission finds that Motorola Mobility infringed EU competition rules by misusing standard essential patents', Press Release IP/14/489 (29 April 2014), available at: http://europa.eu/rapid/press-release_IP-14-489_en.htm?locale=en (accessed 30 April 2014) (Commission decision not yet publicly available). The Commission's actions were triggered by lower court decisions in Germany against Apple in which Samsung and Motorola Mobility were granted injunctions. In March 2013, the investigation of the European Commission convinced the Düsseldorf District Court to refer a similar case on SEPs concerning the 4th generation mobile phone standard to the Court of Justice of the EU (CJEU) with questions regarding the conditions under which claiming an injunction for the enforcement of an SEP against a willing licensee has to be considered abusive. See Case C-170/13 *Huawei Technologies*. The questions asked by the German court are available at: http://curia.europa.eu/juris/document/document.jsf?text=&docid=139489&pageIndex=0&doclang=EN&mode=req&dir=&occ=first&part=1&cid=394895 (31 May 2014). Accordingly, a competition law decision on the use of SEPs from the CJEU can be expected in the foreseeable future.

PART 4

Public procurement and state subsidies

12. Benefits of competition policy in public procurement with special reference to India

S. Chakravarthy

1. INTRODUCTION

For most developing and developed countries, government procurement is of great potential interest as it accounts for a substantial proportion of GDP. But the prevalence of discrimination in this area of government procurement, as well as other practices, creates significant barriers to trade, ultimately adversely impacting the countries' growth and their GDP. Essentially, barriers to efficient and sustainable development are identified as corruption and clientelism in public procurement policies.[1]

The WTO is addressing the problem in the form of its Government Procurement Agreement (GPA). And yet, because of the challenges posed by the problems listed above, the GPA, as a mere 'plurilateral' agreement,[2] has not been adopted and agreed to by a large number of members of the WTO.[3]

This chapter lists the challenges that exist in government procurement and gives an overview of the need for and the features of an appropriate instrument to govern government procurement policies. This chapter also addresses the Indian scenario covering procurement policies, practices and institutions, the reforms undertaken in 2005 and the specific problems and challenges faced by India in this area.

---

[1] R. Wade, 'The System of Administrative and Political Corruption: Canal Irrigation in South India' (1982) *J. Development Stud.* 18; R. Wade, *Governing the Market: Economic Theory and the Role of Government in East Asian Industrialization* (Princeton University Press 2003).

[2] In contrast to 'multilateral' agreements, plurilateral agreements are not part of the mandatory WTO law that is accepted by WTO Members when they join the organization.

[3] Currently the GPA has been signed by 43 WTO Members (March 2014).

2. GOVERNMENT PROCUREMENT, COMPETITION AND ITS SIGNIFICANCE FOR GOVERNANCE[4]

In developed and developing countries, the performance of government procurement impacts governance and the interests of citizens. It cannot be gainsaid that performance is positively impacted if procurement is competition driven. For procurement to be pro-citizen interest and pro-good governance, overt and conscious policies promoting effective competition among potential bidders/suppliers are imperative. Absent such policies, a procurement system is unlikely to be healthy. In turn, healthy operation of competition depends upon measures that effectively exclude collusion among bidders and suppliers. The economist Frédéric Jenny takes this proposition further when he says that promoting competition involves not only preventing collusive practices but also removing barriers that unnecessarily impede healthy competition.[5]

Procurement jurisdictions in many parts of the world accord a high role to competition law. Competition policy and law frown upon collusive practices and bid-rigging. In most competition laws, bid-rigging is prohibited pursuant to the rules against cartelization. Indeed, bid-rigging is often considered illegal *per se*. Such practices are perpetrated even in countries with effective competition regimes, imposing a heavy cost on the governments and their citizens and consumers. Even in jurisdictions that do not recognize *per se* rules, bid-rigging will hardly have any chance of being exempted from the cartel prohibition. Clarke and Evenett have noted that as much as a quarter of documented competition law enforcement actions in developing economies involve bid-rigging in relation to public procurement activities.[6] Anderson, Kovacic and Müller have surveyed the experiences of some developing countries and suggest

---

[4] This section leans on Section 4 of S. Chakravarthy and K Dawar, 'India's Possible Accession to the Agreement on Government Procurement: What Are the Pros and Cons' in S. Arrowsmith and R.D. Anderson (eds), The WTO Regime on Government Procurement: Challenge and Reform (Cambridge University Press 2011) 117.

[5] F. Jenny, 'Competition and Anti-Corruption Considerations in Public Procurement' in OECD (ed.), *Fighting Corruption and Promoting Integrity in Public Procurement* (OECD 2005).

[6] J. Clarke and S.J. Evenett, 'A Multilateral Framework for Competition Policy?' in State Secretariat of Economic Affairs and S. Evenett (eds), *The Singapore Issues and the World Trading System: the Road to Cancun and Beyond* (Swiss State Secretariat for Economic Affairs 2003), also available at: https://www.alexandria.unisg.ch/publications/22224/L-en (accessed 31 December 2013).

that gains (cost savings) from implementation of transparent and competitive government procurement regimes 'can be substantial'.[7] At a Conference of BRIC countries (Brazil, Russia, India and China) in Kazan, the capital of Tatarstan, in early September 2009, an estimate placed the benefit (cost savings) flowing from competition-driven government procurement at US$10 billion.[8] The possibility of bid-rigging is particularly relevant to public sector purchases, given the legal obligations to award contracts by competitive tenders. Further, parties involved in bid-rigging often perceive government to be blind to collusive practices and consequently indulge in bid-rigging while participating in tenders.

Another beneficial dimension of the impact of competition, besides cost savings and protecting the interests of the procuring agencies, government and consumers, is the engendering of integrity in the administrative process of procurement. Massive government procurement regarding food grains, for instance, is handled by an army of functionaries at the villages' and farmers' levels. Many of them are low-paid employees of the government (or of public-sector undertakings) and integrity is not always assured. In procurement operations, rent-seeking activities and corruption at the level of lower order functionaries obviously result in higher prices. Bidders sensing the presence of corruption tend to factor it in while finalizing and submitting their bids. Higher procurement prices result in higher costs for the government and ultimately hamper economic growth and development.[9]

Corruption, as noted in the introduction to this chapter, constitutes a barrier to efficient and sustainable development and is a scourge on the welfare of citizens in many countries, particularly the developing ones. Corrupt practices are a subcategory of the rent-seeking phenomenon, which means the dissipation of a society's resources through activities

---

7 R.D. Anderson, W.E. Kovacic and A.C. Müller, 'Ensuring Integrity and Competition in Public Procurement Markets: A Dual Challenge for Good Governance' in S. Arrowsmith and R.D. Anderson (eds), The WTO Regime on Government Procurement: Challenge and Reform (Cambridge University Press 2011) 681.

8 See also Chakravarthy and Dawar (n. 4 above) 136 (information provided by D. Kumar, former Chairman, Competition Commission of India).

9 K.A. Elliot, *Corruption and the Global Economy* (Institute for International Economics, 1997); A.K. Jain (ed.), *Economics of Corruption* (Kluwer Academic Publishers, 1998), as cited in Chakravarthy and Dawar (n. 4 above) 137.

that enrich individual market participants at the expense of others, without contributing to the welfare of society as a whole.[10]

Corruption is an internal issue for all governments and not just a trade issue. Transparent procedures will reduce the adverse effects of corruption on procurement and incidentally send positive signals to foreign investors. Effective competition can be and is a tool for reducing corruption and imparting integrity in procurement procedures. This in turn enhances the quality of governance. The author's experience supports the views of Anderson et al. that competition policy is highly complementary to the liberalization of national procurement policies,[11] and the links between the two policy areas may be particularly important in the context of developing economies.

3. APPARENT NEED FOR A LEGAL INSTRUMENT TO PROMOTE PRO-COMPETITIVE PUBLIC PROCUREMENT

For promoting competition, transparency, integrity and protecting the state budget in national procurement regimes, an appropriate legal instrument is a *sine qua non*. An instrument that readily comes to mind is the WTO Agreement on Government Procurement (GPA). The GPA is an important international legal instrument that can and will facilitate procurement reform. But it is not the only available tool for countries to address procurement reform. Countries could negotiate procurement provisions in bilateral and regional trade agreements (RTA) or adopt and implement unilateral reforms based on the UNCITRAL Model Law for Public Procurement,[12] for instance. While the GPA offers a stronger and more comprehensive instrument to regulate procurement, its guiding principles – fairness, integrity and efficiency – are similar to those promulgated by international organizations such as the UN, APEC and the OECD, and advocated by NGOs such as Transparency International. The selection of an appropriate instrument and establishment of a scheme of procurement around its principles, despite the costs and challenges that this would involve, would provide an unparalleled opportunity to promote good governance and competition in procurement practices, in

---

10 Anderson, Kovacic and Müller (n. 7 above).

11 Ibid.

12 UNCITRAL Model Law on Public Procurement of 1 July 2011, available at: http://www.uncitral.org/uncitral/en/uncitral_texts/procurement_infrastructure/2011Model.html (accessed 31 December 2013).

addition to important export market opportunities engendering sustainable economic and social development.

4. WHAT THIS INSTRUMENT NEEDS TO CONTAIN

As a general proposition, the instrument should be designed to protect against wasting money in government procurement. It should therefore establish an increased level of competition, transparency and discipline. By providing fair and clear procedures, the instrument should seek to increase efficiency within procurement agencies. This will help check overt corruption while saving finances by increasing efficiency of resource allocation.

This instrument needs to incorporate provisions limiting discrimination in awarding tenders. WTO provisions on national treatment and non-discrimination should inform the overall approach of the instrument towards entities and sectors covered by it. This is likely to engender the general benefits of greater competition – lower prices, better quality and more efficient firms. It cannot be gainsaid that the impact of non-discrimination provisions will be substantial. Baldwin and Richardson note that a ban on procurement discrimination leads to greater imports from foreign suppliers when the domestic industry is substantially or predominantly dependent on the government as the buyer of the goods that it produces for the domestic market, and the price paid by the government exceeds the price paid by domestic private customers to import the same product.[13]

It would be apposite to say that national treatment and non-discrimination commitments such as those set out in the GPA can attract more foreign bidders and are likely to generate the greatest improvements in value-for-money for governments and enable them to spread their scarce budgets further across their populations.

The instrument needs to incorporate a transparent framework of laws, regulations, procedures and practices regarding government procurement. This will likely encourage transparency in the transactions of the procurement agencies and provide non-discriminatory, timely, transparent

[13] R.E. Baldwin, *Non Tariff Distortions of International Trade* (Brookings Institution 1970), 3; R.E. Baldwin and J.D. Richardson, 'Government Purchasing Policies, Other NTBs, and the International Monetary Crisis' in H.E. English and K.A.J. Hay (eds), *Obstacles to Trade in the Pacific Area: Proceedings of the Fourth Pacific Trade and Development Conference* (Carleton School of International Affairs, Ottawa 1972).

and effective procedures enabling suppliers to challenge alleged breaches of the instrument. A government that implements such an instrument is therefore likely to reduce rent-seeking tendencies and corruption. This is likely to lead to procurement being based on more objective criteria, thereby further reducing costs. Greater clarity in the terms and conditions for applying for state procurement contracts is likely to attract larger numbers of both domestic and foreign firms to bid. Small and medium-sized enterprises, which many governments historically seek to protect, would welcome and respond positively to increases in procurement-related transparency.

The instrument could be a bilateral or a regional trade agreement or even a multilateral one. As noted above, the GPA is one such instrument.

5. THE WTO PLURILATERAL AGREEMENT ON GOVERNMENT PROCUREMENT

The GPA is at the moment a plurilateral WTO agreement with only a few WTO Members that have become a party to it. Parties to the GPA get legally guaranteed access to the procurement markets of other GPA signatories. Anderson and Osei-Lah note[14] that this market access is not insignificant. For example, the accession of Chinese Taipei in 2009 has been estimated to bring GPA signatories additional procurement opportunities of more than $20 billion annually.[15] While there is limited potential for some of the poorer developing countries to access the procurement markets of bigger GPA members such as the EU, US or China, there are countries, like India, which have had success in their effort at accessing the procurement markets of other countries. Indian exports have steadily continued to grow rapidly. By 2007, Indian exports were valued at US$100 billion, while merchandise exports from 2005 to 2006 rose by approximately 25 per cent over the previous year. Software

---

14 See R.D. Anderson and K. Osei-Lah, 'Forging a More Global Procurement Market: Issues Concerning Accessions to the Agreement on Government Procurement' in S. Arrowsmith and R.D. Anderson (eds), *The WTO Regime on Government Procurement: Challenge and Reform* (Cambridge University Press 2011) 61.

15 US Trade Representative, 'Ambassador Ron Kirk Applauds Taiwan's Accession to the WTO Agreement on Government Procurement', Press Release of 22 July 2009, available at: http://www.ustr.gov/about-us/press-office/press-releases/2009/july/ambassador-ron-kirk-applauds-taiwans-accession-wto-ag (accessed 31 December 2013).

services constitute a major portion of exports. According to Nasscom, software services exports grew by over 33 per cent from 2005 to 2006 to US$17.3 billion. Demand has been strong in traditional as well as new service sectors – supply management, engineering applications and a host of other such areas.[16] India is not yet a signatory to the GPA and is therefore well placed to take advantage of the export opportunities offered by the GPA. The market access India would gain under the GPA would exceed that in a bilateral or regional trade agreement. An estimate of the possible effect of membership for India places its welfare gain at between 0.3 and 1.7 per cent of the GDP.[17]

If a country were to join the GPA, access to its market for GPA signatories would follow as a consequence. Notwithstanding the legitimate need to provide protection to some sensitive sectors of the economy, this should lead to various benefits flowing from opening up domestic public procurement to competition, including improved value for money from higher-quality goods and services offered by foreign industry and from pressure on domestic firms to improve their own competitiveness as a result of foreign competition. The opening of the national procurement market should also facilitate the transfer of technology in certain high-technology procurement areas.

Finally, membership to the binding plurilateral GPA sends powerful signals to both governments and foreign investors that the signatory WTO Member commits to the principles of transparent, fair and competitive procurement markets. The GPA provisions require the availability of transparent and effective procedural mechanisms to challenge procurement decisions, on the one hand, and of redress to firms that have participated in the bid, on the other hand. Violations of the rules of the GPA can be challenged in the framework of the WTO Dispute Settlement Mechanism, which offers a binding independent forum to any WTO Member that feels its rights under the agreement are being denied. The GPA was revised in 2012.[18] The key elements of interest to developing

---

16 *The Financial Express*, 'Exports Drive India's Growth Story' (17 August 2006) available at: http://www.financialexpress.com/old/fe_archive_full_story.php?content_id=137512 (accessed 31 December 2013).

17 See S.J. Evenett, 'Multilateral Disciplines and Government Procurement', in P. English, B.M. Hockman and A. Mattoo (eds), *Development, Trade and the WTO: A Handbook* (World Trade Organization 2002) 417.

18 Revision of March 2012, which entered into force 6 April 2014 after 11 WTO Members had accepted the Revision Protocol. For further information see WTO, 'Revised WTO Agreement Enters into Force' (7 April 2014), available at: http://www.wto.org/english/news_e/news14_e/gpro_07apr14_e.htm (accessed 30

countries are contained in Article V of the Revised Agreement on Government Procurement. The provision reads:

1. In negotiations on accession to, and in the implementation and administration of, this Agreement, the Parties shall give special consideration to the development, financial and trade needs and circumstances of developing countries … recognizing that these may differ significantly from country to country. …
3. Based on its development needs, and with the agreement of the Parties, a developing country may adopt or maintain one or more of the following transitional measures, during a transition period and in accordance with a schedule, set out in an Annex to its Appendix I, and in a manner that does not discriminate among the Parties:
   a. a price preference programme, provided that the programme:
      i. provides a preference only for the part of the tender incorporating goods or services originating in other developing countries applying the preference or goods or services originating in other developing countries in respect of which the developing country applying the preference has an obligation to provide national treatment under a preferential agreement, provided that where the other developing country is a Party to this Agreement, such treatment would be subject to any conditions set by the Committee; and
      ii. is transparent, and the preference and its application in the procurement are clearly described in the notice of intended procurement;
   b. an offset, provided that any requirement for, or consideration of, the imposition of the offset is clearly stated in the notice of intended procurement;
   c. the phased-in addition of specific entities or sectors; and
   d. a threshold that is higher than its permanent threshold.
4. In negotiations on accession to this Agreement, the Parties may agree to the delay of the application of any specific obligation in this Agreement, other than Article V:1(b), by an acceding developing country while that country completes its implementation of the obligation. …
8. The Parties shall give due consideration to any request by a developing country for technical cooperation and capacity building in relation to that country's accession to, or implementation of, this Agreement.

April 2014). The Revised Agreement on Government Procurement is available at: http://www.wto.org/english/docs_e/legal_e/rev-gpr-94_01_e.htm (accessed 30 April 2014).

6. INDIA – PROCUREMENT POLICIES, PRACTICES AND INSTITUTIONS

The definition of government procurement differs from country to country. In India, it is defined as procurement made for and on behalf of the government, and includes the central government, state governments, public sector undertakings (PSUs) and other public bodies.[19] While data from cross-national studies suggest that government procurement typically constitutes between 10 and 15 per cent or more of a country's total economic activity,[20] in India its overall value is very likely significantly higher given the role of public companies in key sectors of the economy, such as the railways. The value of Indian procurement markets in 2003, according to the World Bank, was estimated to be in the order of US$100 billion, representing over 20 per cent of its GDP.[21]

India's procurement policy has been discriminatory, at least to a degree, as it admonishes government departments and entities to follow a certain hierarchy of preferences. This hierarchy requires them to prefer first the purchase of goods wholly produced in India; second, goods manufactured in India from imported materials; third, purchase from foreign suppliers for which stock is held in India; and last, imported products received for supply through Indian agents or India-based establishments. Participation by foreign firms has been welcomed in particular sectors. Purchasing entities have been accorded the discretion to give price preference to domestically produced products over imported ones and also to articles produced by cottage and small-scale industry over those manufactured by larger ones. For instance, in 1980 the Bureau of Public Enterprises mandated central government ministries and departments as well as PSUs to grant a price preference to PSUs up to 10 per cent, and even more in appropriate cases. If the price offered by a PSU

---

[19] See the Government of India's response to the Questionnaire on Government Procurement Services, WTO Doc. S/WPGR/W/11/Add.14 (7 January 1997).

[20] OECD, 'The Size of Government Procurement Markets' (2002), available at: http://www.keepeek.com/Digital-Asset-Management/oecd/industry-and-services/the-size-of-government-procurement-markets_9789264196308-en#page1 (accessed 31 December 2013) and cited by Chakravarthy and Dawar (n. 4 above) 119, note 7.

[21] World Bank, 'India Country Procurement Assessment Report' (2003), available at: http://web.worldbank.org/WBSITE/EXTERNAL/PROJECTS/PROCUREMENT/0,,contentMDK:20108359~menuPK:84285~pagePK:84269~piPK:60001558~theSitePK:84266,00.html (accessed 31 December 2013).

was within 10 per cent range of the lowest offers, negotiations were held with the PSU and the tender was awarded to it at that lowest offer.[22]

Social responsibility informs the rationale for price preferences in India. Small firms, cottage industries and women's employment schemes operate in economically backward regions and procurement can provide employment to these sectors of the population. The Indian government has used procurement contracts to direct employment towards marginalized groups such as the scheduled castes, for example in labour-intensive public works contracts or by unbundling or splitting up large contracts into smaller packages to enable domestic firms and particularly SMEs to fulfil them. The procurement of specific pharmaceuticals has also been restricted to some PSUs for similar social welfare arguments. PSUs have been protected from competition through reservation, and both central government departments and PSUs have been allowed to grant price and purchase preferences to public sector suppliers.[23]

At the federal level, there is no single law exclusively governing public procurement of goods in India.[24] The federal regulatory framework in place consists of: (1) the General Financial Rules (GFR); (2) the Delegation of Financial Powers Rules (DFPR); (3) the Manual on Policies and Procedures for Purchase of Goods issued by the Ministry of Finance (Manual); (4) government orders regarding price or purchase preference or other facilities to sellers in the handloom sector, cottage and small-scale industries and to central PSUs, and so on; and (5) the guidelines issued by the Central Vigilance Commission to increase transparency and objectivity in public procurement.[25]

Acknowledging the need for enhancing administrative flexibility and ensuring full accountability for the use of public funds and appropriate transparency mechanisms, the Indian government has recently ushered in reforms in the area of procurement by government and its entities. The General Financial Rules (GFR) governing central-level procurement in India have been overhauled, laying down certain basic principles and providing that every authority delegated with the financial powers of procuring goods in the public interest shall have the responsibility and

---

22 Referred to in A. Hoda and B. Suchi, 'Transparency in Government Procurement', Indian Council for Research on International Economic Research in International Economic Relations Working Paper No. 129 (April 2004).

23 V. Srivastava, 'India's Accession to the GPA: Identifying Costs and Benefits' in A. Mattoo and R.M. Stern (eds), *India and the WTO* (OUP 2003) 235.

24 Some Indian states have enacted such laws, for example, Tamil Nadu.

25 See Chakravarthy and Dawar (n. 4 above) 120.

accountability for introducing efficiency, economy and transparency in matters relating to public procurement and for maintaining fair and equitable treatment of suppliers and promotion of competition in public procurement. All government purchases are now mandated to abide by the principles outlined in the GFR. Organizations with a website must publish their tender notices and enquiries on those websites, while those without a website must post the notices on the National Information Centre (NIC) website. Central procurement agencies follow the procedures set out below,[26] depending upon the circumstances and factors underlying the procurement:

The normal procedure for procurement over Rs 2.5 million (one US dollar is approximately fifty Indian rupees) is through open tender. However, department heads have discretion in deciding whether to advertise tenders abroad. Open tenders are invited through advertisements published in the *Indian Trade Journal*, and in two national daily newspapers.

Limited tendering is allowed for procurement up to Rs 2.5 million, advertised to pre-selected approved suppliers. This is also allowed in cases of urgency and where justification is provided by the ministry or department; where it is considered not to be in the public interest to procure goods through open tender; and where the possibility of additional suppliers being tapped is deemed to be remote.

Frequently used goods required by central-government entities on a recurring basis are typically purchased under negotiated (following due process) rate contracts administered by the Directorate-General of Supplies and Disposals (DGS&D) in the Department of Commerce. These contracts are intended to allow the procurement of goods from reliable sources without the need for recurrent tenders. It is important to note that, in principle, there is no preference for domestic as opposed to imported goods for such procurement. Foreign manufacturers may be registered, with or without Indian agents. However, both Indian and non-Indian suppliers must be able to provide after-sales support in India, and the products purchased must be 'suitable for use' in India.

[26] WTO Secretariat, 'Trade Policy Review: India' (2007), WTO-Doc. WT/TPR/S/182/Rev.1. In 2011, the WTO undertook another trade policy review on India, which also covers public procurement policies: WTO Secretariat, Trade Policy Review for India (2011), WTO-Doc. WT/TPR/S/249, available at: http://www.hse.ru/data/2011/11/10/1272142468/India%20-%20s249_e.pdf (accessed 31 December 2013).

For petty purchase of goods or works, cash purchase is resorted to. In such cases, a minimum of three offers must be obtained and the supply contract has to be given to the lowest offer.

The GFR also provides for purchase of goods without requesting multiple offers (up to Rs 15,000) and purchase of goods by local purchase committees, set up by the government department that want to purchase (up to Rs 100,000) (Rule 151 GFR).

Procurement in the railways, postal, telecommunication and defence sectors is subject to specialized procedures but within the overall framework of the GFR. Competition from foreign suppliers is generally permitted in respect of high-technology or high-value items. In the railways sector, foreign firms are free to participate in tenders advertised in India. Payment against such contracts must be made in Indian Rupees on a par with indigenous suppliers. Global tendering is frequently used in procurement of rolling stock, wheels, machinery and plant equipment, including technology transfer.

As a part of the modernization of federal procurement, tender documents have been substantially standardized on the basis of national or international standard specifications. In respect of global tenders, more time is generally given for submission of overseas bids than in the cases of domestic tenders and notices are published or disseminated through Indian embassies.

The reforms of 2005 were designed with the specific objectives of promoting competition and of ensuring fair and equitable treatment of suppliers, yet for political reasons and due to the inherent social-responsibility approach, the preferential policies were retained in practice for central public-sector and micro and small enterprises. The 2007 WTO Trade Policy Review noted that for tenders valued between Rs 50 million and Rs 1 billion, a central public-sector enterprise whose bid is within the 10 per cent range above that of a large private unit is allowed to revise its price downward and is eligible for a contract or parallel-rate contract. Further, micro and small enterprises receive purchase and price preferences in procurement by Central Government ministries and departments and PSUs. Under the purchase-preference system, 358 specified items must be procured exclusively from micro and small enterprises. The price preference system also provides that if the price offered by a micro or small enterprise is not more than 15 per cent above the price offered by a large enterprise, the product must be purchased from the former.[27] Micro and small enterprises are assisted by way of: (i) issue of tender sets free

[27] Extracted from Chakravarthy and Dawar (n. 4 above).

of cost; (ii) exemption from payment of 'earnest money' (deposits); and (iii) waiver of security deposits up to the monetary limit for which the unit is eligible, based on certain transparent criteria.[28]

Transparency takes a back seat for unsuccessful bidders. They are informed of not having been successful through a regret card. The experience of unsuccessful bidders suggests that the competent authority deciding on the tender does not generally furnish reasons for the rejection of their bids. There also is no requirement to publish details of the contracts awarded.

However, India has a good dispute resolution mechanism. In the event of a dispute, the parties are encouraged to resolve differences with the purchaser by mutual consultation. If this fails to resolve the dispute within 21 days, then either the purchaser or the supplier may give notice to the other party of its intention to commence arbitration. If the contract is with a domestic supplier, the applicable arbitration procedure will be conducted under the Indian Arbitration and Conciliation Act 1996. If the contract is with a foreign supplier, the supplier has the option to choose either the application of the Indian Arbitration and Conciliation Act 1996 or arbitration in accordance with the provisions of the UNCITRAL Arbitration Rules. The venue of arbitration is generally the place from where the contract has been issued except when a foreign supplier opts for arbitration in accordance with the provision of UNCITRAL Arbitration Rules, in which case the venue can be a neutral country. Citizens can also lodge complaints with the Central Vigilance Commission (CVC) or with ombudsmen to trigger investigations into alleged acts of corruption in procurement by public officials or politicians. This is complemented by the Right to Information Act 2005, which enables general access to information about procurement decisions within a specified time frame. Internal and external audits of procuring agencies and offices at the federal and local levels are other instruments in place to curb and detect corruption in public procurement. The reports of external audits are made publicly available.[29]

There is one important mechanism for redress for unsuccessful and disappointed bidders. They can avail themselves of the writ jurisdiction of the High Courts and the Supreme Court (Articles 32 and 226 of the

---

28 WTO Secretariat (n. 26 above).

29 ADB/OECD Anti-Corruption Initiative for Asia and the Pacific, 'Curbing Corruption in Public Procurement in Asia and the Pacific' (Asian Development Bank and OECD 2005) 58, available at: http://www.oecd.org/site/adboecdanti-corruptioninitiative/37575976.pdf (accessed 31 December 2013)

Constitution of India). They are entitled to challenge any administrative action that violates fundamental rights.

Having said this, it cannot be gainsaid that, when compared to challenge mechanisms set out in the WTO GPA or most regional trade agreements, the Indian framework for review mechanisms is incomplete and unsatisfactorily defined.[30] This has negative consequences because in addition to providing redress, bid challenges are important self-monitoring and self-implementing mechanisms.[31] They allow those most affected by the failure to apply national procurement laws to have redress, ensuring that problems in the procurement system are identified and addressed quickly and efficiently.

Chakravarthy and Dawar note as follows:

> Overall, while various regulations governing Government purchasing practices exist in India, in general procurement legislation and bid challenge mechanisms in India are incomplete and in places ill-defined. Furthermore, the procurement framework does not have the quality of Parliamentary Law and therefore not all deviations from the rules are subject to judicial review. A 2008 World Bank study on Public Financial Management and Accountability (PFMA) in urban local bodies analysed the linkages that exist between the legislative, budgeting, implementation, reporting and oversight process in urban local bodies in India. The report concluded that the main constraints to strong PFMA in local Government are the weak legal framework, low demand for accountability, lack of incentives for compliance or penalty for non-compliance with existing rules, and limited use of available guidelines.[32]

Despite the 2005 reforms referred to above and the overarching economic reforms of 1991, the Indian procurement framework still lacks elements of transparency, fairness and efficiency that are essential to ensuring sustainable economic and social development.

---

30 See, for background on the WTO requirements in this area, S. Arrowsmith, *Government Procurement in the WTO* (Kluwer Law International 2003) 384–405

31 See D.I. Gordon, 'Constructing a Bid Protest System: The Choices that Every Procurement Challenge System Must Make' (2006) 35 *Pub. Contr. L. J.* 427.

32 Chakravarthy and Davar (n. 4 above) 124.

7. SUGGESTIONS FOR A ROAD MAP FOR INDIA[33]

Given the problems and challenges facing India in the area of government procurement, it needs to posit an appropriate instrument to encompass the elements of transparency, integrity, fairness and efficiency in the public procurement scheme. The GPA is one such instrument, despite reservations on accession to it. Presently, India has decided to become a GPA observer. India could evaluate the pros and cons of joining the GPA and ultimately become a party to it.

As noted further above, the government of India still uses preferential treatment in government procurement as a tool of industrial policy. The existing preferential policy in favour of the small-scale enterprises, PSUs and other organizations is likely to continue as a part of India's strategy for economic development, social responsibility, and protection of the small and vulnerable sections of the society.[34] Discontinuing preferential treatment may not be either desirable or politically feasible. Mention must however be made that it is the declared intention of the Indian government to eliminate purchase preferences. At present the purchase preference policy for PSUs is extended from year to year. Policies of preference to small-scale and cottage industries have continued, although the list of products is gradually being reduced. Accession to the GPA could offer the Indian government the vital legislative push that is needed to overcome inertia and vested interests, while still protecting those sectors of the economy and population that can genuinely benefit from preferences.

Acceding to the GPA poses non-discrimination and national treatment requirements on all tenders above the GPA thresholds on those entities and sectors covered by the Agreement. As an important move to fair and transparent procurement, this necessarily restricts the use of *ad hoc* and discriminatory policies. India needs to strike a balance between its social obligations and the need for non-discrimination and national treatment in procurement policies as mandated by the GPA. This implies that India may negotiate to have specific sectors and agencies (sensitive and critical) excluded from the coverage of the GPA, as the Agreement allows for such exemptions.

The challenge for India, therefore, is in defining those sensitive and critical sectors of the economy that need to be excluded from the

---

33 These suggestions are based on Chakravarthy and Dawar (n. 4 above).

34 C. Raghavan, 'Behind the Talks on Transparency in Government Procurement' in Third World Network (May 2002), available at: http://www.twnside.org.sg/title/twe281a.htm (accessed 31 December 2013).

coverage of the GPA during the accession negotiations. On the obverse side, the Indian government has to mount an effort to form coherent and comprehensive development policies towards sensitive sectors of the economy and society, without compromising on the need for transparency and integrity reforms in these sectors. The more sectors of procurement are sheltered from good-governance principles, the less likely reform measures will be to ensure efficient procurement markets.

It needs to be kept in mind that India's existing carve-out for supplies of specified pharmaceuticals by PSUs may fall foul of the general rules and principles of the GPA. But the relevant issues that arise in the carve-out policies can be addressed in the accession negotiations or under Article XXIII of the GPA to ensure that the Indian government can continue to make available certain drugs and medicines for the poor at affordable prices.

The Indian state governments and PSUs may not have the capacity to adhere to the commitments under the GPA. Problems relating to improper staffing patterns and lack of standardization may compound the said lack of capacity. Furthermore, the legislative framework in most acts of Indian states is not people-centric, promotes archaic practices and needs to focus more on compliance. Weak state laws allow for the exploitation of procurement regimes; therefore standard guidelines, procedures and formats as well as concepts of 'value-for-money' need to be firmly established. Although India has a federal structure and state government purchases are not subject to central government decisions, it should be possible to ask, and encourage through incentives, state governments to conform to the disciplines of such an agreement.[35]

In many cases, as Hoda and Suchi[36] point out, the weakness is not in Indian procurement legislation or policies but in its weak implementation. If the central government is committed to reform, it needs to strengthen implementation through greater oversight and by devising stronger bid-challenge mechanisms.

There will be financial costs in implementing the requirements of the GPA associated with its transparency and procedural requirements. It is important to acknowledge the resource costs not only in terms of setting up new bodies and training staff, but also the costs associated with publishing changes in procurement practices and publishing statistics on procurement decisions. Moreover, the benefits of greater transparency to potential bidders for state contracts are likely to be maximized or fully

35 Srivastava (n. 23 above) 235.
36 Hoda and Suchi (n. 22 above).

realized only when additional steps are taken to ensure due process and to challenge the decisions of procuring entities. This too involves expense and new expertise.

Despite these costs, the benefits of transparency, due process, and rights of appeal would be enjoyed both by potential domestic and foreign bidders for state contracts. Additional costs are typically spread across a country's entire state procurement system and the cost per state purchase may well be very low. These arguments apply with as much force to developing and least-developed countries as they do to other jurisdictions, and some of these costs are a necessary element of reforming a domestic procurement system, rather than being specific to the GPA.

It is interesting to note that in some respects, Indian procurement procedures are already broadly in line with the requirements of the GPA. For instance, the procedures relating to invitation to participate in the intended procurement, selection procedures, time limits for tendering and delivery, submission, receipt and opening of tenders are all in broad conformity with the rules of the GPA. In these cases the problem is with implementation, because the procuring agencies are seen to have deviated from the rules in practice. There have been very few complaints of the absence of rules but many of failure to observe them in letter and spirit. If India accedes to the GPA, such failures may be actionable. This would have a positive impact on the implementation of procurement rules.

While some Indian procurement procedures may be in *de jure* conformity with the GPA requirements, Hoda and Suchi called for the promotion of transparency in procurement transactions and for fostering competition in procurement and supplies.[37] The current practice in government procurement is opaque. Accession to the GPA would provide the welcome clarity and certainty to bidders. It would also improve implementation, because disappointed bidders are those with most interest in having the rules of procurement observed. Again, as Hoda and Suchi note, 'making these changes would really be tantamount to bringing about much needed reform to this area of Government activity'.[38] That is, the costs of accession are typically the costs of reform.

Notwithstanding this debate, once the decision has been taken to exempt a sector of the economy or society from the application of the GPA, there are various flexibilities and exclusions provided to developing countries in Article V of the Revised GPA, in addition to technical assistance during the accession negotiations themselves.

---

[37] Ibid.

[38] Ibid.

8. CONCLUSION

This chapter has identified several areas of procurement policy in India that could benefit from a transparent rule-based system such as that provided by the WTO GPA. Not only does this Agreement include greater enforcement capacity than currently exists in India, but also a fairer, more efficient and more transparent system for spending public funds.

In addition to these good-governance requirements, accession to the GPA would offer India significant access to the procurement markets of the other WTO Members. This presents Indian businesses with a large export potential. It would also allow firms of other GPA Parties to enter the procurement markets that India would be opening up under the GPA, providing for greater competition, value for money, technology transfer and ultimately more efficient use of public money against the backdrop of still widespread poverty in India.

These benefits will not come without costs and risks relating to implementing the provisions and the political backlash that such reform might unleash. Many of the vested interests must be overcome in order to set up any fair procurement regime with integrity and the rule of law, regardless of whether or not it is the WTO GPA. These interests are an obstacle to the implementation of a good procurement system and sustainable development. However, some of these vested interests are also legitimate and make an appropriate claim to preferential treatment from the Indian procurement system. The WTO GPA does not preclude such positive discrimination in any country, particularly for developing countries. The challenge, for India or any accession country, lies in identifying legitimate domestic stakeholders and sectors of the economy that require protection through preferential procurement, either temporarily or for the foreseeable future. Once the negotiators have a coherent strategy on which sectors and elements of the economy and society it wishes to protect, it may negotiate offsets, price preferences or higher thresholds, as set out in Article V of the Revised GPA. A developing country's government may also call for technical assistance and capacity building from the WTO Secretariat and other GPA Members.

To conclude, the government of India's decision to become a GPA observer indicates that it has identified tangible benefits from accession to this Agreement. Firstly, India believes it can take advantage of the access it gains to other Parties' procurement markets, and also that it will benefit from the greater choice it is exposed to by allowing more foreign firms to bid for procurement tenders. Secondly, it is clear that the costs and challenges associated with India's accession to the WTO GPA are by and large the same costs as those associated with implementing comprehensive policies to ensure a transparent, fair and effective domestic procurement system in India. As a first step, India has already shown its commitment to improving its procurement markets and to underpinning its reforms by becoming a GPA observer.

13. Distinguishing state and private subsidies: a closer look at the state character test

Thomas Jaeger

1. SCOPE OF THE ANALYSIS

Approaching the area of state subsidies to private businesses from a fundamental perspective, three questions may be posed. This chapter will answer only one – the last one.

First of all, do we have subsidies at all, are subsidies a prevalent phenomenon? The answer is simply and flatly: yes of course. Virtually all states subsidize their economies and economic operators in one form or another. This is not new: governments have always granted subsidies as a matter of steering economic policies.[1] Subsidization is an age-old phenomenon. What is handed out to whom, when and in what form is a question of sovereign policy choice. Subsidies are a means of economic and competition regulation just like the enactment of laws and other regulatory measures.

A second question, different from the first one (whether subsidies as a steering instrument exist at all) is whether we want subsidies. Are subsidies a good thing or do we prefer subsidy-free competition dynamics? Clearly, subsidies will in most cases (that is, unless they exceptionally compensate for disadvantages suffered by an operator in the public interest) run counter to the logic of competition on the merits. Competition on the merits is, however, something that states typically want to protect on their domestic markets, while they do not care much about it in external trade *vis-à-vis* economic operators in third countries. For

[1] Adam Smith's major work, An Inquiry into the Nature and Causes of the Wealth of Nations, as early as 1776, contained a chapter on 'bounties'; see also L. Rubini, The Definition of Subsidy and State Aid: WTO and EC Law in Comparative Perspective (OUP 2009) 3 (there in n. 1).

example, while the EU has, as will be shown, a rather stringent subsidy control regime in place domestically, export subsidies and domestic price support are not (unless caught by the WTO prohibition also discussed here) necessarily regarded as an evil in the quest for global competitiveness.[2] In fact, whether, in what sectors and to what extent subsidies are good or bad is just as much a matter of policy choice as everything else. However, the policy choice here can be set on a more informed basis by use of economic analysis in particular, delineating the effects of a subsidy in a given context. So the question of whether we want subsidies is to be answered by politicians and/or economists, but not here.

Thirdly, the question arises whether, and how, we shall control the grant of subsidies. This, finally, is a legal question, and the issue that is dealt with in the present chapter. States do not usually control the grant of subsidies in terms of competitive effects. Where subsidy control exists on a national level, it typically takes the form of checking restraints of constitutional competence (in particular of a budgetary or fiscal nature), of legality (legal basis) and of fundamental citizen rights (in particular non-discrimination).[3] Subsidy control is thus an exception to the norm that the state is free to support its economy according to policy choice. But if the choice to control subsidies is made, the way it is done should be right in terms of delivering the results for which the control mechanism has been put in place. As the following analysis will show, this is probably not the case for the WTO regime and certainly not the case for the EU regime.

2. THE RATIONALE BEHIND SUBSIDY CONTROL

Where subsidy control exists, it is pinned against a particular economic background. Actually, there are only two evolved regimes of competitive subsidy control: the regime of the WTO on the one hand and of the EU

---

[2] See only the alleged subsidies granted to the European company Airbus in order to better its competitive position vis-à-vis US-based Boeing, which were brought before a WTO panel by the US and partially found to be illegal. See A. Knorr, J. Bellmann and R. Schomaker, 'Subsidies in Civil Aircraft Manufacturing: The World Trade Organization (WTO) and the Boeing-Airbus Dispute' (2012) *EStAL* 585; G.F. Chianale, 'The WTO Airbus Dispute: Findings of the Panel and of the Appellate Body' (2013) *EStAL* 290.

[3] For the example of subsidy control under the Austrian national system see T. Jaeger, 'Austria' in J. Derenne, A. Müller-Rappard and C. Kaczmarek (eds), *Enforcement of EU State Aid Law at National Level 2009* (Lexxion 2010) 7, passim.

on the other hand.[4] This is an expression of the fact that subsidy control is in fact only needed in the specific setting that trans-national markets are created in and where the functioning of those markets must be safeguarded by protecting competition on the merits between undertakings of different nationalities from state intervention.

Outside of these settings, subsidy control has no place. It could, for example, be argued that subsidy control might help to remedy certain state-induced problems occurring in intra-state markets, such as, particularly, state preferences for state-owned undertakings in relation to privately owned undertakings via financial, factual or regulatory[5] preferences. A closer look, however, soon reveals that subsidy control cannot deliver satisfactory solutions here. State preference of certain undertakings is a problem which goes far beyond the disbursement of benefits (or the forfeiture of revenue) and also encompasses mechanisms such as a preferential legal status (e.g. a specific form of incorporation, special concessions, exceptions from obligations of antitrust, commercial, labor or consumer law, etc.) or preferred contracting (even if the prices established are market compliant). To encompass all this, a more general norm than subsidy control is needed – one that disallows preferences for state-owned enterprises in general. Article 106 TFEU, for example, establishes such a norm and requires that private and state-owned enterprises are treated equally across the board. The same is in fact true in answering concerns that federalist systems might be ridden by some sort of subsidy competition between federal and regional governments or among regions over attracting businesses.[6] Where this occurs, it might be a hint of insufficiencies in the constitutional distribution of vertical competences between the federal and regional levels. So putting a subsidy prohibition and control procedures in place is not necessarily the only, and, in view of the regulatory efforts associated with it, certainly

---

4 Rubini (n. 1 above) 3; G. Schellmann, 'Perspektiven der Beihilfepolitik unter Kommissar Almunia' in T. Jaeger and B. Haslinger (eds), *Jahrbuch Beihilferecht 12* (NWV 2012) 261, 264 ff.

5 In this regard, cf. the problematic hint that preferences accorded in the course of a state's regulatory activity might be state aid free in Case T-575/04 Bouygues [2007] ECR II-2097, para. 138 (concerning telecoms regulation); upheld in this regard by CJEU in Case C-431/07 P. Bouygues [2009] ECR I-2665, paras 42 et seq.

6 For the Chinese case, see also the Chapter by T.K. Cheng in this volume, dealing more generally with restraints of trade exercised by Chinese provinces and lower administrative entities as 'administrative monopolies'.

not the preferred answer. Revisiting and adjusting the constitutional division of competences over policy matters and spending may likewise suffice.

Subsidy control is thus situated in the middle of the two ends of a spectrum of different levels of market integration: Where no full internal market exists, the national borders may still pose relatively more important and more prohibitive boundaries to the competitive behavior of an undertaking than the acts of its competitors situated across the border. Where, therefore, trans-national market integration does not reach beyond a certain state, lesser control mechanisms than subsidy control may suffice to homogenize the conditions of competition between states. Examples here may be taken from regional economic integration zones such as NAFTA, ASEAN and Mercosur, none of which has subsidy rules.[7] In those, not fully integrated, trans-national markets, competition either is safeguarded via mechanisms such as the classic authorization to introduce retaliatory tariffs (Mercosur) or the prohibition of so-called drawback clauses to ensure that customs duties and equivalent charges are paid on any materials and components imported to manufacture a given product (NAFTA, ASEAN and Mercosur) or is subsidy control restricted to certain sectors such as agriculture (NAFTA).[8] At the other end of the spectrum stand fully integrated markets, such as the US or China. Markets in such (genuine, federalist or quasi-federalist) states typically also do not have subsidy control.[9] In the US, for example, the conditions of competition within the federation are *inter alia* controlled via use of the commerce clause, ensuring that certain vital issues for internal competition are laid down by the federal government.

3. BRIEF OVERVIEW OF THE WTO AND EU SUBSIDY REGIMES

The WTO's subsidy rules are predominantly laid down in the Agreement on Subsidies and Countervailing Measures (SCM Agreement).[10] A reference to subsidy control is also contained in Article 9 of the Agreement on

---

[7] Schellmann (n. 1 above) 264 ff.

[8] Ibid.

[9] For the US, see Schellmann (n. 1 above) 264 ff.

[10] On the SCM Agreement in general, see N.S. Bansal, *The WTO after Cancun* (Mittal Publications 2004) 41; J. Flett, A.C. Jessen and K. Talaber-Ritz, 'The Relationship between WTO Subsidies Law and EC State Aid Law' in J.

Agriculture, which does not, however, lay down a divergent definition.[11] The SCM Agreement defines subsidies by seven characteristics: A subsidy is a:

(1) financial contribution
(2) by any public body
(3) involving a benefit
(4) for an enterprise
(5) in a selective manner and which is
(6) export or import-related or
(7) inflicts some other economic injury or serious prejudice.

The initial five requirements are cumulative,[12] the latter two alternative.[13] Certain exempted subsidies exist.[14] WTO subsidy control does not involve individual rights (individuals must complain to their government, which may then raise the case within the WTO);[15] sanctions for illegal subsidies are therefore limited to countermeasures.

In the EU,[16] so-called state aid is defined by five characteristics, which are:

(1) the selectivity
(2) of an economic advantage
(3) granted by the state
(4) to undertakings
(5) which distorts competition and negatively affects trade between Member States.

These characteristics are cumulative: Measures which do not fulfill one of the criteria arc not caught by the prohibition, even if they have

Flett (ed.), *EC State Aid Law: Liber Amicorum for Francisco Santaolalla Gadea* (Wolters Kluwer 2008) 441.

[11] For more, see Rubini (n. 1 above) 108 ff.

[12] Article 1(1) and (2) SCM Agreement.

[13] Articles 3 and 5 SCM Agreement.

[14] Article 8 SCM Agreement.

[15] Article 10 of Council Regulation (EC) No. 597/2009 on protection against subsidised imports from countries not members of the-European Community, [2009] OJ L 188, p. 93. A similar procedure is available under US law.

[16] For more general information about EU state aid rules, for many, see L. Hancher, T. Ottervanger and P.J. Slot, *EU State Aids* (4th edn, Sweet and Maxwell 2012) paras 1-001 ff.

competitive or trade effects equivalent to state aid.[17] Unlike in WTO law, there are no types of subsidies which are exempted from the prohibition *ex ante*, but the possibility of allowing the subsidy due to certain justifications accepted by EU law[18] is checked by the Commission as a matter of standard procedure. In the area of sanctions, also in stark contrast to WTO law, enforcement of the state aid prohibition in the EU internal market is quite effective: competitors may bring state-aid cases before the national courts and violations of the state-aid prohibition are subject to civil sanctions including invalidity of the granting act, recovery and damages and in addition there is public enforcement through the Commission (also directed towards recovery).[19]

In comparison, therefore, the WTO and EU subsidy regimes start from divergent backgrounds, but show some important similarities. In terms of background, WTO rules mainly exist to back up the WTO's tariff provisions.[20] EU state-aid control, by contrast, is an instrument to complete the internal market and harmonize the conditions of competition within that market, thereby, in particular, flanking[21] the fundamental freedoms relating to the free flow of goods, services, persons and undertakings and capital between the EU Member States.[22] Both, however, serve the purpose of ensuring a level playing field among players of different nationalities active on the same or related markets. Those differences in background then translate to stark differences in the area of enforcement. While the EU lays down an individually enforceable and relatively strict prohibition in terms of enforcement power and sanctions, WTO enforcement follows the logic of public international law, thus according no role to private individuals and encountering obstacles of state sovereignty upon enforcement, and can thus at best be described as

---

[17] See Case C-379/98 *PreussenElektra* [2001] ECR I-2099, paras 54 and 61, and (more straightforwardly) Opinion of AG Jacobs to that Case, paras 139 and 150; for more see T. Jaeger, *Beihilfen durch Steuern und parafiskalische Abgaben* (NWV 2006) paras 72 ff.

[18] Articles 106(2) and 107(2) and (3) TFEU.

[19] For more information about EU state aid enforcement, see J. Derenne, A. Müller-Rappard and C. Kaczmarek, 'European Report' in J. Derenne, A. Müller-Rappard and C. Kaczmarek (eds*), Enforcement of EU State Aid Law at National Level 2009* (2010) 2, passim.

[20] Similarly see Hancher, Ottervanger and Slot (n. 16 above) para. 6-002; Rubini (n. 1 above) 40.

[21] See F.J. Säcker, 'Einleitung' in F. Montag and F.J. Säcker (eds), *Münchener Kommentar zum Europäischen und Deutschen Wettbewerbsrecht* (Kartellrecht), Band 3: Beihilfen- und Vergaberecht (C.H. Beck 2011) 2, para 1.

[22] See also Rubini (n. 1 above) 3 ff.

rudimentary. Accordingly, whereas the EU regime sometimes tends to look into even the smallest cases with only doubtful internal market effects,[23] the WTO regime tends to catch only very large subsidy cases. Whereas therefore in the EU regime sometimes even sardines are caught by the Commission's herring trawler, the WTO regime is more adapted to catching whales. Finally, upon first glance, the definition of subsidy (aid) under both regimes likewise is based on similar characteristics: elements like undertaking, benefit, selectivity, state character, figure in both regimes. If looked at more closely, however, the interpretation and scope of these elements diverge significantly. These differences affect the proper functioning of the subsidy prohibition and will form the focus of the remainder of this chapter.

4. STATE-INITIATED RESTRAINTS OF COMPETITION BY MEANS OF SUBSIDIES: IS THE DELINEATION CORRECT?

Subsidy control works right if it delivers on its justificatory logic of establishing a level playing field. This will be investigated here with respect to only one aspect of state-aid control, namely its addressees: What are state-initiated restraints of competition under the WTO and EU subsidy rules and is the definition proper in the sense that the state-initiated measures that should be caught will actually be caught?[24]

Both the WTO and the EU regimes do, as a starting point, apply broad notions of the state as the subject of the subsidy assessment. Article 1 SCM Agreement applies to the state proper (that is, entities vested with sovereign power) as well as 'any public body' and any kind of 'funding mechanism, or [entrusted or directed] private body to carry out one or more of the type of functions … which would normally be vested in the

---

[23] See, for instance, Case C-172/03 *Heiser* [2005] ECR I-1627, paras 32 ff.; for more, see J.L. Buendia Sierra and B. Smulders, 'The Limited Role of the "Refined Economic Approach" in *Achieving the Objectives of State Aid Control: Time for Some Realism*' in J. Flett (ed.), *EC State Aid Law: Liber Amicorum for Francisco Santaolalla Gadea* (Wolters Kluwer 2008) 1.

[24] On the question of a correct delineation of state and non-state measures critically already also H. van Vliet, 'State Resources and PreussenElektra: When Is a State Aid Not a State Aid?' in J. Flett (ed.), *EC State Aid Law: Liber Amicorum for Francisco Santaolalla Gadea* (Wolters Kluwer 2008) 65, passim; T. Jaeger, 'Goodbye Old Friend: Article 107's Double Control Criterion' (2012) *EStAL* 535, passim.

government and the practice'.[25] The same is true under EU law, which also includes in the notion of state aid 'any aid granted by a Member State or through State resources in any form whatsoever'. As under the WTO notion, this is to be interpreted as including any (public or private) entities directed by the state to grant aid.[26]

Under WTO law, the definition of the state as the initial addressee of the subsidy prohibition follows a formal approach: Article 1 SCM Agreement undertakes an exhaustive[27] listing of the types of financial contributions by public (or entrusted) bodies that are to be caught. These are: direct transfers of funds, revenue foregone (such as tax breaks), beneficial purchasing conditions, the creation of a funding mechanism and price support mechanisms. Evidently, however, any formally exhaustive approach runs the risk of gaps: Complex forms of regulatory intervention not contained in the listing, such as the minimum prices or financing obligations, will escape subsidy control.[28]

EU law approaches the issue from the opposite end: in line with an according general approach in EU law, state aid is not defined by any formal standards, but by a functional one. As will be shown, however, this functional approach is not fully implemented, so that eventually we may only speak of a pseudo-functionalist approach – at least in terms of the state element in the EU's aid definition. Generally, the functionalist approach commands that any mechanism shall be caught in which the advantage distributed is 'first ... granted directly or indirectly through State resources ... and, second, ... imputable to the State'.[29] This therefore extends into a double condition, under which the state element is only fulfilled if a measure is initiated as well as financed by the state. Under this approach, measures initiated by private parties are no aid even if the state finances them, whereas *vice versa*, measures initiated by the state, but financed by private parties are not aid either.[30] Financing in

---

25 See also Rubini (n. 1 above) 115 ff. and 130 ff.

26 See, for many, Case C-279/08 P *Commission v. Netherlands* [2011] ECR I-7671, para. 105.

27 See also Rubini (n. 1 above) 108 ff.

28 Ibid., 121.

29 Case C-482/99 *France v. Commission* [2002] ECR I-4397, para. 24; see also Case C-303/88 *Italy v. Commission* [1991] ECR I-1433, para. 11; Case C-279/08 P *Commission v. Netherlands* [2011] ECR I-7671, para. 103.

30 See Case C-379/98 *PreussenElektra* [2001] ECR I-2099, para. 58; similarly already Case 82/77 *van Tiggele* [1978] ECR 25, paras 23 ff.; Joined Cases C-72/91 and C-73/91 *Sloman Neptun* [1993] ECR I-887, para. 19; Case C-189/91 *Kirshammer-Hack* [1993] ECR I-6185, para. 14; Joined Cases C-52/97, C-53/97 and C-54/97 *Viscidio* [1998] I-2629, para. 14; Case C-200/97 *Ecotrade*

particular means that the state must make a financial sacrifice that will diminish the public budget.[31] In fine-tuning the cumulative character of the initial set of conditions of the EU state-aid prohibition, therefore, the state element is split into two and, according to the general logic, both aspects, again, need to be fulfilled in order for the state element as a whole to be fulfilled.[32]

It is due to the double condition that, in the end, the EU's functional approach is probably not much better fit to avoid gaps than the WTO's formal approach. In simple aid constellations, the double condition will not pose a problem, for instance, where direct grants are handed out by a ministry or in the case of tax breaks and other direct forfeiture of public revenue. But for more complex forms, like WTO law, the EU method may encounter limits. If, for example, the state utilizes a third party to disburse the aid, such as public undertakings, private undertakings or even consumers, the state character of an aid measure may effectively be disguised.

Indeed, the decisive element for the double condition in EU law is the question of public control over the measure. Following the logic of the double condition, the means of control are also twofold. There must, firstly, be public control of the decision to grant aid: Did the state influence the third entity towards granting the aid? In practice, this amounts to a low threshold test where even circumstantial evidence of influence *de iure* or *de facto* is sufficient.[33] Secondly, the public must also have control over the means used to finance the aid: Who does the money used to finance the aid belong to? This test asks whether the state can actually use or direct the resources. Here again, indirect control, typically *de iure*, is sufficient: Article 107(1) TFEU 'includes all the

---

[1998] ECR I-7907, para. 35; Case C-295/97 *Piaggio* [1999] ECR I-3735, para. 35.

31 See Joined Cases C-72/91 and C-73/91 *Sloman Neptun* [1993] ECR I-887, para. 19; Case C-189/91 *Kirshammer-Hack* [1993] ECR I-6185, para. 16; Joined Cases C-52/97, C-53/97 and C-54/97 *Viscidio* [1998] I-2629, para. 13; Case C-200/97 *Ecotrade* [1998] ECR I-7907, para. 35; Case C-295/97 *Piaggio* [1999] ECR I-3735, para. 35; Case C-482/99 *France v. Commission* [2002] ECR I-4397, para. 23; Case C-379/98 *PreussenElektra* [2001] ECR I-2099, para. 58; Joined Cases T-425/04, T-444/04, T-450/04 and T-456/04 *France v. Commission* [2010] ECR II-2099, para. 20.

32 See also Case C-345/02 *Pearle* [2004] ECR I-7239, para. 35.

33 See, for example, Case C-482/99 *France v. Commission* [2002] ECR I-4397, paras 50 ff.; Case C-355/00 *Freskot* [2003] ECR I-5263, para. 81; Joined Cases C-328/99 and C-399/00, SIM 2 *Multimedia* [2003] ECR I-4035, para. 33.

financial resources which the State may indeed use to support undertakings. The fact that those resources constantly remain under public control, and therefore are available to the competent national authorities, is sufficient for them to be categorized as State resources'.[34]

The public-initiative leg of the double criterion will, for example, be fulfilled if a local government is closely linked to a local undertaking (e.g. the administration, financing or assets of an airport) and thus there is a clear indication that the undertaking's economic interests are overshadowed by political interests.[35] By contrast, if a legally endorsed professional association is otherwise independent from the public will and thus pursues its own economic agenda, independent measures taken by that association are not considered to be traceable back to public initiative in spite of the special legal status that the state may have accorded the association.[36] As regards control over the means used to finance the aid, the resources of a public undertaking are typically considered as being eventually controlled by the state and therefore as being public.[37] Similarly, the resources of a professional body endorsed by the state will be attributable to the state if it determines the spending of those means.[38]

In most cases, which are also the more simple cases, the two legs of the double criterion will coincide. But this is not always the case. In fact, the double criterion opens loopholes in the sense that an EU Member State can escape the state-aid prohibition if it takes an initiative to grant aid without assuming control over the resources. This problem zone

---

34 Case C-278/00 *Greece v. Commission* [2004] ECR I-3997, para. 52; similarly Case C-83/98 P *Ladbroke* [2000] ECR I-3271, para. 50.

35 See, for example, Case C-482/99 *France v. Commission* [2002] ECR I-4397, paras 50 ff.; Case C-355/00 *Freskot* [2003] ECR I-5263, para. 81; ECJ, Joined Cases C-328/99 and C-399/00 SIM 2 *Multimedia* [2003] ECR I-4035, para. 33.

36 See, for example, Case C-345/02 *Pearle* [2004] ECR I-7239, para. 35.

37 See, for example, European Commission Decision 2002/467/EC of 21 January 2011, Spain: State aid for the Fesa-Enfersa group (Fertiberia), [2002] OJ L 165, p. 1, para. 70; Commission Decision 2002/458/EC of 1 March 2002, Greece: settlement of debts by the agricultural cooperatives in 1992 and 1994 and reorganisation of the dairy cooperative AGNO, [2002] OJ L 159, p. 1, paras 103 ff.; Commission Decision 2004/393/EC of 12 February 2004, Belgium: Brussels South Charleroi Airport, [2004] OJ L 137, p. 1, para. 246; Commission Decision 2011/269/EU of 27 October 2010, State Aid C 14/09 – Hungary: Péti Nitrogénmüvek, [2011] OJ L 118, p. 9, para. 28.

38 See, for example, Case 290/83 *Commission v. France* [1985] ECR 439, paras 14 ff. and 50; Case 67/85 *van der Kooy* [1988] ECR 219, paras 36 and 38.

therefore opens up when pure legal financing obligations, for example by way of parafiscal charges, are created. In such cases the state may lay down a law compelling some undertakings to finance others. The law is clearly a form of state initiative and will therefore easily qualify as public. However, as regards the resources or financing, the money for the aid measure comes from private parties without the state intervening in the payment process. In this regard, the ECJ has confirmed that the creation of a legal obligation alone by the state is not enough to render the financing mechanism public in the sense of the EU state-aid prohibition.[39] If the resources never enter the public sphere, the system escapes the state-aid prohibition for lack of the second leg of the double condition.

Under this doctrine, a financing mechanism will, for example, be deemed public if a parafiscal charge levied under a legal obligation is administered via a public body with discretion as to use or amounts.[40] This is actually the typical case that parafiscal systems are set up throughout the Member States. Similarly, the CJEU has held that a legally endorsed system for trading surplus emissions will also involve public resources.[41] By contrast, a financing mechanism will not be deemed public if there is no public control because the funds are disbursed strictly *inter privatos*, such as in the case of minimum prices (for example, for alcohol)[42] or in the case of a green electricity surcharge paid by final customers to network providers, who then forward the

---

[39] See Case C-379/98 *PreussenElektra* [2001] ECR I-2099, para. 58.

[40] See Case C-206/06 *Essent Netwerk* [2008] ECR I-5497, para. 74; Case T-25/07 *Iride* [2009] ECR II-245, para. 27; see also Commission Decision 2011/528/EU of 8 March 2011, State Aid C 24/09 – Austria: energy-intensive businesses under the Green Electricity Act, [2011] OJ L 235, p. 42, para. 76; Commission Decision 2009/609/EG of 4 June 2008, State Aid 16/04 – Hungary: Power Purchase Agreements, [2009] OJ L 225/53, paras 287 ff.; Commission Decision 2010/460/EG of 19 November 2009, State Aid C 38/A/04 – Italy: Alcoa Trasformazioni, [2010] OJ L 227, p. 62, paras 163 ff.; Commission Decision 2009/476/EG of 28 January 2009, State Aid C 43/02 – Luxembourg: creation of compensation fund for the organisation of the electricity market, [2009] OJ L 159, p. 11, para. 57; Commission Decision 2007/580/EG of 24 April 2007, State Aid 7/2005 – Slovenia: legislation on qualified energy producers, [2007] OJ L 219, p. 9, para 68.

[41] See Case C-279/08 P *Commission v. Netherlands* [2011] ECR I-7671, para. 103.

[42] See Case 82/77 *van Tiggele* [1978] ECR 25, paras 23 ff.; Case T-25/07 *Iride* [2009] ECR II-245, para. 27; Case C-379/98 *PreussenElektra* [2001] ECR I-2099, para. 58; Joined Cases C-128/03 and C-129/03 AEM [2005] I-2861, para. 46.

surcharge to green electricity producers.[43] Another, exceptional, example of a measure not deemed aid because of a lack of public control over resources may be mechanisms where a public body is involved in the administration of parafiscal charges but has no discretion of its own whatsoever as regards the way the money is spent. In this regard, a bonus/malus system for milk levies according to quality, executed by a public body that had no discretion as to use, cause and amount of payments, has been deemed not to involve public resources.[44]

The functionalist approach of the EU to attributing measures to the public or private sphere is thus not indiscriminate. It actually has similar limits as the WTO subsidy definition in that it resorts to a formalistic separation of factually linked actions (initiative and resources). In fact, this separation is quite artificial in that it may entail a legally different treatment of economically comparable situations. Even where the competitive effects of two measures are the same, the formalistic double-control criterion may lead to one being classified as public aid (and thus prohibited) whereas the other is deemed as a non-prohibited private measure. This latter point can be illustrated by way of further examples.

For one instance,[45] the subsidization of the use of combined heat-and-power (CHP) technology by means of a legal financing obligation (surcharge paid by consumers) has been classified by the Commission as not involving aid for lack of control of the German state over the resources of the subsidy.[46] This assessment was rendered against the openly declared aim of the German CHP law to subsidize the construction and production of CHP plants. It was, in other words, not even disguised by the German authorities as being anything but a subsidy for

---

43 See Case C-379/98 *PreussenElektr*a [2001] ECR I-2099, para. 58.

44 See Opinion of AG Kokott on Case C-283/03 *Kuipers* [2005] ECR I-4255, paras 66 ff.

45 The list of examples can, of course, be continued. See, for example, the different treatment of feed-in tariffs in Austria and Germany under Case C-379/98 *PreussenElektra* [2001] ECR I-2099, para. 58 (no aid) versus Commission Decision of 6 July 2006, State Aid N 317/B/2006 – Austria: Support Fee, C(2006) 2964 final, paras 31 ff.; Commission Decision 2011/528/EU of 8 March 2011, State Aid C 24/09 – Austria: energy-intensive businesses under the Green Electricity Act, [2011] OJ L 235, p. 42, para. 76 (all aid).

46 See Commission Decision of 22 May 2002, State aid NN 68/2000 – Germany: Law on the Protection of Electricity generated from Combined Heat and Power, C(2002) 1889 final, p. 3; similarly Commission Decision State Aid N 254/06 – Belgium: 'Panneaux photovoltaïques', C(2006) 4954 final, paras 10 ff.; Commission Decision, State Aid N 608/04 – Belgium: Combined Heat and Power certificates, C(2005) 1318 final, p. 2.

the CHP sector. The reason for the favorable classification of the measure by the Commission was simply the fact that the surcharge for CHP energy was effectuated directly between consumers, suppliers and producers. There was even some public-body involvement present in the case, namely, in terms of checking eligibility for investment aid and in terms of the administration of an aid cap provided for in the law, but since that public involvement did not substantially affect the resources in the scheme, the Commission did not deem this to be harmful. By contrast, only slightly later, a very similar Austrian CHP law for subsidization of the use of CHP technology was qualified by the Commission as involving state aid.[47] The Austrian measure had essentially the same aims and involved similar types of subsidies as the German scheme, but the payout of the subsidy was administered by a public body. That difference was decisive for the Commission to qualify the case in 180 degree opposition to the German case, despite the fact that the competitive effects of the measure were evidently quite similar.

Another instance is the different treatment of certificate-trading schemes in the EU Member States, which are in part deemed to be attributable to the state and sometimes not, depending on the role of the public authorities in the scheme and in full disregard of the question of comparability of competitive effects. In this regard, the Commission deemed that a Belgian scheme for the trading of CHP certificates and backed up by national law was not financed by public resources and thus did not involve aid.[48] The aim of the scheme was to subsidize CHP production. Unlike in the German case, however, the Belgians pursued this aim via free public CHP certificates combined with an obligation for suppliers to acquire a minimum amount of such certificates. If the minimum amount was not reached, sanctions applied. The certificates served as proof of the use of CHP as a production method for the energy and were, alongside the CHP energy, tradable among suppliers. By contrast, the Commission decided that a Dutch scheme for the trading of emission certificates contained state resources and therefore involved aid.[49] The aim of that scheme was, like that of the Belgian one, the subsidization of low-emission industries. To that end, a maximum

---

47 See Commission Decision of 22 May 2002, State aid NN 68/2000 – Germany: Law on the Protection of Electricity generated from Combined Heat and Power, C(2002) 1889 final, 3.

48 See European Commission Decision, State Aid N 608/04 – Belgium: Combined Heat and Power certificates, C(2005) 1318 final, p. 2.

49 See ECJ, Case C-279/08 P *Commission v. Netherlands* [2011] ECR I-7671, para. 103.

amount of emissions per industrial plant was laid down. If exceeded, as in the Belgian scheme, sanctions applied. Unused emission quotas were tradable among plants. The main difference between the Belgian and the Dutch schemes, which prompted the different assessment by the Commission, lay in the fact that the Belgian certificates were seen as attached to the tradable basic product (CHP energy), whereas the unused emission quotas were seen as a separate product alongside the products manufactured in the emission-generating processes. Because the quotas were furnished by the state for free (and thus sanctions were not applied if the industries remained within the quotas), the Commission concluded that state resources were present.

These examples show that the narrow CJEU jurisprudence and according Commission practice under the double criterion for assessing the state character of an aid have the effect of opening loopholes in the prohibition. Whereas very often the attempts of states to escape the state-aid prohibition via a markedly complex design of a measure will not work,[50] sometimes, still, this plan will work out. Even cases involving declared aims of subsidization may escape the state-aid prohibition if the measure is designed in such a way that the state acquires no control over the resources – even if the private parties obliged to finance the aid are (as is typically the case) locked in the scheme. This leads to distinctions between measures that are otherwise comparable in terms of competitive effects and which thus distort the conditions of competition. Like the WTO approach, the EU's approach, therefore, does not deliver a level playing field.

---

[50] Ibid., paras 109 ff.; Case C-206/06 *Essent Netwerk* [2008] ECR I-5497, para. 74; Case T-25/07 *Iride* [2009] ECR II-245, para. 27; also Commission Decision 2011/528/EU of 8 March 2011, State Aid C 24/09 – Austria: energy-intensive businesses under the Green Electricity Act, [2011] OJ L 235, p. 42, para. 76; European Commission Decision 2009/609/EG of 4 June 2008, State Aid 16/04 – Hungary: Power Purchase Agreements, [2009] OJ L 225/53, paras 287 ff.; Commission Decision 2010/460/EG of 19 November 2009, State Aid C 38/A/04 – Italy: Alcoa Trasformazioni, [2010] OJ L 227/62, paras 163 ff.; Commission Decision 2009/476/EG of 28 January 2009, State Aid C 43/02 – Luxembourg: creation of compensation fund for the organisation of the electricity market, [2009] OJ L 159/11, para. 57; Commission Decision 2007/580/EG of 24 April 2007, State Aid 7/2005 – Slovenia: legislation on qualified energy producers, [2007] OJ L 219/9, para. 68; Commission of 6 July 2006, State Aid N 317/B/2006 – Austria: Support Fee, C(2006) 2964 final, paras 31 ff.

5. CONCLUSIONS

As was shown at the outset, subsidy control clearly plays an important role in securing a level playing field in some trans-nationally integrated markets. Depending on the state of market integration, subsidy control may flank tariff control rules (such as in the WTO), but it may also complement the fully-fledged creation of a true internal market (such as in the EU). Markets can do without subsidy control if they show only a low degree of market integration and especially if alternative tariff mechanisms are in place (such as in NAFTA or Mercosur) or if they show, by contrast, a very high degree of political integration at the level of federalist statehood (such as the USA). However, other transnationally integrated markets will typically require subsidy control.

Although the WTO and EU subsidy regimes are only similar upon first glance and in fact differ in relation to the details of the subsidy test, both have flaws. In their attempts to tackle state-initiated distortions of competition in the form of subsidies in the trans-national markets respectively covered, the EU and WTO regimes show similar flaws in spite of their divergent approaches to defining state aid. The EU's functionalist approach, to avoid becoming too indiscriminate in catching state-initiated subsidies, attempts a better fine-tuning than the WTO's formalistic approach, but the EU achieves, at best, a quasi-functionalist result. The approach is not in balance. The EU's state-aid test may be too lax in terms of allowing the circumventing of the state-aid prohibition via legal financing obligations such as minimum prices (as in the case of the German CHP law). Yet at the same time it may also be too harsh when revenue foregone is always classified as aid, even if no public body is actually involved in the scheme (as in the case of the Dutch emissions trading). For this, the EU's test is not free of distortive effects resulting from a legally different treatment of economically comparable aid mechanisms in different Member States.

In consequence, the delineation between private and state subsidy measures produces economically unsound results due to formalistic instead of effects-based assessment criteria under both the WTO and the EU regimes. The WTO mainly shows substantive gaps in the area of complex economic measures flowing from its formal definition approach. In addition it has only a very coarse-meshed enforcement framework. With these traits combined, the WTO system tends to risk under-enforcement. The EU system's functional approach to definitions is, by contrast, partially too lax and partially too tight: it just does not catch the right measures. In that respect, the EU system risks under- as well as over-enforcement. These effects will respectively be leveraged by the very effective enforcement possibilities underlying EU law in general.

Nonetheless, the functional approach is clearly to be preferred over a formal approach in delineating state and private action, such as under WTO law. The functional approach is more flexible and more easily adjustable to changes in the competitive environment. If we accept that the EU system's delineation between state and private action under its functional approach is not right, this still does not make a case against the functional approach in general. It merely indicates that it is time to readjust the concept of state involvement in aid. The remaining formalistic elements in the otherwise functionalist state-character test in the EU should be abandoned. In fact, there is no scenario in which the test for double control over resources really makes sense. Parafiscal subsidy schemes should not be treated like classic minimum prices, since a classic minimum price does not involve purchasing obligations (that is, lock-in of customers). Classic minimum prices without a purchasing obligation will, by contrast, typically not involve aid, as the market share will decrease with an increase in price (that is, substitution will occur).

Therefore, the double criterion should be done away with in favor of a single requirement of proof of public initiative.[51] This will admittedly broaden the scope of application of the state-aid prohibition. In particular, minimum price schemes would, unlike now, be caught, but only insofar as they do involve an economic advantage (that is, to the extent that the price hike is not offset by a loss of market share). After all, this will typically involve situations where customers are locked in. The inclusion of such measures in the scope of the state-aid prohibition appears sensible.[52]

---

51 See already Jaeger (n. 24 above) 537 ff.
52 Ibid., 538.

Index